This book is dedicated to the memory of all the victims of Islamist terrorism, both here and abroad, and to all the brave members of our Armed Forces who have made the ultimate sacrifice, or who have been wounded physically or psychologically, in answering the call to defend our Great Nation from these extremists, be they foreign or domestic. Let us resolve to honor their sacrifice by achieving unconditional victory over the Islamist ideology and preventing future generations of terrorists.

ACKNOWLEDGEMENTS

When I first started this project, my objective was to use my perspective from four decades of operational experience on the Middle East as a member of the intelligence community to offer a roadmap for victory in our war on Islamism. Because I had deep, first-hand knowledge of the Islamist ideology – the kind that many senior officials, politicians, and pundits don't have – I saw this effort as a way to serve my country and to offer a new and innovative strategy for victory that was also realistic and achievable.

But I really had no idea of how to write a book or get it published. I did not have teams of researchers or editors at my disposal. I did not have some ghostwriter or a helpful agent nor any personal fame or celebrity to give me an automatic audience of readers. I've been working in secrecy most of my adult life. Unfortunately, publishers and agents are generally unconcerned with what you write; they are only concerned with how it will sell. It is a business, after all, so when you are an unknown and unpublished author, you have to jump a lot harder and higher if you are to grab the brass ring. I expected lots of rejections and I was not disappointed.

Fortunately, I had a core group of people who believed in me and my manuscript, gave me a chance, and made it possible for this book to be published. I am deeply grateful to them all because this effort could not have succeeded without them.

First and foremost in this group is Colette, my beloved, wonderful wife of 37 years. She is my soulmate and most-trusted advisor and she knows me better than anyone. We have shared tragedies and triumphs. We've had a front row seat to history, both good and bad.

We have lived in foreign cities with unreliable water and electricity and without so much as even a rotary dial telephone. At high-risk locations where hostile surveillance was a known and definite threat, she would provide overwatch for me from our apartment as I inspected my car for bombs every morning before heading off to work. That's love!

In overseas assignments where a job was not available to her, she eagerly volunteered with the Red Cross to help US service members or disabled Arab children, actions for which she was recognized by senior officials. In her career field of occupational therapy, she is still changing the lives of her patients for the better every single day. How cool is that?

So when I first approached her about writing this book, she immediately encouraged me to go forward and her support and confidence have been absolutely unwavering throughout the ups and downs of getting the manuscript written and published. I could not have done it without her. She patiently read and re-read every single rewrite and editing change and offered her objective opinions and criticisms, both good and bad. Your harshest and most-honest critics are often the ones closest to you and in an endeavor such as this, that is a good thing. I cannot imagine my life without Colette and I am so proud and fortunate that she decided to share life's journey with me.

The next person I would like to acknowledge is General Alfred M. Gray, USMC (Ret). General Gray, the 29th Commandant of the Marine Corps, is well-known as a Marine's Marine. He is a legendary leader whose respect for those under his command inspires them to do great things. He is universally admired and held in the highest esteem by those Marines he has commanded or with whom he has served.

As a young officer in the late fifties and early sixties, he had significant influence over the shape and structure of the signals intelligence and electronic warfare field in the Marine Corps that endures to this day. He earned the trust and confidence of senior officials at the National Security Agency and justified the value of signals intelligence and electronic warfare to the Marine Corps leadership and hierarchy. Today the Marines are recognized as leaders and innovators in the SIGINT field and all of us in that military specialty owe General Gray a great debt of gratitude.

I had met the general at several Marine Corps Cryptologic Association reunions and visited with him socially. Since General Gray was a Senior Fellow at the Potomac Institute for Policy Studies, I emailed him one night with a brief description of my manuscript and asked if he thought the Institute might have an interest in publishing it. His reply came back in just 66 minutes and he quickly connected me with all the appropriate people. The manuscript was sent off the next day. This old Sergeant of Marines is humbled and honored beyond measure by General Gray's quick response and willingness to help. I am also grateful to Mike Swetnam, CEO of the Potomac Institute for Policy Studies, for allowing the publication of this work.

Julie Davey is a writing professor at Fullerton College but we first met Julie and her husband, Robert, through our mutual love of aviation. Robert and I are both pilots and we attended the same recurrent training program every year. The aviation connection evolved into a friendship and since both Julie and Robert were published writers, I sought their guidance on getting my manuscript published.

Julie educated me on the publication process and offered loads of encouragement and help for which I am eternally grateful. And to show you what kind of person Julie is, she and a Navy chaplain at Camp Pendleton designed a therapeutic writing program for Marines who have suffered extremely traumatic combat experiences. I am very proud to have friends of that caliber.

I would also like to thank Ms. Sherry Loveless of the Potomac Institute Press. She guided me through the manuscript's editing process and her advice and mentorship definitely made this a much better book. She can cheerfully endure stupid questions from a neophyte author while being a consummate professional in the publication process. Based on my experience, that is a pretty rare talent in the publishing industry.

Last but not least, I have to acknowledge the United States Marine Corps. The Marines took me as an unguided and undisciplined youth and transformed me into a man with the discipline, confidence, focus, and perseverance to confront and overcome any challenge in life. In the Corps, I quickly learned that accountability was equally as important as responsibility. They gave me the education and training that set me on a fascinating career path that I never could have imagined or predicted, one that has served me well throughout my adult life. I've enjoyed my share of successes in life, but the accomplishment that makes me the proudest is earning the title of United States Marine. Many of my best friends are Marines and the Corps' ethos stays with you for the rest of your life.

Without the Marines, my life would have had a far different and less rewarding trajectory. It was in the Marines where I first began learning the ropes of becoming a successful intelligence professional and acquired a spirit of inquisitiveness, innovation, healthy skepticism, perfectionism, and professionalism. I learned the values of honor, courage, and commitment that seem so scarce in the politicized halls of power in Washington today. And, of course, they taught me Arabic before Arabic was cool. I got way more out of them than they ever got out of me. If I die homeless and penniless on the street tomorrow, I'll be the corpse lying at attention in the USMC T-shirt and ball cap. I'm eternally grateful for everything I learned and earned in the Marines.

– David M. Eneboe

IT'S THE IDEOLOGY

HOW TO DEFEAT ISLAMIST TERRORISM ONCE AND FOR ALL

TABLE OF CONTENTS

INTRODUCTION

*"... I know it's hard when you're up to your armpits in alligators
to remember you came here to drain the swamp."*

– Ronald Reagan

A swamp on the edge of town is a breeding ground for all sorts of pests, running the gamut from those that are a mere nuisance to those that can be quite deadly. Insects like mosquitoes and flies are most often just an annoyance and an inconvenience, but sometimes they can pass along diseases like malaria, dengue fever, encephalitis, yellow fever, Zika, and West Nile virus. Although rare, in extreme cases such illnesses may even be fatal. The danger to citizens, their children, and their pets from alligators and venomous snakes is obvious, but even an unexpected encounter with a non-poisonous serpent can be quite a shocking experience to an unsuspecting person. Swamps are nasty places that harbor nasty things.

The swamp ebbs and flows according to the amount of rain that falls every year, which will directly affect the number of pests in the swamp. Rainy years might bring out more mosquitoes and other critters while drier periods can provide some relief from the bugs.

Our imaginary town may put up physical barriers such as walls, berms, and fences in an attempt to keep the gators and snakes away from its citizens and their property. It may undertake measures such as neighborhood fogging to control mosquitoes and other potentially harmful insects while encouraging its residents to wear mosquito repellent, long sleeves, and pants when they go outdoors. The efforts to maintain the barriers and keep up the insect control will cost money and these tasks must be continued into perpetuity. But sooner or later, a cottonmouth or alligator will still find a way to slip past a wall, barrier, or fence and crawl into somebody's back yard. And sooner or later, the insects and mosquitoes will still find a way to bite us no matter what precautions we take. It is a natural and permanent consequence of living next to a swamp.

The swamp and its pests is a perfect analogy to the threat we are facing today from the terrorist ideology of Islamist extremism. Like a swamp, this deviant and perverted ideology provides a fetid breeding ground for all the malevolent pests that constantly buzz around our heads – pests like Al-Qaeda, the Islamic State (IS), Al-Shabaab, and Boko Haram. World events may drive an increase or decrease in terrorism just like rainfall regulates the rise and fall of water in a swamp.

And in this analogy the town situated next to the swamp is our homeland – and really the whole of modern society. Our current counterterrorism strategy is akin to the pest control measures in our hypothetical town. We can erect obstacles to keep out the snakes and gators (e.g., airport security procedures), kill those that we can track down (e.g., Osama bin Laden), undertake fogging to control and contain the mosquitoes (e.g., limited airstrikes against IS), and swat them when they land to bite us (e.g., neutralizing or preventing a terrorist attack). But regardless of what we do, we will never be completely free from the various insects and pests that live and thrive in the swamp (e.g., Islamist terrorists) that are an irritant, at best, and a serious threat, at worst.

Betting solely on counterterrorism measures to fight Islamists is the equivalent of relying exclusively on the bug spray and citronella candles we use in our backyards to guard against bothersome insects and the harmful diseases they may carry. Sometimes they work but more often than not the results are less than satisfying. Even the best counterterrorism measures in the world will not stop every terrorist or every attack every time. They only have to get lucky once – we have to be lucky every time.

It is as if our mythical little town is futilely and frantically trying to surround itself inside a screened-in porch to prevent the bugs from getting in, while the obvious solution is just to just drain the swamp in the first place. Naturally this will require a bit more planning, coordination, and investment, but the tradeoff is the permanent elimination of the source of all these pests (and the risks they carry) instead of just trying (unsuccessfully) to control the pests themselves. It is a one-time, long-term solution instead of an ongoing, short-term accommodation of the nuisance (or threat).

Now, I've been in the intelligence business and working as an Arabic linguist/analyst/collector for a long time — nearly 40 years. I spent a significant amount of that time in the Middle East where I gained a first-hand knowledge of Arab culture, Islam, and the worldview from the Muslim world. Along the way, several colleagues and coworkers of mine were killed in terrorist incidents, which motivated me over the years to learn more about the ideology that was responsible for their deaths. I have always believed that understanding the philosophy that underpins terrorism and extremism is absolutely key to ultimately defeating it. These victims weren't characters in a novel or a movie, they were real people I either met professionally or knew personally. They were dedicated to the ideals of American exceptionalism just like the 3,000 victims of 9/11, the sailors on the USS *Cole* in 2000, the airmen at Khobar Towers in 1996, the Marines in Beirut in 1983, and so many others. Their lives, their deaths, their memories, and their sacrifices deserve so much more than the handwringing and meaningless excuses and disappointing hyperbole that we get from our leaders and decision-makers today.

For decades, I've waited for somebody in Washington to wake up and adopt a comprehensive strategy to eradicate the extremist ideology behind the terror. It hasn't happened. It didn't happen in 1979 when Iranian students poured over the walls of the American Embassy in Tehran — and hundreds of US Marines, diplomats, journalists, and clergy in Lebanon paid the price for that oversight for the next decade. Instead, the government advised those of us serving abroad to wear body armor and vary our times going to and from work. More bug spray, anyone?

Our response to Islamist terrorism since 9/11 has lacked a strategic depth and focus. "Degrading" groups like Al-Qaeda and IS will not solve our problem because another like-minded group will inevitably emerge if we do not delegitimize and destroy the nihilistic ideology that our Islamist enemies embrace. Pest control or pest eradication? Do we want to put up with snakes and mosquitoes the rest of our lives, or do we want to live pest free? I know what my choice is and I know what my fallen comrades deserve.

This is not a history book, although it does contain some salient points of Arab and Islamic history. The observations on history are my own and they reflect my attempt to establish some of the historical, social, and cultural developments that have created the context for today's Middle East. As an analyst I know that there are reasons why things and people are the way they are. One needs to be wary of generalizing, stereotyping, and resorting to absolutes like "always" and "never." Objective knowledge – the truth – really is power. Preconceived notions and uninformed opinions serve to obfuscate the truth and make any objective analysis all but impossible.

This is not a theology book. I am not a Muslim. My thoughts and observations on Islam come from my years of experience working on Islamist terrorism as a linguist and analyst for the intelligence community. I am neither a basher of, nor an apologist for Muslims and I suspect that the majority of Muslims in the world are every bit as concerned about terrorism as we are. We will need them to be our allies in the struggle to defeat extremist ideology. The corrosive philosophy of Islamism originated from within their midst and their cooperation will be the key to defeating it. It cannot be done without them.

America has many more Muslim friends than enemies, but we still must be objective, open-minded, and knowledgeable enough to tell the difference. Muslims in general – and American Muslims, in particular – will have to take a stand to defend their faith. Islamism threatens them every bit as much as non-Muslims.

I often hear people say, "Not every Muslim is a terrorist but nearly every terrorist is a Muslim." So what? In the 1920s and '30s any American could have easily said, "Not every white guy is a bank robber but nearly every bank robber is a white guy." It's an obvious attempt at stereotyping. One of our most egregious strategic mistakes has been tarnishing all Muslims with the same brush while believing that terrorism is the enemy instead of the ideology that breeds it. We haven't taken our eye off the ball – we never had it on the ball in the first place.

At the same time, to portray Islam as only "a religion of peace" is simplistic and Pollyannaish in the extreme. After all, three of the first four of the religion's "rightly-guided caliphs" did not die natural deaths. You don't go through 1400 years of history without good times and bad times, without periods of both violence and peace. To think otherwise is an open defiance of not only human history but human nature, as well.

ON SEMANTICS

This book endeavors to strip away much of today's stereotyping and political correctness in an effort to actually achieve some level of objectivity, a perspective that is sorely lacking in our media and our government. It's the only way for us to recognize, confront, and eliminate the security threat to us posed by the mentality of Islamist extremism.

To that end, let me make some important semantic distinctions. First, I will not refer in this book to Islamist terrorist groups (like the Islamic State or Al-Qaeda) as being *jihadist*. I may cite others who have done so, but I prefer not to use that term. Nor will I refer to their followers and members as *jihadist* or *mujahideen*. Instead, they will be identified as what they really are: Islamists, terrorists, extremists, *Salafists*, or *takfiris* (*takfirists*). The concept of *jihad* in Islam has a positive connotation to the religion's followers but nothing these Islamists are doing can be construed as positive in any way, shape, or form. I believe we have the responsibility to avoid conveying any unintended or accidental legitimacy on the crimes these terrorists are committing so let's stop using *jihadist* and call them what they really are. This is actually step one of my plan and it (along with *takfirism* and *Salafism*) will be discussed in greater detail later in the book.

Second, there needs to be a clear distinction between the adjectives "Islamic" and "Islamist." In this book, any use of the term Islamic will refer to the general history of Islam or concepts related to the practice of its orthodox beliefs, rites, and customs. Islamist, in contrast, will be used to refer to the extreme and intolerant beliefs of those practicing *Salafism* or *takfirism* that fall outside the established and recognized boundaries and norms of Islam. These terms are sometimes used interchangeably in the media or without adequate explanation, and that just creates confusion and needlessly slanders Islam and Muslims. Accuracy is important. We are competing for hearts and minds here.

And finally, I don't like the designations of Muslim American, Black American, Jewish American, etc. To me these terms somehow legitimize the qualification of one's citizenship. Our society and media often seem to place more emphasis on the adjective than the noun it is modifying. We should all be Americans first and foremost and whatever other characteristics with which we might identify should be secondary. In this book I prefer to use the terms "American Muslim," "American Black," or "American Jew," for example. Let's emphasize what unites us first (*E Pluribus Unum!*) and then respect and celebrate our differences. I do not believe that constantly hyphenating and qualifying our citizenship brings our society and our people any closer together. It serves only to divide us.

Here is one more important point in closing. When I was in Marine Corps boot camp 40 years ago, my drill instructors never exhorted us to be losers. It was never okay to be second best. We had to march and drill better than the other platoons in our company and, indeed, even the other recruit training battalions. We had to have the shiniest boots and brass and the sharpest creases in our uniforms. We had to be motivated to fight harder and smarter than everyone else. Our performance on the rifle range or during infantry training just had to be superior. Why? To win! And the reason why Marines are such great warriors is because *they believe that they are the best*. This philosophy, this *ethos* is ingrained in them from the very first day of boot camp and any recruits who don't adopt it will simply wash out at some point. "That's good enough" is not the Marine Corps motto.

Similarly any athlete can train at the gym and reach a certain level of proficiency. But champions become champions because *they believe they are the best*. It's mind over muscle; the power of positive thinking. Whatever you want to call it, they see themselves as winners – they visualize their success. Our nation desperately needs that sort of visualization today so that we can stop wasting time and resources on failed strategies and start winning. It's time for results instead of excuses. It's time for something new instead of more of the same.

America is an exceptional country by any metric. We are winners because we believe in ourselves. But if we want to win the war against Islamism and terror once and for all, there is no alternative to draining the swamp. The good news is that our victory in this conflict is virtually assured and we don't have to wait generations and decades to achieve it – if we are serious about draining the swamp. The bad news is that we will be doomed to a never-ending purgatory of strife and conflict if we keep on doing what we have been doing. And remember this, when we cut through all the political spin and rhetoric we reach a singular truth: *if we're not fighting to win, why are we even fighting?* You don't go to war to "contain" or "degrade" an enemy; you go to war to defeat and destroy him. And make no mistake, we are in a war with the Islamists.

Our leaders in Washington have told us that the nation is "war weary" but I don't think that is really true. What we're weary of is Washington losing battles and foundering in the dark without a clear strategy for victory. I doubt that sentiments about being "war weary" would be expressed if we were tangibly winning this war.

Image Credit: Alex Taliesen.

CHAPTER ONE

IT'S TIME FOR A REALITY CHECK

*"Insanity is doing the same thing over and
over and expecting different results."*

– Anonymous

The first shot in our war against *Salafist* Islamist extremism wasn't fired on
9/11. It actually came on December 29, 1992 when two hotels in Aden,
Yemen were bombed in the belief that they were housing United States
Marines who were on their way to Somalia. In 2008, Osama bin Laden
would take credit for these attacks,[1] although the United States seemed
blissfully unaware of Al-Qaeda's existence in 1992. No Marines were actually there but unfortunately, the attack did claim the lives of a couple of
European tourists.

These terrorists ambitiously took the fight all the way to US soil on
February 26, 1993 when Ramzi Yousef detonated a truck bomb in the
parking garage below the North Tower of the World Trade Center in New
York City. Coincidentally, Yousef's uncle is Khalid Sheikh Mohammed
(yes, the eventual mastermind of 9/11).

In November 1995, a group calling itself the Islamic Movement for
Change claimed responsibility for a car bombing in Riyadh, Saudi Arabia

---

1.   Michael Scheuer, *Through Our Enemies' Eyes: Osama bin Laden, Radical Islam, and the
     Future of America, Revised Edition* (Dulles, VA: Potomac Books, 2006), 147.

that killed five Americans. This group is believed to have evolved from Al-Qaeda in Saudi Arabia.[2]

In 1998, Al-Qaeda operatives carried out the simultaneous bombings of the US embassies in Nairobi, Kenya and Dar es Salaam, Tanzania. These attacks killed over 300 people. In October 2000, the group struck once again in Aden, Yemen with its attack on the USS *Cole* that killed 17 sailors. And, of course, on September 11, 2001, Al-Qaeda killed 3,000 people when its members hijacked four commercial airliners and flew them into the World Trade Center and the Pentagon. Only the heroic actions of the fourth plane's passengers prevented it from striking yet another target. In contrast to 1992, every American now knew who Osama bin Laden was.

The group dispatched shoe and underwear bombers on US air carriers destined for the United States in 2001 and 2009, respectively. From 2002 until 2005, tourist hotels and expatriate housing compounds were bombed in Bali, Kenya, Saudi Arabia, Morocco, Indonesia, and Turkey. In 2009, an Al-Qaeda double agent killed seven CIA officers at Camp Chapman, Afghanistan.

Despite our claims that "Al-Qaeda Central" had been "degraded," the group's affiliate in Yemen attempted to down two cargo aircraft with sophisticated bombs concealed in printers in 2010 (after its failed 2009 "underwear bomber" plot).

In 2013 the North African franchise, Al-Qaeda in the Islamic Maghreb, occupied a natural gas facility at In Amenas, Algeria in a hostage-taking operation in which dozens of expatriate Western workers were eventually killed. Later that same year, Al-Qaeda's East Africa subsidiary – Al-Shabaab – attacked an upscale shopping mall in Nairobi, Kenya in an operation that took the lives of over 60 innocent shoppers.

The above list is by no means all-inclusive. However it is representative of the persistence of the *Salafist*-inspired Islamist extremist threat and it is indicative that whatever we are doing to combat the ideology of that

---

2. "Al-Haramain Brigades/Islamic Movement for Change," Terrorism Research & Analysis Consortium website. Accessed July 13, 2017. http://www.trackingterrorism.org/group/al-haramain-brigades-islamic-movement-change.

extremism is not working. And as long as we don't combat that ideology we are simply dooming ourselves to endless conflict, neither winning nor even ending it.

Think I'm wrong? In 1992 we were faced with a nascent Al-Qaeda and just a handful of sympathizers that had received some form of basic military training from the group in simple, primitive, makeshift camps in Afghanistan. Today we are confronting over 30,000 fanatical extremists in the Islamic State alone, according to CIA estimates cited in the September 12, 2014 edition of *Time Magazine*. That figure was corroborated by Colonel Steve Warren, the *Operation Inherent Resolve* spokesman, in a January 6, 2016 Pentagon press briefing.[3] In addition we must also contend with the likes of *Nusra* Front (which now calls itself *Jabhat Fateh al-Sham* or the Front for the Conquest of the Levant), *Khorasan* Group, Al-Shabaab, Boko Haram, Al-Qaeda in the Islamic Maghreb, and Al-Qaeda in the Arabian Peninsula. None of those groups existed in 1992 or even in 2001 for that matter.

It's time for a reality check. In the near quarter century since the first Al-Qaeda bombings that targeted US interests in Aden, we've invaded and occupied Iraq and Afghanistan. We've mounted hundreds of drone strikes in Pakistan, Afghanistan, Yemen, and now even North Africa. We've killed Al-Qaeda icons such as Osama bin Laden and Anwar al-Awlaki and zapped or captured scores of other militants, commanders, and figureheads in the hinterlands of Pakistan and Yemen. We're flying airstrikes daily against the Islamic State in Iraq and Syria. And yet, the end result is that we are now fighting hundreds of thousands of extremists and their sympathizers from Southwest Asia all the way to the Maghreb instead of just a few dozen in 1992 in the Arabian Peninsula. That doesn't even count the sympathizers and supporters in Western Europe and America. Is this what successful "degrading" is supposed to look like?

We've come up with all manner of technical marvels during this conflict such as the aforementioned drones – unmanned aerial systems that can launch Hellfire missiles from two miles up with extreme accuracy. But

---

3. "Department of Defense Press Briefing by Col. Steve Warren via teleconference from Baghdad, Iraq," US Department of Defense website, January 6, 2016. Accessed July 13, 2017. http://www.defense.gov/News/News-Transcripts/Transcript-View/Article/641754/ department-of-defense-press-briefing-by-col-warren-via-teleconference-from-bagh.

sending an estimated $16 million MQ-9 Reaper[4] to fire a $99,600 AGM-114 Hellfire missile[5] at a couple of insurgents planting a $50 improvised explosive device (IED) still has not won us the war.

To protect our warriors on the battlefield from that same $50 IED, we came up with the mine-resistant ambush protected vehicle more commonly known as the MRAP. Like battleships on wheels, these behemoths were produced in the thousands at around $600,000 per unit and the Pentagon has credited them with saving the lives of 40,000 US servicemen and women.[6] Nevertheless, it's nearly impossible to chase down a nimble enemy scampering through his native countryside on foot when you're in a lumbering vehicle with all the agility of an elephant wearing high heels. And if the point were to protect our warfighters at the very expense of their ability to actually prosecute the war they have been sent to fight, wouldn't it have just been cheaper to keep them home in the first place?

We've even invented kinder, gentler munitions like the Small Diameter Bomb or the GBU-39. This 250-pound smart bomb can be dropped at targets more than 40 nautical miles away from the launching aircraft and the smaller blast will reduce "collateral damage." At $239,000 per bomb, these less destructive weapons still do not come cheap.[7]

All these advanced technological developments and overseas deployments that keep the military-industrial complex chugging along are costing America gazillions of dollars it doesn't have under the pretext of keeping us safe. Unfortunately, we are playing right into the playbook of our extremist adversaries, who wish to draw us into a lengthy war of attrition. If they can't compete with us militarily, the next best thing is to exhaust us economically and politically. There are numerous audio lectures and

---

4. "US Air Force MQ-9 Reaper Fact Sheet," US Air Force website, September 23, 2015. Accessed July 13, 2017. http://www.af.mil/About-Us/Fact-Sheets/Display/Article/104470/mq-9-reaper/.

5. "AGM-114 Hellfire Missile," Aeroweb, April 8, 2015. Accessed July 13, 2017. http://www.fi-aeroweb.com/Defense/AGM-114-Hellfire-Missile-System.html.

6. Chris Rohlfs and Ryan Sullivan, "The MRAP Boondoggle," *Foreign Affairs* Magazine, July 26, 2012. Accessed July 13, 2017. https://www.foreignaffairs.com/articles/2012-07-26/mrap-boondoggle.

7. Small Diameter Bomb," Aeroweb, November 10, 2014. Accessed July 13, 2017. http://www.fi-aeroweb.com/Defense/Small-Diameter-Bomb.html.

publications available on terrorist forums and chat rooms that preach this very principle – I know because I've translated many of them myself. It's classic guerilla warfare strategy right out of Che Guevara and Mao Zedong but we don't seem to have an actual, comprehensive strategy of our own – we're too busy reacting and throwing money at the problem to recognize this glaring fact. And by always reacting to the terrorists and ignoring other strategic fields of the conflict, we've ceded them control of the war's operational tempo. That is not a recipe for our success or victory.

Look at our March 2003 invasion of Iraq and the ensuing eight-and-a-half-year occupation of that country under the pretense of "regime change," the favorite buzz phrase of the period, and the allegations of secret weapons of mass destruction (WMD) programs. We expended the lives of 4,485 US service personnel during the invasion and occupation of Iraq.[8] In addition, nearly *half a million* Iraqis died during the process from 2003-2011 and that figure is believed to be a *low estimate*.[9] Just our direct costs of that war resulted in a price tag of *$2 trillion*.[10]

Was it worth it? Has Iraq become a stable, democratic, friendly ally of the United States? No, and it's worse off now in virtually every respect than it was before we invaded. Instead of a showcase of Western democracy in the Middle East, our meddling created a breeding ground for terrorists and a failed state. How is it that we won every battle yet lost the war? Could the miscalculations of two White Houses and the lack of strategic vision be to blame?

And as far as the war in Afghanistan is concerned – our longest military conflict – the ultimate success of democracy and tolerance in that country after we depart is still very much in doubt. My money is on an eventual reprise of our Iraq debacle if we don't do things according to battlefield conditions rather than some arbitrary deadline that has been set for domestic political considerations.

---

8. As of July 13, 2017 the Iraq Coalition Casualty Count website listed 4,485 US fatalities in Iraq by the end of 2011. http://icasualties.org.
9. Dan Vergano, "Half-Million Iraqis Died in War, New Study Says," *National Geographic*, October 16, 2013. Accessed July 13, 2017. http://news.nationalgeographic.com/news/2013/10/131015-iraq-war-deaths-survey-2013/.
10. Daniel Trotta, "Iraq War Costs U.S. More than $2 Trillion: Study," *Reuters*, March 14, 2013. Accessed July 13, 2017. http://www.reuters.com/article/2013/03/14/us-iraq-war-anniversary-idUSBRE92D0PG20130314.

In fact, when we look at our policy failures in Libya, Syria, and Egypt during the 2011 Arab Spring, we must go all the way back to *Desert Shield/Desert Storm* in 1990-91 to find our last real success in the Middle East.

Amazingly, as the medieval Islamic State barbarians behead, shoot, and crucify their way through Iraq, Syria, Libya, Egypt, Tunisia, France, Belgium, and the United States; as Boko Haram kidnaps and bombs its way across Nigeria; and as Al-Shabaab carries out terrorist operations in Somalia and Kenya, our leaders simply call for these groups to be "degraded."

As the number of Islamist extremist groups has mushroomed in the Middle East and Africa since 1992 and the fighters filling their ranks have swelled from just a handful to tens of thousands, why doesn't Washington have a plan for strategic victory by now?

We have squandered priceless blood and resources in a failed attempt to fight terrorist groups instead of combating the ideology that actually breeds the terrorism. Defeating that ideology and preventing future generations of Islamist terrorists is where the smart money should be going. As a Marine, that's what I think real victory should look like — not just dropping bombs on groups whose members may already have a death wish, anyway.

Overreliance on counterterrorism is not the answer, either. Playing defense alone will not win this war and the evidence of that lies in the fact that even though our government had foreknowledge about the Boston Marathon brothers, the Fort Hood shooter, the underwear bomber, and the Times Square bomber, it still failed to prevent any of those attacks. Moreover, the recent attacks in Paris, Belgium, San Bernardino, and Orlando point to the difficulty of even detecting disaffected lone wolves. Wouldn't it be better to eliminate the ideology that has radicalized them instead of trying to detect and stop them once they have already been radicalized? Isn't an ounce of prevention better (and cheaper) than a pound of cure, especially when that "cure" might involve invading and occupying a Middle Eastern country?

This is a war of hearts and minds if there ever was one and we won't be scoring any points with our target audience by using enhanced interrogation techniques or torture, either. America is much better than that, all the jingoistic slogans and flag waving notwithstanding. Such tactics did not save Mubarak, Al-Assad, or Gaddafi even though they had squads of torturers ripping out prisoners' fingernails (and worse) on a daily basis. Torture just doesn't work and it just does not measure up to our values and ideals. We should not make the mistake of translating our natural human desire for punishment and retribution into official US policy that would short circuit the successful prosecution of our war in the process.

We need to be a beacon of hope and an example to the rest of the world. That can never happen if we subject enemy combatants to torture. America can't very well criticize human rights abuses elsewhere when we are waterboarding people in black site prisons around the world. It's tough to win hearts and minds when our own actions paint us as hypocrites in the eyes of those we seek to influence.

It really is time for a reality check. What we've been doing isn't working. Before we recklessly embark on yet another foolish military misadventure, before we put our great-grandchildren into even more debt by buying more high-tech weapons and toys that won't win our struggle, and before we sacrifice any more of our freedoms under some failed notion that we are making ourselves safer, the time has come for us to be honest with ourselves.

We are losing the war on Islamist extremism because we don't have a real strategy for winning it. The Islamists are exponentially larger in number just since 9/11 and they have metastasized into multiple countries, not just Afghanistan. There are numerous extremist groups now, not just Al-Qaeda. Our job now will be infinitely more difficult because we've been ineffective in countering the terrorist narrative and preventing the expansion of terrorism in the areas where it now flourishes. We're paying the price of "lone wolf" attacks in places like France, Canada, and right here in the United States because we haven't done anything to defeat the ideology.

The Marine in me is angered that I hear no one in Washington ever talking about winning the war against extremism. I hear no one articulating a comprehensive strategy for countering and eradicating the Islamist ideology of hatred, intolerance, and violence. This is America – the world's only remaining superpower – and it is long past time for us to act like it! We won the Cold War not by bombing or "degrading" the militaries of the Soviet Union and the Warsaw Pact nations, but by defeating the communist ideology and forcing the implosion of the Soviet communist economy. We won because while dictators embraced communism and autocracy, their people yearned for democracy and freedom. We won because throngs of people came here from all over the world to live the American dream; nobody wanted to go to the Soviet Union's "workers' paradise." Winning our current battle requires the same strategic vision and patience.

The first step in the process is to be honest about who and what we are fighting. As a linguist, I can tell you that "Islam" in Arabic simply means "submission" and the word does not necessarily distinguish between submission that is voluntary and submission that is coerced. Let's drop the feel-good adjectives from those who claim that Islam is merely a religion of "peace." There is no shortage of violent verses found in the Koran or the oral narratives attributed to Muhammad that exhort his followers to wage war against unbelievers and there are millions of very devout, conservative Muslims who fervently believe this. They believe they can cite 1,400 years of scholarly Islamic jurisprudence to support their beliefs. Sticking our heads in the sand to ignore these facts isn't going to change them, no matter how politically correct we endeavor to be.

But neither does this mean that all Muslims are our enemies or that our war is against Islam itself. All great religions (and societies) have had their own shortcomings and triumphs and Islam is no different. It has had periods of great enlightenment and tolerance and others of great violence. We must avoid falling into the trap of negative stereotypes and recognize that Muslims, like Christians, belong to many different denominations with varying belief structures under several theological schools of thought. These orthodox Muslims represent the overwhelming majority and we will have to find allies among them to help us construct and propagate a successful counter-narrative to that of our terrorist enemies as we roll back their ideology.

To that end, there is respectable, recent polling evidence to show that most Muslims are just as worried about the spread of Islamist radicalism as we are.[11] And why shouldn't they be? The terrorists are often bombing, beheading, and crucifying right there in the Muslims' own backyards. We'll look at this in greater detail later in the book.

Next we have to be honest with ourselves that we are fighting a war with extremism that must be fought on all fronts. It must be fought in cyber-space, social media, television, and wherever our message can be sent. Their narrative must be confronted and defeated everywhere. With a nod to former President Bill Clinton and his campaign advisor James Carville, "It's the ideology, stupid."

We have made the strategic mistake of framing our conflict as a war on terrorism – the Global War on Terror (GWoT). In doing so we have completely missed the boat on what our real objective is and how we should go about achieving it. The terrorism that is plaguing the world from an increasing number of Islamist extremists is but a consequence of their radical and intolerant philosophy and ideology. Terrorism is only a symptom of the disease, not the disease itself. The only way our war can be won is through a Global War on Islamism (GWoI). If we delegitimize and eliminate radical Islamism, we will delegitimize and eliminate the terrorism that springs from it.

Unfortunately, what we have been doing is merely prolonging and even perpetuating the war by limiting our strategy to one of counterterror-ism and limited military action. It's a colossal waste of money, as well. Even though counterterrorism is an important element of our fight, it doesn't do any good when it isn't catching known terrorists and pre-venting them from carrying out their attacks. We have a shameful track record in this regard. Ineffective counterterrorism is just as bad as no counterterrorism at all.

Military action must inevitably be part of our comprehensive strategy but we must be smarter in how we employ it. Our misadventures in Iraq and Afghanistan have cost us trillions in expenditure and thousands of precious lives, yet served only to exacerbate our plight. By occupying Muslim lands as a non-Muslim power, we have made the situation much worse. Our

---

11. "Muslim Publics Share Concerns about Extremist Groups," Pew Research Center Survey, September 10, 2013. Accessed July 13, 2017. http://www.pewglobal.org/2013/09/10/muslim-publics-share-concerns-about-extremist-groups/.

occupation has fostered resentment and that resentment has only created more terrorists. Once again, we played right into our enemies' hands when they claim that America and the West is at war with Muslims and their religion. This isn't rocket science; it's sociology and human nature. How would we feel if America were occupied by a foreign power?

Pinprick airstrikes against the Islamic State and tying our hands behind our backs by promising never to have "boots on the ground" in Iraq and Syria certainly sent the wrong message to our allies and adversaries alike. This kind of rhetoric might play well to segments of the US domestic audience but it telegraphs to IS and others that we aren't really serious in our desire to defeat them once and for all. It actually encourages them to step up their war against us. After all, if you're hell-bent on martyrdom anyway, what do you have to lose?

Our leaders – elected and appointed – are letting us down. According to the episode of the CBS news program *60 Minutes* that aired on May 1, 2016, our politicians in Congress are spending half or more of their work-week "dialing for dollars" and making fundraising calls even as they cannot agree on a real budget for our government. Such misplaced priorities are not a Republican or Democrat problem, they are a systemic Washington problem. We are at war so let's act like it. Let's wake up, get our heads out of our hindquarters, and resolve to confront our enemy on *every* field of battle and not be satisfied until we are ultimately triumphant over the medieval ideology that seeks our destruction. The American people – and our very way of life – deserve nothing less. Period.

The Marine Corps holds fast to three core values: honor, courage and commitment. I think they would serve us all well in the crisis we are facing today.

Honor: The Merriam-Webster online dictionary defines honor as "respect given to someone who is admired" or "high moral standards of behavior." These aren't the qualities that the overwhelming majority of Americans use to describe their Congressional delegates from either house, irrespective of party affiliation. Congress's approval ratings have been in the toilet for years because most of us don't think our senators and representatives are honest to begin with, let alone doing the jobs to which we elected them. The politicians aren't doing anything to restore our trust and confidence in them, either.

Honor is about doing the right thing – even when nobody is watching. The members of Congress can and must do better if the institution is to serve the best interests of our nation and its people. If they don't, we the people should boot them out.

Courage: The Merriam-Webster online dictionary defines courage as "the ability to do something that you know is difficult or dangerous" or "mental or moral strength to venture, persevere, and withstand danger, fear, or difficulty." While we should expect this definition to apply to our politicians and policymakers, it must also apply to all of us. We must all have the courage to face our challenges honestly and objectively, free of any perceptions and stereotypes that may be colored either by personal bias or political correctness but not based on fact.

Courage and honor have a symbiotic relationship. It's nearly impossible to "do the right thing" with honor unless one also has the moral courage to do so. Likewise courage and the ability to "withstand danger, fear, or difficulty" similarly require honor and "high moral standards of behavior." You cannot have one without the other.

Most of all, we must have the courage to abandon the status quo for some new and innovative thinking. Fortunately, this is exactly the sort of thing at which the American people excel. We are optimists by nature whose gaze is firmly fixed on the future. The challenges we face also offer opportunities and we must not be afraid to seize them. Americans will never accept the medieval, seventh century *Weltanschauung* of the Islamists and, quite frankly, neither will most of the world's Muslims. We are not alone in our fight.

Commitment: This seems pretty self-explanatory. If we are going to be successful in defeating and eradicating the threat from radical Islamist ideology, then we must be committed to seeing our strategy through. And we must have the honor and courage to sustain that commitment *without backing down.* As Americans, we all must be committed to the war effort in order to achieve victory. It's not just for members of our armed forces or the CIA. Popular support was critical for winning World War II and it's even more crucial for winning our war against a nebulous, shadowy enemy who, nevertheless, is just as committed to our defeat as any Japanese or Nazi soldier ever was.

We've spent trillions of dollars on invasions and long-term occupations of Iraq and Afghanistan and neither of those brought us any closer to victory against our Islamist foes. On the home front our vast counterterrorism enterprise has been unable to adapt effectively to our enemies' shift from grand, 9/11-style attacks to the lone wolf incidents that are becoming more and more frequent. And whenever we fail, the answer is always to throw more money at the problem rather than examining whether or not we are fighting the right war with the right tools against the right enemy.

We've had a succession of administrations going all the way back to that of Bill Clinton whose responses to the acts of *Salafist*-inspired terrorism have been limited primarily to the tactical level: retribution and counterterrorism. We have battled groups like Al-Qaeda without successfully engaging the ideology and radicalism that is their *raison d'etre*. That's why we now see a variety of *Salafist* extremist groups that have metastasized in the region and whose influence and reach is now threatening the West. What we don't comprehend is that they believe they win just by not being completely eliminated.

We invaded Afghanistan in 2001 to topple the Taliban and deny the country as a safe haven for Osama bin Laden and Al-Qaeda. But then what? What was the plan? What was the overall strategy? What were the conditions of victory? As this conflict has bogged down to become America's longest war, after a decade-and-a-half do we even still know what victory there will look like? Or will this be like our military disasters in Vietnam and Iraq where we will struggle to find an excuse – any excuse – just to get out of there?

Exit strategies are for losers. We should never be committing American military men and women to action in risky enterprises unless we have a clear strategy for victory and a viable plan for achieving it *before the first shot is ever fired*. The application of military force must be *one part of an overarching strategy*, not the only tool in the toolbox. It is a tool that should be used sparingly since the problem is not intrinsically a military one. We're not doing so well in this regard.

There's plenty of blame to go around, too. The Republican administration of George W. Bush set the stage for the mess in Iraq today when it decided to invade the country in 2003. I never met a single intelligence community analyst who thought that the invasion was justified or even a good idea. That administration's failure to comprehend the cultural dynamics of the country and the strategic ramifications of our invasion and occupation were worrisome evidence that the world's only remaining superpower had lost its geopolitical and geostrategic mojo.

The Democrats haven't done any better. President Obama became to the Global War on Islamism what Lyndon Baines Johnson was to the Vietnam War. Like Johnson, he had no strategy for victory. As I mentioned, he imposed limits on how we could fight the Islamic State in Iraq and Syria. These were self-imposed political restraints that guaranteed we would have to fight the terrorists with at least one hand tied behind our back just like Johnson defined what targets we could and could not bomb in Vietnam. In the same mercurial fashion by which Johnson started and stopped bombing campaigns, President Obama sought to arbitrarily end wars based solely on a calendar date that had absolutely no relevance to the battlefield situation. Can you imagine a real military strategist like Douglas MacArthur or George Patton making those kinds of mistakes in World War II? A wise leader would give his military whatever resources are needed to ensure victory, not impose political constraints that will only guarantee that we'll waste money we don't have in an inadequate effort that we won't win.

Like Johnson, Obama's White House had a reputation for micromanaging the Pentagon's military operations in Iraq and Syria. Despite a record number of staffers on its National Security Council, that council failed to articulate a strategy against Islamism while focusing instead on fighting this or that group. The administration claimed that its bombing campaign had significantly degraded the Islamic State, but if that really were the case, why did the group suddenly appear in Libya beheading Egyptian Copts? Why did it gain traction in Egypt? Why did it spread to Yemen and Tunisia? We seem to be making the same mistake of believing we can contain the phenomenon of Islamist violence without strategically defeating its root cause – the ideology. As Yogi Berra put it, "It's *déjà vu* all over again."

Barack Obama had his own "Mission Accomplished" moment when he grabbed the headlines and television screens to pat his administration on the back for killing Osama bin Laden. It was as if the terrorist's elimination would somehow pronounce the benediction to the Global War on Terror. Frankly the killing of bin Laden is comparable to the killing of Admiral Isoruku Yamamoto – the architect of the attack on Pearl Harbor – in 1943. It didn't end the Second World War, but the man Americans perceived to have started it was brought to justice.

This book offers a roadmap out of the dysfunctional morass in which Washington finds itself. It provides a guide for combating the extremism of today and – most importantly – preventing the radicalization and terrorism of tomorrow. That must be our strategic objective.

We're at a critical moment of truth and we must acknowledge that what we have been doing isn't working. We are facing many more terrorists and extremists now, and in more parts of the world, than we did in 1992 or even in the immediate aftermath of 9/11. It's time to rethink, reboot, and reposition ourselves to fight and achieve strategic victory in the Global War on Islamism. Just like fire creates its own wind, victory creates its own momentum. We have to *think* like winners. *That* is what America and Americans will support and *that* is what they deserve – nothing more, nothing less!

Ronald Reagan is often criticized by the left and idolized by the right, but nobody can deny that the guy really was the Great Communicator. He had a way with words that resonated with the American public.

He once said, "Here's my strategy on the Cold War. We win, they lose." Pretty simple. And guess what? We won and they lost. Maybe there's a lesson in that.

Today we have hordes of blue-suited "experts" on every cable channel telling us what we should be doing. Yet, with all this bloviating we are still no closer to victory than we were in 1992, or even after 9/11. All this white noise doesn't provide clarity; it just makes the issue more difficult than it needs to be.

If we defeat the Islamist ideology, we will defeat the terrorism that it breeds. And contrary to the doom and gloom from the blue suits, this does not have to be a war lasting many generations. Our victory is already all but assured and this book offers an achievable strategy for getting us there.

14

CHAPTER TWO

ENVIRONMENT IS EVERYTHING

*"It ain't what you don't know that gets you into trouble.
It's what you know for sure that just ain't so."*

– Mark Twain

One of seventeenth-century English poet and priest John Donne's most famous lines is, "No man is an island, entire of itself." We are all products of our environment; we are shaped and molded by our cultures, our societal mores, our religious values, our families, our educational systems, and our life experiences. This is true for every human being on the planet. We all share the same biology but our individual environments create the lens through which we all view and interpret the world around us.

We justifiably see the perpetrators of the terrorist attacks against America on 9/11 as our enemies, but they didn't carry out their attacks in a vacuum. They didn't just wake up one day and decide to martyr themselves for their cause by hijacking commercial airplanes and flying them into the Pentagon and the twin towers of the World Trade Center in New York. Each of those terrorists was a product of his own environment who responded to the ideology of Osama bin Laden (and others before him) and each was willing to sacrifice himself, believing that he was doing so in the cause of Allah. If we are to defeat this ideology, then we must first gain a fundamental grasp of the environment from which it is born. We must know our enemy in order to fight and defeat him.

This necessity has been confirmed by no less a military authority than the ancient Chinese general Sun Tzu, "Hence the saying: If you know the enemy and know yourself, you need not fear the result of a hundred battles. If you know yourself but not the enemy, for every victory gained you will also suffer a defeat. If you know neither the enemy nor yourself, you will succumb in every battle."[12]

To understand the fabric and context of our enemies' environment we have to review some history. We often tend to generalize and stereotype Arabs and Muslims without really knowing who they are. Pundits and commentators with only a few seconds to make a point in our fast-paced media world can sometimes convey the impression that all Muslim Arabs are terrorist fanatics or that nearly every teenaged Arab youth aspires to be a suicide bomber. Similarly, we hear words like "caliphate" used with grim foreboding that indicates the end of the world is nigh. But yet we've had 1,400 years of Islamic history involving caliphates, empires, and dynasties of all different kinds in the Middle East, and for the most part they looked very different than what is happening in Iraq and Syria today. In fact, much of that period was marked with a great deal of scientific and cultural advancement, education, and tolerance. The violence we see quoted in Koranic verses and the oral passages attributed to the Prophet Muhammad himself actually pertain to Arab-on-Arab violence in seventh century Saudi Arabia when the prophet and his followers sought to Islamize the entire Arabian Peninsula.

What seems to have coalesced out of the ashes of 9/11 is a sense of *us* versus *them*. This is a classic social psychology response where an in-group (i.e., Americans) perceives a threat from an out-group (i.e., Muslims). The in-group will tend to stereotype all members of that out-group and view them all as a potential threat. Perhaps this was inevitable after President George W. Bush declared, "Either you are with us, or you are with the terrorists," in his address to a joint session of Congress on September 20, 2001 in the immediate aftermath of that terrible tragedy.

This spawned a spate of Muslim bashing in our country that, for some, has apparently turned into a profitable cottage industry. Dehumanizing an enemy makes them easier to hate but stereotyping is dangerous and unfair. The actions of Al-Qaeda, Islamic State, or Al-Shabaab do not represent mainstream Islam.

---

12. Sun Tzu, *The Art of War*, trans. Lionel Giles (Blacksburg: Thrifty Books, 2009), 79.

Our war is against *extremism in the name of Islam*, not Islam itself. Our enemies are *Islamists*, not Muslims. This is a very important distinction because we aren't going to solve our problem by attacking every Muslim nation on earth. Better and smarter engagement with mainstream Islamic countries and the discarding of stereotypes (ours and theirs) will go a long way toward fixing this. This topic will be addressed in much greater detail later in the book.

So, if we are to formulate and execute a successful strategy for eradicating Islamist extremism around the world, we must be willing to abandon our stereotypes and look at the problem objectively. After all, there are an estimated 1.6 billion Muslims in the world[13] with just under three-and-a-half million in North America.[14] The overwhelming majority of these individuals are not extremists and do not themselves have a positive view of extremists and extremism. They do not want to trade in their modern conveniences to live in the seventh century.

Just like there is a diversity of beliefs among Christians in a broad range of denominations in the Protestant, Orthodox, and Catholic branches of the faith, there is a similar diversity of beliefs under the various denominations of *Sunni* and *Shia* Islam. While our media constantly focuses on the atrocities of the extremist Islamic State, the BBC's "Trending" blog reported on November 25, 2014 that some Muslim moderates are surprisingly turning to social media to reject implementation of the *Sharia*. There is no one-size-fits-all stereotype of a Christian and the same holds true for Muslims.

There is hard evidence to back this up. In September 2013, the Pew Research Global Attitudes Project published the results of a survey conducted from March 3 - April 7, 2013 of 11 Muslim publics. The survey consisted of face-to-face interviews with nearly 9,000 Muslims in Egypt, Indonesia, Jordan, Lebanon, Malaysia, Nigeria, Pakistan, the Palestinian territories, Senegal, Tunisia, and Turkey. The survey showed widespread concern over the growth of "Islamic extremism" and a clear

---

13. Drew DeSilver and David Masci, "World's Muslim Population More Widespread than You Might Think," Pew Research Center, January 31, 2017. Accessed July 13, 2017. http://www.pewresearch.org/fact-tank/2013/06/07/worlds-muslim-population-more-widespread-than-you-might-think/.

14. *Ibid.*

rejection of suicide bombing in the name of Islam. Some findings of the survey included:

- Two-thirds of the survey's respondents were either somewhat or very concerned about "Islamic extremism" and those concerns had increased from the previous year in five of the countries polled: Pakistan, Jordan, Tunisia, Turkey, and Indonesia.

- More than half of those questioned (57%) across the entire sample had an unfavorable opinion of Al-Qaeda, Osama bin Laden, and other extremist groups.

- Strong majorities in several of the aforementioned Muslim countries opposed violence in the name of Islam. Nearly nine in ten respondents in Pakistan and approximately eight in ten respondents in Indonesia, Nigeria, and Tunisia expressed their belief that "suicide bombings or other acts of violence that target civilians are never justified."[15]

But while we in the West and a majority of Muslims share a common concern for increasing Islamic extremism, that has not translated into better relations between *us* and *them*. In a separate 2011 study entitled, "Muslim-Western Tensions Persist," Pew reported:

> *Muslim and Western publics continue to see relations between them as generally bad, with both sides holding negative stereotypes of the other. Many in the West see Muslims as fanatical and violent, while few say Muslims are tolerant or respectful of women. Meanwhile Muslims in the Middle East and Asia generally see Westerners as selfish, immoral, and greedy – as well as violent and fanatical.*[16]

---

15. "Muslim Publics Share Concerns about Extremist Groups," Pew Research Center Survey, September 10, 2013. Accessed July 13, 2017. http://www.pewglobal.org/2013/09/10/ muslim-publics-share-concerns-about-extremist-groups/.

16. "Muslim-Western Tensions Persist," Pew Research Center Survey, July 21, 2013. Accessed July 13, 2017. http://www.pewglobal.org/2011/07/21/muslim-western-tensions-persist/.

As to the reasons for the poor relations between Muslims and the West, the Pew study found (not surprisingly) that the two sides mostly blame each other for the lack of better ties. For example, Muslims in the Middle East and elsewhere in the *ummah* who believe that their relations with the West are poor overwhelmingly blame the reasons for those bad relations on the West. However, while most Americans and Europeans similarly put the blame for poor relations on the Muslims, "significant numbers" do acknowledge Western responsibility for the disharmony and discord between the two sides.

Both Westerners and Muslims agree that the Muslim nations should be more prosperous economically than they currently are, but the Muslims put the blame for this problem squarely on the shoulders of Western policy. A median of 53% across the entire survey believed U.S. and Western policies are "one of the top two reasons why Muslim nations are not wealthier." [17]

So, it's interesting to see that Europeans, Americans, and Muslims share a concern and an unfavorable attitude toward Islamist extremism yet these Westerners and Easterners still view each other with a healthy degree of mutual suspicion and skepticism. This mistrust undoubtedly contributes toward the absence of a unified effort mounted by both East and West to combat and defeat extremism and extremist ideology.

DIFFERENT CULTURES FROM DIFFERENT ENVIRONMENTS

Arab history goes back to the dawn of human civilization. If we begin with the Semitic Arab Bedouins of the Arabian Peninsula, we find a homogenous tribal culture with very little ethnic diversity. In his excellent "*The Arabs: A Short History*," Philip Hitti explains:

> *Ethnic purity is a reward of a most ungrateful and isolated environment, such as central Arabia affords. The "Island of the Arabians"* [i.e., the Arabian Peninsula] *furnishes an almost unique example of uninterrupted relationship between populace and soil. If immigrations have ever taken place into Arabia resulting in successive waves*

---

17. *Ibid.*

of settlers ousting or submerging one another – as in the case of India, Greece, Italy, England and the United States – history has left no record of them. Nor do we know of any invader who succeeded in penetrating the sandy barriers and establishing a permanent foothold in this land. The people of Arabia, particularly the Bedouins, have remained virtually the same throughout all recorded ages.[18]

Hitti goes on to emphasize the tribal nature of the Bedouin society:

The clan organization is the basis of Bedouin society. Every tent represents a family; members of one encampment constitute a clan. A number of kindred clans grouped together make a tribe. All members of the same clan consider each other as of one blood, submit to the authority of one chief – the senior member of the clan – and use one battle-cry. Blood relationship – real or fictitious (clan kinship may be acquired by sucking a few drops of a member's blood) – furnishes the cohesive element in tribal organization.[19]

This tribal and clan culture extends well outside of the Arabian Peninsula into Iran and other parts of Southwest Asia, Iraq, and Syria and it is also predominant in many of the desert cultures of North Africa. Libya, for example, has dozens of Arab and Berber tribes and while the Arab tribes date from the early expansion of Islam in the seventh century, many of the Berber tribes can trace their lineages back to antiquity.

This tribal society is a necessity in a harsh desert environment where a person or even a family unit would not be able to survive on its own for very long. These tribes are egalitarian in nature where a family will have its own personal possessions inside its tent (swords, clothing, jewelry, tools, etc.) but collective resources like water wells and grazing land belong to the tribe. Each clan has a chieftain – the clan's respected leader – and these chieftains represent their respective clans on a tribal council. This council, in turn, handles matters such as adjudicating disputes between member clans, relations with other tribes, and any major decision that would affect the entire tribe.

---

18. Philip K. Hitti, *The Arabs: A Short History*, (Chicago: Henry Regnery Company, 1970), 7.
19. Hitti, 17.

This is a form of representational government but without the physical institutions and characteristics that are associated with the US or Western form of democracy. According to the website of the Saudi Mission to the European Union, such councils form a part of Saudi governance to this very day:

> *In the Majlis, weekly meetings that are open to all, members of the general public can approach the King and leaders at the local, provincial and national levels to discuss issues and raise grievances.*[20]

In contrast to this traditional and conservative societal structure in much of the Middle East, the history and society of the United States is quite different. While Christopher Columbus may have discovered the New World in 1492 (the Vikings may have preceded him with their settlement at Vinland in Newfoundland but they did not survive and stay), the real history of America – as we know it today – began with the Pilgrims stepping off the *Mayflower* at Plymouth Rock in 1620.

Our environment evolved quite differently from that of the Arabs. When the United States of America declared its independence from Great Britain on July 4, 1776, it was clear that these states were forming a new country based on the concept of Westphalian sovereignty that emerged from the Peace of Westphalia in 1648 wherein sovereign states coexist under a framework regulated by international law. This is still the fundamental basis by which modern states are supposed to control acts of aggression and settle disputes.

The Declaration of Independence makes this quite clear:

> *We hold these truths to be self-evident that all men are created equal, that they are endowed by their Creator with certain inalienable Rights, that among these are Life, Liberty, and the pursuit of Happiness. That to secure these rights, Governments are instituted among Men, deriving their just powers from the consent of the governed* [emphasis added].

---

20. "Government," website of the Saudi Mission to the EU in Brussels, Belgium. Accessed July 13, 2017. http://ksamissioneu.net/en/government/.

Following the American victory over the British in 1783 in the War of Independence, the 13 original colonies – now the United States of America – set out to lay the foundations of the newly-born country's government and laws. The end result was the United States Constitution that took effect as the supreme law of the land in 1789. And with this Constitution as our guide, over the next 228 years, America developed into an ethnically, religiously, and culturally diverse society, although not without many sacrifices, tribulations, and sufferings of its people. In fact, we still face setbacks as we endeavor to build that diverse form of American society.

This highlights some key differences between *us* and *them*. America was founded from the very beginning as a modern sovereign nation with a government, institutions, and laws. We have (eventually) reached the point where everyone under those laws has equal status, regardless of race, color, or creed. As a "nation of immigrants," we have a diverse society that still enjoys a great degree of homogeneity in which we all consider ourselves Americans; *E Pluribus Unum*: "Out of many, one."

Conversely, the traditional tribal society in many Arab lands goes back to the beginning of recorded time. This is structured along family and clan lines and is designed for nomadic tribes in an arid and unforgiving desert environment to survive. Here homogeneity rules the day and outsiders are seen as either fair game or a threat. And despite the fact that these societies are very egalitarian (at least to tribe members), there is no formal government whose powers are clearly divided and separated along clear lines of authority. Absolute power rests with clan chieftains and tribal councils. Whatever laws do exist are based on either tradition or religion and there are few, if any, brick-and-mortar institutions.

MIDDLE EAST HISTORY

Our country's history only goes back about 400 years but the Middle East has a history that spans many millennia. During that time the region has seen many great empires rise and fall. The Middle East has a reputation for being a violent and turbulent region and that reputation is undeniably deserved. It has always been a tough neighborhood where finishing second might mean your head winds up displayed on a pike.

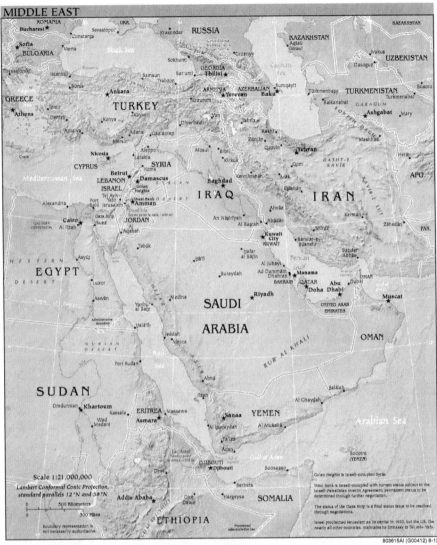

The World Factbook 2013-14. Washington, DC: Central Intelligence Agency, 2013.

As the birthplace of human civilization, the Middle East has witnessed every form of human behavior – both good and bad. It has been home to ancient wonders of the world like the Hanging Gardens of Babylon, the Great Pyramids, and Great Library of Alexandria. Mankind invented early forms of writing such as cuneiform in ancient Mesopotamia and hieroglyphics in ancient Egypt. The rise of agriculture along the banks of the great rivers of Iraq and Egypt was the catalyst that created the first settled civilizations and transformed humanity from hunter-gatherers to agrarian farmers with domesticated livestock. Nevertheless, these early civilizations (and their agriculture) depended on ample water resources. The arid deserts like those in the interior of the Arabian Peninsula remained the exclusive realm of the tribes.

But the evolution of civilization also had a dark side in the form of competition between societies and peoples for domination over limited agricultural and economic resources and greater regional power. With greater power came greater wealth. The Sumerians, Assyrians, Akkadians, and Babylonians all had their day in ancient Iraq, superseding one another. The spheres of influence sometimes overlapped between competing empires like the Assyrians and ancient Egyptians so these clashes and wars sometimes took place far from home.

Thus, it is fair to say that the history of the Middle East really is a composite and a mosaic of the evolution of human society and human civilization, with all the good and bad that goes along with it. However, the advent of Islam was a singular event in Arab history, one that unified nomadic Arab tribesmen and transformed them into conquering holy warriors that rapidly spread eastward and westward in the name of their religion. For the purpose of this discussion, Arab history prior to Islam is largely irrelevant.

ISLAM

Islam began as a uniquely Semitic Arab religion. According to Islam, the Koran (Arabic for "The Recitation") was revealed in Arabic by the angel Gabriel to an Arab prophet, Muhammad, who belonged to the Quraysh tribe in Mecca. Arabic is still the only sanctioned language of the Koran since the rhyme and meter of the Koran's verses (which is very important in a literary and poetic language such as Arabic) cannot be replicated in other languages. The five-daily calls to prayer and even the ritual supplications by Muslims – regardless of their ethnic origins and linguistic abilities – are also to be uttered in Arabic for the same reason. Young boys around the world who are sent to religious *madrassahs* (Arabic for schools) to memorize the Koran are required to memorize and recite it in Arabic regardless of their own native language.

The religion unified the nomadic tribesmen of the arid Arabian Peninsula as nothing had before. Muhammad managed to Islamize a good portion of the peninsula prior to his death. Islam became not just a religion but provided the framework for a heretofore nonexistent Arabian state:

> *Thus by one stroke the most vital bond of Arab relationship, that of tribal kinship, was replaced by a new bond, that of faith. Herein lies one of the chief claims of Muhammad to originality. A sort of Pax Islamica was instituted for Arabia. The new community was to have no priesthood, no hierarchy, no central see. Its mosque was its public forum and military drill ground as well as its place of common worship.*[21]

From the death of Muhammad in 632 through 661, the Islamic conquest had spread to the Atlantic Ocean in the West all the way to the Indus Valley in the East. In the span of 29 years, the Bedouins of the Arabian Desert had occupied much of the known world but this did not necessarily mean that they successfully converted the conquered peoples to their faith.

In some cases, these peoples had already been oppressed by other rulers. They saw the Arabs as less tyrannical and, thus, a better alternative to the status quo. Islam was still primarily an Arabic religion that found little resonance with non-Arabs. Moreover, the Bedouins were initially enchanted and preoccupied with many of the luxuries and comforts they found in places they conquered like the Sassanid Empire in Mesopotamia and Persia.

Hitti writes:

> *Not until the second and third centuries of the Moslem [sic] era did the bulk of the people in Syria, Mesopotamia and Persia profess the religion of Muhammad. Between the military conquest of these regions and their religious conversion a long period intervened. And when*

---

21. Hitti, 40.

they were converted the people turned primarily because of self-interest – to escape tribute and seek identification with the ruling class.[22]

It appears that Islam, as a form of worship, was something of a hard sell to non-Arabs for the first couple hundred years. The religion's exclusive use of the Arabic language certainly limited Islam's acceptance and appeal to non-Arabs that had been conquered by the Muslims.

Muhammad's death in 632 raised questions about who would succeed him as the leader of the faith. This is where the first great split came in the religion; *Shia* Muslims regard Ali – Muhammad's cousin – as his rightful successor while *Sunni* Muslims regarded one of the prophet's oldest companions – Abu-Bakr – as the proper choice.

In any case, the first four caliphs (from the Arabic word for "successor") after Muhammad's death formed the Rashidun Caliphate from 632-661. "Rashidun" means "rightly-guided" caliphs but that term was obviously one of dispute at the time. Only the first caliph, Abu-Bakr, died a natural death. The other three were killed as cliques and factions within the new faith jockeyed for position. The first three ruled the budding empire from the Arabian Peninsula while the fourth caliph, Muhammad's cousin Ali who was favored to succeed him by the *Shia*, moved his capital to Iraq. With Ali's death in 661, Islam's caliphate underwent a drastic transformation.

The Rashidun Caliphate gave way to the Umayyad Caliphate in 661 and this became the first real dynasty in Islamic history. From its capital in Damascus, this caliphate reigned with a remarkable degree of tolerance for Christians and Jews, in particular, and non-Muslims, in general, from 661-750. It marked a turning point where science, literature, art, and medicine began to become a higher priority than warfare and conquest.

This period saw the beginning of Arab science, the first treatise on medicine coming, characteristically, by way of a translation by a Jew of a Greek tract composed by a Christian priest in Alexandria. Alchemy, like medicine, one of the few sciences in which the Arabs later made a distinct contribution, was one of the disciplines early developed.

---

22. Hitti, 61.

Poetry and music flourished in the court at Damascus, the latter over the protest of conservatives, who linked music and song with wine-drinking and gambling as diversions forbidden by the Prophet.[23]

In 750, the Abbasids toppled the Umayyads, although a branch of the Umayyads continued to rule in Cordoba, Spain until 1031. The Abbasids viewed the Umayyad tolerance toward non-Muslims as being unfair to the Muslims themselves and believed the penchant for poetry and wine in Damascus was nothing short of licentious decadence. The Abbasids shifted the capital of the Islamic empire to Baghdad, the seat of their caliphate.[24]

With the loss of Spain to the surviving Umayyads, the Abbasid Caliphate saw its influence wane in the West with the advent of the *Shiite* Fatamid Caliphate in Cairo. Nevertheless, they remained in strong control over Mesopotamia and Persia through their capital in Baghdad, which became a sophisticated center of science, trade, and culture for the next 500 years.

But the Abbasid Caliphate and Baghdad – and with them the Golden Era of Islamic History – met their own violent end on January 29, 1258 when the Mongols, under the command of Genghis Khan's grandson Hulagu, invaded, sacked, and destroyed Baghdad and killed virtually everybody in the city (except the Christians).

The New Yorker published a vivid account of the Mongols' brutality written by Ian Frazier in its April 25, 2005 edition. According to Frazier, Hulagu's men carried out a seven-day killing spree that slaughtered anywhere from two hundred thousand to over a million Muslims in the city (depending on the source). The caliph's palace was put to the torch and the fragrance of the smoke from its burning beams of rare woods filled the air for dozens of miles. The caliph himself was wrapped in a carpet and trampled to death by horses since there was a fear that some natural disaster, like an earthquake, might occur should his spilled blood touch the earth. Precious jewels, gold, and silver were piled high around Hulagu's tent and "so many books from Baghdad's libraries were flung

---

23. Hitti, 101.
24. Hitti, 101.

into the Tigris that a horse could walk across on them." The river ran black with ink and red with blood.[25]

And although the Mongols may have delivered the death blow to Baghdad and the Abbasids, Islam continued to survive.

The Mamluke Dynasty or Mamluke Sultanate ruled from 1250-1517 and there is some academic disagreement over whether it was a continuation of the Abbasid Caliphate (since the Mamlukes had been loyal to the Abbasids prior to the sacking of Baghdad). Since the seat of power for the Mamlukes was Cairo and not Baghdad, and the Mamlukes had no family ties to the Abbasids, characterizing them as an extension of the defeated Abbasids seems inappropriate. The Mamlukes were a warrior caste made up of slaves ("mamluke" means "owned" or "possessed" in Arabic) whose exact origins are unclear but they are known to have existed by at least the ninth century in the Abbasid Caliphate. These soldier-slaves held no allegiance to any Arab tribe or clan and, therefore, were thought to be immune from any potential conspiracy or palace intrigue against the ruler. They eventually formed much of the Islamic military soldiery because, as foreign slaves, they had no power base of their own.

The capital of the Mamluke Sultanate was Cairo and they succeeded in turning back the Mongol invaders after their successful invasion of Baghdad and they also acquitted themselves well in battle against the Crusaders. They eventually were defeated in 1517 by the armies and artillery of the Ottoman Empire, although the Ottoman Turks eventually absorbed the Mamlukes into their own forces.

The final chapter of Islamic rule in the Middle East was the Ottoman Empire, which existed from 1517-1924. This was a non-Arab caliphate whose decline and fall marked the end of a regime and a religious empire that had lasted 1300 years, beginning with the *blitzkrieg* of Arab Bedouin armies to the east and the west in the seventh century. During the halcyon years of the Umayyad and Abbasid Caliphates, the Middle East and Spain enjoyed periods of great social and scientific enlightenment at a time when Europe was still in the Dark Ages.

---

25. Ian Frazier, "Invaders: Destroying Baghdad," *The New Yorker*, April 25, 2005. Accessed July 13, 2017. http://www.newyorker.com/magazine/2005/04/25/invaders-3.

While Islam as a religion had little appeal among Europeans, they were certainly among the beneficiaries of Arab learning:

> ...*Moslem* [sic] *learning entered Western thought at many a point. Moslem Spain wrote one of the brightest chapters in the intellectual history of medieval Europe. Between the middle of the eighth and the beginning of the thirteenth centuries, as we have noted before, the Arabic-speaking peoples were the main bearers of the torch of culture and civilization throughout the world, the medium through which ancient science and philosophy were recovered, supplemented and transmitted to make possible the renaissance of Western Europe.*[26]

An important takeaway from this quick historical review is that Muslims have collectively viewed Islam as a religion, a culture, and a state for 1300 years. For many Arabs and Muslims today, their allegiance is to their faith first. Any loyalty to a nationality or a ruler is secondary to their commitment to their religion because nationalities, in the Westphalian sense, did not exist for much of their history. And the modern boundaries that exist between many Arab nations today were actually drawn by the Western Powers in the nineteenth and twentieth centuries.

SECULARISM AND ARAB NATIONALISM

Secularism in the Arab world started to gain traction with the concept of Arab nationalism. With the gradual breakdown of the Ottoman Empire, Western countries began increasing their contacts and influence in the Middle East. Christian-governed Lebanon housed US and European Christian universities in the 1850s and 1860s and Lebanon welcomed European and American merchants and traders. It became a conduit for Western political thought into the region.

The concepts of political democracy and nationalism encouraged struggles for national independence and represented a major break with the region's past. The Arab nationalist movement began with Lebanese Christians and Syrian intellectuals who were spurred on by a revived

---

26. Hitti, 174-175.

interest in the classical Arabic language and literature and the glory of Arabic civilization and Islamic history. The modern goal, however, was not Pan-Islam but Pan-Arabism.[27] Here again, we see Arabs seeking a collective identity rather than a patriotic one.

Arab nationalism and Pan-Arabism waxed and waned in the wake of World War I and the final dissolution of the last vestiges of Ottoman rule. Britain and France attempted to establish monarchies in Syria, Iraq, Transjordan, and Egypt that were largely resented by their respective populations.

After World War II, Arab nationalism once again gained steam as turbulent events roiled the Middle East. The creation of the Jewish State of Israel in 1948 on Palestinian soil sparked fear and alarm among the Arabs and a series of Arab nationalist leaders and movements took center stage in response. Some examples of how Arab nationalism and secularism have performed in the Arab world follow:

1. EGYPT

Gamal Abdel-Nasser, the first Pan-Arabist leader, became president of Egypt in 1956 after helping to overthrow the monarchy in 1952. He was widely regarded as an icon of Arab unity and dignity and a staunch anti-imperialist who delighted in thumbing his nose at the West. Abdel-Nasser was also a populist president who carried out agrarian, housing, and welfare reforms that made him extremely popular with ordinary Egyptians.

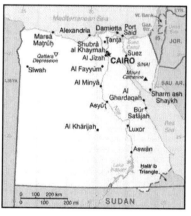

The World Factbook 2013-14. Washington, DC: Central Intelligence Agency, 2013.

However he was far less successful in his international gamesmanship. His nationalization of the Suez Canal Company in 1956 precipitated a disastrous military response from Britain, France, and Israel even though

---

27. Hitti, 260-261.

many in the Arab world saw it as a victory because Abdel-Nasser had stood up to the Europeans. His neutralist attitude and support for socialism did not make him a favorite of President Eisenhower or subsequent US leaders. Under Abdel-Nasser's administration the Egyptian military was completely devastated in the 1967 Six-Day War with Israel.

At the Arab level, Abdel-Nasser's attempt at a political union with Syria in the United Arab Republic failed after only four years largely because of his lack of understanding Syria's internal problems. He became entangled in Yemen's civil war from 1962-1967 in a misadventure that has been called Egypt's Vietnam.

Nevertheless, Gamal Abdel-Nasser ruled Egypt by force of his charisma and direct connection to the Egyptian people alone. He established few state institutions prior to his death in 1970.

His successor, Anwar El-Sadat, would almost immediately attempt an even more grandiose Arab unity scheme between Egypt, Sudan, Syria, and Libya but this effort was also doomed to fail. Sadat ruefully discussed the abortive Confederation of Arab Republics in his autobiography.[28]

Sadat's grand accomplishment was the 1973 Yom Kippur War in which Egypt was able to utilize strategic surprise and break through Israel's vaunted Bar-Lev Line on the eastern side of the Suez Canal. Sadat likely overestimated Syria's military performance and underestimated the US response in the war and the Egyptian forces were eventually contained and defeated. But Sadat had avenged Egypt's total humiliation by Israel in 1967 and, indirectly, laid the framework for his future peace negotiations with Israel and the recovery of Egypt's Sinai Peninsula.

The 1977 visit to Israel by Sadat that culminated in the Camp David Accords and a peace treaty with Israel made the Egyptian leader far more popular abroad than at home. The treaty was viewed by Arabs and Egyptians alike as a catastrophic breach of Arab solidarity against the Zionist enemy and it ultimately led to his demise when he was assassinated

---

28. Anwar el-Sadat, *In Search of Identity*, (New York: Harper and Row Publishers, 1977-78), 215-218.

by Egyptian Islamists while viewing the annual military parade com-
memorating the great October 1973 victory – his finest hour.

Sadat's death paved the way for his vice president, Muhammad Hosni
Mubarak, to take the reins of power. Mubarak was a lackluster air force
general with few military accomplishments to his name. He made a good
choice as a vice president because he had no personal or military power
base from which to threaten the president.

Mubarak had all the charm and charisma of a lump of bread dough.
The primary accomplishment of his nearly three decades in power was to
leave Egypt in shambles, with a legacy consisting of economic stagnation,
skyrocketing unemployment, and widespread corruption.

He went ahead with the crackdown on Islamists and the Muslim
Brotherhood that had started with Abdel-Nasser and continued with
Sadat. Egyptian prisons were frequently cited for human rights violations
and torture during Mubarak's tenure. His public image became one of a
corrupt, despotic tyrant who was completely disconnected from the woes
of his people. The popular Egyptian revolution of the wider 2011 Arab
Spring toppled him from power in just over a couple of weeks and he,
along with his sons and some senior government officials, fell from their
seats of power like rotten apples from a tree.

An interim Supreme Council of the Armed Forces (SCAF) stepped into
the resulting vacuum to run the government while a popular electoral
process was organized to democratically elect an Egyptian president for
the very first time. The process of selecting candidates for the presidential
ballot, their platforms, their backgrounds, and virtually everything else
about Egypt's first presidential election was discussed nearly constantly
on Egypt's media with a combination of optimism and euphoria. The
people were finally going to have their say and Egypt would once again
be propelled to the forefront of the Arab political world through its
embracement of the democratic process.

Mohamed Morsi, with ties to Egypt's Muslim Brotherhood, defeated
Mubarak's last prime minister, Ahmed Shafik, in the election but with
Morsi's victory, Egypt's first experiment in democracy quickly began to
unravel. He stacked the Constituent Council responsible for drafting
a new Egyptian constitution with Islamists, granted himself unlimited

powers, and authorized himself to govern outside of any judicial oversight. His authoritarianism enraged Egyptians who feared they had simply toppled one dictator for another – and an Islamist one at that. The people once upon a time might have granted Abdel-Nasser such sweeping power, but not Morsi.

The army toppled Morsi in July 2013 after just one year in office, resulting in the concurrent imprisonment of both of Egypt's former presidents – Mubarak and Morsi – and the eventual accession to the presidency of Field Marshal Abdul Fattah El-Sisi in June 2014 with over 95% of the vote. As if to drive the final nail in Egypt's democratic experiment, Sisi's victory was widely viewed as a sham election both inside and outside of Egypt.

Egypt's secular governments from Abdel-Nasser onwards have not fulfilled the original promises of Arab nationalism and Pan-Arabism. There was no more charismatic Arab nationalist than Gamal Abdel-Nasser when he assumed Egypt's presidency in 1956. Egypt was the leading nation in the Arab world at the time, yet for all his oratorical skills, his reputation for standing up to the West, and his strong roots to Egypt's common people, Abdel-Nasser failed miserably in his attempt with the United Arab Republic. His meddling in Yemen was a catastrophic misadventure and he suffered crushing military defeats in 1956 and 1967.

Sadat never got anywhere with the Confederation of Arab Republics and his eventual separate peace with Israel alienated Egypt from the rest of the Arab world for decades. Presidents Mubarak, Morsi, and Sisi are/were simply strong-men dictators of various stripes. Through it all, the life of ordinary Egyptians just got worse and worse as the economy swirled down the toilet.

If Abdel-Nasser couldn't pull it off, probably nobody can. Arab nationalism and Pan-Arabism can never be achieved without Arab unity and that remains but a shimmering mirage on the desert horizon. Many Arab countries have their own intrinsic problems related to their unique social and economic dynamics that simply aren't suited to being managed under a Pan-Arab union. But even more than that, the autocratic secular Arab rulers are loath to sacrifice their own wealth and personal interests on the altar of Arab unity and Arab nationalism.

2. LIBYA

The next aspirant to don the mantle of
Pan-Arabism was Muammar al-Gaddafi. The ebullient and mercurial son
of a nomadic goatherd, Gaddafi's childhood and adolescence set him on a path
toward activism. As a young secondary
school student – the first in his family
– many of his teachers were Egyptians
and he began to take a serious interest
in Arab nationalism and Pan-Arabism
because he viewed Gamal Abdel-Nasser
as a hero.[29]

The World Factbook 2013-14. Washington,
DC: Central Intelligence Agency, 2013.

Gaddafi dropped out of university and enrolled in Libya's Royal Military
Academy, believing it to be a pathway toward making social and political
change in his country and he and some like-minded colleagues went on
to form their own version of Abdel-Nasser's Free Officers. In 1969 they
mounted a bloodless coup that deposed King Idris while he was abroad
and abolished his absolute monarchy. Gaddafi proclaimed the establishment of the Libyan Arab Republic.

As a staunch anti-imperialist, Gaddafi was suspicious and scornful of the
West in general. As evidence of his Pan-Arab inclinations, at the end
of 1969 he established the Arab Revolutionary Front with Egypt and
Sudan with a view toward political unification[30] but Abdel-Nasser's death
in 1970 and the failure of the Confederation of Arab Republics in 1971
ended any practical moves toward a Pan-Arab union.

During his 42-year rule, Gaddafi continued to embrace both Pan-Arabism
and Pan-Africanism. He compiled his own worldview of nationalism,
socialism, Islam, and social equality into his own political ideology in
1973 called "The Third Universal Theory" but it was more commonly
known as his "Green Book."

---

29. Bruce Ronald St. John, *Libya: From Colony to Revolution*, (Oxford: Oneworld, 2011),
     136.
30. St. John, 186.

Despite Libya's growing importance as an oil exporter from the '70s onward, the country has never wielded great political influence in the Arab world. The 2014 edition of the "CIA World Factbook" reports a population of around 6.2 million and a gross domestic product (GDP) of $73.6 billion estimated in 2013, ranking it 85th in the world. The per capita contribution to GDP is only $11,300, putting it in 109th place in the world.

In comparison, according to that same "CIA World Factbook" Egypt has a population estimated at 86.89 million and a GDP of $551.4 billion (28th in the world), although its per capita GDP is even worse than Libya's at $6,600, ranking it a lowly 144th.

Moreover, most Arab leaders kept their distance from Gaddafi during the four decades he ruled Libya. His connections to international terrorism and his close associations to African despots like Idi Amin made him something of an outcast among his counterparts elsewhere in the Arab world and did little to bolster his Arab nationalist credentials. His demise at the hands of his own people in October 2011 was likely met with more sighs of relief than regret.

3. IRAQ

The Arab *Baath* ("Renaissance") movement was an Arab nationalist ideology that was the product of the theories of three Syrians: Zaki al-Arsuzi, Michel Aflaq, and Salah al-Din al-Bitar. This ideology was predicated on Arab nationalism and Pan-Arabism and it called for the unification of Arab countries into a single, unified, Arab state. This ideology led to a *Baath* Party in Iraq and Syria but the single party quickly broke down into two branches, one for each country, because of political differences between the sides. (There

The World Factbook 2013-14. Washington, DC: Central Intelligence Agency, 2013.

35

were branches of the party in many Arab countries for a brief time but the movement never gained that much traction outside of Iraq and Syria).

When Hafez al-Assad became president of Syria he usurped the *Baath* Party and turned it into his own tool for running the country. It was transformed into a cult of loyalty to Assad and his family where Assad's principles of government trumped those of traditional Arab nationalism. Moreover, as a member of the minority *Alawite* sect – an offshoot of *Shia* Islam – Assad never really had any strong credentials as a Pan-Arabist in a *Sunni* majority Arab world.

Saddam Hussein was not known as an ardent supporter of Gamal Abdel-Nasser's brand of pan-Arabism, so when he became president of Iraq in 1979 he began to put his own spin on *Baathism*. In his version of the ideology, Saddam combined Iraqi nationalism with Arab nationalism that praised the Iraqi nation's values from ancient Mesopotamia all the way to the present day. This was an Iraqi-centric form of nationalism that used Iraq's resistance against the Ottoman, British, and US hegemony as models for the rest of the Arab world. Some have referred to these principles as Saddamist *Baathism* and they were likely fundamentally influenced by the leader's xenophobia, since he rarely traveled outside of the country.

Ever the narcissist, Saddam seemed to fancy himself as a modern-day Salah al-Din (Saladin in English), the legendary Muslim liberator of Jerusalem who turned the tide against the Crusaders at the Battle of Hattin in 1187. Although both men shared Tikrit, Iraq as their birthplace, they could not have been more different. Salah al-Din was a Kurd and a charismatic leader and skilled battlefield general with a heroic place, at least in Islamic and Arab history.

For his part, Saddam Hussein was not Kurdish but Arab. Under Saddam, the Iraqi army would seek to displace and ethnically cleanse vast areas of Iraqi Kurdistan and resettle them with loyal Iraqi Arabs. The Iraqi president's conduct of the 1980-1988 Iran-Iraq War, the rout of his forces from Kuwait in 1991, and the rapid military collapse of Iraq during the 2003 US-led invasion are clear testaments to his utter lack of military tactical or strategic prowess. Moreover, the man ruled by absolute terror and held the entire country, its population, and its society in his iron grip. Instead of having charisma, he instilled only fear. His place in history will forever be one of infamy – particularly among the Kurds and *Shiite* populations of his own people.

Like a chameleon, Saddam wrapped himself in the mantle of Arab nationalism, Iraqi nationalism, and even Islam whenever the situation suited him. After his strategic miscalculation of the Arab and Western response to his 1990 invasion of Kuwait, Saddam desperately portrayed his fight against the Crusader West as the "Mother of All Battles."

But in the end he was none of those things. He was a ruthless thug who ruled Iraq the same way as a 1920s Chicago gangster ran his territory. His menacing shadow eclipsed the entire country where the bullet and the noose awaited anyone who even hinted at dissent.

4. LEBANON

Let's take a look at secularism from a different angle. Beirut was once seen as the pearl of the Middle East. It was a cosmopolitan and sophisticated city that was a melting pot of Eastern, Western, Arab, European, Islamic, and Christian cultures. But despite its promising potential it has become yet another example of what could have been, but isn't.

The World Factbook 2013-14. Washington, DC: Central Intelligence Agency, 2013.

Lebanon gained its independence from French rule in 1943. According to the 2014 edition of the "CIA World Factbook," the country's population of 5.8 million is the most diverse in the entire Middle East with 54% Muslim (evenly split between *Sunnis* and *Shia*), 40.5% split among various Christian denominations, 5.6% Jews, and the remainder divvied up among Baha'is, Hindus, Buddhists, and Mormons. The country has 18 different recognized sects.

Power is shared among these factions of the population with the presidency being reserved for a Maronite Christian, the office of prime minister for a Sunni Muslim, and the speaker of parliament being filled by a *Shiite*. This arrangement goes back to the unwritten National Pact in 1943 where President Bechar al-Khouri (a Maronite Christian) and Prime Minister Riad al-Solh (a *Sunni* Muslim) agreed verbally to this method of sharing power among the various sects.[31] On the surface, Lebanon would seem to be a model of tolerance, diversity, and power sharing, a place where secularism would be the only successful form of governance. After all, it was the gateway of modern Western political and democratic thinking into the Middle East and Arab world in the latter half of the nineteenth century.

But most of its post-independence history has been one of violence and war. Muslim factions rebelled against the Christian government in 1958 in the first instance of sectarian infighting that ruptured into full-scale civil war from 1975-1990. The 1948 creation of the modern State of Israel displaced thousands of indigenous Palestinians into Lebanon as refugees and their descendants have continued to resist the Israeli occupation of their homeland in a variety of political and military groups ever since. This resistance, in raids mounted from Lebanese territory, sparked Israeli invasions of Lebanon in 1978 and 1982.

It has also fallen victim to regional proxy warfare. In 2006 guerillas from Iran's Lebanese proxy – *Hezbollah* – sparked a 34-day war with Israel when they began firing rockets at settlements in northern Israel. Scattered hostilities often still break out between Israel and *Hezbollah*.

The ongoing civil war in Syria has also spilled over into Lebanese territory where supporters and opponents of the Al-Assad regime in Damascus clash. Syria itself occupied Lebanon from 1976-2005 and was only forced out after being implicated in the assassination of then-Prime Minister Rafik Hariri.

In fairness, Lebanon's location in a particularly turbulent part of the region has not been helpful. However, the country's power-sharing structure among several different powerful factions has left its central government

---

31. "Lebanon: Constitutional Law and the Political Rights of Religious Communities," The Law Library of Congress, Library of Congress. Accessed July 13, 2013. http://www.loc.gov/law/help/lb-religious-political-rights/political-rights-of-religious-communities.pdf.

impotent and unable to deal with the crises that result when these various sects (or outside parties) take up arms against themselves.

THE ORIGINS OF *SALAFIST* MILITANCY

Since *Salafist* militancy represents a clear and present danger to the Western free world today, it's important to understand its roots and origins. And there is a noticeable and noteworthy Saudi connection to many of these, especially when we get to the Al-Qaeda era.

Islam was far from being a religion of peace during its early days. The Prophet Muhammad himself spent the last ten years of his life leading military campaigns to spread the faith and reclaim his home city, Mecca, from where he was forced to emigrate. He personally took part in 27 military raids and ordered some 73 more.

In some of these raids, Muhammad simply planned to attack caravans in order to acquire greater financial resources. In others, he plotted to assassinate persons who had insulted him through poetry or mocked or criticized him in other ways. The prophet was not necessarily always portrayed as a forbearing and forgiving sort of fellow and the *Salafist* militants of today seem to be cut from the same cloth. It certainly provides some strong historical context for the Islamists' desire to assassinate those who have resorted to cartoons to denigrate the prophet's image or reputation. In its earliest days in the cradle of the Arabian Peninsula, it seems Islam was long on militancy and short on tolerance. That's not an allegation or an assertion; it's a historical fact. It was a time when Muhammad and his followers not only had to fight to spread their religion, they had to fight just to survive.

After Muhammad's death and the One True Faith had conquered their desert peninsula, the Arab tribesmen raced east and west to triumph over empires large and small. Within the span of a century, they had claimed nearly half of the known world for Islam – a truly amazing feat. This Islamic conquest and the creation of an Islamic empire did not happen though direct mail marketing or some kind of ancient public relations campaign. It happened because thousands of militant Arab tribesmen took to their steeds and spread their faith by the tips of their swords and spears. These desert nomads had always enjoyed a penchant for raiding before Islam and the religion merely gave that penchant a tighter focus and a larger purpose.

With the rapid expansion of the empire and the eventual relocation of the seat of the caliphate to Damascus, the harsh and austere nature of a religion that was bred from a harsh and austere desert society began to change. Islam matured and evolved as the seat of the caliphate moved in turn from Damascus to Cordoba, Baghdad, Cairo, and Istanbul. The militant, unbending, and unforgiving character of the faith mellowed under the influences of a plethora of caliphs who were quite urbane and sophisticated for their time, unlike the unruly Bedouins of the desert.

As we noted earlier, Islam went through some truly golden periods where scientific, medical, and other important texts of the Greek and Roman periods were translated into Arabic and preserved. Muslim scientists and astronomers made significant discoveries and Christians, Jews, and other religious and ethnic minorities enjoyed a great degree of autonomy and tolerance. Caliphs built grand and beautiful mosques, ornate palaces, and schools of science and learning. This "civilized" Islamic culture was a long way from the austere desert Islam as practiced by the Bedouins. This sophistication and even luxury stands in sharp contrast to the Islamic State of today, the Taliban, and Al-Qaeda in the Islamic Maghreb, who have devoted themselves to the destruction of art and culture and dispensing with any education save the memorization of the Koran.

But like with any major religion, human beings have a habit of coming to different interpretations of any divine message and the practices it requires. Even as Islam had softened from the militant early years of its expansion, some eventually began to see that softening as a religious weakness and a heretical departure from the unyielding orthodoxy of the Islam of Muhammad's time. This gave rise to *Salafism*, a movement aimed at returning to what was believed to be "pure" Islam, the way the religion was practiced by Muhammad, his companions, and the first generations of Muslims; the faith that was not embellished by any of the modern "innovations." This movement's name was coined from the Arabic word *salaf*, which means "ancestors" or "predecessors."

The first real proponent of *Salafist* ideology was a fourteenth century Islamic scholar named Ibn Taymiyyah. He was born in Turkey in 1263 and he received a broad secular and religious education. He became an Islamic scholar and jurisprudent affiliated with the Hanbali school of thought – the most conservative and traditional of the four main *Sunni* schools. He lived during a very tumultuous time for Islam as it confronted the Mongol invasions of Iraq and Syria. He called on all Muslims to wage *jihad* – holy war – against the Mongols as a compulsory duty.

His disdain for many of what he called "innovations" that had been made to the religion often got him into trouble with the Islamic authorities of his day. He scorned any attempt at using discursive rationalization to reach religious rulings on questionable matters and believed in relying solely on the examples of Muhammad and his companions for such questions. Ibn Taymiyyah also disapproved of the *Shiite* custom of visiting the tombs of so-called saints. He saw it as a form of idolatry. His vision and his creed was to practice Islam in its "pure" form, the way Muhammad and his companions had done so in the seventh century. He died in 1328 while imprisoned for his beliefs inside the Citadel in Damascus.

To this day, Ibn Taymiyyah is a revered figure among *Salafists*, who refer to him as the "Sheikh of Islam." They often cite his rulings as justification for their militant actions.

Roughly 400 years after Ibn Taymiyyah's death, a stern preacher from the Nejd region of central Saudi Arabia picked up his *Salafist* banner and similarly called for a return to the puritanical form of Islam as practiced in its earliest times. He condemned those who made offerings to dead saints and prophets as polytheists and he preached about the "oneness" of God – monotheism. God was God and He had no associates or equals among mankind.

This preacher was named Muhammad Ibn Abdul-Wahhab and he was heavily influenced by the teachings of Ibn Taymiyyah and his successors. And like Ibn Taymiyyah, his fundamentalist views on Islam got him into trouble. He destroyed a grave said to be of one of Muhammad's companions that was revered by locals (probably because pilgrims visiting the grave generated revenue for them) and he organized the stoning of a woman for adultery.

These actions got him expelled from his hometown but he was invited to settle in a neighboring city by a young, local chieftain named Muhammad bin Saud. The two established a pact in 1744 that gave Abdul-Wahhab responsibility for religious affairs and established Saud as the area's military commander, paving the way to the establishment of the first Saudi state ruled by the House of Saud.

This relationship between the Saudi family and the puritanical *Wahhabi* brand of Islam continues to the present day. *Wahhabi* Islam is the country's state-sponsored religion. It is taught in schools and forms the bedrock of just about every aspect of Saudi culture and daily life. Shops must close at prayer times. Censors dutifully excise any questionable images or scenes from magazines, movies, and television shows. Women out in public must be accompanied by a male guardian. The consumption of alcohol is completely banned in the country and harsh punishments – like beheadings – are held in public to deter any aberrant behavior. Any other religions are either banned or strictly controlled to the point of being nearly invisible to the population. Don't even think of trying to proselytize.

But in the early days of the twentieth century, Saudi Arabia was still an isolated and desolate kingdom whose main claim to fame was hosting the annual pilgrimage of Muslims to Mecca. The country's vast petroleum resources remained undiscovered until the mid-1930s and even then, it wasn't until the post-World War II economic boom that the Saudis began to enjoy significant oil wealth. That wealth would become more significant later in that century.

The next phase of militant Islam's evolution took place in Egypt. Hassan al-Banna was born in 1906. The son of a Hanbali imam, Banna was heavily influenced by the Egyptian revolution of 1919. This experience gave him a nationalist, as well as a political awakening that would serve him a few years later in 1928, when he established the Muslim Brotherhood.

The Brotherhood began as just one more of the many Islamic charitable and social organizations that were operating inside Egypt at the time. The difference was that Banna tied his organization into the network of other popular businesses, mosques, and associations while speaking out against the heavy British presence and influence in the country. His Islamic message was interconnected with pan-Arabism, Arab

42

nationalism, and anti-colonialism and it began to resonate strongly with the Egyptian people.

The Muslim Brotherhood continued to gain support and popularity with the Egyptians and the Egyptian monarchy began to see the organization as a real threat. The Brotherhood had made a name for itself in mobilizing support for the 1936 Palestinian Revolt and had sent fighters to fight in the 1948 Arab-Israeli war. The monarchy banned the movement in 1948 and Banna was assassinated under dubious circumstances late that same year.

Nevertheless, the Muslim Brotherhood was a seminal event in the progression to Islamist militancy. The organization combined pan-Arabism and pan-Islamism with strident anti-colonialism – in this case a strong anti-British sentiment. It did not hesitate to encourage its members to take up arms to defend Islam and Arabs whenever the situation required it. Its popularity and political clout encouraged successive Egyptian governments to maintain the ban on the Muslim Brotherhood until after the toppling of Hosni Mubarak.

With its strong social, educational, and charitable institutions and its reputation as a fierce defender of Islam, Arabs, and Muslims the Brotherhood has continued to be a strong player in Egyptian society even though it was driven underground. Moreover, chapters and branches of the Brotherhood have been established in many other countries all over the world. The Muslim Brotherhood is the pioneer of modern political and militant Islam. Although it is not really accurate to categorize it as either a purely *Salafist* or *Wahhabist* organization, the Brotherhood has enjoyed significant financial support from *Salafists* and *Wahhabists* in the Arabian Peninsula.

The next stop in the evolutionary chain of modern Islamist ideology is another Egyptian, Sayyid Qutb. He is widely regarded as one of the most prominent and influential Islamist thinkers of modern times. A prolific writer, Qutb wrote around two-dozen books on his Islamist concepts and extensive commentaries on the Koran. His thoughts and ideas were heavily influenced by Hassan al-Banna and Qutb was a leading figure in the Muslim Brotherhood for a time. Such infamous Islamists as Osama bin Laden and Anwar al-Awlaki are known to have read at least some of his works.

The man studied in the United States for two years where he developed a strong dislike for America and Americans. He found them superficial and materialistic and devoid of any sort of the moral and ethical values with which he was familiar. Living in Greeley, Colorado, Qutb also claimed to encounter a fair amount of racism and prejudice as a person of color living among a white majority. Moreover, he was angered by America's unbridled support for the creation of Israel and its displacement of the Palestinians.

Qutb and the Muslim Brotherhood were initial supporters of Gamal Abdel-Nasser and the Free Officers Movement in 1952 that deposed Egypt's monarchy, which they saw as an un-Islamic puppet regime of the British. However Abdel-Nasser was suspicious of the Brotherhood and had no use for it. He tried to entice Qutb into accepting a position in the Egyptian government as a means to control him but Qutb refused all Abdel-Nasser's invitations.

Eventually, in something of a show trial, Qutb was convicted of plotting to assassinate Abdel-Nasser along with a handful of other alleged co-conspirators from the Muslim Brotherhood. He was hanged in 1966.

Qutb's brother, Muhammad, became an influential Islamist in his own right. After his release from an Egyptian prison, Muhammad emigrated to Saudi Arabia to become a professor of Islamist studies. He continued to promote his brother's writings and ideas and is known to have socialized with Al-Qaeda leaders Osama bin Laden and Ayman al-Zawahiri.

Much of today's Islamist ideology conforms with Qutb's thinking. His books are often cited as *Salafist* references. He believed that there was no need for any form of secular government or governance whatsoever; the *Sharia* provided all that was needed. He considered that humanity had only two choices: Islam or ignorance and he was critical of Muslims who were attracted by Western materialism. Qutb thought that all Muslims were obliged to take up the armed struggle against this ignorance and materialism and any Muslim who failed to do so was just another infidel.

The creation of the State of Israel in 1948 was yet another polarizing event on the path to radicalism. The Arabs were decisively defeated in 1948 and Israel even managed to invade Egypt and temporarily occupy the Sinai Peninsula during the 1956 Suez Crisis. The Arab world was further humiliated in the Six-Day War of 1967 when Israel captured the Gaza Strip, West Bank, all of Jerusalem, the Golan Heights, and the Sinai Peninsula. While Egypt may celebrate the 1973 October War and its successful breaching of Israel's Bar-Lev Line along the Suez Canal as a great victory, most Egyptians also seethe at the memory that the war ended with Israel's surrounding of Egypt's Third Army in the vicinity of Ismailia and the subsequent advance of Israeli forces to within 60 miles of Cairo.

The perceived usurping of Palestinian territories and Islamic holy sites along with a steady stream of humiliating military defeats inflicted on the Arab armies have made Israel the focus of intense hatred and resentment in the Arab world. Regardless of the peace treaties Israel has signed with Jordan and Egypt, at the popular level the Arabs still harbor a deep hatred of the Jewish state. The fact that no resolution to the Palestinian-Israeli conflict has been reached nearly 70 years after Israel's creation means that this dispute remains an open wound. And Israel's annexation of more Palestinian lands on which to construct new Jewish settlements and its merciless pounding of Palestinians in Gaza serves to constantly rub salt into that wound.

It should come as no surprise, then, that the Islamists' calls to drive Israel "into the sea" find a great deal of receptivity among just about everybody on the Arab street. Peace with their Jewish enemies has not delivered the promised economic boon to most of them and, ultimately, the Middle East is all about and eye for an eye and a tooth for a tooth, regardless of whether one is Jewish or Arab.

The last half of the twentieth century was a very turbulent period in the Middle East, with most Arabs and Muslims being on the receiving end of that turbulence. In 1979 two major events took place that would have seismic repercussions for years to come.

The first event was the return of Ayatollah Khomeini to Iran in February of that year and his creation of the Islamic Republic of Iran. Khomeini's vehement hatred of the United States and his stated goal of exporting his Islamic revolution translated into a brand of *Shiite* militancy that confronted and plagued the United States in Lebanon for most of the 1980s, as we previously discussed. Nevertheless, a resurgent and militant Iran – no longer contained by a *Sunni* Iraq – has stoked Arab fears that have manifested themselves in the *Sunni-Shiite* civil war we see playing out in Iraq today. Iranian and *Hezbollah* support for the *Alawite* regime in Damascus and Iranian military participation in Iraq's attempt to reclaim territory lost to the Islamic State just adds more fuel to that fire. A more in-depth discussion of the *Sunni-Shia* rift will follow shortly.

The second significant incident of the year marked yet another turning point in the evolution of *Sunni* militancy. It was the Soviet invasion of Afghanistan in December.

The importance of the Afghanistan war to the evolution of the modern *Salafist* militancy and radicalism simply cannot be downplayed or minimized. The Soviet invasion and occupation of the country was the catalyst that drove a devout young *Salafist* and Saudi (there's that connection again) named Osama bin Laden to establish the *Maktab al-Khidamat*, the "Afghan Services Bureau" through which bin Laden raised funds and recruited Arab fighters for the Afghan war effort against the Russians. These fighters – and eventually bin Laden himself – went into Afghanistan as *Sunni* Muslim volunteers who hailed from all over the Middle East and the rest of the world. Their goal was to drive the godless Soviets out of a Muslim nation.

Somewhere in the process they became *Salafist* zealots who would emerge from the crucible of the Afghan war to call themselves the Arab Afghan *mujahideen*. This was the genesis of the modern, militant, so-called *jihadist* movement and the birth of Osama bin Laden's Al-Qaeda. These Arabs who had bought into *Salafism* with every fiber of their being were ready and willing to return to their homelands and carry on with their own brand of *jihad* there once the victory in Afghanistan had been won.

Even though the actual success of these Afghan Arabs on the battlefield was negligible, their reputation was secured. Their inflated contribution to driving one of the world's two superpowers out of Afghanistan in a single stroke avenged all the Israeli humiliations and defeats suffered by the Arab armies and gave them confidence in their cause. More importantly, it gave their ideology tremendous credence and credibility to many others in the Muslim world who were eager to restore honor and dignity to the *ummah* after years of perceived disgrace at the hands of the immoral West and Zionist Israel – and even from the corrupt autocratic and dictatorial

Arab secularists. If Allah could lead the *mujahideen* to victory against the Russians, He could do the same against America and the Zionists. It was clear proof of the righteousness of the *Salafist* ideology and its *jihadist* cause.

The triumph over the infidels galvanized bin Laden into redoubling his efforts against the West. It didn't take long for the Saudi zealot and his nascent Al-Qaeda organization to pin the target on Uncle Sam's back. The group's 1992 opening salvo against the United States in Aden, the 1993 World Trade Center attack, the 1998 African embassy bombings, the USS *Cole* suicide mission, and the 9/11 attacks on New York and Washington gained him much greater fame and notoriety in anti-US circles and made him an icon of restored Arab and Muslim pride among many. But without the Afghan war, the world may never have heard of Osama bin Laden, Al-Qaeda would never have existed, and the *Salafist jihad* would have required some other spark to get it going.

A second key development of the Afghan war was that it brought Saudi Arabia front and center onto the world stage as a main financial supporter of the various Afghan factions fighting the Russian occupiers. The Saudi government matched US funding to Afghan rebel groups dollar for dollar during the war, something that was confirmed by the chief of the Afghan Bureau in Pakistan's Inter-Services Intelligence.[32] While none of the official US or Saudi funding was ever used to aid bin Laden or the Afghan Arabs, there is evidence that Saudi Arabia and others provided funding to these Arab fighters in a separate, clandestine effort. In his book "Understanding Terror Networks," Marc Sageman, based in Islamabad, Pakistan during the war wrote:

> *No U.S. official ever came in contact with the foreign volunteers. They simply traveled in different circles and never crossed U.S. radar screens. They had their own sources of money and their own contacts with the Pakistanis, official Saudis, and other Muslim supporters, and they made their own deals with the various Afghan resistance leaders. Their presence in Afghanistan was very small and they did not participate in any significant fighting.*[33]

---

32. Mohammad Yousaf; Mark Adkin. *The Bear Trap: Afghanistan's Untold Story* (Lahore: Jang Publishers, 1992), 81.
33. Marc Sageman. *Understanding Terror Networks* (Philadelphia: University of Pennsylvania Press, 2004), 57-58.

So, in bin Laden and the Afghan Arabs, the Saudis found a Muslim group whose *Salafism* was essentially identical to the *Wahhabism* of the Kingdom. Here was a chance to support Arabs sympathetic to the Saudi religious ideology who would eventually go back to their homes throughout the Middle East. In helping them, the Saudis not only fulfilled what they saw as a religious duty to spread the "pure" version of Islam, but they hoped to expand their own influence in the Arab world at the same time.

In 1990, Iraqi President Saddam Hussein invaded Kuwait. As the United States built a coalition of Muslim nations to drive Saddam out of the tiny Gulf country, it began a steady buildup of military forces in Saudi Arabia that was sanctioned by the Saudi government, which viewed Saddam as a threat. Bin Laden saw this Western presence on the Arabian Peninsula as a defilement of Muslim holy land and his protestations to Saudi officials on the matter led to harsh disagreement and his fall from grace with his *Wahhabi* masters. Nevertheless, he did remain popular with an extremely conservative segment of the Saudi population who shared his displeasure with the massive US and Western presence.

The eruption of Somalia's civil war shortly after the conclusion of *Desert Storm* with yet another US intervention in a fraternal Muslim nation infuriated bin Laden even more. It was the final straw for him as he began his active terrorist campaign against America in 1992.

The perceived string of successes by Al-Qaeda and its founder boosted their popularity in the region immensely. Although many Americans wouldn't have recognized Osama bin Laden's name until after 9/11, he was becoming a cult and folk hero in the Muslim world. Finally there was a man and a group that was tweaking the nose of the Great Satan and giving it a dose of its own medicine. Finally there was hope that the tide was turning, hope that by humiliating and defeating the United States the Arabs and Muslims would finally succeed in righting the wrong represented by Israel's illegitimate existence on Palestinian Arab and Muslim territory. Bin Laden enjoyed a level of popularity in the Arab world not seen since the days of Gamal Abdel-Nasser.

When we invaded Afghanistan shortly after the events of 9/11, there was a short grace period when most of the Muslim world expected such a US response. However the resentment began to build when we toppled the

Taliban – who had hosted Osama bin Laden – but then we didn't leave. Our subsequent occupation of the country has even made many moderate Arabs and Muslims suspicious of our ultimate motives. In that part of the world this occupation merely proves the veracity of the *Salafist* and terrorist narrative in the eyes of many.

Finally our invasion and occupation of Iraq in 2003, as part of our misbegotten quest for nonexistent WMD, did more to boost the *Salafist* recruiting cause than anything bin Laden could ever have hoped for. We threw out the *Sunnis* who had ruled the country for half a millennium and replaced them with the apostate *Shiites*. We were the superpower bull in the Mesopotamian china shop and our clueless focus on establishing a completely alien, Western form of democracy did nothing but ignite *Sunni-Shia* sectarian passions and hatred to the point of civil war.

With the loss of Iraq as its natural buffer against Iranian influence and the rise of a confrontational Iran that has been fomenting strife all around Saudi Arabia in Bahrain, Iraq, and Syria, not to mention the kingdom's own Eastern Province, the Saudis have felt the need like never before to mobilize radical *Sunnis* to counter their archenemy across the Gulf. In their quest to depose the *Alawite/Shiite* regime in Damascus, did they provide funding to the *Nusra* Front, Al-Qaeda's franchise in Syria? Did they initially support Islamic State for the same reason? There are rumors that unidentified Saudis showed up on the Turkish side of the Syrian border with bags of cash for *Salafist* extremists in these groups, but so far none of that has been proven.

On the bright side, it does seem as if the Saudis may finally understand that they have played a historical role the creation of a *Salafist/Wahhabist* Frankenstein. They shut off support for Egypt's Muslim Brotherhood, going as far as to brand the organization un-Islamic. The kingdom has been a lukewarm member of the coalition against the Islamic State but the rulers do seem to realize that the radical ideology that they helped to create decades ago is also now a threat to them and the modern Saudi state. They now state that the ideology is "misguided" and not connected to Islam in any way. One can only hope that the Custodian of the Two Holy Mosques will now be as helpful in confronting and removing the threat as his predecessors were in creating it in the first place.

49

HISTORICAL VIOLENCE IN THE MIDDLE EAST

Hardly a day goes by where we don't see or hear media reports about gruesome violence in the Middle East. It may fool us into thinking that the region has somehow become a more violent place after the 2011 Arab Spring.

The Islamist terrorists have discovered their own "shock and awe" campaign over the last dozen or so years: videos showing the beheadings of Western prisoners and hostages or the immolation of others in a cage. The ubiquity and anonymity of the Internet allows these terrorists to upload the videos, disseminate them via social media, and strike fear into the hearts of Western infidels thousands of miles away. The worldwide web gives them a platform and a global reach that allows them to get everyone's immediate attention. This instant, laser-like media focus is a terrorist's dream come true.

In addition, everybody has a cellphone with a camera nowadays. As a result, we have seen videos of five years of atrocities coming out of the Syrian civil war, clips of brutal *Sharia* justice in places like Yemen and Mali, and Somalia, and the mass shootings, beheadings, and crucifixions carried out by the Islamic State group in Iraq and Syria. The violence itself hasn't necessarily increased; there are just more graphic images of it that are being uploaded to the Internet.

Naturally, this suits the terrorists' purposes just fine. A gullible international media can portray them as being nearly invincible with a global reach so they don't have to cultivate (or prove) that image themselves. The media aspect will be discussed in greater detail later in the book. However, it is worthwhile to remember that violence in the Middle East predates Islam by many millennia. As we've noted, the region and its Fertile Crescent is the land from which our human civilization sprang forth and the history of that civilization includes an awful lot of blood and guts.

There is no shortage of war stories when it comes to ancient civilizations. We can find downright apocalyptic events in the Bible, alone. In Genesis, the very first book of the Old Testament, we find the story of God's destruction of the sinful cities of Sodom and Gomorrah by raining fire and brimstone down upon them. This is destruction on a citywide scale.[34]

Another complete city is destroyed in the story of Joshua and the Battle of Jericho. The Israelites circled the city seven times on the seventh day according to God's instruction, blew their trumpets, and the walls of the city fell. They were commanded to put every man, woman, child, and beast inside the city to the sword and collect all the gold, silver, bronze, and iron for God's treasury.[35]

In the Bible's account of Noah and the Great Flood, God went so far as to kill every living thing on the face of the earth in a catastrophic flood – and it doesn't get any more catastrophic than that.[36]

Not to be outdone, the Book of Revelations at the very end of the Bible warns us about the final battle during the End Times – the Battle of Armageddon.[37] Here, a river of blood will flow up to the height of a horses' bridle for 200 miles.[38]

From the Bible and antiquity we can fast forward to the Crusades. These were a series of wars and campaigns aimed at protecting sacred Christian sites in the Holy Land as well as defending the seat of Byzantium Christendom itself in Constantinople. The Crusades lasted from about 1095 to 1291 and (for the most part) did not go particularly well for the early Christians.

But violence and bloodshed in the Middle East hasn't just been limited to rival ancient empires and religious wars, there has been plenty of brutality in the region just since the end of the Second World War. In fact, some secular Arab leaders seem to have been even more bloodthirsty than their Islamic era counterparts.

It is difficult to top the brutal example of Saddam Hussein in this regard. His 23-year dictatorship was characterized by an eight-year war with Iran, a disastrous 1990 invasion of neighboring Kuwait, and an ensuing decade

---

34. Genesis 19:1-29.
35. Joshua 6:1-27.
36. Genesis 6:1 – 9:17.
37. Revelations 16:16.
38. Revelations 14:20.

of standoff with the United Nations and international community over his alleged weapons of mass destruction programs. That culminated in the 2003 US invasion and occupation of Iraq and the toppling of Saddam's government. Along the way he also ruthlessly repressed uprisings by the majority *Shiites* and killed 5,000 Iraq Kurds in the village of Halabja with chemical weapons in a single attack.

ABC News compiled a long list of Saddam's crimes immediately after the Iraqi dictator was hanged and it concluded that the number of his victims might range as high as half a million, although exact numbers will probably never be known.[39] In addition to this tally, the dictator is also at least indirectly responsible for the deaths of Iraqis and Iranians during the 1980-1988 Iran-Iraq War and the deaths of Iraqi children who died due to the international trade sanctions that were imposed on Iraq after *Desert Storm.*

While Saddam liked to portray himself in turn as a Bedouin tribesman, a modern-day Salah al-Din, a wise general, and a benevolent leader, his actual track record ranks him closer to another infamous figure in Iraq. That would be Hulagu, the Mongol warlord who sacked Baghdad in 1258, destroyed everyone and everything in the city, and had the Abbasid caliph trampled.

The Assad family in neighboring Syria is another secular dynasty that is known for its brutality. The patriarch of the family, Hafez al-Assad, started out as a young air force pilot but he constantly worked his way up the ladder of the Syrian branch of the *Baath* Party. He reached the top in 1971 when he became president of the country.

As a member of the *Alawite* sect of the *Shia* branch of Islam, the Assad regime was not popular with the *Sunni*-majority population of Syria. He sided with Iran in the 1980-1988 war with Iraq and invaded neighboring Lebanon in 1976 to intervene in that country's civil war.

Hafez al-Assad violently put down several *Sunni* uprisings during his presidency that culminated in a showdown with *Sunni* members of the Syrian Muslim Brotherhood in the city of Hama in 1982. Assad sent in

---

39. "List of Saddam's Crimes is Long," *ABC News*, December 30, 2006. Accessed July 13, 2017. http://abcnews.go.com/WNT/IraqCoverage/story?id=2761722.

the tanks and up to 20,000 *Sunnis* were killed in Hama. Much of the city was left in ruins.[40]

When Hafez died in 2000, his young son Bashar al-Assad succeeded him as president. The West initially viewed Bashar as a London-educated moderate and a potential political reformer. But the eruption of the Syrian civil war in 2011 has shown him to be every bit as ruthless a dictator as his father was. In February 2016, an article on the Public Broadcasting Service website cited an estimate by the Syrian Center for Policy Research that 470,000 had died in the Syrian conflict.[41]

Bashar's kill tally may be lower than Saddam's now, but it is likely to rise. The Syrian civil war shows no signs of abating anytime soon.

And, of course, let's not forget Libya's Muammar al-Gaddafi. The final count in the death toll of his victims might not compete with Saddam Hussein or the Assad regime, but the Libyan dictator certainly wasn't a slacker. He had a penchant for dabbling in terrorism: the 1988 bombing of Pan Am 103 over Lockerbie, Scotland with the deaths of 259 people; the 1989 bombing of a UTA airliner over the Sahara Desert with the deaths of 170 passengers and crew; and a former aide claimed Gaddafi was responsible for downing a Libyan airliner in 1992 that resulted in the deaths of 157 victims.[42] In 1986 his henchmen bombed the La Belle Disco in a Berlin, Germany suburb that killed two US soldiers and a Turkish woman.[43]

During his 42-year reign of terror, the dictator was also very unforgiving of any dissent at home. He was especially concerned about those Libyans

40. Jason Rodrigues, "1982: Syria's President Hafez al-Assad Crushes Rebellion in Hama," *The Guardian*, August 1, 2011. Accessed July 13, 2017. https://www.theguardian.com/theguardian/from-the-archive-blog/2011/aug/01/hama-syria-massacre-1982-archive.

41. Priyanka Boghani, "A Staggering New Death Toll for Syria's War – 470,000," website of the Public Broadcasting Service, February 11, 2016. Accessed July 13, 2017. http://www.pbs.org/wgbh/frontline/article/a-staggering-new-death-toll-for-syrias-war-470000/.

42. Christopher Olgiati, "Libya: Muammar Gaddafi's Secrets Finally Revealed," *BBC News*, February 3, 2014. Accessed July 13, 2017. http://www.bbc.com/news/world-africa-25979532.

43. Daniel Scheschkewitz and Nick Amies, "Berlin's La Belle Nightclub Bombing Remembered 25 Years on," *Deutsche Welle News*, April 4, 2011. Accessed July 13, 2017. http://www.dw.de/berlins-la-belle-nightclub-bombing-remembered-25-years-on/a-14965254.

seen to be traditional, devout Muslims. An eyewitness account of the notorious Abu-Salim Prison massacre in 1996 when the regime gunned down more than 1,200 prisoners was given to *Al-Jazeera* in 2011, shortly after Gaddafi's death.[44]

The regime's fear of Islamists was well founded since the Libyan Islamic Fighting Group had coalesced into a potent opposition force. From its origins in the early nineties from the conservative Muslim roots of eastern Libya, the group enjoyed numerous fighters with battle experience from the Afghan war and a network of support in Libya and elsewhere in the Middle East and it made three unsuccessful attempts to assassinate the Libyan leader.[45] No wonder Gaddafi was worried.

But while the Abu-Salim Prison massacre may have been carried out in secret, Gaddafi recognized the importance of terror as a tool of control, beginning with his first public execution in 1984. It was broadcast live on Libyan state television for maximum effect.

A macabre circus atmosphere prevailed over the event. The execution was held in a Benghazi basketball stadium and thousands of Libyan school-children had been bused in to view what they believed would be a trial. These children were shown pumping their fists in the air and chanting revolutionary slogans.

A Libyan student, Sadiq Hamed Shwehdi, was accused of plotting against the Gaddafi regime while studying aeronautical engineering in the United States. With fear in his eyes, the man, with his hands already bound behind his back, confessed to the crowd and was then summarily hanged on a makeshift gallows inside the stadium. Various grainy clips and scenes of the execution are still available online[46] and at least one print media

44. Evan Hill, "Libya Survivor Describes 1996 Prison Massacre," *Al-Jazeera English*, July 13, 2017. Accessed October 30, 2014. http://www.aljazeera.com/indepth/features/2011/09/201.192.23521462487.html.

45. Ian Black, "The Libyan Islamic Fighting Group – From al-Qaida to the Arab Spring," *The Guardian*, September 5, 2011. Accessed July 13, 2017. http://www.theguardian.com/world/2011/sep/05/libyan-islamic-fighting-group-leaders.

46. Reportage by Peter Bouckaert, "How Gaddafi Used to Hang People in Benghazi," *YouTube* published July 19, 2011. Accessed October 5. 2016. http://www.youtube.com/watch?v=5RO159SSJSc.

account of the story indicates Shwehdi had to be subsequently killed in a hospital because the hanging itself was botched.[47]

The regime continued the practice of public executions as a means of deterring any internal dissent. While we cannot know Gaddafi's final "kill tally," it is safe to assume he and his regime were very proficient in the use of fear as an effective tool of control against his own people.

Another observation about the megalomaniacs of Saddam Hussein, the Assad family, and Muammar al-Gaddafi: they all had ongoing WMD programs.

THE SUNNI-SHIA RIFT

No review of the current social environment in the Middle East would be complete without a discussion of the widening *Sunni-Shia* rift in the region. This is a critical religious dynamic in areas where a natural fault line exists between the two main branches of Islam such as in Iran, Iraq, Bahrain, Syria, Lebanon, and Yemen. Saudi Arabia also is home to a large *Shiite* minority in its Eastern Province. In addition, it has been a major root cause of *Sunni Salafist* militancy.

As we briefly noted earlier, the origin of the split between these two groups goes all the way back to the earliest days of Islam and the process of selecting the rightful successor to lead the faith after the death of Muhammad in 632. The *Sunnis* believed that Muhammad's successor should be among those who had followed his traditions and emulated him (i.e., one of the prophet's "Companions") while the *Shiites* believed that the new leader should have come from within the prophet's own family and household.

While the *Sunnis* and the *Shia* do diverge on various major theological points and practices in Islam, those differences are not what interest us here. What is important is that each side views the other as being an apostate and a heretic who has turned its back on the true faith. Both the *Sunnis* and the *Shia* see this as an unpardonable sin of the worst kind.

---

47. "Awful Journey into Mind of Dictator Muammar Gaddafi," *The Australian*, March 14, 2011. Accessed July 13, 2017. http://www.theaustralian.com.au/news/world/awful-journey-into-mind-of-dictator-muammar-gaddafi/story-e6frg6so-122.602.0713120.

At least that is the current narrative, which seems to be borne out by the bloody fighting between the two sects.

When relations between the two are examined through an objective, historical prism rather than a black-and-white ideological one, it would seem that the two sides have mostly coexisted peacefully for rather a long time. In countries like Iraq, for example, there has been widespread intermarriage between *Sunni* and *Shia* families – something that would be unthinkable if this were a full-blown 1400-year-old religious war. Jews, Christians, and Muslims have all had to live together in the Middle East during the last millennium and a half and periods of religious tolerance marked the Umayyad, Abbasid, and especially the Fatamid Caliphates. Yes, there were periods of strife but these were the exception rather than the rule. Something shifted in the latter half of the twentieth century that upset the balance of this relatively tranquil relationship.

Perhaps the most disruptive event to this traditional coexistence was the 1979 overthrow of the shah of Iran by the Iranian Revolution that was led by Ayatollah Khomeini. The stern-faced cleric, who became the Supreme Leader in the ensuing Islamic Republic of Iran, quickly purged the country's government and culture of any secular influences and he became the symbol of modern Islamic extremism, particularly in the eyes of the West.

Khomeini and his militant and unforgiving brand of *Shiism* were wildly popular in Iran, especially among the country's working class who had felt ignored and marginalized under the shah and now enjoyed the retribution that was being visited upon his former officials and supporters. The concept of "an eye for an eye" predates Islam and goes all the way back to the Torah and the Old Testament, so Khomeini's execution and punishment of those who were seen as oppressors under the shah met widespread acceptance from those Muslim faithful who had been the oppressed. It was populist justice at its best in a region where vengeance is a very real religious concept.

But Khomeini wasn't satisfied with merely establishing his Islamic Republic of Iran, he almost immediately turned his wrathful visage outward and proclaimed the United States the "Great Satan" and Russia the "Lesser Satan." He sanctioned the 444-day takeover of the US embassy in Tehran in November 1979 by Iranian students. Suddenly Khomeini had catapulted the *Shiites*, who represent only about 10% of the Muslim

56

population, out of the shadows and into the world's catbird seat by tweaking the whiskers on Uncle Sam's chin.

The Supreme Leader called for Iran's Islamic revolution to be exported worldwide. That motivated Saddam Hussein, with a sizable *Shia* majority population of his own, to invade Iran in 1980 and fight an eight-year war that ended in an exhausted stalemate. It is important to remember that while *Sunni* Iraq and *Shiite* Iran were fighting each other in this war, the conflict was still officially at the level of countries and state actors. Although Saddam saw any exportation of Iran's revolution to Iraq as a potential threat, he was also inspired to attack Iran by his belief that the Iranian armed forces had been severely weakened by Khomeini's purge of those perceived as the shah's loyalists. The Iraqi president also had territorial ambitions of his own, so the war itself was not solely a sectarian conflict.

Despite the grueling Iran-Iraq war, the Islamic Republic and Khomeini continued to export and promote militant *Shiism* in the region. With the creation of its Lebanese proxy *Hezbollah* ("The Party of God"), Iran was able to extend its influence into Lebanon and even engage the Zionist archenemy in guerilla warfare. In fact, it's fair (and somewhat ironic) to say that *Shiite Hezbollah* developed and pioneered most of the tactics of *Sunni* Islamist violence that we see today. During much of the eighties, *Hezbollah* fighters kidnapped and/or killed American diplomats, journalists, military personnel, and even clergy. They introduced the tactic of suicide truck bombings at the American Embassy in Beirut and the US Marine barracks in 1983. And they have gone beyond being just a paramilitary organization to become a major political force in the diverse political spectrum that exists inside Lebanon.

The emergence of Ayatollah Khomeini in Iran and the rise of his radical, aggressive, and revolutionary brand of *Shiite* Islam and its projection outside of the country was the first disruptor to *Sunni-Shia* coexistence in the final half of the last century. This new threat rang alarm bells in the conservative *Sunni* strongholds of Saudi Arabia and the other Gulf Arab states and even in Cairo.

In response to this *Shiite* Iranian resurgence, the *Sunni* Arab countries in the Gulf formed the Gulf Cooperation Council in 1981 to foster political, economic, commercial, scientific, and technical cooperation, unity, and exchange among the countries and their peoples. The GCC, as it became known, also included a joint military element whose purpose was to deter aggression against any of the member states. Any potential threat to the GCC was seen as coming from Iran, as it is the only non-Arab and non-GCC member state on the Arab/Persian Gulf.

In comparing the GCC's senior member, Saudi Arabia, to the Islamic Republic of Iran, the two countries could not be more different. Under Khomeini, the Islamic Republic operated under what he termed the *Velayet-e-Faqih* ("Guardianship of Islamic Jurists") form of government where senior clergy were responsible for running all the nation's affairs.

In contrast, Saudi Arabia was a traditional and conservative monarchy that was the absolute antithesis of being in any way, shape, or form revolutionary. Saudi King Khalid was anything but a charismatic figure and the Saudis' attention was primarily directed inward (with the exception of its oil industry) since the king is, nominally, the Custodian of the Two Holy Mosques (i.e., the mosques in Mecca and Medina).

During the Iran-Iraq War, Saudi Arabia and the other GCC states were firmly in Iraq's camp. They provided extensive financial support to Iraq and paid for it by boosting their own oil production, aiming to further debilitate Iran by lowering oil prices.

In short, when the Islamic Republic of Iran came onto the scene in 1979 led by a fiery *Shiite* cleric who made no secret of his desire to unify the Muslims of the world under his banner, the stage was set for the *Sunni-Shia* showdown that we are seeing today.

The next disruptive force in the *Sunni-Shia* balance appeared on the *Sunni* side with the arrival of Osama bin Laden in Pakistan in 1979 – the same year as Khomeini's return to Iran. Bin Laden had gone to Pakistan to help support the *mujahideen* fighting the Soviets in Afghanistan. He set up offices in various Arab countries to recruit fighters and used his own money to finance the purchase of weapons and other necessities for the Afghan war.

By the mid-eighties bin Laden had begun to sporadically take part in combat operations against the Russians. The Al-Qaeda group had been created sometime around 1988 and by the time the Soviets left Afghanistan in 1989, bin Laden was seen as a charismatic and selfless *mujahid* who was willing to sacrifice his own wealth "in the cause of Allah."

It's interesting to note the similarities between bin Laden and Khomeini. Both men had a vision of uniting first the Muslims, and then the whole world, under their own banner of Islam. They were both charismatic leaders who were idolized by their followers. Both took advantage of the simmering resentment in the Islamic world against the West, in general, and the United States, in particular, and used it to great effect.

America did have a history of meddling in Iranian domestic affairs after World War II and when the students overran and occupied the American Embassy in Tehran in 1979, it was portrayed as a nest of spies. In a nation famous for weaving ornate rugs and carpets, Iranians painstakingly reconstructed classified documents from individual strands of paper taken from the embassy's shredders as proof of America's injustice and iniquity. The "Death to America" chants were (and still are) a trademark of pro-government demonstrations inside Iran.

The trigger point for bin Laden was the US military presence on the Arabian Peninsula after the eviction of Iraq from Kuwait in *Desert Storm*. He viewed US troops as "infidels" – those who did not believe in Islam – and their existence in Saudi Arabia – the birthplace of Islam and home to its holiest shrines – as a defilement of the Muslims' sacred lands. In his opinion, they were nothing more than a modern equivalent of Byzantium's medieval Crusaders.

And of course America's overt, blatant, and unconditional economic, military, and political support for Israel – "the Zionist entity" – at the expense of the Arab Muslim Palestinians did little to endear it to either the Arab or Islamic worlds. It frequently made the United States a target of derision and hatred in the region, at least at both the *Sunni* and *Shiite* popular levels.

As previously pointed out, Khomeini's protégés in Lebanon's *Hezbollah* introduced the concept of *istishhad* – martyrdom – in their suicide bombings against the American Embassy and Marine barracks in Beirut in 1983. It wasn't a totally new idea. During the Iran-Iraq War, waves of

Iranian *basij* marched and ran in human waves through Iraqi minefields, sacrificing themselves to clear the way for regular army soldiers to follow behind them.

At some point between the mid-eighties and mid-nineties of the last century, the tactic of suicide bombing – *istishhad* – made the jump from *Shiite* Islam to the *Sunnis* and the Palestinian Islamic Resistance Movement – Hamas – made the first such *Sunni* attacks in Israel in 1994. It has become a trademark of Islamist extremist terror ever since.

Bin Laden and Al-Qaeda embraced *istishhad* and suicide bombings and used them to assault the United States with the twin US embassy bombings in Kenya and Tanzania in 1998, the USS *Cole* attack in 2000, and the events of 9/11 the following year. With that, bin Laden became the global icon and proponent of *Sunni* extremism and terrorism around the world just like Khomeini had done on the *Shiite* side.

The US invasion of Iraq in 2003 became another definitive and significant disruptor in *Sunni-Shia* coexistence that actually escalated to open conflict between the two factions within a single national population. Although a minority population, the *Sunnis* had first been put in administrative control of Iraq by the Ottoman Empire in the early sixteenth century to prevent the spread of Persian *Shiite* Islam westward into the *Sunni* empire. After the defeat and subsequent fall of the Ottomans after World War I, the *Sunnis* continued running the country under the British Mandate. When the Iraqi monarchy was overthrown and replaced by the secular *Baath* movement, the party's powerbase was almost exclusively the domain of *Sunni* Iraqis.

The first official act of the Coalition Provisional Authority after toppling the Saddam Hussein regime was to disband the army and de-*Baathify* the Iraqi government. The end result of those decisions was to remove the *Sunnis* – the people who had run Iraq for 500 years – from power with a single stroke of a pen. As the *Sunnis* were increasingly pushed out of the government and disenfranchised by the *Shia*, tensions and violence began to mount. By 2006 the fighting between *Sunnis* and *Shia* had nearly reached the point of open civil war and it was all our fault.

The *Sunnis* in the vast Anbar province in the west of Iraq turned to Al-Qaeda for assistance. The xenophobic *Sunni* tribes began fighting an insurgency against the foreign US occupier while also fighting a sectarian battle against its archenemies in Baghdad – the *Shiites* now running the country. And as Al-Qaeda started to take on the leading role in the insurgency, the brutality of the violence exploded exponentially. Torture, beheadings, and kidnappings became the order of the day.

By creating a partnership with the *Sunni* tribes to fight Al-Qaeda and restore some order in Anbar through what became known as the Awakening Councils, the US military was able to eventually drive Al-Qaeda in Iraq underground. After that the US presence in the country acted as something of a brake on *Sunni-Shia* violence, but when the Americans left in 2011 the situation between the two sides quickly broke down again. This allowed Al-Qaeda in Iraq to resurrect itself and transform into the even more violent Islamic State in Iraq and Syria (ISIS), fill the void in Anbar, and even take its battle to the *Shiite* apostates in Syria. It eventually identified itself simply as the Islamic State and adopted a methodology and a degree of violence so extreme that even Al-Qaeda disavowed it.

The final disruptor came in 2011 in the form of the Arab Spring. Widespread corruption, political discontent, economic stagnation, and unemployment had caused tensions in the Arab world to reach the boiling point by the end of 2010 and the beginning of 2011. When the Tunisian street vendor Mohamed Bouazizi doused himself with gasoline and set himself on fire after a government inspector confiscated his wares, it triggered a sympathetic reaction from one end of the Middle East to the other. Mass protests and demonstrations erupted first in Tunisia, where the country's president, Zine El Abidine Ben Ali, was quickly ousted.

The groundswell of revolt rippled into Cairo next and toppled President Hosni Mubarak in just 18 days. Libya's revolution began in February and eventually toppled Gaddafi in August of 2011 and the Syrian revolution – and now civil war – began in March of 2011. President Ali Abdullah al-Saleh was deposed in Yemen, although he was granted immunity from prosecution.

Numerous other Arab countries saw protests and demonstrations and in several countries the violence broke down along *Shia-Sunni* lines.

In Bahrain pro-democracy *Shia* demonstrators clashed day and night with the *Sunni* government's security and police forces in the tiny Gulf kingdom. Learning from the example of Egyptian youth, the Bahraini protestors began using cellphone video to record acts of police brutality against the demonstrators and disseminating it via social media. This attracted Western media attention and the government quickly asked for troops from fellow GCC member Saudi Arabia to enter Bahrain and restore order. Despite some political concessions by the government, this conflict is split right along *Sunni-Shia* lines and it continues at a low boil.

The Saudi military occupation of Bahrain also prompted the *Shia* minority in Saudi Arabia's Eastern Province to protest in support of their religious brethren in Bahrain. The city of Al-Qatif has been a focal point for *Shia* unrest, particularly after the Saudis shot, arrested, and eventually executed Nimr al-Nimr, a very popular *Shiite* cleric who promoted anti-government protests in the city.

From the very beginning, the Syrian revolution and ensuing civil war almost immediately fractured into *Sunni* opposition to a corrupt *Shia Alawite* regime. Once again graphic images and videos of violence perpetrated by both sides were quickly uploaded to the Internet and social media sites. In a conflict marked by daily massacres, humanitarian atrocities and suffering, and even chemical warfare the constant media and image battle has kept passions white hot among combatants and their respective supporters ever since the fighting broke out. The Syrian arena has been distinguished by its first acknowledged Al-Qaeda affiliate (*Nusra* Front – now the Front for the Conquest of the Levant) and the even more brutal Islamic State in Iraq and Syria (ISIS) and both have overshadowed the Free Syrian Army (and its many offshoots), an allegedly moderate secular and *Sunni* opposition to the Bashar al-Assad regime.

Yemen's revolution may have officially started in January 2011 but the *Sunni* government has been fighting an on-again, off-again insurgency with Houthi rebels in the north for about a decade. The Houthis are members of the Zaidi sect of *Shia* Islam who are seeking greater autonomy from the central government and by 2010 the fighting had reached the point of Saudi military intervention in Yemen against the Houthi rebels. Recently, the Houthis were even able to occupy the capital of Sanaa and much of the country down to Aden in the south, so there does not appear to be a decisive end to this dispute anytime soon. (And, of course, Yemen has also been fighting Al-Qaeda in the south of the country with US assistance.)

And Iraq has splintered into a *Sunni-Shia* civil war since the end of 2012. The perceived persecution and disenfranchisement of the *Sunni* tribes in northern and western Iraq by the *Shiite*-dominated government threw open the door for ISIS (now IS) to take territory and expand its influence all the way to a very nervous Baghdad.

If all that wasn't bad enough, there has been dramatic rise in the tone and tenor of *Sunni-Shia* hate speech in the Muslim world. A 2013 *BBC Arabic* video production was aired in March 2014 entitled "Freedom to Broadcast Hate" that examined the problem of *Sunni-Shia* hate speech. The program (broadcasted in English) highlighted six Islamic religious satellite television channels that are exploiting the press freedoms gained from by Arab Spring to stoke the flames of sectarian violence.[48]

While the claim that *Sunnis* and *Shia* have been at each other's throats for 1400 years is clearly inaccurate, the tensions between the two have ratcheted up steadily ever since the Iranian revolution became the Islamic Republic of Iran and Ayatollah Khomeini began exporting his revolution to the region. Given the *Sunni-Shia* nature of the civil wars in Iraq, Yemen, and Syria and the escalation of hate speech by both sides, this rift shows no signs of rapprochement in the foreseeable future. As this conflict engulfs other ethnic and religious minorities and human atrocities on both sides continue to mount, it will likely get much worse before it gets better.

ISRAEL AND THE PALESTINIANS

Finally, no discussion about the cultural and social environment in the Arab and Muslim world can be complete without understanding the importance of the Israeli-Palestinian conflict. It has been the 800-pound gorilla in the room ever since the modern State of Israel was established in 1948. For the purposes of this discussion, our focus is on the more than 700,000 Palestinians who were displaced by the creation of the

---

48. "Survey of Palestinian Refugees and Internally Displaced Persons 2006-2007," website of the United Nations Information System on the Question of Palestine (UNISPAL), dated June 2007. Accessed July 13, 2017. https://unispal.un.org/pdfs/Badil_06-07Survey.pdf.

Jewish state in their homeland.[49] Another 200,000 were displaced in the 1967 Six Day War.[50] According to a factsheet about Palestinian refugees on the website of the Negotiations Affairs Department of the Palestine Liberation Organization (PLO), these original displaced persons and their descendants now number more than 6.5 million, constituting "the world's oldest and largest refugee population, making up nearly one-fourth of the entire refugee population in the world."[51]

Although Jerusalem in Palestine is home to Islam's third holiest shrine, the Al-Aqsa Mosque, the Palestinian cause is primarily a nationalist one. The cause to establish an independent Palestinian state within the 1948 borders and expel the "Zionist entity" took on a militant tone in the late 1950s when Yasser Arafat and a close circle of supporters founded Fatah. The name was an Arabic reverse acronym of the Palestinian National Liberation Movement (*Harakat al-Tahrir al-Watani al-Filistiniyah*) that also translates to "conquest" or "victory." It was under Arafat's Fatah that the Palestinian armed struggle against Israel began.

With today's media spotlight focused on all things IS and Islamist extremist terrorism, it would be easy to forget that the United States was a target of Palestinian nationalists long before the Islamists came on the scene. As the primary political, military, and financial supporter of archenemy Israel, the Palestinians saw America and its citizens as justified targets in their cause.

American airliners in the Mediterranean would become frequent targets in the seventies and eighties after two fighters from the Popular Front for the Liberation of Palestine (PFLP) hijacked TWA 840 in 1969 and diverted it to Damascus. One of the hijackers – a diminutive young woman named Leila Khaled – would become an icon of Palestinian resistance after that hijacking.

---

49. "Survey of Palestinian Refugees and Internally Displaced Persons (2002)," website of the United Nations Office for the Coordination of Humanitarian Affairs, Occupied Palestinian Territory, dated April 21, 2003. Accessed July 13, 2017. https://www.ochaopt. org/documents/opt_prot_badil_studey_survey_of_refugees_idp_2002.pdf.
50. "Palestinian Refugees," Negotiations Affairs Department of the Palestine Liberation Organization. Accessed July 13, 2017. http://www.nad-plo.org/etemplate.php?id=258.
51. *Ibid.*

The PFLP's Dawson's Field mass hijacking operation the next year included two American commercial aircraft. Three out of four of the hijacked aircraft (including a TWA Boeing 707) were landed in a remote part of the Jordanian desert while the fourth (a Pan American 747) was taken to Cairo. These aircraft were later destroyed although all the hostages were subsequently freed. Leila Khaled and her accomplice failed in their attempt to commandeer an Israeli El Al flight as part of the operation and she was captured and taken into custody.

In 1974, flight TWA 841 was destroyed off the west coast of Greece by what the National Transportation Safety Board later ruled to be a bomb placed in the cargo hold. The incident killed all 88 persons on board but the actual identity of the perpetrator has never been definitively proven, although Palestinians were the likely suspects.

A bomb planted under a seat on TWA flight 840 in 1986 exploded killing four Americans – including an infant – on the plane. The aircraft was able to land safely and the bombing was believed to be the work of the Palestinian guerilla group Abu Nidal.

Then there is the particularly reprehensible incident in 1985 when four members of the Palestine Liberation Front hijacked the cruise ship *Achille Lauro*. The Palestinian terrorists shot American Leon Klinghoffer as he sat in his wheelchair and then dumped his body overboard.

These acts of terrorism by Palestinian "freedom fighters" did absolutely nothing to build any sympathy among Americans for their cause. If anything, they had the opposite effect by actually working to foster and cement even stronger US-Israeli ties at the expense of any empathy for Palestinian suffering. In fact, the word "terrorism" in the sixties, seventies, and eighties of the last century conjured up images of armed Palestinian fighters in groups like the PLO, PFLP, Abu Nidal, and Black September in the minds of most Americans who felt that these "terrorists" deserved whatever retribution could be wreaked upon them by Israel or the United States for what they saw as their despicable and cowardly crimes. It simply increased the resolve of American public opinion against supporting anything related to the Palestinian cause.

Nevertheless, the United States began pushing the peace process between Israel and the Palestinians shortly after its *Desert Storm* victory over

Saddam Hussein in 1991. The Madrid Conference later that year sought to restart negotiations between the two parties and the Oslo Accords in 1993 actually initiated the process of attempting to reach a peace based on two existing United Nations Security Council Resolutions. While the accords achieved the mutual recognition of Israel and the PLO, they did not ultimately result in peace between the Israelis and Palestinians. A whole host of negotiations, summits, and roadmaps over the ensuing years has not brought about independent statehood for the Palestinians and enduring peace and security for Israel. Each side blames the other for this failure but the status quo remains.

Despite its attempt at peacemaking, the United States has never been seen as a just and fair broker in the peace process by the Palestinian and Arab side. They believe that America has too long a history of supporting Israel diplomatically, politically, economically, and militarily. Israel flies American jets and attack helicopters and shoots American rifles. And the Arabs are the ones those weapons are most often targeting.

Moreover, on the issue of weapons of mass destruction and Saddam Hussein, the Arabs saw a tremendous double standard in the way the United States (and the United Nations) dealt with Iraq while completely overlooking the existence (albeit unacknowledged) of Israel's nuclear and ballistic missile arsenal.

The Arabs see Washington's tepid admonishments to Israel about expanding its West Bank and Jerusalem settlements as mere lip service while the Israelis have gone about building their "wall of racist separation" (as the Palestinians call it) without suffering any consequences. Palestinian and Arab protestations over land seizures and house demolitions continue to fall on deaf ears in Israel and the United States.

Particularly after 9/11, Americans have a dim view of Palestinian attacks and suicide bombings. We don't see these acts as blows being struck against an occupying power (i.e., Israel), we simply see more Arabs committing the same kinds of terrorism that were used against us on September 11, 2001. Only this time they are attacking a US ally (i.e., Israel). And when it comes to terrorism and suicide operations, Americans are simply uninterested in whether such operations are religious or nationalist in nature. We see it as a cowardly, heinous act against innocent people by despicable criminals. It makes us hate them, not sympathize with their cause.

Obviously, the Arabs have different sentiments and emotions on this issue that factor into the calculus of their general view of the West and their specific view of the United States. The longer the Israeli-Palestinian conflict goes on, the more America's image will suffer among Arabs and Muslims.

This has become an intractable conflict in which neither side is sufficiently willing to pay the cost of a comprehensive peace. The Palestinians seek a return to 1948 and 1967 borders and the right of refugees displaced in 1948 to return to (and repossess) the properties from which they fled. They demand the return of Jerusalem to Palestinian control. These are "red lines" – inviolable positions – in the Palestinian peace negotiations.

Good luck with that. Israel would never agree to these terms. If the displaced Palestinians were allowed to return, the Israelis fear it would erase the Jewish nature and identity of their modern state. They are certainly unwilling to allow these refugees to simply come back and repossess and reoccupy their homes. Moreover, Jewish control over Jerusalem is simply non-negotiable. These are Israeli "red lines."

While the Palestinians wave resolutions of "international legitimacy" from the UN Security Council supporting their territorial claims, the Israelis remain in control and in possession of the land – and, as the old saying goes, "possession is nine-tenths of the law." Their continued absorption of, and expansion into the disputed territory will eventually make it virtually impossible for any future Israeli government to surrender it back to the Palestinians, regardless of how many pieces of paper they have from the UN. That seems to be a part of the Israeli plan – and it's working.

The human cost of this perpetual tragedy is portrayed on the faces of Israelis mourning the victims of some Hamas rocket attack or a suicide bombing and those of Palestinians grieving over sons and husbands killed in an Israeli airstrike in Gaza. The suffering only serves to make each side more stubborn. No matter how much we push and cajole, no negotiations or talks held for our benefit will ever go anywhere as long as neither side is willing to pay the price for peace – period. It's pure political narcissism and hubris on our part to believe otherwise. Nevertheless, we lose nothing by remaining engaged with both sides and encouraging them to talk.

THE ARAB WORLDVIEW AND EXTREMISM

When one takes a long view of Arab culture and history and the totality of the environment from which it has evolved, it should give us an understanding that the Arabs have a much different worldview than our own. They have experienced nearly 12 millennia of human civilization with all the good and evil that has come with it. They have taken their turns as both the conquerors and the conquered, the victors and the vanquished.

Many Arab societies like those in Iraq, Syria, the Arabian Peninsula, and much of North Africa have their roots in a familial tribal hierarchy that may be egalitarian, but not necessarily democratic (at least not by our definition). These tribal societies were homogenous, largely nomadic, and enjoyed very few physical institutions. Carving an austere and difficult life out of a harsh and hostile desert environment required strong leadership by the chief and the collective efforts of the clan or tribe just to survive, let alone prosper. Maybe this trait is partially responsible for the number of post-war autocratic regimes in the Middle East.

Islam evolved into the perfect religion for the wandering tribesmen of the Arabian Peninsula. It incorporated many pre-Islamic desert traditions and combined them with existing elements of Christianity and Judaism. Islam provided a conduit for these tribes to go beyond family and blood relationships and form a larger society of Muslims in which all the aspects of their daily lives were governed under the rubric of an overarching religion. For simplicity's sake (an important consideration of the nomadic tribal existence), everything could be managed out of the mosque: education, worship, governance, marriages, judicial affairs, property transactions, and even medical treatment. An early Muslim's life would have revolved around the mosque.

The early days of human civilization were the days of empires: Babylonians, Assyrians, and ancient Egyptians. When Islam swept eastward and westward from Arabia after Muhammad's death, it created an empire just like the other civilizations that had preceded it. The Islamic Empire and its series of caliphates were made up of Muslims who didn't primarily think of themselves as Syrians or Iraqis or any other nationality. The empire or caliphate's citizens were ranked in a caste system that was ordered by ethnicity and religion. Ethnic Arab Muslims were at the apex.

Non-Arab Christian and Jewish converts to Islam were next, followed by non-Muslim Christians and Jews and non-Muslims who were neither Christians nor Jews at the bottom.

It is worth remembering that even today many Arabs do not have a strong national identity. Many of the boundary lines in today's Middle East were drawn by Western powers under the early twentieth-century Sykes-Picot Agreement or the British and French Mandates. These powers added even more changes and amendments to the map after World War II. Egypt is a prominent exception to this rule with a modern state structure that goes back two centuries under the Muhammad Ali dynasty but this is not the case in the majority of Arab countries.

Our modern system of states and international law is a byproduct of the Peace of Westphalia in 1648 that established a new political and diplomatic order in Europe. The Islamic Empire had already endured for 1,000 years by that time and, although it was on the decline, it still had another 300 years to go.

One of the seminal concepts of Islam is that it is both a religion and a state (in Arabic this is called *deen wa dawla*). Here the Koran and Islamic law provide the precepts and principles of governance without the need for any secular intervention. Thus, the Arab's identity as a Muslim takes precedence over any affiliation or loyalty to an artificial, manmade, national entity. Here the Koran defines human rights, not the United Nations. Political parties are unnecessary because there is no need for elections – the *Sharia* forms the basis of government and law.

While we in America attempt to separate church and state, Islam does the exact opposite; it fuses religion and the state into a single entity. In our heterogeneous and diverse society, we endeavor to respect everyone's individual religious beliefs by avoiding any pretext at a state religion but in the homogenous society of many Muslim countries, Islam casts its dominating shadow over all aspects of daily life.

Do modern Muslims aspire to unification under a single caliphate? A recent BBC article indicated that many do. The article referenced a 2006 Gallup poll of Muslims in Egypt, Morocco, Indonesia, and Pakistan that reported two-thirds of the respondents supported the unification of all

Islamic countries into a single caliphate. These are mainstream Muslims, not extremists. The article speculated that the motivation for a new caliphate came from an association of the historical caliphates with periods of Muslim unity and greatness. This is far different from the situation in which most Muslims find themselves today.[52]

Moreover, Muslims' experience with life under secular forms government has not been very favorable, either. Arab nationalism and pan-Arabism never lived up to their promises and *Baathist* regimes in Iraq and Syria turned into oppressive and tyrannical dictatorships.

Nevertheless, results from the same polling suggest that Muslims do believe that democracy can coexist with Islamic rule and the *Sharia*. That 2006 Gallup poll indicated that a majority of respondents in ten Muslim countries wanted to see the *Sharia* as at least the basis for legislation, but they acknowledged that "freedom of speech" was one of the elements they most admired about Western societies. What many Muslims appear to be seeking is a democracy that incorporates freedoms in a manner that is still consistent with Islamic values.[53]

Even as Muslims and Arabs may believe they can adapt democracy to coexist with Islam, there is one phenomenon that is widely rejected in traditional, conservative societies: globalization. This is widely seen as the blatant Westernization of the unique Arab and Muslim identity and it is anathema to conservative Arabs, who regard globalization as the equivalent of "assimilation by the Borg."

We've seen from the 2011 and 2013 Pew research surveys cited earlier in this chapter that both Muslims and we in the West share a concern over the growth of Islamist extremism and that we both recognize relations between us are bad, although we point the finger of blame at the other side. Muslims see many Westerners as "greedy" and "immoral" while we in the West generally characterize Muslims as "fanatical" and "violent."

---

52. "What's the Appeal of a Caliphate?," *BBC News Magazine*, October 26, 2014. Accessed July 13, 2017. See http://www.bbc.com/news/magazine-29761018.
53. Dalia Mogahed and Geneive Abdo, "Islam and Democracy," The Gallup Organization, 2006. Accessed July 13, 2017. http://media.gallup.com/WorldPoll/PDF/GALLUPMUSLIMSTUDIESIslamandDemocracy030607.pdf.

In fact, four in ten Americans even admit to prejudices against Muslims living in the United States.[54]

But every environment produces its own misfits, malcontents, miscreants, and monsters. Our own environment has produced such notable examples as Charles Whitman, who shot and killed 16 people from the bell tower of the University of Texas in Austin in 1966, Lee Harvey Oswald, who assassinated President John F. Kennedy in Dallas in 1963, and the infamous Charles Manson.

More recently, our society has produced the perpetrators of the 1999 massacre at Colorado's Columbine High School, the 2007 Virginia Tech shootings, the 2011 Tucson attack on a US congresswoman, the mass killings in 2012 at the Newtown, Connecticut Sandy Hook Elementary School, and the mass shootings the same year at a theater in Aurora, Colorado. Twelve people were killed when a former Navy reservist opened fire at the Washington Navy Yard in 2013. And a disturbed young man shot and killed nine people at the Emmanuel Baptist Church in Charleston, SC in 2015. In fact, there have been 889 victims in 130 separate incidents since 1966.[55]

European society has spawned its own mass murders. Adolf Hitler's Nazi Germany killed six million Jews, Slavs, and others deemed "undesirable" by the master race. Josef Stalin is commonly thought to have executed at least three million during his administration of the Soviet Union.

And of course, the brutality of Japanese soldiers throughout the Pacific Theater of World War II is well documented. The Middle East and Islam do not enjoy a monopoly on violence.

In any society there will be persons who feel like they don't "fit in" with everybody else. They may not have a large circle of friends and so they may feel alienated and unimportant. There are thousands of teenagers

---

54. Lydia Saad, "Anti-Muslim Sentiments Fairly Commonplace," The Gallup Organization, August 10, 2006. Accessed July 13, 2017. See http://media.gallup.com/WorldPoll/PDF/AntiMuslimSentiment81006.pdf.

55. Bonnie Berkowitz, Lazaro Gamio, Denise Lu, Kevin Uhrmacher, Todd Lindeman, "The math of mass shootings," the Washington Post website, June 6, 2017. Accessed July 13, 2017. https://www.washingtonpost.com/graphics/national/mass-shootings-in-america/.

and young men in the United States who feel this way and they have thousands of counterparts in the Middle East and the Arab world. It is a phenomenon that is not uncommon during adolescence.

Adam Lanza, the Newtown shooter, was a classic example of a troubled young man with few friends. A December 14, 2012 portrait of Lanza in the "*New York Times*" by David Halbfinger painted the picture of a loner with a personality disorder who shunned attention. According to a November 25, 2013 *ABC News* report, he became obsessed with mass murder articles and memorabilia and violent video games that role-played mass shootings.[56] He went from fantasizing about killing and murder to actually carrying it out on December 14, 2012 when he killed his mother and then went to the school where he killed six staff and 20 children — instantly catapulting himself from anonymity to infamy.

Now think of a similar disaffected, alienated, and, perhaps, maladjusted young man in a Middle Eastern country who becomes obsessed with watching videos of IS violence in Iraq and Syria. Such a person may develop feelings of anger against his society. For once in his life he may want to become a part of something larger than himself, something that gives him a sense of worth and importance.

The young man sees the respect and attention given to IS in the international media, the kind of respect and attention for which he yearns himself. He sees enticing images and videos on social media and begins to read IS propaganda and study its deviant religious ideology. He sees the aggressive nature of IS actions as proof of its strength. He dreams about "punishing" others. His limited understanding of Islamic orthodoxy and Arab history makes him particularly vulnerable to Koranic verses and *hadith* texts that have been hand-picked by IS recruiters in their propaganda to appeal to him. My suspicion is that many of these recruits don't have a thorough knowledge of Islamic theology in the first place. The potential recruit is well down the road of radicalization before he even knows it.

---

56. Colleen Curry, "Sandy Hook Report Offers Grim Details of Adam Lanza's Bedroom," *ABC News*, November 25, 2013. Accessed July 13, 2017. http://abcnews.go.com/US/ sandy-hook-report-inside-gunman-adam-lanzas-bedroom/story?id=21009111.

If we are to believe numerous Western news stories and analyses, this is how IS has been successfully recruiting young people from the Middle East, North Africa, Europe, Asia, and even the United States. These youth see membership in IS – even with the prospect of martyrdom and death – as giving themselves a purpose in a heretofore nihilistic and purposeless life. Many of them are seeking certainty and order in a very uncertain and disorderly world.

Teenage rebellion may actually be a human behavioral phenomenon that transcends our respective cultural and societal environments. Young men in particular seem particularly inclined in their late teens and early twenties to establish their own identity, one separate from their parents. They may rebel against authority and push a parent's envelope by breaking rules. This behavior is probably a normal phase of "growing up" and becoming an adult.

Unfortunately, there may be a few that harbor darker thoughts and behavioral problems that push them down a self-destructive path. We've seen it at Newtown and Columbine and we're seeing it in Iraq and Syria. But unlike Newtown and Columbine, there are no police to come to the aid of the victims of IS violence in Raqqa, Mosul, Kobani, or Fallujah.

When you add former Iraqi *Baathist* military officers to this influx of willing, brainwashed recruits, you get a potent combination. These are officers who lost everything when the Coalition Provisional Authority put them out of work. They may have faced persecution under a vengeful *Shiite* government in Baghdad that lusted after *Sunni* blood. And if they actually did serve under Saddam Hussein, they may already have been involved with mass executions and ethnic cleansing. Just the sort of experience the Islamic State was looking for.

At the end of the day, Americans and Arab Muslims come from much different social, cultural, and religious environments. Our differences often cause us to see the world contradictorily and our stereotypes may perpetuate our mutual suspicions. Yet as human beings, we may have more in common than we think.

The preceding review – which really incorporates only the highlights – emphasizes the complexity of the environment from which the contemporary Arab and Muslim cultures have emerged. Each Arab country has its own unique cultural, religious, economic, and political dynamics that should never be ignored and we must resist the urge to stereotype them at all costs.

As stated earlier, this is not a war against Islam, it is a war against extremism. It is a war of hearts and minds if ever there was one. We will need the help of Arabs and Muslims if we are to prevail and eradicate the scourge of Islamist extremist ideology and make this a better world for us all. This is the silver lining. In any challenge, there is also opportunity.

CHAPTER THREE

THINGS YOU MAY NOT KNOW ABOUT ISLAM

"God has no religion."

– Mahatma Gandhi

Islam is the last of the three great Abrahamic monotheistic religions (preceded by Judaism and Christianity) and its adherents – Muslims – believe their faith represents God's final, complete, and universal message to all of mankind. It is believed that the message of Islam was dictated to Muhammad, Islam's prophet, by the angel Gabriel over a period of nearly a quarter of a century. It was eventually written down and recorded as the Koran (meaning "The Recitation" in Arabic). These verses or scriptures in the Koran and the compiled accounts of the Prophet Muhammad's words, deeds, and behavior known collectively as the *ahadith* (singular – *hadith*) comprise the religion's holy books. Rather than using the Arabic plural, for ease of understanding the singular *hadith* will be pluralized herein simply by appending the letter "s" to the word (e.g., *hadiths*).

All the world's religions share one problem: their divine messages ultimately must be interpreted and understood by the human mind. This is the weakest link in any religion as its specific message may often be interpreted in many different ways, for various reasons, by many of its followers. As Mahatma Gandhi also said, "God reveals His truth to instruments that are imperfect." It all goes back to each of us having our own three-pound universe sitting atop our shoulders so it's possible to have seven billion different opinions on any one subject.

Just like Judaism and Christianity, Islam has its own share of contradictions and paradoxes that have been the subject of controversy and intense study and debate through the ages. Sword verses, peace verses, Meccan and Medinan verses, and the subject of the abrogation and supersession of various verses in the Koran have sparked discussion and disagreement among many Islamic scholars over the course of centuries. The fact that Islam is divided into *Sunni* and *Shia* branches and each of those branches has its own individual denominations only serves to highlight the diversity of opinion on issues and scriptures that non-Muslim Westerners may find confusing and contradictory.

To begin with, some important, fundamental differences that distinguish the Koran from both the Bible and the Torah should be introduced. First and foremost, the Koran is considered to contain the spoken Word of God. Through the angel Gabriel, God gave his message to Muhammad *in Arabic*. Therefore, His message can only truly be interpreted and comprehended by studying the original, Arabic text. Translations into other languages may be useful for non-Arab Muslims as a means of *beginning to understand* the faith, but they will always be imperfect because God conveyed His message in Arabic. Congregational prayers are always uttered in Arabic for this same reason, even in mosques outside the Arab world.

The Koran's use of the Arabic language is central to a couple of other significant points. Arabic has long been a language of poetry, music, and storytelling. In pre-Islamic days, illiterate Bedouin tribesmen would have sat around the campfire at night listening to poetry, stories, or songs that would have been handed down orally from one generation of poets and storytellers to the next. This tradition was well established. At the dawn of Islam in Arabia, most of these tribesmen had no knowledge of how to read or write.

In fact during the period immediately preceding the advent of Islam, Arabic as a written language was only taught in two locations in Arabia: a Jewish-operated school at Yathrib (i.e., pre-Islamic Medina) and Najran, where a "bishop" was said to the "the schoolmaster." [57] Hence, nomadic Bedouins would not have had any opportunity to learn written Arabic in the first place.

---

57. M.C.A. Macdonald (ed.), *The Development of Arabic as a Written Language.* (Supplement to the Proceedings of the Seminar for Arabian Studies 40). Oxford: Archaeopress, 2010, 1.

Muhammad was no different from them. The Koran itself confirms that he was "unlettered" or illiterate. The use of the adjective "*ummi*" in the Arabic text leaves no doubt to this:

> *Those who follow the Messenger, the unlettered prophet, whom they find written in what they have of the Torah and the Gospel, who enjoins upon them what is right and forbids them what is wrong, and makes lawful for them the good things and prohibits for them the evil and relieves them of their burdens and the shackles which were upon them. So they who have believed in him, honored him and followed the light which was sent down with him — it is those who will be successful.*[58]

Why would The Most High God have used an illiterate man as the vessel for receiving His final and universal message? The only logical answer to this intriguing question is that the Koran (i.e., "The Recitation") was not originally intended to be written down in a book that the majority of Bedouin tribesmen would not have been able to read, anyway. No, these revelations and scriptures were to be *memorized* by the early Muslims and then *recited* in the tradition of the pre-Islamic Bedouin poetry, stories, and songs.

The evidence of this tradition continues to this very day where young Muslim boys all over the Muslim world are still sent to a *madrassah* (Arabic for "school") where they will learn to memorize and recite the Koran in its entirety. Even though they may not speak or even understand Arabic at all, they will memorize the entire book and learn to recite it properly in Arabic. In many remote parts of the world, this may comprise the child's only formal education.

These recitations in classical Arabic include tonal inflections and a rhythm that imparts a lyrical, musical character to the verses that is particularly pleasing to an Arab or Eastern ear and this musical quality could not be properly replicated if the Koran were translated into any other language. Competitions are held throughout the Arab and Muslim world every year for the best and most beautiful recitations of the Koran.

---

58. Koran 7:157.

Further evidence of the oral tradition of these scriptures comes from the fact that no one even thought of collecting the various *suras* (chapters) and compiling them in written form until well after Muhammad's death. Uthman Ibn Affan, one of Muhammad's companions and the third rightly-guided caliph, has been credited by many Muslims for compiling the first standardized version of the Koran known as the "Uthman Codex" in order to preserve the text as Muhammad's companions began to die off. Actual documentary evidence of this, however, is scant. The oldest known Koranic manuscript is believed to have been found during the renovation of the Great Mosque of Sanaa, Yemen and a radiocarbon analysis of the manuscript's parchment dates it to approximately 671.[59]

There are numerous good English translations of the Koran; the majority of these were done in the 20th century. However, when a non-Arabic-speaking Westerner attempts to read the Koran, he or she will encounter some puzzling – and maybe even annoying – features.

For example, the 114 *suras* of the Koran are not arranged in any particular order. They do not follow a standard chronological or historical pattern. With the exception of the very first *sura*, they are essentially arranged by length from the longest to the shortest. To the Christian or Jew, who may be used to the books of the Old Testament following a historical sequence, this can be quite confusing. We must remember that while the separate *suras* collectively make up the Koran, the intention is for them to be recited individually. The Koran is not a book that proceeds in linear fashion from a set beginning to an established end. It was meant to be a compendium of Muhammad's revelations more than a stuffy, religious reference book.

Non-Arabic-speaking Westerners are also often befuddled by the extent of repetition in the verses of the Koran. Once again, we must remember that the words and verses are intended to be recited in Arabic according to strict rules of inflection and intonation. If we think of these verses in the context of lyrics in a song or lines in poetry, we can then understand that this repetition may serve a linguistic purpose or objective in the original language that is not at all evident in the English translation.

---

59. Behnam Sadeghi and Uwe Bergmann, "The Codex of a Companion of the Prophet and the Qur'ān of the Prophet." *Arabica* 57 No. 4 (2010) 353.

As for the content of the Koran, it establishes the primary elements and beliefs of Islam. It confirms the existence of the eternal, omnipotent, and omniscient One True God (i.e., monotheism) who has no equal and this is a central pillar of the faith. The verses of the *suras* offer guidance on how mankind is to live their lives in service and in worship to God, this being man's sole reason for existence. There are also religious lessons drawn from Muhammad's contemporary history.

Naturally, the Koran shares many commonalities with the Torah and the Old and New Testaments of the Bible. It contains accounts of many of the Old Testament prophets and Jesus is also ranked as one of God's prophets. Its scriptures provide guidance on what is right and wrong and although it does not codify the Ten Commandments as such, each commandment is contained in individual verses and *suras* throughout the book.

Like the Bible, the Koran also often refers to the End Times and the Day of Judgment as being an apocryphal event. Muslim believers will enjoy an afterlife in paradise and sinners will burn for eternity in hellfire.

With the exception of the verses involving Muhammad's contemporary history, it would be fair to say that most Christians and Jews familiar with the Old Testament or the Torah would recognize much of the Koran's content and find it to be very similar to their own scriptures.

THE HADITHS AND SUNNAH

The Koran warns the Muslim faithful that it does have some verses that are literal and some that are allegorical or metaphorical, but it does not tell them which ones are which:

> *It is He who has sent down to you, [O Muhammad, the Book; in it are verses [that are] precise – they are the foundation of the Book – and others unspecific. As for those in whose hearts is deviation [from truth], they will follow that of it which is unspecific, seeking discord and seeking an interpretation [suitable to them]. And no one knows its [true] interpretations except Allah. But those firm in*

knowledge say, "We believe in it. All [of it] is from our Lord." And no one will be reminded except those of understanding.[60]

To help Muslims – especially the early followers – better understand some of these scriptures and principles, the Koran recommended that the believers should look to the behavior and conduct of the Prophet Muhammad as a helpful example:

There has certainly been for you in the Messenger of Allah an excellent pattern for anyone whose hope is in Allah and the Last Day and [who] remembers Allah often.[61]

So, the Koran itself established the precedent of using the prophet's words and deeds as a means of illustrating various religious concepts and encouraging the emulation of his behavior.

During his lifetime, Muhammad was surrounded by a number of early disciples who became his close associates and these friends and disciples became known as Muhammad's companions. These were men who accompanied Muhammad on military campaigns, spent considerable time with him, and worked with him to spread and preach Islam as a religion.

These companions and other contemporaries of Muhammad at the time would relay the words and deeds of the prophet in oral narratives (i.e., *hadiths* in Arabic) that, in the best traditions of seventh century Arabia, were handed down verbally from one person or generation to the next. Nearly 200 years after Muhammad's death these narratives were finally written down, corroborated, and then compiled in books by a series of Islamic scholars.

Each *hadith* is comprised of two parts. The actual account of Muhammad's saying or action is called the *matn* in Arabic. This is the actual body of text.

The second portion is called the *isnad* and it is the chain of corroborating evidence that confirms the authenticity of the *hadith*. Here will be listed

---

60. Koran 3:7.
61. Koran 33:21.

the original observer 'A' who narrated it to person 'B,' who narrated it to person 'C,' and so forth. Scholars worked to verify that the individuals identified in the chain of narration lived at the appropriate times and that each narrator knew his recipient. *Hadiths* that can be confirmed in this manner all the way back to Muhammad are known as "authentic." Others with less (or no) corroboration may be graded as "good," "weak," or "fabricated."

Many of the prophet's sermons, deeds, speeches, or comments were witnessed by more than one person so ten people witnessing one of Muhammad's sermons and providing their own narration or account of it would comprise ten different *hadiths*. Many of these repetitions were dropped in compiling the *hadith* collections but there are still approximately 7,000 narrations of Muhammad's sayings and actions that make up the main body of *hadiths*.

These accounts have been compiled in six volumes to which the *Sunnis* refer as "The Six Books." The most authentic collections are found in *Sahih Al-Bukhari* and *Sahih Muslim* but all six books represent canonical sources of *Sunni* Islamic jurisprudence. For their part, the *Shia* use three completely different *hadith* collections.

These individual *hadiths* provide examples of the prophet's behavior, actions, ideas, and thinking. These volumes and collections are Islam's approximate counterpart to the four gospels of the New Testament that chronicle the ministry of Christ on earth. Jesus was known for his parables; Muhammad was known for his *hadiths*. Along with the Koran, these narratives collectively form the basis of the *Sunnah* – the way of life that Muslims should emulate based on Muhammad's teachings and actions. It is from the word *Sunnah* that we derive the adjective *Sunni*.

ABROGATION

Both the Bible and the Koran contain verses that, when taken individually and isolated from their respective contexts, seem to convey contradictory messages. This encourages supporters and detractors alike to cherry pick certain verses that will support their arguments. Scriptures can be like statistics – you can always find one to justify your case. Can one verse supersede another?

The subject of abrogation, where a later verse or scripture supersedes or abrogates an earlier verse or scripture, is a controversial one in both Christianity and Islam. Many Christian theologians believe that there are passages in the New Testament that abrogate portions of the Old Testament, especially with respect to the various elements of Jewish law in the Old Testament. One of the most common examples here is Christ's Sermon on the Mount in the Gospel of Matthew chapters 5, 6, and 7. Here Christian theologians and scholars have extensively discussed whether these teachings by Christ have abrogated the Law of Moses in the Old Testament and, of course, there is no universal agreement on this issue.

Islam has its own share of debate on this topic, too. Some Islamic scholars have expressed an opinion that up to 200 verses of the Koran have been abrogated while others put the figure at only a handful – or none at all. Unfortunately this inevitably boils down to a matter of human interpretation. It's up to our personal three-pound universe again. In neither faith do we have an actual verse from God that says, "I decided to change my mind."

The *suras* and verses of the Koran are roughly divided into two groups: the Meccan and Medinan verses. These groups are reflective of the periods in Muhammad's life as Islam's prophet. God began revealing His message to Muhammad when the prophet lived in Mecca. These early *suras* are generally shorter in length and more universal in nature and they represent a time when Muhammad first began preaching and attempting to gain followers. Since the *suras* in the Koran are mainly arranged from longest to shortest, many of the *suras* at the end of the Koran actually predate the ones toward the beginning. This can add to the reader's confusion because verses at the beginning of the Koran may abrogate others toward the end of the holy book (at least according to some Islamic scholars). That just seems backwards to many people (myself included).

But after Muhammad and his followers began facing persecution in Mecca, he was invited to emigrate to Medina and establish an Islamic city-state. Thus, the Medinan verses are said to be more legalistic since he was laying the legal foundation of a Muslim state during this period.[62]

So, can verses in the Koran be abrogated or superseded? The Koran itself alludes to this possibility:

> *We do not abrogate a verse or cause it to be forgotten except that We bring forth [one] better than it or similar to it. Do you not know that Allah is over all things competent?*[63]

But while the above verse generally leaves the door open for abrogation, unfortunately it is left up to human interpretation whether or not any verses in the Koran have been abrogated and, if so, which ones and which verses supersede them. And nowhere does the controversy over abrogation become any hotter and more intense than it does over the so-called Sword Verse.

The verse in question is the fifth verse of the ninth *sura*:

> *And when the sacred months have passed, then kill the polytheists wherever you find them and capture them and besiege them and sit in wait for them at every place of ambush. But if they should repent, establish prayer, and give zakah, let them [go] on their way. Indeed, Allah is Forgiving and Merciful.*[64]

Ironically, this verse is often cited both by critics of Islam and Islamist extremists as justification for their respective positions. The critics use this specific verse as *prima facie* evidence that Islam is a religion of violence and that the Koran preaches that all non-Muslims should be killed. The extremists and terrorists use this and other, similar verses as a divine instruction to kill the unbelievers "wherever" they are found.

---

62. John Gilchrist, "The Meccan and Medinan Verses," in *Muhammad and the Religion of Islam (Vol. 1)* (Benoni, RSA: Jesus to the Muslims, 1986), 149.
63. Koran 2:106.
64. Koran 9:5.

Moderate Islamic clerics and scholars disagree with the extremist view, believing that they have plucked the verse out from its historical context. For example, Sheikh Jamal Rahman, a contemporary Muslim cleric and a member of the "Interfaith Amigos" – a trio composed of Muslim, Jewish, and Christian clerics – expressed his opinion in 2010 that "the verse is seriously limited and defined by its historical context." During the seventh century, the tiny community of Muslims in Medina was under constant attack from their archenemies, the Quraysh tribe in Mecca, who were usually better armed than the fledgling Muslims and in superior numbers.

Sheikh Rahman also believed that the textual context of the so-called Sword Verse is also very important because it "softens" the verse's "sharp edges." For example, the preceding verse says: "Fight in the way of God with those who fight you, but begin not hostilities. Lo! Allah loveth not aggressors," (Koran 2:190).

Similarly, the verses immediately following the Sword Verse say: "…but if they cease, God is Oft-forgiving, most Merciful… let there be no hostility… and know that God is with those who restrain themselves," (Koran 2:192-194).

Rahman concluded that the Sword Verse actually pertains to defensive fighting only and if an attacker stops fighting them, the Muslims must stop fighting, too. Nevertheless, he was bothered by the injunction to "Kill the unbeliever" in the verse and wondered why the "All-Powerful God, who has infused every human with divine breath and holds every human heart between divine fingers" would ever order anyone to kill another human of His creation.[65]

Even though contemporary, moderate scholars like Rahman have determined, according to their interpretations, that the context of this verse applies specifically to a defensive war against the polytheists of Mecca, this *sura* is the penultimate chapter of the Koran based on chronological order. There are other scholars throughout history that have interpreted that the chronology of this verse gives it supersession over earlier, more

---

65. Sheikh Jamal Rahman, "Making Peace with the Sword Verse," *Yes! Magazine*, October 13, 2010. Accessed July 13, 2017. http://www.yesmagazine.org/blogs/interfaith-amigos/making-peace-with-the-sword-verse.

peaceful verses. One thing is certain, however. The controversy over this verse among Muslims is bound to continue for a long time.

In contrast, many Islamist extremists already see Christians as polytheists since they worship the Holy Trinity of God the Father, Jesus the Son, and the Holy Spirit. The message of monotheism – the Oneness of God – is absolutely central in the Koran and there are numerous scriptures to that effect. In fact, the Koran classifies such polytheism as an unpardonable sin:

> *Indeed, Allah does not forgive association with Him* [i.e., polytheism]*, but He forgives what is less than that for whom He wills. And he who associates others with Allah has certainly fabricated a tremendous sin.*[66]

And the extremists have even more specific justification for fighting against Christians and Jews just a few verses down from the aforementioned Sword Verse in the same *sura*:

> *Fight those who do not believe in Allah or in the Last Day and who do not consider unlawful what Allah and His Messenger have made unlawful and who do not adopt the religion of truth* [i.e., Islam] *from those who were given the Scripture* [i.e., Jews and Christians] *– [fight] until they give the jizyah* [i.e., a tax imposed on non-Muslims] *willingly while they are humbled.*

> *The Jews say, "Ezra is the son of Allah"; and the Christians say, "The Messiah is the son of Allah." That is their statement from their mouths; they imitate the saying of those who disbelieve [before them]. May Allah destroy them; how are they deluded?*[67]

In addition to these verses from the Koran, the extremists also have a variety of *hadiths* on *jihad* and fighting available to them. Here are just a couple of examples:

---

66. Koran 4:48.
67. Koran 9:29-30.

*It is reported on the authority of Abu Huraira that he heard the
Messenger of Allah (may peace be upon him) say: I have been commanded to fight against people till they testify to the fact that there
is none worthy of worship (in truth) but Allah, and believe in
me (that) I am the messenger (from the Lord) and in all that I
have brought. And when they do it, their blood and riches are
guaranteed protection on my behalf except where it is justified by
law, and their affairs rest with Allah.*[68]

*It has been narrated by 'Umar b. al-Khattib that he heard the
Messenger of Allah (may peace be upon him) say: I will expel the
Jews and Christians from the Arabian Peninsula and will not leave
any but Muslim.*[69]

Ultimately, the matter of abrogation seems to be one that is mostly
academic. Those Muslims having an inclination toward moderation
and tolerance will seek out and cite verses and *hadiths* that support
their beliefs while those who espouse violence will find scriptural justifications for their actions. Since there is no universal consensus on the
subject, Muslims' attitudes on abrogation likely mirror their personal
religious beliefs.

TAQIYYA

Although both Christian and Islamic theologians and academics have
debated their various positions on abrogation regarding their respective
scriptures for many years – and will likely continue to do so – the concept
of *taqiyya* is one that is exclusive to Islam. No apparent equivalent exists
in either Judaism or Christianity.

The Arabic word *taqiyya* means "caution" or "prudence" but in Islamic
religious terms the word has evolved to mean dissimulation or deception. It allows Muslims to lie about, or even deny their faith and commit
unlawful acts if they believe themselves to be under threat of persecution. Most often *taqiyya* has been viewed as a *Shia* tactic since they have

68. *Sahih Muslim* 1:31.
69. *Sahih Muslim* 19:4366.

historically been a minority in the Muslim world and their communities in the *Sunni* Muslim countries have often faced maltreatment, harassment, and persecution. In this contest then, *taqiyya* would allow a *Shiite* to feign being a *Sunni* – and even deny being a *Shiite* – in order to avoid persecution.

Even though the word itself does not appear in the Koran, the concept of dissimulation and deception does have scriptural justification:

> *Let not believers take disbelievers as allies rather than believers. And whoever [of you] does that has nothing with Allah, except when taking precautions against them in prudence.*[70]

Accordingly, Muslims may take non-Muslims as allies only "as a precaution" and a prudent measure. Furthermore, the Koran explicitly allows Muslims to outwardly dissemble their faith as long as they remain believers in their hearts:

> *Whoever disbelieves in Allah after his belief... except for one who is forced [to renounce his religion] while his heart is secure in faith. But those who [willingly] open their breasts to disbelief, upon them is wrath from Allah, and for them is a great punishment.*[71]

The Koran also sanctions Muslims' consumption of unclean foods when it is *by necessity*:

> *He has only forbidden to you dead animals, blood, the flesh of swine, and that which has been dedicated to other than Allah. But whoever is forced [by necessity], neither desiring [it] nor transgressing [its limit], there is no sin upon him. Indeed, Allah is Forgiving and Merciful.*[72]

---

70.   Koran 3:28.
71.   Koran 16:106.
72.   Koran 2:173.

Now while *taqiyya* has usually been portrayed as a course of survival employed by minority *Shiites* living under *Sunni* rule, there are some who consider the use of *taqiyya* far more widespread and akin to an everyday Islamic doctrine, not just a ploy to be used as a means to escape persecution. Such observers point out that *Sunni* communities in the West frequently consider themselves to be isolated and facing many of the same persecutions and threats as have the *Shia*. They cite ample evidence from respected *Sunni* legists that not only authorizes the practice but deem it almost obligatory in almost any dealings between Muslims and non-Muslims. (Note there is a semantic difference where *taqiyya* is usually reserved for the *Shia* but the *Sunnis* have a nearly identical concept called *idtirar*, which translates to "coercion." It allows them to use deception and dissimulation as a survival tactic, too. For the purposes of simplicity, however, we will use *taqiyya* to refer to both denominations' use of deception.)

One such individual is Raymond Ibrahim, who wrote a lengthy essay on *taqiyya* in the Winter 2010 edition of the *Middle East Quarterly*, a publication of the conservative American and pro-Israel Middle East Forum think tank. The article identified Mr. Ibrahim as the associate director of the organization but he is also a frequent commentator on Islam in general, and so-called radical Islam, in particular.

In his article, Ibrahim cited justification from the Koran, the *hadiths,* and early Islamic history all the way up to contemporary writers and scholars for Muslims to employ deception and dissimulation in most, if not all of their dealings with non-Muslims. Deception was a permissible – even laudable – element of war, after all.[73]

In addition, according to Ibrahim *taqiyya* allows Muslims to break treaties and truces and say one thing to your non-Muslim enemies while saying something completely different to your Muslim countrymen.

As an example of this, Ibrahim cited an incident where PLO leader Yasser Arafat was allegedly criticized for conceding too much to Israel during the negotiation of a peace treaty. While addressing a group of Muslims in South Africa, Arafat responded to that criticism by comparing his

---

73. Raymond Ibrahim, "How *Taqiyya* Alters Islam's Rules of War," *Middle East Quarterly*, Winter 2010, 3-13.

negotiation of the peace treaty with Israel to the Prophet Muhammad's treaty with the Quraysh in Mecca, which Muhammad later broke. Ibrahim was implying that Arafat would break his treaty with the Israelis if "something better" were to come along or if the Palestinians became strong enough to continue their fight against the Jewish state.[74]

Ibrahim also referenced evidence of Osama bin Laden employing *taqiyya* by claiming that Islamist terrorism toward the West originates from grievances in how Muslims have been treated.

He claimed that whenever the Islamists like bin Laden make statements to America or the West, they excuse their own terrorism as being merely "reciprocal treatment" for years and decades of Israeli and Western tyranny against Islam and Muslims. However, when they address an audience of Muslims, they portray this terrorism as a "religious obligation," not something that is a response to any "military or political provocation."

For instance, Ibrahim stated that Osama bin Laden would often list the "oppression of the Palestinians" and other political injustices against Muslims by the West as the motivation for his war, using cause-and-effect justifications that most Westerners would recognize and understand. But in his remarks and statements to other Muslims, bin Laden distilled his true justification down to various Koranic verses that enjoin Muslims to stop fighting "infidels" only after they submit to Islam. Ibrahim quoted the founder of Al-Qaeda as saying: "Battle, animosity, and hatred – directed from the Muslim to the infidel – is the foundation of our religion.[75] Politics and grievances had nothing to do with it; they were just for show for the infidel West.

So, Ibrahim concluded that any Islamist or Muslim who believes Islam to be at war with the West is permitted to deceive non-Muslims and lie to them in order to protect himself and advance the cause of Allah. It is nothing short of obligatory on them to do so. (Here it should also be noted that Western politicians are also known for employing what we can categorize somewhat tongue-in-cheek as "artful speech" to tailor and customize their remarks to some particular audience. We may not call it *taqiyya*, but we do have our own terms for this practice.)

---

74. *Ibid.*
75. *Ibid.*

And since we're dealing with the concept of *Sunni* Muslims using artifice and deception to survive and prosper while living as a minority in the West, there is another somewhat paradoxical point that should be borne in mind. Islam divides the world into two realms, one that is governed according to God's law – the *Sharia,* and one that is not.

The former is described in Arabic as the *Dar al-Islam,* which means "the realm of Islam" or "the realm of submission." These are the lands and territories of the earth that are under Muslim rule.

The second realm in Arabic is the *Dar al-Harb,* which means "the realm of war." In other words, any lands or territories on the face of the earth that are not governed according to the *Sharia* fall under the category of "the realm of war." Of course, this infers that Muslims must be at war with everybody outside "the realm of submission" (i.e., all non-Muslims) and it contrasts sharply with Muslim moderates and Western pundits eager to portray Islam as a "religion of peace."

Neither of these two terms is found in either the Koran or the *hadiths.* Their origin has been attributed to Abu Hanifa, the early Islamic scholar who founded the Hanafi school of Islamic jurisprudence (one of the four main schools of *Sunni* Islam). Some contemporary moderate clerics have downplayed the significance of these terms – especially since there is no scriptural support for them – but they have been used widely by other Muslim jurists in their rulings over the past 1300 years.

Although these terms are not considered to be "radical" (at least in the current sense of the word) since they can be traced all the way back to the eighth century, they do appear prominently in the writings, lectures, and rulings of the Islamist extremists and terrorists. These contemporary radicals are the ones who believe themselves to be in a state of war with the entire non-Muslim world. To moderate scholars, the terms *Dar al-Islam* and *Dar al-Harb* may have relatively benign connotations but to an Islamist these terms convey nothing short of battle lines.

But here is the tricky bit. Certainly any *Sunni* or *Shiite* Muslim could find a wealth of Islamic legal rulings that would allow that Muslim to lie, cheat, steal, deceive, and commit otherwise unlawful acts in his dealings with a non-Muslim – especially in the *Dar al-Harb* (like the United States or Western Europe). Do all Muslims in the West engage in *taqiyya* in everything they do on a daily basis? Of course not. But our Islamist enemies certainly would not hesitate to do so.

DEEN WA DAWLA

We've touched on this subject before. In Arabic, *deen wa dawla* literally translates to "a religion and a state." It refers to the fact that Islam was meant first as a religion, but also it was intended to form the basic framework and institution for a state and its governance. In the world of the Arabian Desert, under Islam the mosque would become not just a house of worship but a courthouse, a school, a hospital, or whatever body or organization the people needed.

This concept worked well for a homogenous, Bedouin, clan-based society living in a sparsely populated and barren wilderness. It doesn't seem to be such a natural fit in a Western, Westphalian world order that is governed by manmade international laws. In its original, seventh century form, Islam had no obvious, natural accommodation for democracy, secular civil and human rights, or the religious freedoms that are so essential in Western countries with diverse and heterogeneous populations. In short, *deen wa dawla* does not really allow for the separation of state and religion, a fundamental element of modern Western democracy. By definition, it requires any Islamic state to be a theocracy in which every aspect of daily life and even international relations are governed by the *Sharia* and the *Sunnah*. Any questions or ambiguities are ultimately decided by Islamic scholars and jurists.

This puritanical form of Islam does not really exist today. Even very strict Islamic states like the Kingdom of Saudi Arabia and the Islamic Republic of Iran do have their own legislative bodies that create, recommend, and enact laws. The constitutions of many Arab countries may claim to use the Koran and *Sharia* as a basis and reference for their legislation, but they also rely quite heavily on secular Western law. This is an unavoidable necessity in an increasingly globalized world where political, economic, and diplomatic disputes are tried in the various formal international courts of law and informal forums of public opinion.

At the individual and personal level, however, *deen wa dawla* may mean something quite different. For many Muslims it means that their loyalty is to their faith first and foremost, not to their state and there is data to back this up.

July 2006 polling by the Pew Research Global Attitudes Project found that majorities of Muslim populations both in Europe and in the Muslim world self-identified first as Muslims over the nationality of their country of residence. Here are some of the survey's key statistics:

• *In Great Britain, 81% of Muslims self-identified as Muslim rather than British.*

• *In Spain, 69% of Muslims self-identified as Muslim rather than Spanish.*

• *In Germany, 66% of Muslims self-identified as Muslim rather than German.*

• *In France, there was an almost even split where 46% identified first as Muslim and 42% considered themselves to be primarily French.*

• *Solid majorities in Muslim countries also primarily self-identified as Muslim over any nationality, e.g., Pakistan (87%) and Jordan (67%). The percentage in Turkey was 51% but that was a sharp rise from 43% the previous year.*

• *In contrast, 90% of Indians self-identified as Indian rather than Hindu.*

• *Interestingly, in the United States, 42% of Christians said they self-identified as Christians first rather than Americans.*[76]

An interesting conclusion that we can draw from this particular Pew Research survey is that solid majorities of Muslims not only in Western

---

76. "Muslims in Europe: Economic Worries Top Concerns About Religious and Cultural Identity," Pew Research Center Survey, July 6, 2006. Accessed July 13, 2017. http://www.pewglobal.org/2006/07/06/muslims-in-europe-economic-worries-top-concerns-about-religious-and-cultural-identity/.

Europe, but also in Muslim countries, think of themselves as Muslims first, before identifying themselves by nationality or as a citizen of any state.

Among Muslim immigrant communities in the West, this might seem unsurprising and even fairly natural. The countries of Western Europe and even the United States do not have Muslim majorities and have never been considered part of the Islamic world. Many of the Muslim immigrants who have settled there have done so to escape economic, political, or humanitarian hardships in their homelands. They have no deep ethnic ties or roots to the West and, as a result, they may actually feel somewhat disconnected, alienated, and disenfranchised in a new and unfamiliar, heterogeneous culture that is completely different from that of their homelands.

But the real takeaway here is that even in Pakistan, Jordan, Egypt, and Turkey – all very prominent countries in the Islamic world – the majority of respondents self-identified (sometimes overwhelmingly) as Muslims rather than citizens of their respective countries. After 1400 years of Islamic empire in one form or another in which individual states and nations were nonexistent (at least in the Westphalian sense), a majority of Muslims still identifies with being a follower of Islam over being the citizen of a country whose very existence and boundaries may be largely a Western creation of the 19th and 20th centuries.

They may love their homelands for ethnic, cultural, and religious reasons but this isn't patriotism in the same way that we understand it. Muslims are part of the *ummah* – the international collective of Muslims in the world – and this *ummah* transcends any national identity or sense of patriotism. This is a crucial point if we in the West are to have any hope of attempting to grasp their *Weltanschauung*.

In the West, we somewhat tritely blame the Muslims of intolerance when there is an outcry over a European cartoonist lampooning the prophet, for example. After all, political cartoonists and satirists in the West have been doing this sort of thing for hundreds of years. What's the big deal in the Muslim world? It's just a cartoon!

Let's say a political cartoonist in a US newspaper uses his or her pen to incite the ire of the paper's Republican or Democrat readers. If the cartoonist is syndicated, the image might wind up annoying a few hundred thousand or even a couple million readers. But, people in Germany, Italy, France or Scotland won't care and all the hubbub and commotion will die back down just as quickly as it erupted. Controversy is the very purpose of political commentary and satire. And most people in the West do not primarily self-identify with their political party.

But when a Western cartoonist draws a cartoon that openly ridicules Islam or its prophet, that cartoonist is raising the ire of over *one-and-a-half billion* Muslims, not just a few Republicans or Democrats. Many of the countries in the Muslim world do not have diverse populations and the punishment for blasphemy or heresy in those countries is often death. While we may like to tout our freedom of expression and freedom of speech, we should be mindful that "letting it all hang out" will likely provoke a violent response among a majority of the world's Muslims – *Sunni* and *Shia* alike – and it will do little to help us in the struggle of hearts and minds. Just because we *can* do something doesn't necessarily mean that we *should* do it. The January 2015 *Charlie Hebdo* massacre in Paris is a great example.

Those French terrorist tragedies notwithstanding, the strategic importance of this isn't limited to just a couple of offensive cartoons by French or Danish satirists. We invaded Iraq – a Muslim nation – in March of 2003 and settled in for an eight-and-a-half-year occupation. Our soldiers humiliated Iraqi prisoners at Baghdad's notorious Abu Ghraib Prison, but these actions didn't just insult and offend a few dozen million Iraqis or a couple hundred million Arabs. They offended *one-and-a-half billion* Muslims. They offended the entire *ummah*.

Let me put this into a more familiar context. As a military veteran, I don't appreciate seeing somebody burning an American flag as a form of "expression." It angers and insults me. That person may be within the law when he strikes a match to Old Glory but doing it outside the local American Legion, a VFW post, or a military base is not likely to be a good idea. Those who have served this great nation, put their lives on the line, and made a personal sacrifice for that person's right to express himself will still want to beat the tar out of him for destroying a symbol that they hold dear.

When a few Western journalists or celebrities take it upon themselves to insult the entire Muslim world in a cartoon or some other endeavor, they are evoking the same response from 1.6 billion Muslims that a handful of American veterans or military personnel would feel if they saw someone setting fire to their flag. Is such a cartoon helpful, should it make us proud to publish it? It may bring a few ignorant people some short-term notoriety and celebrity but such sad and misguided actions only hurt our cause; they don't help it.

The civil war in Iraq has pitted *Sunni* against *Shiite* and created a breeding ground for Islamist extremism and terrorism that threatens an explosion of bloody sectarianism throughout the Arab and Muslim worlds. While we in the West are shocked when we endure occasional, scattered acts of terrorist violence – the so-called "lone wolf attacks" – thousands of innocent people in the Muslim world are suffering brutal and savage ethnic and religious pogroms in unending orgies of violence and death. Dozens die in Baghdad car bomb explosions nearly every day. Is an insulting cartoon going to make his or her life any better? Is it going to attract him to our cause? If not, why do it?

When Muslims in Iraq, Syria, Lebanon, Somalia, or Yemen are in pain and torment, the rest of the *ummah* is in pain and torment with them. They identify with each other Muslim-to-Muslim and Arab-to-Arab.

As a non-Muslim and non-Arab country, we will always be the odd man out in the Middle East. If we are to restore our tarnished reputation, recognizing the primacy of self-identification as a Muslim before any nationality is absolutely essential in the strategic calculus of our policy options and decisions in the Middle East, North Africa, and Southwest Asia.

In many countries of the Muslim world, the populations have never had the basic building blocks of our form of democracy. They have not experienced generations of the First Amendment, they have often spent their lives living under autocracy and dictatorship, and their religion may be the focal point of their lives. It offers a little solace and escape from an otherwise austere and difficult life. While we might have a measured and tolerant response to an offensive cartoon or editorial, we cannot and should not expect the same from the world's Muslims who have a much more black-and-white view of the world and whose life experiences do not match our own.

America's penchant for political narcissism often motivates us to view the world through the prism of our own secular values and expect that other cultures vastly different from our own will inevitably see the world in the same way we do. This has been, and continues to be a strategic shortcoming by our pundits and policymakers alike. Even though they may have separate denominations and follow different theological schools of thought, on matters involving offense or insult to Islam or its prophet, the 1.6 billion Muslims of the *ummah* will collectively rally to defend their faith. If you don't want a snake to bite you, just leave it alone. Don't go poking at it with a stick.

CHAPTER FOUR

WHY ARE WE A TARGET?

*"Our motto, which we are not afraid to repeat
year after year, is 'Death to America'!"*

– Hassan Nasrallah, Leader of Hezbollah

Lots of times Americans ask themselves, "Why do these terrorists hate us so much? We buy the Arabs' oil. We kicked Saddam Hussein out of Kuwait and made Iraq a democracy. Every time there is an earthquake or other natural disaster in the Muslim world, we are among the first to render assistance. We've welcomed persecuted political refugees from the Middle East into our country. Our Agency for International Development has helped many Arab and Muslim countries with US taxpayer-funded economic, scientific, medical, and technical assistance. What have we ever done to them to deserve being a target for their terrorist attacks?"

Certainly that is a logical question from our point of view, but that is part of our problem in understanding Islamist terrorism. We often use a Western logic matrix as a tool for predicting terrorist behavior (e.g., "If we do 'A,' then they will respond by doing 'B.'"). Our thought process is built around the concept of causality or cause and effect, where we think that we can execute some action to cause some physical consequence or result. Our adversaries use a much different calculus.

To the terrorists it is not the consequence of any action that is important since they believe that God/Allah has already ordained the result. The important thing is the performance of the act itself. This is confirmed by no less an authority than Ayatollah Khomeini in his 1988 "Letter to

Clergy" in which he responded to criticism about his handling of the Iran-Iraq war: "We do not repent, nor are we sorry for even a single moment for our performance during the war. *Have we forgotten that we fought to fulfill our religious duty and that the result is a marginal issue?*"[77] [Italics added for emphasis.]

From the terrorists' viewpoint, performing the actual act of martyrdom (or terrorism, as we see it) is the only thing that has significance. God has already decided whether any enemies or unbelievers will be killed (and how many). In fact, God has already decided the outcome of the terrorists' struggle. Thus, the performance of the act of martyrdom itself is all that matters.

In contrast, we take a causal approach where the probability of some action is based on the likely result (or effect) of that action. For example, dropping bombs on a convoy of Al-Shabaab fighters is not seen as very worthwhile unless we are going to kill or injure as many of them as we can. For us, the act is less important than the result. While the above questions certainly seem relevant to us, they are completely irrelevant to our adversaries. Our extremist enemies hate us for who we are and what we represent, not so much because of what we do (or don't do). They hate us because we stand for everything that they stand against. They view the world through a medieval, seventh century, religious prism that is completely inconsistent and incompatible with our twenty-first century worldview. It is impossible to reconcile the two.

To the extremists, the fact that we have not embraced their strict, unflinching, uncompromising interpretation of Islam has made us an "enemy of Allah." Therefore, we are worthy only of hate and destruction and the Koran has given the following instruction on how to deal with "enemies of Allah" like us:

> *And prepare against them what force you are able and strings of horses by which you may terrify the enemy of Allah and your enemy and others besides them whom you do not know [but] whom Allah*

---

77. Baqer Moin, *Khomeini: Life of the Ayatollah* (New York: St. Martin's Press, 2000), 285.

knows. And whatever you spend in the cause of Allah will be fully repaid to you, and you will not be wronged.[78]

So, not only do these extremist terrorists hate us as an enemy of Allah, the above scripture enjoins them to fight against us. To them it is not an option; it is a sacred duty.

We seek a future that betters our society with advances in science, medicine, and technology. We believe in social equality and fairness with basic human and civil rights that are to be protected by the government. This is embodied in the US Declaration of Independence:

> *We hold these truths to be self-evident, that all men are created equal, that they are endowed by their Creator with certain unalienable Rights, that among these are Life, Liberty, and the pursuit of Happiness. That to secure these Rights, Governments are instituted among Men, deriving their just powers from the consent of the governed, that whenever any Form of Government becomes destructive of these ends, it is the Right of the People to alter or to abolish it, and to institute new Government, laying its foundation on such principles and organizing its powers in such form, as to them shall seem most likely to effect their Safety and Happiness.*

The Islamist extremists do not believe in government by man in any form and they certainly have nothing but scorn and disdain for the rights set forth above. They believe that God's law – the *Sharia* – is perfect. According to their ideology God has no associate. He has no partner and no equal. Since God gave us His *Sharia*, mankind has no right to establish any other government or legislate any other laws because God's law is perfect and it cannot be amended, changed, or modified by man. Any attempts by man to usurp God's divine authority are nothing but acts of heresy and blasphemy that are only deserving of death. In the Islamist mentality, this is a pillar of their belief over which there can be no argument, discussion, or compromise.

---

78. Koran 8:60.

Moreover, by and large they are not focused on a brighter future for humanity because their gaze is aimed squarely and exclusively at the past. On the *Sunni* side, virtually all Islamist extremists can be considered *Salafists* (at least semantically) because they seek to turn the clock back to the first three generations of Muslims. The terms *Salafist* and *Salafism* originate from the Arabic word *salaf*, which means "ancestors" or "predecessors." This desire stems from this statement attributed to the prophet Muhammad in the *hadith* texts (versions of which appear in several passages):

> *The Prophet was asked, "Who are the best people?" He replied: The people of my generation, and then those who will follow (come after) them, and then those who will come after the later (generation).*[79]

Their objective is to emulate the time of Muhammad and the two generations of Muslims that followed. They oppose modernity and everything it represents. Imagine life in Afghanistan under the Taliban and this gives a pretty good picture of the *Salafist* ideals. No music, no television, no art, and public executions in the stadium every Friday.

Women must be cocooned and covered from head to toe and they are not allowed in public without a male relative as a guardian. Wives should be considered property and have approximately the same rights as livestock. Girls have no need for schooling whatsoever and the only education necessary for boys is the memorization of the Koran.

Thieves have their limbs amputated and adulterers are stoned to death. Marriages are arranged like a business transaction virtually without regard for a girl's age or feelings. Once married, wives (and eventually the children) can be beaten at will by their husbands. The man can treat them as his property rather than treating them with love and care as human family members.

The extremists and *Salafists* have no wish to see advances in science, medicine, or technology because that was unimportant in the prophet's

---

79. *Sahih al-Bukhari*, 8:78:652.

time. Our unique form of American democracy, epitomized by Abraham Lincoln in his Gettysburg Address as "government of the people, by the people, and for the people," is absolute anathema to them. It is heresy and apostasy because they believe that government in any form is the sole and exclusive domain of the *Sharia* – period. Any human tinkering with the *Sharia* must be met unquestionably with *takfir* (Arabic for branding someone as an infidel or unbeliever), which is punishable by death. And in their own extremist version of Islam, anybody who does not believe the same way they do is branded an infidel and often killed right on the spot.

The Islamists' views and ideology are absolutely uncompromising and unwavering and any well-meaning Westerner who believes that any reasoning with these extremists is possible is woefully misinformed and sadly mistaken. We are not going to sacrifice any portion of our future to accommodate them and they are not going to sacrifice any portion of their *Salafist* past to accommodate us. Our philosophies are not only vastly different they are mutually and universally incompatible and completely contradictory in every way. It's like the collision of matter and anti-matter in a science fiction movie.

The *Salafists* will hate us just because we are not *Salafists* like them. It doesn't matter if we send first aid to a remote village stricken by an earthquake because both the earthquake and the dead and injured victims have already been ordained by God. Drilling a well to supply villagers in a rural area with water or offering them medical and health care will likewise be rejected for the same reasons. And even if they do enjoy taking our assistance and our money, they will still hate us because we are not fundamentalist, puritanical, *Salafists* like them. We are not part of their tribe, their group. It's a simple as that.

Since we've been reminiscing about life under the Taliban in Afghanistan, let's take a brief look at what we have accomplished there during our country's longest war. We are training and standing up a national army and police force in the country. The country is now governed by a democratically elected president and a bicameral parliament legislates laws and regulations. These both emanated from the 2004 Afghan Constitution.

But the central government has little influence outside a handful of major cities. In the remote valleys in the wilds of Afghanistan, many villagers want nothing to do with either the central government or the United States. There the Taliban still roam freely and officials of the central government are seen as US lackeys and infidels. They (like US troops) are outsiders in a very closed society that views outsiders with a healthy dose of suspicion and distrust, as it has done for centuries.

Members of the new army and police, if they do not desert their posts, have been involved in numerous so-called "green on blue" attacks against American and Western military personnel. Police officers in rural Afghanistan are commonly seen as corrupt and have not gained either the trust or respect of many Afghans. After 15 years of US occupation, many Afghans do not trust us and we dare not trust them.

Even our attempts to rein in the cultivation of opium poppies in Afghanistan has been a failure. It's hard to convince farmers to plant wheat or potatoes in a country that has neither a system of roads to get such crops to market, or even a national market in which to sell them. Afghan farmers are already quite skilled and proficient at raising poppies while the planting and harvesting of corn, for example, takes more equipment and water.

The poppies are much more profitable for the farmers and the opium is relatively easy to collect, transport, and sell. In fact, even after 13 years of US occupation, the 2014 opium harvest was expected to be at a record high.[80] And the good Muslim farmers are not raising the poppies and opium for their own consumption, after all. They're just collecting money from unbelievers – infidels – who will actually be the ones to use the narcotic. Taking money and property from infidels is sanctioned by the Koran, so where's the harm in that?

Let's see a show of hands from everyone who believes that Afghanistan will be a stable, diverse, tolerant, flourishing beacon of democracy in the region five years after we leave.

---

80. "Afghanistan Opium Harvest at Record High as NATO Withdraws," *BBC News*, November 12, 2014. Accessed July 15, 2017. http://www.bbc.com/news/world-asia-30017898.

We've already seen how this movie ended when we left Iraq in 2011 after an eight-and-a-half-year occupation. Afghanistan will probably not be any different unless we learn carefully from our mistakes and omissions from that Iraq disaster.

Our lengthy occupations of both countries have certainly had a negative effect on our image in the Muslim and Arab worlds. We have been seen as Western/Crusader occupiers of Muslim countries who are endeavoring to impose Western values and forms of government upon them. This has further inflamed passions and emotions in the region and made us targets of even more hate.

The US attempts at nation building in Iraq and Afghanistan have been dismal failures. In most locations inside Iraq the lights aren't on any longer now than they were over a decade ago under Saddam Hussein. The *Sunni-Shia* violence in the country – that is largely our fault – kills dozens of Iraqis every day. This kind of widespread, open, and random terror did not happen when Saddam was in charge.

After a humiliating, lengthy occupation we left Iraq with more problems and in worse shape than it was in when we invaded in 2003. Iraqis of all stripes were happy to see our backs in 2011 and the only reason we hear any cries for help from them now is because the *Shiites* in Baghdad fear being overrun by IS. They still hate us but they want our help in order to save their own skins.

We may have had the best of intentions after toppling Saddam in 2003. We promised to keep the lights on. We promised to rebuild a country that had been devastated by war and years of economic sanctions. We promised to establish a strong, inclusive, democratic government. But by the time we left Iraq in December 2011, none of those promises had been fulfilled and the country slid back into the hellish chaos and violence that we see today.

Now after 16 years of making the same promises in Afghanistan, we are looking for a way out and we have failed there, too. Despite our best intentions, many Afghans still dislike us (especially in the isolated, rural areas) and they will be happy to see us go.

Indeed, the results of our misbegotten occupations of Iraq and Afghanistan seem to confirm the admonition in the following verse of the Koran:

O ye who have believed, do not take the Jews and the Christians as allies. They are in fact allies of one another. And whosoever is an ally to them amongst you, then, indeed, he is one of them. Indeed, Allah guides not the wrongdoing people.[81]

This helps to explain why many Muslims prefer to keep us at arm's length. At best we are seen as meddling, well-intentioned, bumbling aliens in that part of the world; at worst we are invading and occupying Crusaders. Either way, any further attempts by the United States at nation building on its own or hegemonic democratization (based on the US model of democracy) in the Middle East will ultimately work against us.

While the *Salafist* extremists will simply hate us because we are not *Salafist* extremists like them, other Arabs and Muslims will hate (or at least resent) us for what they regard as sticking our foreign, Christian noses into their business. If the situation were reversed I'm sure we would feel the same way.

With that said, there are many Muslims and moderates who are eager for American help in eradicating the Islamist ideology. But they are reluctant to come forward until we lose the image of a foreign occupier. Whether we like it or not, that puts us into the same classification as Israel.

ISRAEL AND PALESTINE

We touched on the subject of Israel and Palestine in the preceding chapter. Although the situation in Iraq and Syria with the Islamic State currently dominates the news, the Palestinian issue has been a long-term cause and *casus belli* of the Muslims and the Arabs. It has festered for almost 70 years because there has never been a successful resolution to the conflict that goes all the way back to the creation of the modern State of Israel

---

81.   Koranic verse 5:51.

and the ensuing displacement of Palestinian refugees. It certainly remains on the front burner of the Palestinians and many other Muslims today.

These groups have long complained that the international community has treated Israel with a double standard compared with other international conflicts and disputes in recent history. The Negotiations Affairs Department of the Palestine Liberation Organization even authored a report on the matter in a September 2002 publication entitled: "Double Standards: How the International Community has Taught Israel that it is Above the Law." The BADIL Resource Center for Palestinian Residency and Refugee Rights excerpted that report and cited numerous examples of these double standards in how the international community has supported the return of refugees in other recent conflicts such as the Tutsis in Rwanda, the Kosovars, and those who had fled South Africa during the fight against apartheid. The report concluded:

> *The right of Palestinian refugees to return home to mainland Israel or to the occupied territories has been a key demand of the Palestinians since 1948. As can be seen, in 1948 and 1968, Israel faced demands from the international community to ensure the right of return for refugees whose movements stemmed from those particular conflicts. However subsequently these international demands have diminished and there have been attempts to declare this as a non-negotiable issue in Israel-Palestine peace negotiations. Such a practice would, however, fly in the face of all other precedents.*[82]

I am neither defending the PLO's report nor detracting from it, but the United States should give some objective consideration to the organization's viewpoint on these matters as part of its own calculus for a settlement of the Israeli-Palestinian issue. It takes two to tango and for any negotiations to succeed.

---

82. UN and International Protection, website of BADIL Resource Center for Palestinian Residency and Refugee Rights. Accessed July 15, 2017. http://www.badil.org/en/publication/periodicals/al-majdal/item/1035-un-and-international-protection.html.

An October 2002 article in *The Economist* examined many of the claims made in the PLO report and pointed out a key difference between UN Security Council resolutions on Iraq and those on the Palestinian-Israeli issue:

> *The UN distinguishes between two sorts of Security Council resolution. Those passed under Chapter Six deal with the peaceful resolution of disputes and entitle the council to make non-binding recommendations. Those under Chapter Seven give the council broad powers to take action, including warlike action, to deal with "threats to the peace, breaches of the peace, or acts of aggression". Such resolutions, binding on all UN members, were rare during the cold war. But they were used against Iraq after its invasion of Kuwait. None of the resolutions relating to the Israeli-Arab conflict comes under Chapter Seven. By imposing sanctions—including military ones—against Iraq but not against Israel, the UN is merely acting in accordance with its own rules.*[83]

The Economist went on to say that Palestinians do understand the distinction between Chapter Six and Seven resolutions, and the fact that none of the latter has been passed against Israel is a prime complaint. Nevertheless, there are many in the world (not just the Palestinians) who view the issue as being one of right and wrong and see the Palestinians as being long overdue to have a state of their own. They attribute the double standard by which their conflict has been treated to the constant US economic and diplomatic support for Israel even as the superpower was laying the foundation in the Security Council for military action against Iraq at the time. And on the issue of nuclear weapons, Iraq had been a signatory to the Non-Proliferation Treaty (NPT) while Israel never signed the agreement.[84] The Chapter Six/Seven distinction has never meant much to the Palestinian (or Arab) double standards argument, either. It's a black-and-white issue of right and wrong.

---

83. "Double Standards," *The Economist*, October 10, 2002. Accessed July 15, 2017. http://www.economist.com/node/1378577.
84. *Ibid.*

The fact that America failed to find any kind of weapons of mass destruction in Iraq – after justifying its 2003 invasion of the country on its suspicions that Saddam Hussein still had illicit WMD programs – did little to burnish America's image in the Arab and Muslim world. In a July 28, 2003 editorial by Aftab Kazmil, the Al-Ain bureau chief for *Gulf News*, the author blasted the US double standard in dealing with the WMD programs of Israel and Iraq:

> *Turning a blind eye towards the nuclear weapons programme [sic] of Israel, the U.S. administration considers it as a measure in "self-defence"[sic]. For many Arab and Muslim countries this is a "double standard" and they are even viewing the roadmap for the Middle East suspiciously.*

Kazmil chided the Bush administration's inability to actually justify its military invasion of Iraq and its "wrong intelligence" and "botched efforts" at finding any WMD in the country. Such failures could not bring a "good name" to U.S. policies or garner international support until those policies "hold legal and moral authenticity and the backing of a judicious and unbiased government."

This feeling of an American double standard in its treatment of Arabs and Israelis was the subject of a February 21, 1998 *New York Times* article by Steven Erlanger. The article cited Arabs and Arab-Americans who were complaining of American hypocrisy in its dealings with Arab states and Israel. Erlanger wrote:

> *They say Washington is willing to bomb Iraq to enforce Security Council resolutions but does not even criticize Israel when it flouts the Council. And Israel possesses weapons of mass destruction — nuclear weapons — but this draws no overt criticism from Washington.*

Erlanger quoted James J. Zogby, the president of the Arab American Institute in Washington, as saying: "The perception of an American double standard has undercut U.S. credibility and that of the Arab governments who are allied to the United States." This had left the ordinary Arab on the street feeling "angry and alienated."

Zogby went on to lament the fact that our Arab allies in *Desert Storm* believed they had an understanding that the United States would push for a resolution of the Palestinian-Israeli conflict after the end of the war but this had not happened. He added, "The Arabs get threats and force, and Israel gets compassion and aid."

The Arabs and Muslims don't care about the Chapter Six or Seven differences in Security Council resolutions on Iraq and Israel. The fact that Iraq was an NPT signatory and Israel has never signed the treaty is irrelevant to them. They are not interested in splitting legal hairs; they are only interested in what they see as justice.

As the Palestinians see it, Washington has not been able to be an honest and fair broker in the peace process. They do not believe America has forced Israel to abide by its obligations from Oslo forward. It has not forced Israel to stop seizing Palestinian territory nor has it prevented Israel from expanding its settlements in the occupied territories.

The Palestinians, Arabs, and Muslims see America and Israel as being two peas in the same pod. This causes resentment, frustration, and anger with the Arab on the street that has eventually developed into a general feeling of antipathy and mistrust toward the US, at best, and all-out hatred of us, at worst. Since there is still no foreseeable end to the conflict, this anti-American sentiment will continue to simmer for some time.

IRAN

By the early 1950s the world had become the geopolitical and geostrategic chessboard of the Cold War and the Middle East and Persian/Arabian Gulf region was becoming a very active competitive arena between East and West. The secular Arab *Baath* movement was becoming increasingly popular in many Arab countries as Arab nationalism and socialism began to take root in the newly independent countries of the region. Many of these countries had been former colonies of European states and had a general mistrust of the Western powers, seeing them as colonialists and imperialists. This feeling of general aversion toward Europe and America along with early dabbling in socialist forms of government gave many of these Arab states a pro-Soviet orientation.

Nevertheless, the West still held the major oil-producing countries of the Arabian Peninsula and the Persian Gulf firmly within its orbit. Saudi Arabia, Iran, and the other sheikhdoms of the Gulf were monarchies whose rulers enjoyed absolute power and saw membership in the Western camp as being in their best personal interests. In return, America and Britain benefitted from nearly exclusive access to the Gulf's oil wealth through the Arabian-American Oil Company (ARAMCO) in Saudi Arabia and the Anglo-Iranian Oil Company (AIOC) in Iran.

This lucrative oil business was, naturally, extremely important to America and Great Britain as post-war reconstruction eventually gave way to economic recovery that was fueled by their access to cheap energy. Both parties were loath to see this applecart upset.

While this cozy relationship continued unabated with the West's Arab clients in the Gulf, storm clouds began forming on the horizon for Britain's AIOC in Iran with the emergence of Dr. Mohammad Mossadeq, a secular democrat and Iranian nationalist with a vision of a strong, independent, democratic Iran who supported nationalizing Iran's petroleum industry as a way to finance reforms and improve life for his countrymen. This position made him extremely popular with Iranians, many of whom worked for AIOC for paltry wages and lived under appalling conditions even as the company (i.e., Britain) was taking far more than its share of oil revenue out of the country.

Iran's parliament nationalized the oil industry and the holdings of AIOC in 1951 and Mossadeq became prime minister a few months later. He traveled to New York to defend Iran's move at the United Nations where he showed that British revenues on Iranian oil in 1950 alone totaled more than it had paid Iran for the past 50 years. He presented documentary evidence to support the nationalization at The Hague the following year. The action made Mossadeq popular in much of the world and put him on the cover of *Time Magazine* twice.[85]

For their part, the British didn't stand idly by while the Iranians nationalized the AIOC. They eventually pulled their technicians out of the country, crippling Iran's ability to actually produce the petroleum, and exerted international pressure to prevent Iran from selling its oil. The near shutdown of oil money caused economic hardships for Iran but the shah's attempt to remove Mossadeq as prime minister backfired in 1952 when huge numbers of Iranians took to the streets to support the well-liked Iranian nationalist.

The British unsuccessfully tried to covertly foment unrest in Iran as a means of toppling Mossadeq. Their opening came in 1953 when they were able to convince the new Eisenhower administration that the Mossadeq government's instability threatened to put Iran into the communist camp.

Britain's activation of the "communist" alarm bell was all it took. The CIA came up with *Operation Ajax*, which accomplished the toppling of Mossadeq in 1953. Full details about the operation were eventually declassified by the agency and are now available online.[86]

We may have engineered a successful coup in Iran in 1953 under the dubious pretext of keeping a valuable square on the chessboard from falling under communist – and potentially Soviet – control, but we lost the support of the Iranian people in the process. Even according to Radio Free Europe/Radio Liberty, the US ouster of the first democratically elected government in Iran "is widely credited with fueling the hostility against the West that culminated decades later with the 1979 Islamic

---

85. Mohammad Mossadegh [sic] Biography, The Mossadegh Project. Accessed July 15, 2017. http://www.mohammadmossadegh.com/biography.
86. Malcolm Byrne, ed. "The Secret CIA History of the Iran Coup, 1953," The National Security Archive, The George Washington University, November 29, 2000. Accessed July 15, 2017. http://nsarchive.gwu.edu/NSAEBB/NSAEBB28/.

Revolution."[87] Consistent with much of our contemporary policy in the Middle East, in 1953 we won the battle but lost the war.

With the return of Ayatollah Khomeini in 1979 and his establishment of the Islamic Republic of Iran, simmering resentment against the United States became open hostility, as evidenced by the takeover of the US embassy in Tehran in November 1979. Over the course of the next three-and-a-half decades, US-Iranian relations went from bad to worse and our strategic position on that chessboard went tail over teakettle. On the bright side, at least we had the good fortune to watch our erstwhile Cold War adversary, the Soviet Union, implode and disappear.

Our history of backing the wrong horse in Iran and ignoring the Iranian people has hurt us immensely. We suffered the bombings of the US embassy in Beirut and the Marine barracks in that city by Iran's *Hezbollah* proxy in 1983. In 1987 and 1988 we attacked Iranian oil platforms in the Gulf and one of our cruisers – equipped with state of the art air defense radars and weaponry – shot down a civilian Iranian airliner by mistake. Over the years we have financed Iranian opposition groups and, of course, we tightened our economic sanctions on the country as our concerns about Iran's nuclear program mounted. After 60 years of animosity between us, what are Iranians' contemporary attitudes toward America?

In 2011, the RAND Corporation published the results of a telephone survey of 1,002 Iranians constituting a "nationally representative sample" of the country's population. The survey's objective was to assess Iranian public opinion on matters relevant to US-Iranian relations and the polling itself had been conducted in December 2009. When asked whether they favored or opposed the reestablishment of relations with the United States, 45% of respondents expressed opposition to such a move and 39% voiced their support. However, RAND also took into consideration those who were more comfortable with the survey compared with those who weren't (fearing that the Iranian government might be monitoring

87. "Aftershocks Of Iran's 1953 Coup Still Felt Around The World, 60 Years Later," Frud Bezham. *Radio Free Europe/Radio Liberty*, August 15, 2013. Accessed July 15, 2017. http://www.rferl.org/content/iran-coup-mossadegh-cia-60th-anniversary/25076552.html.

the phone call). Among those who were most comfortable answering the questions, 43% of respondents favored restoring relations with America and 41% were opposed.[88] Still a pretty even split.

The RAND survey also indicated that 52% of respondents believed that the 1953 Mossadeq coup still shaped very negative attitudes toward the United States. A majority still expressed negative views of the US government and its policies but despite that, 52% of respondents had a positive view of the American people. Nevertheless, 65% disapproved of American cultural influences in their country. Relevant to the current tensions, a solid majority of Iranians also believed in their "national right" to possess nuclear technology for civilian purposes.[89]

Another 2009 poll by World Public Opinion queried a similar number of Iranians by telephone. According to this survey's results, 63% of those asked favored a restoration of US-Iranian diplomatic relations, although eight out of ten expressed mistrust of America and three-quarters of respondents opined that the United States seeks to impose its culture on Iran's Muslim society. A majority of 51% did express positive feelings about the American people.[90]

In February 2012, Gallup polling found that only eight percent of Iranians approved of the US leadership. Its survey revealed that while nearly half (46%) of respondents favored cutting ties with countries that imposed economic sanctions on Iran, 31% did not. Gallup interpreted this positively, believing that a "sizable minority" still saw value in pursuing the diplomatic track to resolve the country's isolation.[91]

On September 27, 2013, Max Fisher reported in the *Washington Post Worldviews Blog* that *CNN* had set up a camera on a Tehran street to quiz

88. Sara Beth Elson and Alireza Nader, "What Do Iranians Think? A Survey of Attitudes on the United States, the Nuclear Program, and the Economy." RAND Corporation, 2011. Accessed July 15, 2017. See http://www.rand.org/pubs/technical_reports/TR910.html.
89. *Ibid.*
90. "Iranians Favor Diplomatic Relations With US But Have Little Trust in Obama," World Public Opinion, September 19, 2009. Accessed July 15, 2017. http://worldpublicopinion.net/iranians-favor-diplomatic-relations-with-us-but-have-little-trust-in-obama/.
91. Julie Ray, "Opinion Briefing: Iranians' Outlook for U.S. Relations," Gallup, Inc., February 28, 2012. Accessed July 15, 2017. http://www.gallup.com/poll/153002/opinion-briefing-iranians-outlook-relations.aspx.

everyday Iranians about their feelings toward America. While this was not a scientific poll, many Iranians expressed favorable attitudes toward the American people. Their opinion of US foreign policy, however, was universally quite negative. They see US policy toward Iran as "bullying" and confrontational. This does seem generally consistent with the results of the earlier surveys.

The American government may say that its dispute is with the Iranian government and not its people, but the preceding figures demonstrate that Washington has made little progress in convincing the Iranian public of its good intentions toward them. Our government is still paying for the Mossadeq misadventure from 60 years ago.

The much-extended, arduous negotiations with Iran that eventually resulted in a less-than-perfect agreement on the country's nuclear program are testament to the depth of the mutual enmity and mistrust between the US and Iranian governments. There are those in the US and the West who claim that the agreement was "the best that could be done" under the circumstances while numerous other Republican (and even some Democrat) voices in Congress (along with the Israeli prime minister) condemn the agreement and predict that it will open the way for Iran to build "the bomb." Only time will tell.

To me the elephant in the room is whether or not ending the economic sanctions on Iran will provide torrents of cash to pour into its regional meddling and terrorist adventures. That threat is arguably more urgent and immediate than the nuclear program ever was and it remains to be seen whether the price we pay for controlling Iran's nuclear program will be to suffer greater Iranian-sponsored terrorism and power projection in the region. Once again, a lack of long-term strategic vision may come back to haunt us.

(On a side note, it seems pretty clear that Iran has its own image problem in the rest of the world. A Pew Research Center publication from June 2013 reported, "Majorities in most of 39 countries surveyed have an unfavorable opinion of Iran, and most say Tehran does not respect the personal freedoms of its people. Meanwhile, any nuclear ambitions harbored by the Iranian government continue to draw strong opposition from Western countries, as well as neighboring states in the Middle East."[92])

Both governments have a long way to go. The "Death to America" chants in Tehran demonstrations won't be going away anytime soon.

THE ARAB SPRING

During the presidency of George W. Bush, the hegemonic democratization of the Middle East was administration policy. The White House believed that encouraging our form of democracy in the region would allow Arabs under repressive, autocratic regimes to finally have a voice in their own government and their own affairs. They would finally be able to enjoy freedoms that we have long taken for granted in the West. Democracy in the Arab world would usher in a new era that would sweep away the root causes of terrorism and the lion would lie down with the lamb forevermore.

The concept ignored a glaring deficiency: the building blocks necessary for constructing a democracy, as we know it, are virtually non existent in most of the Arab countries. As we've seen in the preceding chapter, our form of Western democracy has never been an intrinsic element of Arab political thought or culture. The policy should have been recognized as a non-starter right off the bat.

First, there is no freedom of speech. There is no free press in most of the Arab world. Governments have ministries of information that tell the media what they can and cannot say. Even the freedom to assemble in many Arab states was (and still is) strictly curtailed under various emergency laws.

Next, women in the Arab world are generally regarded to be second-class citizens. In Saudi Arabia they cannot even drive cars. Their abilities for

---

92. "Global Views of Iran Overwhelmingly Negative," Pew Research Center, June 11, 2013. Accessed July 15, 2017. http://www.pewglobal.org/2013/06/11/global-views-of-iran-overwhelmingly-negative/.

holding jobs are limited and they will usually be paid far less than a man for doing the same work. (And while we're on the subject, let's not forget women in America did not even have the right to vote until ratification of the 19th Amendment to the US Constitution in 1920.)

In the homogenous world of Arab Muslim society, ethnic and religious minorities are often the victims of blatant discrimination. They may be restricted from owning property and face outright social stigmas. (Our track record on civil rights has also been pretty spotty. Slavery was not abolished until the adoption of the 13th Amendment in 1865. The 14th Amendment in 1868 denied states' powers to "make or enforce any law" that would abridge the rights or privileges of any of its citizens and the 15th Amendment gave the newly-freed former black slaves the right to vote, banning any state from denying that right on the basis of race or color. Even the United States took until 1964 to pass an all-encompassing Civil Rights Act and we still have our own civil rights issues today.)

While we may believe in the separation of church and state, the same is not true in Arab countries. Islam is the state religion and most countries will at least acknowledge the *Sharia* as the basis for all their legislation. And while some of these countries allow followers of other religions to practice their faiths, there is no doubt that they are doing so as a minority. Their rights and freedoms will therefore be marginalized.

In countries like Saudi Arabia there is no true religious freedom. Church buildings must not be outwardly recognizable as such. Christian missionaries can face prison (or worse) for proselytizing Muslims. In fact at one time it was technically even against Saudi law to send a Christmas card in the Saudi mail system.

Human rights as we know them are almost completely absent in that part of the world. If a person is arrested, there is no automatic right to an attorney or speedy trial. Torture is often the rule when prisoners are interrogated. Food and medical care for people who have been incarcerated in the Arab world are often well below the minimum standards in the West. Even when a country's constitution spells out a person's rights, a corrupt government and judiciary may still completely disregard those rights.

Add to this the potential for government corruption, the lack of a free economy, restrictive and discriminatory investment laws, absolute central planning, and a host of other differences and it's clear that US-style democracy was just not ready for prime time during the administration of President George W. Bush. The raw ingredients were just not there. They still aren't and won't be for generations to come.

This ill-conceived policy, conjured up by policymakers who were absolutely clueless about the Middle East and its history and cultural dynamics, was pretty much dead on arrival. The administration's 2005 selection of "soccer mom" Karen Hughes as the State Department's Undersecretary of Public Diplomacy to bring democracy to the Arabs was an absolute flop. She had zero knowledge of the language, religion, culture, or customs and so had no way of actually connecting with her target audience. It simply highlighted our own ignorance and had all the trappings of a domestic public relations campaign rather than serious foreign policy. You could almost see question marks in cartoon bubbles above Arab leaders' heads.

Moreover, most Arabs bristled at what they saw as yet another American plan to impose something upon them. Once again, we were telling them what to do and how to do it even though they had no ambitions or desire to be just like us. It was arrogant and ignorant hubris at its absolute worst. It smacked of Christian missionaries bringing the gospel to African heathens and the Arabs wanted nothing to do with it.

As we shot ourselves in one foot by unwisely portraying ourselves as trying to preach the gospel of democracy to the heathen Arabs, we completely lost sight of another important fact. Many of the most reviled and despised autocratic regimes in the Middle East were actually those of our allies in the region. Bang! There went our other foot.

There was no better example of this than Egypt's Hosni Mubarak. In power since 1981, he had a reputation among most Egyptians as a corrupt president who was grooming his son to take over the family business. Mubarak surrounded himself with a cabal of corrupt ministers, judges, and other officials. The select elite at the top of Egyptian society got richer while the middle class imploded and the poor got poorer. The economy was in shambles and unemployment – especially among young people

– was through the roof. Human rights abuses in Egypt were nearly as common as weather reports. Yet the United States would look the other way and stand firmly by its friend and client, Hosni Mubarak, nearly until the very end even though his regime was the absolute antithesis of democracy and used its emergency law to conveniently suppress freedoms and liberties for decades.

Another great example of the non-democratic nature of our allies in the region is Saudi Arabia. Like most of the Arabian Gulf countries, the Saudis are a hereditary monarchy. They have no interest in allowing any sort of government or legislative representation to ethnic or religious minorities in the country. The country is a quasi-theocratic state where stern Islamic clergy play a prominent role. However Saudi dissidents (and Islamist extremists) characterize the Saudi royal family as being corrupt and un-Islamic. The country is ruled with an iron fist and it has few, if any, democratic traits. But all the king has to do is whistle and Uncle Sam will show up, hat in hand, eager to reassure them.

At the very southern tip of the Arabian Peninsula, President Ali Abdullah Saleh ruled the troubled country of Yemen as his own personal fiefdom. Widespread government corruption, economic stagnation, a restive south-ern Yemen that aspired to secede from the hated north, the intermittent Houthi rebellion in the northwest, and a nascent Al-Qaeda presence in the south and west of the country added up to a failing state in constant turmoil. Saleh was disliked by just about everyone in Yemen – except us.

In Morocco, King Hassan II was another Arab ruler with a miserable human rights record yet he was a staunch US ally.

Washington even came to believe that Libya's Muammar al-Gaddafi – the man who had killed hundreds of Americans over Lockerbie, Scotland and in a Berlin disco – had somehow "reformed" and become a useful partner with the United States in the war on terror that followed 9/11. Libya was certainly no democracy and Gaddafi was no friend of the United States.

It's hard enough to push Western democracy on a region of wary and non-receptive populations. It becomes downright impossible when your chief allies in the Arab world are corrupt dictators who are reviled by the

117

very people we are trying to democratize. It was an incredibly obtuse policy that ignored realities on the ground in the Middle East that were crystal clear to the Arabs but apparently totally invisible to a naive White House and State Department. It's embarrassing when our hubris is only exceeded by our ignorance.

The Arabs have a much different concept of democracy than ours. In most cases, they simply equate it with a popular revolt that topples a hated, autocratic dictator who has been in power for years – even decades – and allows those who have been repressed and oppressed by that ruler to take power. It is about the people punishing and seeking retribution from that deposed tyrant because the principle of revenge and vengeance is ingrained in the Arab (and even Islamic) culture. At least in the beginning, it is all about the worm turning and the issues of constructing public institutions of democracy that are so significant to us (e.g., a free press, human rights, independent judiciary, etc.) are secondary to them at that stage.

Rather than our misguided attempts to externally impose the US brand of democracy on the Arabs, the Arab Spring was an indigenous revolution that quickly gained traction in the Middle East. The dissidents used social media to great effect in rallying popular support to their demonstrations and protests. Some of these protests were peaceful and others turned violent. Extensive conventional media coverage and snowballing social media usage spread the revolution from one country to another. But in a matter of days, weeks, and months, massive demonstrations in places like Tunisia, Egypt, Libya, and Yemen deposed rulers and regimes that had been in power for decades – and who had been regarded as US allies or pro-Western.

The rapid eruption of the Arab Spring caught America totally off guard and completely flatfooted and it scrambled frantically to respond. Initially it tried to stand by some of its friends and patrons like Hosni Mubarak, but as Mubarak's position and strength eroded there were calls for America to take a stand "on the right side of history." Nevertheless, our hesitancy and uncertain response wound up disappointing just about everyone in Egypt.

In fairness to Washington, however, the deposed rulers themselves like Zine al-Abdine Ben Ali and Hosni Mubarak never saw this coming, either – and they were in a position to tap telephones, read emails, and torture jailed prisoners. The depth and breadth of the revolution, along with its rapid pace, took everyone by surprise – even the revolutionaries. It was a spontaneous eruption of emotions, passions, and frustrations that had been bottled up inside the populations of these countries for decades and once the genie got out of that bottle there was no way it was going back in. It was a raw, populist explosion – a human wave – that left no doubt as to the will of the people. It wasn't what we would call democracy, but it may ultimately lead to a form of it in some countries.

In both Tunisia and Egypt, the people just wanted to be rid of their despots. But there was a significant Islamist opposition waiting in the wings in both countries and the White House and State Department were unsure and wary of the ramifications if they came to power. Washington was particularly concerned about the Muslim Brotherhood coming out of the shadows in Egypt to govern the country openly. This conjured up images of the chaos in Iran in 1979 when America's then-main ally in the region, Shah Reza Pahlavi, was toppled and replaced by a vehemently anti-American Islamic Republic of Iran. America's crystal ball hadn't worked so well then, either.

Egypt has been a critically important US ally in the Middle East for decades, ever since President Sadat signed a peace treaty with Israel. A review of the aftermath of the Arab Spring in that country demonstrates the challenges that Washington faced in reacting to fast-moving events while it also highlights the challenges that democracy faced during the same period. The country's first democratic experience didn't turn out so well.

With Mubarak's ouster on February 11, 2011 the Egyptian military announced that it was dissolving parliament and suspending the constitution on February 13, 2011. The Supreme Council of the Armed Forces (SCAF) moved to fill the power vacuum in the country left by the president's resignation, temporarily leaving Mubarak's cabinet in place to help run the country. The SCAF indicated it planned to govern Egypt for a six-month period, or until presidential elections were held. The move was seen favorably by a majority of Egyptians since the military was a widely respected institution in the country.

On April 30, 2011 the Muslim Brotherhood – long banned under Mubarak, Sadat, and even Gamal Abdel-Nasser – formed its own political party. To allay fears that the party would be dominated by religious ideology, *Los Angeles Times* reporter Amro Hassan reported on April 30, 2011 that then-Brotherhood politburo member Mohamed Morsi had said, "The party will not be Islamist in the old understanding" whatever that meant. At the time, the party planned to take part in parliamentary elections but it had no plan to put forth a candidate for the presidential elections. Nevertheless, the legitimization of the Muslim Brotherhood and its ability to openly take part in elections set the stage for polarizing the secular and Islamist communities in Egypt.

Washington's concerns grew in January 2012 when almost three-quarters of the seats in the parliamentary elections were won by various Islamist parties. Still, the country remained under firm military rule. However, in yet another twist on Egypt's path to democracy, the country's Supreme Constitutional Court dissolved the Islamist-dominated parliament just days before the presidential elections, setting the stage for a confrontation and showdown between the SCAF and the Islamists.

On June 24, 2012 the Muslim Brotherhood candidate, Mohamed Morsi, was declared the first democratically elected president in Egyptian history after defeating Hosni Mubarak's last prime minister, Ahmed Shafik. This quickly set the stage for a showdown between the SCAF and President Morsi as the now-banned Islamist-dominated parliament reconvened in defiance of the military rulers. This situation escalated further in November when Morsi granted himself nearly total judicial and legislative powers, in essence making himself an Islamist dictator who was beyond the law. This caused civil unrest and rioting between Egypt's secularists and Islamists to worsen considerably.

The secularist anger mounted even further when the new Egyptian constitution, written by another Islamist-dominated council, was approved in a referendum that the secularists believed was corrupt and fraudulent. As Morsi and the Islamists increasingly attempted to tighten their grip on power, the breaking point was reached on the first anniversary of Morsi's inauguration on June 30, 2013 when hundreds of thousands of Egyptians gathered in protest outside the presidential palace. On July 3, 2013 the Egyptian army announced it had removed Morsi from power and suspended the constitution, evoking scenes of joy in the capital's Tahrir Square that were reminiscent of those when Mubarak was ousted.

Protestors supporting the now-deposed president set up their camps at *Al-Nahda* Square and *Rabiaa al-Adawiya* Square in Cairo. On August 14th, the military moved in to break these camps up in clashes with the demonstrators that turned violent. Hundreds of protestors were killed.

SCAF strong man, minister of defense, and supreme military commander Abdul Fattah El-Sisi, who played the leading role in Morsi's ouster, succeeded him as president in June 2014. Despite clamping down harshly on the Islamists, he still faces a determined opposition from Islamist extremists in the Sinai and those Egyptians disappointed and disenfranchised by Morsi's removal. Meanwhile, the now-banned Muslim Brotherhood has slipped comfortably back into the shadows – its normal operating environment for most of its history.

Egypt's failed experiment with democracy poses some questions about the future of that form of government in the Middle East. Do a majority of Arabs actually prefer having a strong leader over selecting one through the ballot box? Osama bin Laden must have thought so when he once said: "When people see a strong horse and a weak horse, they will naturally want to side with the strong horse."

All the ups and downs and twists and turns on the Egyptian domestic scene must have given the White House whiplash. Trying to decide whether or not to call Morsi's ouster a coup or whether it should release military assistance to Egypt put Washington in a delicate situation. Eventually it saw a staunch anti-Islamist in Sisi and decided to back him. But America's image was already tarnished by three decades of supporting, and propping up one leader – Hosni Mubarak – who was the epitome of corruption in his countrymen's eyes. After the dust of Egypt's revolution and turbulent foray into democracy had settled, America found that it had few friends left in the restive country.

Even prior to Morsi's removal, the results of a September 2012 Gallup poll indicated a clear negative attitude toward the United States by a majority of Egyptians. The statistics showed that in most years since 2005, fewer than one in five Egyptians have approved of US leaders. Moreover, most Egyptians (83%) felt that America would not let people in the region determine their own political future. A similar percentage even expressed opposition to US aid to the country.[93]

As for Egypt itself, May 2014 polling by the Pew Research Center confirms the country remains divided about its current path. Nearly three-quarters of the respondents were dissatisfied with the country's current direction and only 54% expressed a positive view of President Sisi. A sizeable minority – 38% – still holds a positive view of the Muslim Brotherhood. Fifty-nine percent of respondents believed that democracy was still a preferable form of government but 54% believed that a stable government was more important even if it wasn't fully democratic.[94]

These figures certainly show that while Egyptians today don't necessarily hate us, they do not like us very much, either. They are not in a mood to appear beholden to us for accepting our aid. After our track record in the region, they are distrustful of us and prefer government (and internal) stability over democracy. President Sisi undoubtedly senses this and prefers to keep America at arm's length. Meanwhile, we have a long road ahead of us if we want to rebuild trust with Egypt.

---

93. Dalia Mogahed, "Opinion Briefing: Egyptians Skeptical of US Intentions," Gallup, Inc., September 21, 2012. Accessed July 15, 2017. http://www.gallup.com/poll/157592/opinion-briefing-egyptians-skeptical-intentions.aspx.
94. Richard Wike, "Key Takeaways from Our Egypt Survey," Pew Research Center, May 22, 2014. Accessed July 15, 2017. http://www.pewresearch.org/fact-tank/2014/05/22/key-takeaways-from-our-survey-of-egypt/.

NOW FOR SOME GOOD NEWS

While the results of Arab and Muslim public opinion polls over the past few years have shown that respondents have generally had a negative view of the United States. In July 2014 the Pew Research Global Attitudes Project reported that most areas of the world had a positive view of the United States except in the Middle East, where only 30% of those asked held America in a positive light.

In the Middle East we had the most favorable rating in Tunisia, scoring 42%, and the least favorable rating in Egypt, where we plummeted from a 30% favorable rating in 2006 to only 10% in 2014. Surprisingly our favorability rose in the Palestinian territories from 16% in 2013 to 30% in 2014 likely out of hopes for a restart of the peace process with Israel. On the negative side, confidence in most Arab countries in President Obama's ability to do the right thing in world affairs has been steadily decreasing since 2009.[95]

But with challenges also come opportunities. Public opinion poll results allow us to see the areas on which the Arabs view us the most negatively and give us an opportunity to devise strategies for improving our image. While Western pollsters like Gallup and the Pew Research Center have provided some good results, perhaps the best and most honest data comes from the surveys conducted by the Arabs themselves.

For example, the Arab Center for Research and Policy Studies (ACRPS) in Doha, Qatar carried out its 2014 Arab Opinion Index from January to July with face-to-face interviews of 26,618 respondents from 14 Arab countries – including 5,466 Syrian refugees and internally displaced persons. The 14 countries were Mauritania, Morocco, Algeria, Tunisia, Libya, Egypt, Sudan, Palestine, Lebanon, Jordan, Iraq, Saudi Arabia,

---

95. "Chapter 1: The American Brand," Pew Research Center, July 14, 2014. Accessed July 15, 2017. http://www.pewglobal.org/2014/07/14/chapter-1-the-american-brand/.

Yemen and Kuwait. The index reported some predictable results, but others were rather surprising:[96]

- 45% of respondents viewed the revolutions of the Arab Spring positively while a surprising 42% did not. Those with negative views were primarily influenced by the loss of life, the failures of these revolutions to achieve their goals, and the destruction, chaos, and instability resulting from the Arab Spring.

- Nevertheless, 60% of those surveyed believed that the Arab Spring was going through a difficult phase but that it would eventually achieve its objectives.

- On the Syrian civil war, 68% of Arabs expressed the view that "it would be better for Syria if Bashar al-Assad stepped down."

- Respondents expressed fears regarding the rise of both secular and Islamist governments. Thirty-seven percent were concerned about the rise of secular political movements while 43% were fearful over the rise of political Islamists. The survey interpreted this as indicative of the polarization of Arab society with the recognition that the inability of the two trends to cooperate would be an obstacle to any democratic transition.

- A whopping 73% of Arabs voiced support for democracy as a system of government but they also supported authoritarian rule (14%), Islamic *Sharia* (30%), representative government of Islamist parties (27%), and representative government of non-religious parties (30%).

- Pan-Arabism is still alive and well. The index indicated conclusively that an overwhelming majority of Arabs view themselves as "citizens of one nation" that is divided by "artificial borders." Eighty-one percent of respondents expressed this view compared to only 14% who see the Arab people as distinct, separate nations.

---

96. "Findings From the 2014 Arab Opinion Index, the Largest-ever Survey of Arab Public Opinion, to be Announced in Doha September 24," Arab Center for Research and Policy Studies, Doha Institute, September 22, 2014. Accessed July 15, 2017. http://english.dohainstitute.org/content/0613fa41-1994-4009-b8de-5d7cac2b306c.

- In this poll, approximately 36% of respondents had either a positive or somewhat positive view of the United States. This compared with 57% for Turkey, 52% for China, 47% for France, 37% for Russia, and 17% for Iran.

- Eighty-seven percent of those polled described themselves as religious or very religious but they also firmly supported tolerance toward the followers of other faiths. A solid 70% did not believe any person or group had the right to declare these followers of other religions "infidels."

Stanford University's Center on Democracy, Development, and the Rule of Law used data from the respected Yemen Polling Center (YPC) to gauge support for democracy in Yemen. YPC found that support for democracy, as a form of governance, was surprisingly strong. Its data, collected from 2006-2010, showed that around eight out of ten Yemenis were supportive of democratic government. However additional data indicated that the slow pace of democratic reforms in Yemen – even prior to the Arab Spring – had caused some people to lose faith in the democratic process by 2011.[97]

Perhaps most optimistically, a November 2014 paper by the Doha-based Arab Center for Research and Policy Studies found that a majority of Arabs oppose the Islamic State and support airstrikes against it. ACRPS surveyed 5100 respondents in seven Arab countries and found that 85% of those surveyed held negative views of the group while only 11% saw the group in a positive light. As to the reasons why IS enjoyed backing from its supporters, 55% believed it was because of the group's military achievements, its readiness to challenge the West, its opposition to the regimes in Iran, Syria, and Iraq, and its perceived support for the *Sunni* community.[98]

---

97. Chris Miller, Hafez al-Bukari and Olga Aymerich, "Democracy, Political Parties, and Reform: A Review of Public Opinion in Yemen," Center on Democracy, Development, and the Rule of Law, Stanford University, no 126, October 2012. Accessed July 15, 2017. http://cddrl.fsi.stanford.edu/sites/default/files/No_126_Yemen_English.pdf.

98. "A Majority of Arabs Oppose ISIL Support Air Strikes on the Group," Arab Center for Research and Policy Studies, Doha Institute, November 11, 2014. Accessed July 15, 2017. http://english.dohainstitute.org/content/6a355a64-5237-4d7a-b957-87f6b1ceba9b.

While 59% expressed support for the US-led coalition's airstrikes on IS, only 22% believed that the coalition could achieve its objectives. Unfortunately, a majority also believed that the ones who stood to gain from the coalition were the United States, Israel, Iran, and Syria. This negative attitude is explained by the Arab public's skepticism of US policy in the region, particularly toward the Palestinians and the Syrian civil war.[99]

CONCLUSIONS

What conclusions can we take away from this data? First, our inability to orchestrate a just and lasting settlement to the Palestinian-Israeli conflict since the Oslo Accords of 1993 has done considerable damage to our reputation among the Arabs in the Middle East and Muslims elsewhere in the world. We enjoyed a groundswell of good will in the region after we put together a joint East-West coalition to expel Saddam Hussein out of Kuwait in 1992. Our Arab partners in that coalition had the tacit understanding that resolving the Palestinian issue would be next on our list of things to do.

Despite over two decades of road maps, agreements, and on-again, off-again negotiations, we have not been able to bring the two sides to reach a permanent agreement. The Arabs see Israel as the 51st US state in the region and they believe we have not exerted sufficient pressure on the Israelis, as evidenced by the expansion of Jewish settlements, the construction of the Israeli wall of separation, harsh military operations against Hamas in Gaza, and a host of other perceived injustices against the Palestinians.

The Palestinians themselves don't differentiate between Chapter Six and Chapter Seven UN Security Council Resolutions. They believe the West, in general, and the United States, in particular, have treated their cause unfairly and with a double standard compared with other recent conflicts around the world. In their eyes, they are the aggrieved party in the dispute and they are disappointed that America is unwilling to "lean on" its Israeli ally to finally settle the crisis in a just and satisfactory fashion.

---

99. *Ibid.*

In addition, the polling indicates that the Arabs remain generally skeptical of US policy in the region. The long-term US occupations of Iraq and Afghanistan have not left either country with a visibly better future than it had prior to our invasion. We still have a chance to change that in Afghanistan; in Iraq it is too late.

Our long history of backing rulers that have been seen as tyrants and despots by their people was not helped by our missteps after the Arab Spring. Our indecision and hesitancy over Mubarak's fate in Egypt, our reluctance to support anti-regime forces in Syria, and our leadership from behind during Libya's revolution have all left the Arabs questioning whether America is able to exert a positive influence on the region's events any more.

In Iran, public opinion strongly favors Iran's right to a peaceful civilian nuclear program. Iranians have negative opinions on US policy, seeing America as trying to bully Iran into giving up its peaceful nuclear power program. We have a long history of clashing with Iran all the way back to 1953 and this has led to deep distrust and suspicion over Washington's official policies and intentions with regard to Iran and the region, as a whole.

On the plus side, the polling indicates a majority of Arabs believe that democracy is their preferred form of governance. They want to have the freedoms of speech and assembly and other political freedoms that we enjoy but they don't necessarily want a US-style democratic government. A majority of Arabs desire a form of democracy that is consistent with Islamic values, one that embraces human rights but also allows a prominent role for Islam.

While many are disappointed that the revolutions of the Arab Spring have not fully achieved their goals, there is optimism that the Arab Spring is going through a difficult period and these revolutions will ultimately prevail.

Most Arabs share our concern over the rise of Islamist extremism and they support the fight against the Islamic State, although they are dubious of our intentions and abilities to achieve our goals. A clear majority demonstrates a tolerant attitude toward non-Muslims and opposes branding anyone who is not a Muslim an "infidel" or unbeliever.

Even in Iran, a majority of those polled had a favorable view of the American people. It's our government and its policies that they don't like.

There really is some good news here. The Arab surveys and polls do seem to show that we share some common ground with solid majorities in the Arab world on several important issues. If we can build on the areas where we agree, continue to remain actively engaged on the Palestinian peace process, and cooperate with the Arabs and Muslims against the Islamist extremist ideology that threatens them as much as it threatens us, then the prospects for boosting our standing in the region will improve greatly. It will require some concrete actions on our part (not just more empty rhetoric) to begin restoring their faith in US policy. But the hearts and minds component in defeating this ideology is incredibly important and we will need the Arabs' help in this endeavor if we are to succeed. I keep reiterating this because it is so vital to our mutual war against Islamist ideology.

CHAPTER FIVE

THE PROBLEM: WE AREN'T FIGHTING TO WIN

"Self-obsession is at the heart of our insanity."

– *Narcotics Anonymous*

After 9/11 America got scared. Al-Qaeda's own "shock and awe" campaign claimed 3,000 innocent lives in New York, Pennsylvania, and Washington, DC in just a couple of hours. Terrorism was no longer some abstract concept that threatened American military personnel or diplomats abroad. It wasn't just about some obscure European or Palestinian faction that did something terrible to people in some far-off land. Suddenly it endangered all of us right here at home and it forever changed the paradigm of our daily lives. Al-Qaeda and Osama bin Laden had smacked us with a two-by-four right between the eyes and finally got our attention.

There can be no dispute that September 11th was a huge intelligence failure. The 1993 World Trade Center bombing attempt, the 1998 African twin embassy bombings, and the USS *Cole* attack proved that Al-Qaeda was serious in its hatred for America. Nearly a decade of bin Laden's own *fatwas* and rhetoric surely left no doubt of the malevolence of his intentions toward all Americans. There were no innocent Americans in his eyes; we were all fair game and there were people in the intelligence community who knew it but for the most part, our nation and our government were taken completely by surprise by the 9/11 attacks.

Those events sent a shockwave through us all. The president was kept airborne in Air Force One – just in case. Nobody knew if the attacks were over or if there were more to come. The vice president was hustled into an underground bunker. Commercial aviation in this country was completely shut down for days and general aviation was crippled for weeks. We were scared that another shoe was going to drop and since we had already been taken by surprise once, we all feared that we could be taken by surprise once again. We just didn't know. Then came the anthrax letters in October. Were they part of the 9/11 plot? Would nuclear bombs in shipping containers be next? Every day there was a new worst-case scenario. And in the aftermath of those dark days, our existing government infrastructure had not only completely failed to warn us of the attacks, it was seemingly impotent in our defense when those attacks were executed. These were troubled times inside the Beltway that quickly gave way to finger-pointing and assigning blame. Politicians fretted that the intelligence community had failed to "connect the dots" and that the individual intelligence agencies that comprised the community were unwilling to share their information and intelligence with each other. It seemed like the only solution would be a wholesale restructuring of the government's intelligence and security apparatus. Under the best of intentions, the administration of President George W. Bush created an entirely new department – the Department of Homeland Security – whose sole mission was to protect this nation. Some existing bureaucracies like the Coast Guard and Federal Emergency Management Administration were reshuffled, reorganized, and folded under the DHS umbrella while other, new ones were created. Its first secretary was the no-nonsense ex-governor of Pennsylvania, Tom Ridge. The message was clear: DHS was there to keep America and Americans safe. We weren't going to let another 9/11 happen.

In its review of the intelligence community's performance the 9/11 Commission recommended the creation of a Director of National Intelligence (DNI) position to better supervise and oversee the country's various intelligence agencies and improve their performance. The Office of the Director of National Intelligence was created in 2004 as yet another agency to assist the DNI in the performance of his/her mission.

Now given the government's unacceptable performance on 9/11, I can certainly understand the desire and need for improvement. But in the decade-and-a-half since these new bureaucracies were created, how have they performed? Are we any safer now than we were on 9/11? And while counterterrorism is extremely important, is it the key to victory in our war against Islamism?

ARE WE SAFER NOW THAN WE WERE ON 9/11?

The short answer is: sort of. On 9/11 we were largely ignorant of the terrorist threat from Al-Qaeda and Islamism. We had seen plenty of warning signs, but we were taken by surprise as 19 mostly-Saudi hijackers took control of four commercial jetliners and changed our country forever just as the Pearl Harbor attack had done 60 years earlier. Both of these assaults had come from enemies who had been rattling our cage for years and yet we still hadn't taken the threat seriously at the official level.

So, we are now somewhat safer because post-9/11 we do have a general, strategic awareness of the scale of the Islamist terrorist threat to our country. It's no longer something bubbling under the surface that is only recognized and acknowledged by a smattering of intelligence analysts but completely ignored by our policymakers. The threat from terrorism has taken its place front and center in everyone's minds. That is a good thing inasmuch as threats can only be countered effectively when they are recognized and assessed objectively.

Another positive is that our intelligence agencies have become very adept at monitoring various social media, chat rooms, and other virtual meeting places where terrorists and their sympathizers like to hang out. We can examine the resources, videos, and reference materials they may post online and we can follow messages and discussion threads to see what they are saying. These things may give us some valuable insights into possible strategies and tactics that they may be considering for future attacks against us.

This is often called monitoring the extremists' "buzz" or "chatter" and we use it as a very broad and blunt threat indicator. When terrorist buzz or chatter increases, we suspect that the reason for the rise in activity may be that the participants believe some significant event might soon take place. There may be rumors inside the terrorist community that some big operation is underway. If the buzz or chatter spikes around the time of a major US holiday or occasion, we will probably hear warnings from our government to be vigilant even if there is no information or indication of a specific threat or attack. Likewise when the buzz decreases, it is often interpreted as a sign of reduced threat.

The problem with the buzz or chatter volume is that it incorporates all of cyberspace. That means that there are thousands of sympathizers out there who may be clamoring for an attack around Christmas or the Fourth of July, for example, even though no specific actual operation has been planned. The terrorists' rumor mill is often as inaccurate as our own so since the buzz level doesn't provide the intelligence community with any specifics, its usefulness as a threat indicator is pretty limited.

Since we know that Al-Qaeda and Islamic State might like to strike us on a noteworthy or important date or day, if the chatter builds around a holiday or a major event it will invariably make our officials nervous. In this situation some of the terrorists might actually artificially boost the chatter level just to keep us worried and force us to spend money on elevated security preparations even when they have nothing planned. It costs them nothing to do so but it costs us money we really can't afford only to counter a threat that doesn't even exist, in this case. They're just pulling our chain but it does allow them to study our reactions and preparations and that may assist them in their planning of future terrorist operations.

It's a little like the old days during the Cold War when either we or the Soviets would send some jets screaming toward one of the other side's air defense sites to see how quickly it would react and what it would do. The jets would be recalled or turn away before any shooting started or missiles launched, but it was a way to gauge the enemy's reaction in case actual hostilities ever broke out. The frequency and intensity of such operations might fluctuate depending on how good or bad US-Soviet relations were at the time.

At best, terrorist chatter is a very broad indicator. At worst, it is a disinformation technique that can offer our enemies a peek into our counterterrorism strategies and preparations.

And it's not like the nature and scope of the terrorism threat hasn't changed significantly since 9/11. After the events of September 11, 2001 we were focused on what were called low-probability, high-consequence attacks like the use of a "dirty bomb" or even chemical or biological weapons. In fact the viability of terrorists using WMD of all kinds was constantly being assessed. There were rumors that old Soviet "suitcase nukes" had made it into the hands of Al-Qaeda and worries that former Soviet nuclear and biological facilities (and scientists) were vulnerable to exploitation and recruitment after the fall of the Soviet Union since bin Laden was thought to have piles of money and the former Soviet scientists were broke. Given that 9/11 had led to 3,000 US dead and a significant impact on our national psyche, it was believed that Al-Qaeda and Osama bin Laden would be eager to carry out some other kind of mass-casualty attack. The intelligence community is still concerned about this even today.

After 9/11 it seemed like Al-Qaeda became obsessed with attacking commercial jetliners. Shoe bombs, underwear bombs, and printer cartridges cleverly disguising explosives were all used in attempts to down passenger aircraft. Luckily all these failed because of the poor design of the bomb, the ineptitude of the bomber, the intervention of other passengers, or just good luck on our part. For a while the terrorists even considered the surgical implantation of some type of explosive device inside the body of a bomber in order to escape detection at the airport. That sort of plot has some rather daunting complications of its own. How do you plant toxic explosives into a person and keep him alive long enough to kill himself on a commercial airline flight?

The success of the 9/11 attacks boosted the popularity of Al-Qaeda among anti-American Arabs overnight. But while the organization may have coveted another such success, it just never managed to pull it off. In the meantime Al-Qaeda Central was under attack and its ability to plan and execute such grand operations was severely curtailed. Operational planners and commanders were steadily killed or captured until the original Al-Qaeda did not represent much of a threat. It didn't go away though; it just morphed into something different.

Al-Qaeda in the Arabian Peninsula (AQAP) headquartered in Yemen had a talented bomb-maker on its staff. He designed a body bomb that was intended to assassinate a Saudi security official and the famous printer cartridge bombs that were intended to down commercial aircraft. The bombs were ingenious but his novel attempts failed.

But where AQAP succeeded beyond anyone's wildest imagination was when it first started publishing its English, online magazine called *Inspire*. First published in the summer of 2010, *Inspire* represented a quantum shift in Al-Qaeda's strategy. The slick online magazine specifically targeted disaffected Western youth and encouraged them to rise up and commit individual acts of terrorism in the Al-Qaeda cause, what it called its *jihad*. Editions of the magazine offered instructions on how to make bombs and explosives from household items and even encouraged its readers to use a car to run people down in a crowd. If your homemade bomb-making skills aren't up to par, you can't get any less complicated than that. In one fell swoop Al-Qaeda had established its brand, boosted the numbers of young sympathizers, and changed the strategic focus of its terrorism. Why waste time on complex, failure-prone operations when you can encourage dozens of people to commit sympathetic acts of terror on their own? The new focus on individual attacks was a game changer and it greatly complicated our counterterrorism efforts.

The subsequent rise of the Islamic State and its unparalleled use of the Internet and social media to disseminate its propaganda has taken the threat of individual terrorism – so-called "lone wolf attacks" – to an unprecedented level. The greatest threat now comes from some heretofore-unknown perpetrator carrying out an isolated attack in a restaurant, a church, or a shopping mall. Such small-scale, limited operations involve persons who remain below the counterterrorism radar. They might not have a police record and others may not even believe them to have become radicalized. And since their operations are often extremely simple, there may be no digital trail on the Internet that leads back to online bomb-making manuals or some terrorist leader or recruiter.

Are we safer now than we were on 9/11? I believe we're much safer from the low-probability, high-consequence attacks like those of 9/11. Subsequent terrorist attempts at similar operations have all failed. Commercial jetliners now have hardened cockpits and some pilots are even armed. The somewhat lackadaisical and haphazard airport security situation that preceded 9/11 has been replaced by a much more stringent and standardized approach where passengers receive far greater scrutiny before they are allowed to board their flights. But let's not forget that the more complex a terrorist operation is, the more likely it is to fail of its own accord. A complex plan is much more difficult to execute and the best evidence of that is that the passengers on at least one of the four planes hijacked on 9/11 were able to thwart the terrorists from carrying out their plan.

On the negative side we are far less safe today from these lone wolf attacks. They are becoming increasingly common and our counterterrorism enterprise does not have a great track record in detecting or stopping them. Expect that trend to continue even as law enforcement will endeavor to counter such threats.

At the strategic level, however, there is much more to this issue that never seems to be discussed.

THE PROBLEMS WITH COUNTERTERRORISM

There are two big problems with seeing counterterrorism as some kind of silver bullet in our fight against Islamism. First, counterterrorism is limited to playing defense. It seeks to protect us from terrorist attacks while doing absolutely nothing to prevent the spread of the terrorism itself. It's like relying on hot chicken soup to get over a cold rather than doing whatever it took to avoid getting the cold in the first place. I don't wish to downplay or minimize the importance of our counterterrorism enterprise to our national security but I don't think it's healthy to overestimate it, either. Playing defense doesn't win wars and the best defense is usually a good offense.

Let's look at this a different way. Islamism is often compared to a cancerous or malignant ideology and I couldn't agree more. If we take that analogy one step further, isn't it more beneficial to try and prevent cancer in the first place? Isn't it wiser to get in the habit of using sunscreen to prevent melanoma rather than trying to successfully treat an advanced case once it occurs? Aren't your odds of living a long and healthy life enhanced by not smoking to begin with? Is chemotherapy or radiation going to give you those same odds once you are diagnosed with lung cancer?

Prevention is almost always more successful than treatment. Similarly preventing terrorism and radicalization at its source will be much more effective and successful than trying to defend against it. But doing that requires policy decisions and actions that go far beyond the tactical level of counterterrorism. It requires eliminating the ideology itself and that cannot be done by introducing a new x-ray scanner at airports or limiting how much toothpaste a passenger can bring aboard a commercial airliner. Counterterrorism by itself just does not go far enough. It is not a strategic tool.

The counterterrorism enterprise in this country is primarily a collection of law enforcement and security organizations that are augmented by various intelligence resources that have a counterterrorist mission. The sole focus of this enterprise is to protect the United States and its people against terrorist attacks and it doesn't matter whether those attacks may come from Islamist terrorists or Puerto Rican nationalists. The law enforcement, intelligence, and security entities within the enterprise will naturally assess the levels of the various threats differently but they are committed to defending us against any threat. That is their job.

As its name suggests, the Department of Homeland Security (DHS) is the prime federal government entity responsible for protecting America and its citizens. It defines its vital mission as securing "the nation from the many threats we face. This requires the dedication of more than 240,000 employees in jobs that range from aviation and border security to emergency response, from cybersecurity analyst to chemical facility inspector. Our duties are wide-ranging, but our goal is clear – keeping America safe."[100]

A number of federal law enforcement, security, and disaster response organizations fall under the DHS umbrella such as:[101]

- Citizenship and Immigration Services

- Customs and Border Patrol

- Coast Guard

- Federal Emergency Management Agency

- Federal Law Enforcement Training Center

- Immigration and Customs Enforcement

- Transportation Security Administration

- Secret Service

---

100. "About DHS," Department of Homeland Security website. Accessed July 15, 2017. http://www.dhs.gov/about-dhs.
101. "Operational and Support Components," Department of Homeland Security website. Accessed July 15, 2017. http://www.dhs.gov/components-directorates-and-offices.

In addition, DHS liaises with a number of "primary and recognized fusion centers" in states and major urban areas. According to the DHS website:

A primary fusion center typically provides information sharing and analysis for an entire state. These centers are the highest priority for the allocation of available federal resources, including the deployment of personnel and connectivity with federal data systems...[102]

The DHS website goes on to list 53 "primary fusion centers" in the states, the District of Columbia, Guam, Puerto Rico, and the Virgin Islands.[103]

It goes on to identify yet another 25 "recognized fusion centers" in major urban areas around the country. These are fusion centers not designated as "primary" that may be set up by state governments instead of the federal government.[104]

But DHS is not alone in performing the counterterrorism role in the United States. The Department of Justice is another major player in protecting the nation against terrorism. According to the department's budget request data for fiscal year 2015, the Department of Justice "is comprised of approximately 40 components that have a broad array of national security, law enforcement, and criminal justice system responsibilities."[105] The budget request sought $27.4 billion to fund 116,788 employees.[106]

Not to be outdone, the Office of the Director of National Intelligence operates the National Counterterrorism Center (NCTC) out of a spiffy, new, modern complex in McLean, Virginia. As of July 13, 2017, according to the homepage of the NCTC on the DNI website, its mission is:

---

102. "Fusion Center Locations and Contact Information," Department of Homeland Security website. Accessed July 15, 2017. http://www.dhs.gov/fusion-center-locations-and-contact-information.
103. *Ibid.*
104. *Ibid.*
105. US Department of Justice Budget Overview for FY 2015, Department of Justice website. Accessed July 15, 2017. http://www.justice.gov/sites/default/files/jmd/legacy/2013/11/21/fy15-bud-sum.pdf.
106. *Ibid.*

We lead and integrate the national counterterrorism (CT) effort by fusing foreign and domestic CT information, providing terrorism analysis, sharing information with partners across the CT enterprise, and driving whole-of-government action to secure our national CT objectives.

One of the things NCTC does is maintain a watch list of terrorist names. Called the Terrorism Identities Datamart Environment (TIDE), a fact sheet available on the NCTC section of the Director of National Intelligence website current as of February 1, 2017 stated this watch list contained the identities of 1.6 million names, including about 16,000 US persons.[107] Names may be duplicated because of spelling variations. Since spy and intelligence agencies are notoriously shy about their facts and figures, we have to rely on a February 2011 Congressional Research Service Report to learn it has a headquarters staff of "more than 500 personnel."[108] The center's aforementioned homepage does identify its 17 "key partners" from the federal government.

Since counterterrorism inside the United States is largely viewed as a law enforcement matter, it's interesting to view the total number of federal law enforcement officers that can be put to bear at any given time. The Bureau of Justice Statistics (BJS) issued a report in June 2012 entitled "Federal Law Enforcement Officers, 2008" that cited data from the 2008 Census of Federal Law Enforcement Officers conducted by the bureau. The report summarized:

In September 2008, federal agencies employed approximately 120,000 full-time law enforcement officers who were authorized to make arrests and carry firearms in the United States. This was the equivalent of 40 officers per 100,000 residents. The number of federal officers in the United States increased by about 15,000,

---

107. "Terrorist Identities Datamart Environment," National Counterterrorism Center section of Director of National Intelligence website, February 1, 2017. Accessed July 13, 2017. https://www.dni.gov/files/NCTC/documents/features_documents/TIDEfactsheet10FEB2017.pdf.

108. Richard A. Best, Jr., "The National Counterterrorism Center (NCTC) – Responsibilities and Potential," website of the Federation of American Scientists, February 1, 2011. Accessed July 13, 2017. https://fas.org/sgp/crs/intel/R41022.pdf.

or 14%, between 2004 and 2008. Federal agencies also employed nearly 1,600 officers in the U.S. territories in 2008, primarily in Puerto Rico.[109]

The report went on to add:

> *... The four largest agencies, two in the Department of Homeland Security (DHS) and two in the Department of Justice (DOJ), employed about two-thirds of all officers. Overall, DHS and DOJ agencies employed about 4 in 5 federal officers.*[110]

BJS went on to report on the numbers of state and local law enforcement officers in the United States in 2008, citing the findings of the Census of State and Local Law Enforcement Agencies for that year:

> *In September 2008, state and local law enforcement agencies employed more than 1.1 million persons on a full-time basis, including about 765,000 sworn personnel (defined as those with general arrest powers). Agencies also employed approximately 100,000 part-time employees, including 44,000 sworn officers.*[111]

But even the local, state, and federal governments aren't the only ones in the counterterrorism game. Since 9/11 an entire industry has sprung up to feed the insatiable appetite of the counterterrorism bureaucracy. Many thousands of employees from private companies and commercial contractors assist their federal counterparts. The extensive "Top Secret America" investigation by *Washington Post* journalists Dana Priest and William Arkin in 2010 showed how the entire federal counterterrorism enterprise had become a growth industry for the private sector:

- Some 1,271 government organizations and 1,931 private companies work on programs related to counterterrorism, homeland

---

109. "Federal Law Enforcement Officers, 2008," Bureau of Justice Statistics website. Accessed July 15, 2017. http://www.bjs.gov/content/pub/pdf/fleo08.pdf.
110. *Ibid.*
111. "Census of State and Local Law Enforcement Agencies, 2008," Bureau of Justice Statistics website. Accessed July 15, 2017. http://www.bjs.gov/content/pub/pdf/csllea08.pdf.

security and intelligence in about 10,000 locations across the United States.

- An estimated 854,000 people, nearly 1.5 times as many people as live in Washington, D.C., hold top-secret security clearances.

- In Washington and the surrounding area, 33 building complexes for top-secret intelligence work are under construction or have been built since September 2001. Together they occupy the equivalent of almost three Pentagons or 22 US Capitol buildings – about 17 million square feet of space.

- Many security and intelligence agencies do the same work, creating redundancy and waste. For example, 51 federal organizations and military commands, operating in 15 American cities, track the flow of money to and from terrorist networks.

- Analysts who make sense of documents and conversations obtained by foreign and domestic spying share their judgment by publishing 50,000 intelligence reports each year – a volume so large that many are routinely ignored.[112]

If Priest and Arkin are to be believed, we have created a counterterrorism juggernaut composed of 1,271 government organizations and 1,931 private companies in 10,000 locations around the country. Add to that the roughly one million federal, state, and local law enforcement officers and only the Pentagon exceeds this entity in size. Bearing in mind that these statistics are several years old and today's figures are undoubtedly higher, does that sound nimble, agile, and responsive to you? And it's all focused tactically on defending the nation from terrorist attacks. One wonders if there is any strategic component aimed at defeating the ideology that produces the terrorism in the first place.

What we do know of large government bureaucracies is that they never go away. Their only objective is to grow ever larger and perpetuate

---

112. Dana Priest and Willian Arkin, "Top Secret America," *Washington Post*, July 19, 2010. Accessed July 15, 2017. http://projects.washingtonpost.com/top-secret-america/articles/a-hidden-world-growing-beyond-control/.

themselves. All those government organizations are comprised of little bureaucratic fiefdoms that are competing with each other for more and more resources and money. This bloated bureaucratic beast will never die. It's a Beltway Bandit's dream.

We have placed a lot of eggs in a basket that cannot win this war for us. In fact, it has no vested interests in winning – that would threaten the beast's very existence. Playing to win would be bureaucratic suicide. The system in its current form is part of the problem, not part of the solution.

The second major problem I have with counterterrorism is that we haven't been very good at it. There's no shortage of high-profile evidence for this.

Let's start with the April 15, 2013 Boston Marathon bombing by the two Tsarnaev brothers. This incident killed three persons and injured more than 170.

The *Boston Globe* newspaper did a five-month investigation on the brothers that it published on December 15, 2013. The paper chronicled the dysfunctional nature of the whole family and the difficulty they experienced as a Chechen family adapting to life in America after allegedly escaping persecution in their homeland in 2003. The troubled path of the older brother, Tamerlan, toward radicalization was firmly established and the FBI investigated him after being tipped off by the Russians, who had intercepted a conversation between Tamerlan and his mother, Zubeidat, in which they allegedly mentioned *jihad*. But after a three-month investigation, the FBI closed the case in 2011 and was merely satisfied to add their names into a terrorism database. That was it.

Foreign Policy magazine looked at the FBI's handling of this investigation in an April 25, 2013 article entitled "Did the FBI Bungle the Tsarnaev Case?" Author David Gomez analyzed what the FBI did and what it was authorized to do, in view of the fact that the Tsarnaev brothers were US persons under the law. The FBI opened what was called a Foreign Police Cooperation case after the Russians informed them about the alleged *jihadist* conversation. But the Russians never responded to requests for further information from the FBI and the bureau never found any solid evidence of involvement in a terrorist activity so the case was eventually closed. Gomez concluded that the FBI had played by the rules at the time and had not "bungled" the case.[113]

Here is a case where a suspected terrorist is reported to the FBI, which then carries out a perfunctory investigation and closes the file. Two years later he and his brother set off two pressure cooker bombs at the Boston Marathon, kill or maim scores of innocent people, shoot a policeman in cold blood, and hijack a man's car. The FBI did what it was supposed to do according to the procedures of the day, but it still failed to stop the crime.

There is more evidence of incidents that could have been stopped but weren't.

In 2009, US Army Major Nidal Malik Hasan opened fire on his fellow soldiers at Fort Hood, Texas killing 13 persons and wounding 30 more. It turned out that Hasan had also attracted the interest of the counterterrorism establishment.

According to Priest and Arkin, Hasan's behavior at Walter Reed Army Medical Center, where he had received training as a psychiatrist, had become "increasingly strange." He allegedly warned commanders that Muslims should be allowed to "leave the Army" or they would risk "adverse events." Hasan was also known to be exchanging emails with a "radical cleric in Yemen" who was under surveillance by US intelligence agencies.

But the Army's counterintelligence organization, the 902nd Military Intelligence Group, was not following up on any of these worrisome clues. Instead of performing its counterintelligence mission, the unit's commander focused on "assessing general terrorist affiliations in the United States," duplicating the efforts of the Department of Homeland Security and the FBI's terrorism task forces. The 902nd's efforts to collect intelligence on Hezbollah, Iran's Revolutionary Guard, and Al-Qaeda "student organizations" did not provide any information that the Pentagon didn't already know. Instead of red-flagging Hasan's activities, the unit wasted its time duplicating the work of others while failing in "the much more

---

113. David Gomez, "Did the FBI Bungle the Tsarnaev Case?," *Foreign Policy Magazine*, April 25 2013. Accessed July 15, 2017. http://www.foreignpolicy.com/articles/2013/04/25/ fbi_tamerlan_tsarnaev_investigation.

challenging job of trying to identify potential *jihadist* sympathizers within the Army itself."[114]

The Christmas Day 2009 case of the underwear bomber, Umar Farouk Abdulmutallab, is yet another incident where the US counterterrorism enterprise dropped the ball. The bomber's own father sounded the alarm over his son's radicalization to Nigerian authorities who then took the man to meet directly with the CIA station chief in the Nigerian capital.[115] US officials put the bomber's name on a watch list of terrorism suspects but never added it to the country's no-fly list.

So there was no reason to prevent Abdulmutallab from boarding Northwest Airlines Flight 253. Far from the complex terrorist operations of 9/11, this was meant to be an extremely simple operation where a single terrorist would set off explosives that had been concealed in his underwear. And despite the alert from the top CIA official in Nigeria, it wasn't our counterterrorism enterprise that stopped Abdulmutallab from perpetrating a terrorist tragedy and killing hundreds of people. It was a vigilant passenger onboard the aircraft.

Then-White House counterterrorism advisor (and later CIA director) John Brennan later stated: "We didn't follow up and prioritize the stream of intelligence because no one intelligence entity, or team or task force was assigned responsibility for doing that follow-up investigation." And in true bureaucratic fashion, then-Director of National Intelligence Blair lobbied Congress for "more money and more analysts to prevent another mistake."[116]

In another mulligan by the federal counterterrorism apparatus, Faisal Shahzad attempted to set off a car bomb in New York's Times Square on May 1, 2010. Shahzad, an American of Pakistani origin, traveled to Pakistan for terrorist training and contacted the US-born Al-Qaeda cleric, Anwar al-Awlaki, in Yemen (and other terrorist notables) via the Internet

---

114. Priest and Arkin, "Top Secret America."
115. Dana Hughes and Kirit Rada, "'Underwear Bomber's' Alarming Last Phone Call," *ABC News*, December 31, 2009. Accessed July 15, 2017. http://abcnews.go.com/WN/bombers-phone-call-father/story?id=9457361.
116. *Ibid.*

all without attracting any attention from anyone in law enforcement, from the federal level on down.[117]

There are plenty of similar examples but these four prominent incidents I've referenced above represent glaring indictments of our existing counterterrorism enterprise. Only fate and good fortune prevented the Times Square bombing and the Abdulmutallab attempt from resulting in a large loss of life. We weren't that lucky in San Bernardino or Chatanooga in 2015 or at the Pulse Nightclub in 2016. They are all indicative of the same kind of bureaucratic incompetence that led to 9/11 in the first place.

Our government has too much bloat and blubber to be effective at performing virtually any of its responsibilities. Look no further than the 2014 hacks of the sensitive personal data of nearly 22 million current and former federal employees from the Office of Personnel Management (OPM). Then there are the hacks of confidential taxpayer information from the Internal Revenue Service. And let's not forget that Edward Snowden walked out of a supposedly ultra secure facility with over a million classified documents in his pocket. How can this be happening with all the money we're spending playing defense?

The intelligence, law enforcement, and counterterrorism communities will justifiably point to the difficulty in sifting through dozens, hundreds, and even thousands of potential terrorism suspects in order to identify those who are truly serious threats. They will also respond that their successes happen quietly, without any public attention or fanfare, while their failures and shortcomings are often front-page headlines. That's true, too.

But despite over a million federal employees, contractors, and federal, state, and local law enforcement officers and billions of dollars of new infrastructure and the latest technical hardware, we still seem to strike out at least as often as we succeed. It will be impossible for this system to find every needle in every haystack every time. We taxpayers should start asking ourselves whether there is a better and more effective way

---

117. Richard Esposito, Chris Vlasto and Chris Cuomo, "Sources: Shahzad Had Contact with Awlaki, Taliban Chief, and Mumbai Massacre Mastermind," *ABC News*, May 6, 2010. Accessed July 15, 2017. http://abcnews.go.com/Blotter/faisal-shahzad-contact-awlaki-taliban-mumbai-massacre-mastermind/story?id=10575061.

of protecting ourselves that does not involve the erosion of personal privacies and freedoms. And while effective counterterrorism must be an important part of our playbook, it will not be the key to our victory in this war.

FIGHTING WARS WITHOUT A STRATEGY LEADS TO DEFEAT

History has clearly shown us that when we fight wars without any strategy whatsoever we lose, and when we fight wars with a strategy for victory we win. But having the wrong strategy is just as bad as having none at all. And make no mistake about it, our Global War on Islamism is a war that we must not only take seriously, but one that requires a comprehensive strategy if we are going to win it. I don't think any of us would relish the consequences if we were to lose.

In order to make my point, let's first take the example of the Vietnam War. It was a war that lacked any semblance of a strategy for achieving victory. President Lyndon Johnson was so worried about some action in Vietnam starting World War III with Russia or China that he made victory in Vietnam impossible. You can't make strategic bombing targets off limits and expect to win. You can't call arbitrary halts to the bombing and expect to win. You can't have the White House compiling the lists of bombing targets every day and expect to win. And when the overarching strategy of fighting the war is based solely on avoiding a new war with another superpower, defeat is pretty much assured.

Historians have rendered their verdicts on the Vietnam War. It was a strategic blunder by the United States with a defeat that has had lasting effects on our society, our politicians, our foreign policy, and our military. The lack of a strategy for victory created a quagmire of confusion over what we were really doing there. US soldiers would fight and die to take some godforsaken hill in the middle of nowhere only to withdraw and give it back to the enemy for no reason whatsoever. Formations of B-52 bombers would fly the same routes at the same times to and from Hanoi during the Christmas bombing. It was more akin to an airline schedule than a bombing run and it's pretty hard not to incur losses when the enemy knows where you're coming from and when. This is not the way to prosecute a war and achieve victory.

145

Without a strategic plan for victory, our loss in Vietnam came as no surprise. The only surprise comes in how long we managed to continue the war effort under such dismal circumstances and with such devastating results. Thus, from the Vietnam experience we can deduce that the prosecution of any war without a clear strategy for winning that war will likely result in defeat with an unacceptable cost in lives and assets, and all its accompanying long-term emotional, cultural, and societal baggage. If there is any one takeaway from the Vietnam conflict, it is that we must never again fight another war without a strategy for victory on day one. Plans almost never survive first contact with the enemy in warfare but the strategic objectives will still remain the same. Plans change but strategies endure.

FIGHTING WARS WITH A STRATEGY LEADS TO VICTORY

In contrast to our sobering experience in Vietnam, we also have some shining examples of what happens when we do have a winning strategy and we execute it.

The best example of this is World War II. America did employ a grand strategy during the Second World War that was summarized in winning the war in Europe first, and then defeating Japan. From the US Army's initial defeat at Kasserine Pass, the British and American armies eventually pushed Germany's renowned *Afrika Korps* out of North Africa. The US Eighth Air Force mounted daylight strategic bombing raids on targets throughout Nazi Europe that whittled away the enemy's industrial infrastructure and eroded his ability to wage war. At night the British Royal Air Force carpet-bombed German cities, killing thousands of civilians and sapping their will to support Hitler and his war effort.

In contrast to the constant pummeling inflicted upon the Third Reich's industrial heartland, American factories were free and unfettered to churn out ships, tanks, and airplanes in the tens of thousands, supplying not only our own forces but those of our allies (like Russia) as well. We steadily strangled Hitler's supply lines by mercilessly bombing occupied Europe's road and rail networks and Allied naval and air assets defeated his U-boat wolfpacks in the Atlantic – Germany's only real threat to our logistics.

As the war progressed, we became stronger and stronger while the *Wehrmacht* became weaker and weaker. By the time of the Allied D-Day invasion on June 6, 1944 the Russians already had Germany's army in full retreat along the Eastern Front. The Normandy invasion put the final nail in the Axis Powers' coffin and while the fighting was often brutal and desperate, the Allies' strategy of wearing down the German war machine and avoiding a war of attrition ensured their ultimate success.

The US campaign in the Pacific during World War II was no less strategic. Beginning with the Doolittle Raid on April 18, 1942 America quickly began taking the war to the Japanese themselves. The raid itself didn't do much damage but it gave a much-needed shot in the arm to sagging American morale at home and it brought surprise and disgrace to Japan, whose military leaders believed their island to be impregnable against such an attack.

In the Battle of Midway in June 1942, the United States Navy inflicted losses in ships and aircraft upon the enemy from which the Japanese would never recover. In August of the same year US Marines landed on Guadalcanal in the Solomon Islands as the first stop of an island-hopping campaign that eventually drove the Japanese forces from the Gilbert, Marshall, and Mariana Islands all the way back to the Japanese home islands of Iwo Jima and Okinawa.

From airstrips on desolate islands like Tinian we mounted massive B-29 raids on Japan in mid-1944 that culminated in the firebombing of major cities like Tokyo. These raids inflicted huge losses on the Japanese while the Americans suffered relatively few casualties. Japanese industrial production was all but eliminated even before the atomic bombs fell on Hiroshima and Nagasaki in August 1945.

The United States emerged from World War II not only as a victor but also as the dominant military, economic, and political power in the entire post-war world. We devised and executed a detailed, comprehensive strategy for a military campaign that spanned the entire globe and we settled for nothing less than the unconditional surrender of Germany, Italy, and Japan. There was a roadmap for absolute victory with the achievement of incremental benchmarks of success. In both the European and Pacific Theaters, we stopped *reacting* to events relatively quickly and began *controlling the operational tempo* – meaning we went on the offensive and took the fight to our enemies and we didn't stop until they were *completely vanquished*. This is exactly the kind of commitment that is missing from our counterterrorism-based effort today.

There's something else about our World War II strategy that bears remembering. We led an international effort with global allies like Great Britain and Russia and regional allies in various theaters around the world. We didn't win the war on our own and we didn't have to fight it alone, either.

In a similar vein, we will need both strategic global and regional allies in our war against the ideology of Islamism. We cannot fight and win this war on our own nor do we have to.

SOME INTERESTING PARALLELS BETWEEN WORLD WAR II AND THE WAR ON ISLAMISM

Since we've just seen how a clear, comprehensive strategy was critical to our victory in World War II, it's also interesting to note some of the parallels between that conflict and our war against Islamism:

Surprise attacks

We were plunged into what was considered an existential conflict with the surprise attack on December 7, 1941 against Pearl Harbor by the Empire of Japan in much the same way as the unexpected attacks on 9/11 against the World Trade Center and the Pentagon. The Japanese attack killed around 2,400 Americans[118] and the Al-Qaeda attacks killed 2,977.[119] Both incidents unified Americans across the political and social spectrum and

---

118. "Pearl Harbor Casualties," PearlHarbor.org website. Accessed July 15, 2017. http://www. pearlharbor.org/history/casualties/pearl-harbor-casualties/.
119. "September 11th Fast Facts," *CNN*, September 7, 2015. Accessed July 15, 2017. http:// www.cnn.com/2013/07/27/us/september-11-anniversary-fast-facts/.

galvanized citizens to action – in both cases spurring America's youth to join the military in a spirit of patriotism.

Warning signs

Both of these wars had warning signs leading up to the Pearl Harbor and 9/11 attacks. Japan invaded Manchuria in 1931 and parts of China in 1937. In the decade leading up to World War II Japan made no secret of its desire and strategic goal to drive what it saw as Western imperialists like the United States and Great Britain out of Asia. And in September 1940, one year after Hitler's invasion of Poland that sparked the Second World War, Japan concluded the Tripartite Pact with Germany and Italy that formed the Axis Powers.

By the spring of 1941, it is well known that President Franklin Roosevelt was actively cooperating with the British against the Germans and the US Navy was escorting naval convoys to England and actively firing on U-boats that sought to interdict this shipping, although the Germans were still reluctant to shoot back. It seems a logical conclusion that Roosevelt was anticipating American involvement in the European war against Hitler so it would also seem probable that he foresaw war with Japan, as well, after its conclusion of the Tripartite Pact with Germany and Italy.

Our war against Al-Qaeda should also have come as no surprise.

On August 7, 1998 Al-Qaeda really introduced itself to the mainstream American public when it carried out the twin bombings of the US embassies in Nairobi, Kenya and Dar es Salaam, Tanzania. The Nairobi bombing killed 224 (including 12 Americans) and wounded 4,650. The attack in Dar es Salaam killed ten Tanzanians.[120] Then-President Bill Clinton responded to the attacks by firing some 75 Tomahawk cruise missiles at alleged terrorist targets in Afghanistan and Sudan almost two weeks later due to the "imminent threat" posed to the United States by Osama bin Laden and his Al-Qaeda organization.[121]

---

120. "1998 U.S. Embassies in Africa Bombings Fast Facts," *CNN*, July 27, 2015. Accessed July 15, 2017. http://www.cnn.com/2013/10/06/world/africa/africa-embassy-bombings-fast-facts/.
121. *Ibid.*

On October 12, 2000 – a scant 11 months before the attacks of September 11, 2001 – suicide bombers from bin Laden's group ripped a hole in the hull of the USS *Cole* as it was in port for refueling in Aden, Yemen. The blast killed 17 US sailors and injured 39 others.[122]

In a chilling harbinger of things to come, the *Washington Post* reported in July 2004 that the December 4, 1998 edition of the President's Daily Brief warned President Clinton of an Al-Qaeda plot to hijack US airliners "in an effort to force the United States to release imprisoned conspirators in the 1993 World Trade Center attacks."[123]

And bin Laden himself declared war on America in the February 23, 1998 *fatwa* issued by his World Islamic Front:

> *The Arabian Peninsula has never — since God made it flat, created its desert, and encircled it with seas — been stormed by any forces like the crusader armies spreading in it like locusts, eating its riches and wiping out its plantations. All this is happening at a time in which nations are attacking Muslims like people fighting over a plate of food. In the light of the grave situation and the lack of support, we and you are obliged to discuss current events, and we should all agree on how to settle the matter.*

> *No one argues today about three facts that are known to everyone; we will list them, in order to remind everyone:*

> *First, for over seven years the United States has been occupying the lands of Islam in the holiest of places, the Arabian Peninsula, plundering its riches, dictating to its rulers, humiliating its people, terrorizing its neighbors, and turning its bases in the*

---

122. "USS *Cole* Bombing Fast Facts," *CNN*, September 24, 2015. Accessed July 15, 2017. http://www.cnn.com/2013/09/18/world/meast/uss-cole-bombing-fast-facts/.

123. Susan Schmidt, "1998 Memo Cited Suspected Hijack Plot by Bin Laden," *Washington Post*, July 18, 2004, A17.

Peninsula into a spearhead through which to fight the neighboring Muslim peoples.

If some people have in the past argued about the fact of the occupation, all the people of the Peninsula have now acknowledged it. The best proof of this is the Americans' continuing aggression against the Iraqi people using the Peninsula as a staging post, even though all its rulers are against their territories being used to that end, but they are helpless.

Second, despite the great devastation inflicted on the Iraqi people by the crusader-Zionist alliance, and despite the huge number of those killed, which has exceeded 1 million... despite all this, the Americans are once again trying to repeat the horrific massacres, as though they are not content with the protracted blockade imposed after the ferocious war or the fragmentation and devastation.

So here they come to annihilate what is left of this people and to humiliate their Muslim neighbors.

Third, if the Americans' aims behind these wars are religious and economic, the aim is also to serve the Jews' petty state and divert attention from its occupation of Jerusalem and murder of Muslims there. The best proof of this is their eagerness to destroy Iraq, the strongest neighboring Arab state, and their endeavor to fragment all the states of the region such as Iraq, Saudi Arabia, Egypt, and Sudan into paper statelets and through their disunion and weakness to guarantee Israel's survival and the continuation of the brutal crusade occupation of the Peninsula.

All these crimes and sins committed by the Americans are a clear declaration of war on God, his messenger, and Muslims. And ulema have throughout Islamic history unanimously agreed that the jihad is an individual duty if the enemy destroys the Muslim countries. This was revealed by Imam Bin-Qadamah in "Al – Mughni," Imam al-Kisa'i in "Al-Bada'i," al-Qurtubi in his interpretation, and the shaykh of al-Islam in his books, where he said: "As for the fighting to repulse [an enemy], it is aimed at defending sanctity and religion, and it is a duty as agreed [by the ulema]. Nothing is more sacred than belief except repulsing an enemy who is attacking religion and life."

On that basis, and in compliance with God's order, we issue the following fatwa to all Muslims:

The ruling to kill the Americans and their allies — civilians and military — is an individual duty for every Muslim who can do it in any country in which it is possible to do it, in order to liberate the al-Aqsa Mosque and the holy mosque [Mecca] from their grip, and in order for their armies to move out of all the lands of Islam, defeated and unable to threaten any Muslim. This is in accordance with the words of Almighty God, "and fight the pagans all together as they fight you all together," and "fight them until there is no more tumult or oppression, and there prevail justice and faith in God."

This is in addition to the words of Almighty God: "And why should ye not fight in the cause of God and of those who, being weak, are ill-treated (and oppressed)? — women and children, whose cry is: 'Our Lord, rescue us from this town, whose people are oppressors; and raise for us from thee one who will help!'"

We — with God's help — call on every Muslim who believes in God and wishes to be rewarded to comply with God's order to kill the Americans and plunder their money wherever and whenever they find it. We also call on Muslim ulema, leaders, youths, and soldiers to launch the raid on Satan's U.S. troops and the devil's supporters allying with them, and to displace those who are behind them so that they may learn a lesson.[124]

FANATICISM AND SUICIDE

Another interesting parallel from World War II and the war on Islamist extremism is the use of suicide forces by both the Japanese and radical terrorists. Both the Japanese and the terrorists even used religion as a justification for suicide.

In the Japanese military, the *samurai* spirit and code of *Bushido* required death instead of capture or defeat and the perceived shame that would be brought upon oneself, one's family, the Japanese military, and most damningly, the Japanese emperor. Japanese kamikaze pilot Yasuo Kuwahara summarized the philosophy as follows:

"A samurai lives in such a way that he will always be prepared to die." Every Japanese fighting man knew these words. "We are expendable." "Be resolved that honor is heavier than the mountains and death lighter than a feather." This was all part of the timeless pattern, an ancient and revered religious philosophy, national Shintoism.[125]

Nowhere was this ideology of suicide over capture more apparent that in the series of island invasions in the Pacific Theater during the Second World War. In most cases, very few Japanese soldiers were taken prisoner at the end of each operation. For example, in the November 1943 Battle of Tarawa, only 17 Japanese prisoners of war were taken out of a total garrison of 4,836 soldiers.[126] A year later at Peleliu, out of an original force of 11,000 Japanese only seven soldiers and 12 Japanese sailors were taken

---

124. Travis McGee post on September 9, 2001 (1:17:25 PDT), "Text of Fatwa by Bin Laden Ordering Moslems [sic] to Kill Americans," *Free Republic.* Accessed July 15, 2017. http://www.freerepublic.com/focus/f-news/530420/posts.

125. Yasuo Kuwahara and Gordon T. Allred, *Kamikaze: A Japanese Pilot's Own Spectacular Story of the Famous Suicide Squadrons* (New York: Ballantine Books, 1957) 124.

126. "Casualties," Tarawa on the Web website, January 14, 2001. Accessed July 15, 2017. http://tarawaontheweb.org/caschart.htm.

prisoner.[127] And at Iwo Jima, "Fewer than 250 Japanese soldiers out of a force of more than twenty-one thousand survived the fighting."[128]

When we think of Japanese suicide attacks, we most often we think of the infamous *kamikaze* pilots who began aiming their planes at American and Allied naval ships in mass attacks beginning in the latter half of 1944. Translated as "Divine Wind" the term originally referred to typhoons that had thwarted Mongolian invasion fleets in the thirteenth century.

For their part, Islamist terrorists have also embraced the suicide weapon in the form of a car or truck bomb or a person wearing a vest containing explosives. Since suicide is prohibited in Islam, those espousing radical Islamist views usually refer to what we call "suicide bombing" as *istishhad* – martyrdom – because the intent of the act is not to kill oneself but to fight in the cause of God and death comes only as a consequence of that fight. The Muslim Public Affairs Council provides some rather ambiguous and non-committal guidance on the matter.

On the one hand, the council states that Islam views suicide "strictly as sinful and detrimental to one's spiritual journey." But since humans are prone to committing mistakes, God will forgive and expiate their sins if they are "truly sincere in repentance." On the other, it acknowledges that some hold the opinion that the act of death in the course of *jihad* is not suicide, but rather martyrdom. The council says that there is Koranic scripture to counter this view since those who kill innocents are "wrong-doers and transgressors," but recognizes that some people do claim that Islam permits "the use of suicide" against the unjust if one feels "no other option" is available.[129]

Like the divine message in any religion, one can select individual verses and scriptures to support just about any opinion. Those citing the Koran's prohibition on suicide may cite:

---

127. Eugene B. Sledge, *With the Old Breed, at Peleliu and Okinawa* (Novato, California: Presidio Press, 1981) 155.
128. James A. Warren, *American Spartans: The US Marines: A combat history from Iwo Jima to Iraq* (New York: Free Press, 2005) 35.
129. "Religious Views on Suicide," Muslim Public Affairs Council website. Accessed July 15, 2017. http://www.mpac.org/programs/anti-terrorism-campaign/islamic-views-regarding-terrorism-and-suicidem/religious-views-on-suicide.php.

And spend in the way of Allah and do not throw [yourselves] with your [own] hands into destruction. Do good; indeed Allah loves the doers of good. (Koran 2:195).

Those supporting the martyrdom angle can cite the following verse:

Do not consider those who have been killed in the cause of Allah as dead. Rather, they live with their Lord who sustains them. (Koran 3:169).

Given the breadth of the chasm that separates the *Sunni* and *Shia* branches of Islam and each side's burning hatred of the other, it's interesting to note that the modern use of suicide bombing began with the *Shia* and then was later embraced by the *Sunnis*. For example Iran's *Shia* proxies like *Hezbollah* and the Islamic *Jihad* Organization carried out attacks against US interests like the 1983 suicide truck bombings of the US embassy and Marine barracks in Beirut.

The modern *Sunni* concept of martyrdom and suicide bombing likely began after the Israeli occupation of Palestine where Palestinian resistance fighters – *fedayeen* – attacked Israeli targets inside occupied Palestine and Israel as well as the interests of Israel and its allies abroad. These *fedayeen* (literally "those who are willing to sacrifice themselves") began to appear in such movements as the Palestine Liberation Organization, Black September, and a myriad of other factions. These were the fighters the West viewed as terrorists who hijacked airliners and were responsible for the deaths of Israeli athletes at the Munich Olympics in 1970.

Initially there was an intrinsic difference between *Shia* martyrs and *Sunni fedayeen*. The *Shia* were willing to die in sacrifice to, and for the advancement of their Islamic cause. Evidence of this is the example I cited previously of thousands of Iranian *basijis* being marched through minefields during the 1980-1988 Iran-Iraq War so that those minefields could be cleared for Iranian assault troops to attack the Iraqis. They had to be prepared to sacrifice themselves for the sake of Iran, Ayatollah Khomeini, and *Shiism*, because it would clearly be a suicide mission.

155

Similarly, Lebanese *Shia* suicide bombers were endeavoring to rid their land of any US, Western, or Israeli presence and influence while advancing the role, influence, and prestige of *Shiism* in their homeland.

The concept of the *Sunni feda'y* (i.e., singular form of *fedayeen*), on the other hand, started out a little differently – especially in the context of the Palestinian cause. These *fedayeen* saw themselves dying for their cause primarily as a last resort. They wanted to hijack airplanes to gain concessions from Israel or Israeli allies; the threat of crashing these planes and killing themselves and everybody else aboard was a means toward achieving their ultimate goal but it was not the goal itself. These *fedayeen* operations were about advancing the goal of Palestinian independence and nationalism, not advancing an Islamic or Islamist agenda of any sort. Most often these operations sought the release of other *fedayeen* comrades imprisoned or jailed in various countries around the world.

Of course both the *Sunni* and *Shia* have long since adopted the tactic of using a suicide bomber – *shahid* – as a way of attacking their enemies. The concept of the *fedayeen*, i.e., the fighters who primarily wanted to live to fight another day, faded from popular usage as the Palestinians began sending suicide bombers to attack Israeli bus stops and restaurants in the early nineties. The *feda'y* was almost universally replaced by the *shahid* and now both the *Sunnis* and *Shia* in Iraq use suicide bombers to kill each other by the dozens on a daily basis.

It's also coincidental to note the similarities in the effects from the Japanese and Islamist use of suicide fighters. According to the Pacific War Online Encyclopedia, Japanese *kamikaze* attacks killed nearly 5,000 Allied servicemen and wounded another 4,800. Around 4,000 Japanese died in these attacks – about 125 *kamikaze* aircrew died for each Allied warship sunk.[130] While they were an effective terror weapon and had a great psychological effect on Allied naval personnel, the *kamikaze* attacks did not turn the tide of the war in Japan's favor. These attacks were fearsome and inflicted a terrible human cost, but they had no strategic effect on the war.

---

130. "Kamikazes," Pacific War Online Encyclopedia website. Accessed July 15, 2017. http://pwencycl.kgbudge.com/K/a/Kamikazes.htm.

Likewise, three-and-a-half decades of Islamist suicide bombings in the Middle East and around the world have killed tens of thousands of people and wreaked billions of dollars of damage yet they have had no *strategic* effect. The Palestinian territories (sans the Gaza Strip) are still occupied by Israel. Although the Lebanese civil war has officially ended, the various secular and religious factions inside that country are still using suicide bombers as the preferred tool with which to jockey for position. In fact, in just about any Arab or Middle Eastern country that is wracked by domestic unrest, the suicide bomber is nearly always a key player that adds to the population's misery but does very little to achieve an end result.

Existential Conflicts

Both World War II and the war on Islamist extremism can be seen as existential conflicts, but that isn't really accurate in the classical sense. If America had not prevailed during the Second World War, the most probable outcome would have been that we would have lost our access to Europe and the Pacific. Western Europe might have remained a Nazi fortress, Great Britain might have been subjugated, and Russia might have become marginalized but America is a vast country that is isolated by great oceans. The limited manpower resources of Germany and Italy would have made it unlikely they could have successfully occupied the United States.

During the war, we felt we were in a race with Germany to develop an atomic bomb but, realistically, the Nazi effort was mediocre at best. Even if the Third Reich had managed to construct one or two weapons they would not have had a means of delivering them to the United States (although they could have used them against England or Russia). Germany never managed to run the gauntlet of Allied air power in Britain and at sea to drop a single conventional bomb on the United States. Flying all the way across the Atlantic to drop a nuclear weapon on New York or Washington would have been out of the question.

German rockets were unreliable and inaccurate. Their ranges were limited to a few hundred miles and they relied on highly corrosive fuels that were extremely difficult to handle. As a result, German intercontinental ballistic missiles (ICBMs) were completely unfeasible and the fuel problem prevented any thought of launching them from a ship or U-boat.

A Nazi victory would have meant that America would have been cut off from its pre-war allies and friends in Europe, but left largely intact. Any defeat would have had political fallout in the United States but I doubt whether some kind of pro-German regime would suddenly have sprung up in America after years of bitter warfare.

Japan was always more interested in its own Asian-Pacific empire than in occupying the United States; its reason for the war was to expel America and the West from Asia, not occupy it. A Japanese victory would likely have cut us off from the Philippines, China, Malaysia, Indonesia, and the rest of the continent. We might have been pushed back from Hawaii. But, again, Japan would have been more interested in occupying its Asian-Pacific realm than conquering America. Even with its Asian interests truncated America would still have remained an integral nation on the North American continent. A post-war pro-Japanese government in the United States would have been even more unlikely than a pro-German one. Japan was the country that started our war with its attack on Pearl Harbor, after all.

Russia would have been pushed back farther to the east and the nations of Eastern and Central Europe would have been German possessions instead of Soviet ones. Our Cold War might have been replaced with a continuing ideological struggle between a victorious *Nazism* and a Russian communism on the defensive. Certainly Asia would look much different under the domination of the Empire of Japan but China would likely still have eventually emerged as a competitor for regional influence in the continent.

Existentially, the end result would have been that we would not have become what we did. We would not have been the post-war power that shaped the world. We would have been marginalized and isolated in a much different post-war world.

The Islamists, for their part, don't have the resources or capability to wipe us off the map, either. They don't have bunkers full of atomic bombs and silos of ICBMs pointed in our direction yet they have had a cumulative effect on our lives. This can be measured in the loss and erosion of personal liberties and freedoms in exchange for "security." Each time we lose a little freedom under the guise of making us safer, the Islamist terrorists score a little victory while we suffer a defeat. We actually make them stronger by hyping the threat.

The Islamists can, however, carry out coordinated, small-scale attacks inside our country that could erode our freedoms and liberties even further. What happens if they were to start a campaign of attacking soft targets like bus stations, restaurants, shopping malls, or churches? Imagine having to pass through a metal detector before you go shopping just because of some previous terrorist incident or perceived threat.

There are many things that terrorists could do that would deter us from going to a theater, attending a ballgame, having a Fourth of July picnic in the park, or even walking the dog after dinner. They don't have to destroy us with some Hollywood-inspired WMD attack when we can be cowed by simple lone wolf operations and uncertainty. That is what terrorism is all about so I guess that's existential enough for me. I want my old America back – the one with personal liberties and without the terrorism fears.

There is another angle to the lone wolf terrorist issue that needs some objective discussion. We already have a problem in our country with lone gunmen carrying out mass shootings and killings of innocent people who have absolutely nothing to do with Islamism or any other political cause. We have plenty of recent examples, for example:

- The April 20, 1999 Columbine High School massacre. Students Dylan Kliebold and Eric Harris killed 12 students and one teacher and injured over 20 others and then committed suicide. They were not Muslims or Islamists.

- The April 16, 2007 mass shooting carried out by Seung-Hui Cho at Virginia Tech University that killed 32 people and wounded nearly two-dozen others. Cho committed suicide. He was an emotionally troubled young man but he was neither a Muslim nor an Islamist.

- Jared Lee Loughner opened fire outside a Tucson, AZ supermarket on January 8, 2011 and seriously wounded US Representative Gabrielle Giffords and 18 others. He killed six. He was diagnosed as paranoid schizophrenic after his arrest but he was not a Muslim nor was he an Islamist

- On July 20, 2012 James Holmes opened fire inside a theater in Aurora, CO. He killed 12 and injured 70 others. He was mentally disturbed and used an insanity defense at his trial but he was not an Islamist or a Muslim.

- The infamous Sandy Hook Elementary School shooting took place in Newtown, Connecticut on December 14, 2012. Shooter Adam Lanza killed 20 children and six school staff before turning his gun on himself and taking his own life. Lanza had known emotional problems but he was neither a Muslim nor an Islamist.

- A mass shooting occurred at the Umpqua Community College in Roseburg, OR on October 1, 2015. Christopher Harper-Mercy killed nine people and wounded another nine before fatally shooting himself in a gun battle with police. Like the previous examples, this shooter may have had emotional issues but he was not a Muslim or Islamist.

- On June 18, 2015 a young man named Dylann Storm Roof walked into a Bible study and prayer group and the Emanuel African Methodist Episcopal Church in Charleston, SC. He opened fire on the group with a handgun and killed nine. He is alleged to be a white supremacist and racist but he was neither a Muslim nor an Islamist.

- On February 20, 2016 a series of random shootings killed six people and wounded two more. The shootings were attributed to a 45-year-old Uber driver named Jason Brian Dalton. He is neither a Muslim nor an Islamist.

I've got a problem with our focus on institutionalizing "lone wolf terrorism" by Islamist militants and somehow categorizing it differently than the crimes and mass murders carried out by gunmen such as those in the above examples. Bear in mind that these are just eight out of dozens of recent mass murder incidents in this country that had absolutely nothing to do with Islamists or Muslims yet these eight examples took the lives of over 100 innocent Americans. How can we not consider mass shootings at a school, church, or theater anything but domestic terrorism? What makes a potential mass shooting by a lone wolf Islamist more terroristic than a mass shooting by a mentally unstable young American male? Dead is still dead. Aren't Americans still killed or injured either way?

In my view troubled shooters like Adam Lanza or Jared Loughner are just as much of a lone wolf terrorist as Muhammad Youssef Abdulazeez, the perpetrator of the Chattanooga recruiting and military reserve centers on July 16, 2015 that killed six (including Abdulazeez) and wounded two. The shooter was a naturalized US citizen of Arab ethnicity from a conservative Muslim family. That has served to paint him as a violent Muslim extremist. But Abdulazeez also suffered from substance abuse and mental issues – just like most of the Americans on the above Murderers' Row.

The larger question to me is, "why are so many young American men so emotionally and mentally troubled? What causes so many of them to pick up a gun and go on a shooting spree one day?"

Our media and government like to portray the lone wolf terrorist as a unique and different type of boogeyman. It's justification for pumping a steady stream of money we don't have into the counterterrorism establishment in the blind and false belief it will somehow keep us safer. It's blatant sensationalism, a misdirection of scarce resources, and it's just plain wrong. The overall requirement on our authorities is to protect *all* American lives. The lives that may potentially be taken by homegrown, mentally unstable lone gunmen are just as important as those that might be taken by a so-called "lone wolf terrorist." There is no sliding scale of value on a victim's life based on some bureaucratic, political definition of what constitutes terrorism.

Bear in mind, the motives might be different but the *modus operandi* of such attacks are pretty much the same regardless of whether the shooter is a domestic crazy or a terrorist. That's what law enforcement should be focusing on. Let's drop sensationalist adjectives, protect lives, and keep politics and religion out of it. That's what the taxpayers are paying for.

TERRORISM IS AN EMOTIONAL RATHER THAN A STATISTICAL THREAT

When you look at the true statistical scale of the threat from Islamist terrorism versus other causes of preventable death in the United States, there are some surprising comparisons that one rarely hears reported in the media. For example, a September 2013 story by ProPublica reported on the number of deaths in America resulting from medical mistakes. The report began by citing a 1999 Institute of Medicine paper that estimated up to 98,000 patients die every year because of mistakes in hospitals. The Office of the Inspector General for Health and Human Services in 2010 reported that hospital care contributed to the deaths of *180,000 patients a year just in Medicare*. ProPublica then cited a 2013 paper that estimated patient deaths from medical mistakes at *between 210,000 and 440,000 per year*, making medical mistakes the third leading cause of death in America.[131]

In contrast, the Boston Marathon bombing in 2013 – the only Islamist terrorist attack to cause death that year – resulted in three deaths. Therefore, even if we take the extremely conservative 1999 estimate of 98,000 deaths each year from medical mistakes, *the number of Americans killed by medical mistakes in 2013 was 32,000 times greater than the number of those killed by terrorism.*

In 2014 the Veterans Health Administration scandal broke in which it was revealed that *dozens* of US veterans had died while waiting for medical appointments even as bureaucrats allegedly manipulated the records to make it appear that those patients did not experience untimely delays in seeing their doctors. This purported misrepresentation supposedly allowed those VA employees and bureaucrats to collect millions in bonuses. Thus, potential VA malfeasance that year ostensibly killed more Americans – veterans, of all people – than terrorism.

---

131. Marshall Allen, "How Many Die From Medical Mistakes in U.S. Hospitals?," ProPublica website, September 19, 2013. Accessed July 15, 2017. http://www.propublica.org/article/how-many-die-from-medical-mistakes-in-us-hospitals.

Similarly, the National Highway Traffic Safety Administration reported 32,719 fatalities on US roads from traffic accidents in 2013.[132] So, *nearly 11,000 times more Americans died in traffic crashes than from terrorism in 2013.*

But while the average American may face a far greater statistical threat of death or bodily injury from getting behind the wheel of his or her car or going into the hospital than from terrorism, those are risks with which everyone is familiar. Cars with advanced safety equipment and good driving habits can mitigate much of the driving risk and close monitoring of medical care by a patient or the patient's family can do the same during hospital stays. Even though these things kill more of us every year than terrorism, these are dangers that we understand. Nobody is actually trying to kill us in these cases and we can do relatively simple things to protect ourselves.

Terrorism is different because, by its very definition, the objective is to instill a visceral fear in its victims. You don't expect to be shot at a work Christmas party or a nightclub just because of your nationality or religion. There isn't very much you can personally do to prevent such a horrendous thing from happening. A seatbelt can't protect you from acts of terrorism and, sometimes, neither can the government.

I can understand the public's disproportionate fear of terrorism. Any time a terrorist attack takes place – here or elsewhere in the West – the event is saturated by media coverage. Television analysts often point fingers and assess blame even before the smoke has cleared. People want to know why their government and their authorities did not prevent the attack – and justifiably so. Terrorism is a crime and fighting crime is a government responsibility. But it's a fact of life that governments cannot always predict or prevent terrorist attacks (or other crimes). No government will ever have a 100% success rate.

That is why our counterterrorism measures must be complemented by the elements in this book to delegitimize and eliminate the Islamist ideology

---

132. "2013 Motor Vehicle Crashes: Overview," National Highway Traffic Safety Administration website, December 2014. Accessed July 15, 2017. https://crashstats. nhtsa.dot.gov/Api/Public/ViewPublication/812101.

at the strategic level. That is our best way to prevent future generations of vulnerable youth from succumbing to radicalization. I believe it is fair to say that those who become radicalized are actually terrorism's first victims and we should be doing all we can to prevent that from happening.

THE BEST DEFENSE IS A GOOD OFFENSE

The United States is the most powerful country the world has ever seen in every respect: militarily, economically, politically, and culturally. America's "brand" is the one most recognized throughout the globe. Everybody from Azerbaijan to Zimbabwe is familiar with Coca-Cola, Apple, and Michael Jackson. We invented the automobile and the airplane and landed men on the moon not once, but six times! We are the ones who created rock-and-roll, jazz, and the Internet. Yet we wring our hands and dither over what to do about the IS, a band of barbaric thugs using savagery and fear to turn the clock back to the Dark Ages in parts of Iraq and Syria. Sadly, the country that invented advertising, public relations, and Madison Avenue is getting whipped in the information war by a bunch of *takfirists* with social media savvy.

In World War II we *attacked our enemies on every field of battle.* We fought them on land, on (and under) the sea, and in the air. We used propaganda to great effect and sold war bonds to finance the effort. The people at home shared in the sacrifice made by those actually fighting through rationing programs that limited their own access to critical goods like tires, gasoline, automobiles, and even foods in order to support those at the front with whatever they needed for victory. As a people, Americans were united in fighting evil wherever it appeared and they were resolved that *we would win.*

Our president, Franklin Roosevelt, was committed to nothing less than complete victory. The fact that the American people overwhelmingly reelected him to an unprecedented fourth term left no doubt that they were equally resolved and steadfast to triumph unconditionally over the Axis Powers. There simply was no other option.

This commitment and certainty in the cause is what is missing in our country today. We face indecision in Washington about how to fight and defeat Islamist extremism because there is no obvious strategy for doing so. We often hear our leaders tell us what we *cannot* do rather than articulating a willingness to allocate the resources to achieve ultimate victory. This type of behavior does little to inspire any confidence that our government has a plan for winning this fight.

As the anticipation built that the long-awaited Iraqi offensive to retake Mosul from Islamic State was close at hand, we steadily boosted the number of US military forces in Iraq in the roles of trainers, advisors, and support personnel. But is there a plan for governing Mosul once IS is driven out? Will the largely *Shia* Iraqi Army refrain from the retributions it committed against *Sunnis* in its liberation of Tikrit?

Aside from liberating Mosul and, ultimately, the Syrian city of Raqqa and the *de facto* capital of Islamic State, what is our strategy for fighting and containing the group's offshoots in Yemen, Tunisia, Libya, Egypt, Afghanistan, and even parts of Asia? Simply reacting to our enemies sets the stage for one little shooting war after another that will cost us billions upon billions of dollars and still leave us with no strategic victory in sight. It is the result of fighting individual groups instead of targeting the strategic objective of their common Islamist ideology.

If we are to prevail in our *war* on Islamist and *takfirist* extremism, if we are to defeat our enemies and *put an end to their deviant beliefs once and for all*, then we need to go beyond the defense of counterterrorism and a limited offense that focuses only on fighting groups. Yes, counterterrorism is necessary but our existing enterprise will require greater speed, precision, and agility if it is to become more successful. Having a million cleared government employees – each with their individual chains of command in a myriad of different agencies – seems somewhat antithetical to the nimbleness that the counterterrorism mission requires. Moreover, shifting resources to delegitimize and eliminate the ideology that generates the terrorist groups to begin with will ultimately pave the way to making our counterterrorism mission more effective and less expensive.

At the same time, greater emphasis on offense should not mean overreliance on our military. We've seen that our 2003 invasion of Iraq did much to contribute to the environment of *Sunni-Shia* bloodshed and *Salafist* extremism that we are seeing there today. We will not win this war with air – and drone strikes or special forces raids. Defeating Islamism is an ideological issue, not a military one. Our judicious use of military force must be augmented with broader efforts at the popular, religious, and diplomatic levels.

Strategic vision and strategic planning in Washington have become lost arts that must be resurrected. President Franklin Roosevelt wasted no time agonizing over what restrictions he should place on how America could prosecute World War II. He had a commitment to unconditional victory with a clarity of vision that he communicated eloquently and enduringly to the American public. He and his administration crafted and implemented a strategy that focused all of America's military, industrial, agricultural, political, and cultural might on defeating the Axis Powers. I believe we would benefit from a similar dedication and single-mindedness today.

The phalanx of presidents, politicians, pundits, professors, and pontificators that has paraded through the past 35 years of our history doesn't seem any closer to a strategy for winning the war on Islamist extremism now than we were in 1979 when Iranian students took over the American Embassy in Tehran. As someone who has learned the language, spent years in the Middle East, studied the religion and the extremists' ideology, and worked on Arab and Middle East issues for four decades, the remaining chapters in this book are dedicated to my strategy for achieving victory over Islamism. They are dedicated to a future where the Islamist ideology has been relegated to the ash heap of history; a future in which we no longer face the threat of Islamist terrorists or Islamist groups. At the risk of repeating myself, that's what I think victory should look like.

THE PLAN

Image Credit: www.Pixabay.com
SteenJepsen

CHAPTER SIX

STEP ONE: LET'S STOP CALLING TERRORISM JIHAD

"The devil can cite Scripture for his purpose.
An evil soul producing holy witness
Is like a villain with a smiling cheek,
A goodly apple rotten at the heart.
O, what a goodly outside falsehood hath!"

– William Shakespeare, *The Merchant of Venice*

The first element in the strategy to defeat the ideology of Islamist extremism is one that can be accomplished immediately and doesn't cost a single penny. Nevertheless, it is a step that will have a profound impact on our struggle. We must recalibrate and rethink our ubiquitous use of the word *"jihad"* in referring to our terrorist enemies and their actions.

In order to understand the importance of this step, we need to know what *jihad* means. The definition of this Arabic word has evolved considerably over time from its initial use in the Koran and that's the problem. In the West, the word is widely understood only to mean a holy war by Muslims against non-Muslims. However, Islamic scholars and jurists over the years have rendered many different meanings and conflations of the word, so *jihad* in today's lexicon has a much more diverse connotation and usage from that found in Islam's holiest book.

At its simplest level, the word *jihad* translates to "struggle." This may be a personal struggle such as a person resisting sinful temptation. It may be the collective struggle of a people, such as Muslims struggling or striving to practice their faith in a hostile environment. There are many verses in the Koran that use the verbal form of the word to "struggle" against unbelievers (i.e., non-Muslims) but the actual noun – *jihad* – only appears in a couple of the book's scriptures (Koran 9:24 and 60:1). This "struggle" against unbelievers has been conflated by some as meaning a holy war against non-Muslims, although that definition is never unequivocally stated in the Koran itself.

Adding to this ambiguity, the term *jihad* is often used in the context of "struggling" in the cause of God (*jihad fi sabil lillah*). Many Islamic scholars have also conflated *jihad fi sabil lillah* with *qital fi sabil lilllah* (fighting in the cause of God). Thus, some online English translations of the Koran (and many clerics) make no distinction between *jihad* in the cause of God and fighting in the cause of God, although the Arabic text is very clear. Like any religious or divine message, it is open to mankind's interpretation. God may have known what He wanted to say but men hear only what they want to hear.

Here is an analogy, for the purpose of illustration. Christians have their own form of *jihad* (as it was defined in the Koran) in struggling to resist worldly temptations and doing their best to live their lives in accordance with God's commandments and instructions. In broader terms, people of faith in any religion try to do the same. The Koran just has a word for it.

Islam is an Abrahamic religion like Christianity and Judaism and it has its own Day of Judgment. Although each faith may have different versions of the concept, the central point for each is that every one of us must account for the actions of our lives to God or Allah. I know Muslims who hold a similar view of the Day of Judgment where every Muslim will be held accountable to Allah for what is in his or her heart, not whether or not he or she was a follower of Osama bin Laden or Ayman al-Zawahiri. The Koranic idea of *jihad* is more about doing the right thing in one's life, regardless of the difficulty. It isn't about killing unbelievers.

Nowhere is the meaning of *jihad* more diverse than among Muslims themselves. This was borne out in the 2002 Gallup Poll of the Islamic World in which Muslims were asked to explain what *jihad* meant to them. Given the almost universal negative connotation of *jihad* among Western non-Muslims, the poll's results were both surprising and interesting.

The poll surveyed over 10,000 adults in predominantly Muslim countries. All but 674 of those questioned were Muslims and they were asked to define *jihad* in just one or a few words. A "significant minority" of the respondents referenced *jihad* as "sacrificing one's life for the sake of Islam/God/a just cause." Interestingly, this response was the "most commonly identifiable pattern" in four non-Arab countries (Pakistan, Iran, Turkey, and Indonesia) but it was only expressed as an "outright majority" in Indonesia.

In the survey's four Arab countries (Lebanon, Kuwait, Jordan, and Morocco) there were no such militaristic responses at all. *Jihad* was most often described in these countries as a "duty toward God" or a "worship of God." This is a surprising result given the amount of religious violence we see in the Middle East and the Arab world.

Some of the other descriptions included "a commitment to hard work," "struggling to achieve a noble cause," and "promoting peace, harmony or cooperation, and assisting others." The survey concluded that among the global collective of Muslims, "the concept of *jihad* is considerably more nuanced that the single sense in which Western commentators invariably invoke the term."[133]

While Muslims' definition of the word may differ, the above poll does show that they have an overwhelmingly positive view of *jihad* as a religious duty. Whatever their individual interpretation may be, they collectively see it as some form of struggle in a righteous cause.

---

133. Richard Burkholder, "Jihad – 'Holy War', or Internal Spiritual Struggle?," Gallup, Inc., December 3, 2002. Accessed July 15, 2017. http://www.gallup.com/poll/7333/jihad-holy-war-internal-spiritual-struggle.aspx.

Candidly, many Muslims – to some degree – will acknowledge a militaristic aspect to the word. While the context of *jihad* in the Koran may be less specific and more nebulous and spiritual in nature, there is no doubt from hundreds of *hadiths* that the Prophet Muhammad considered his fight and war against the unbelievers – the infidels – to be a form of *jihad*. In fact, the *Sahih al-Bukhari* collection, which is considered the most authentic of the six major collections of *hadiths*, has an entire book on *jihad* with nearly 300 *hadiths* (Volume 4, Book 52, entitled: "Fighting for the Cause of God (*Jihad*)"). Here the context of *jihad* is invariably the act of going off somewhere to take part in a battle of Muslims against non-Muslims and this usage is consistent throughout Al-Bukhari's entire *hadith* collection.

This collection is quite significant because it was compiled by a Persian named Muhammad al-Bukhari who used a painstaking methodology to authenticate all the narratives, tracing them all the way back to the prophet himself, his companions, or other early Muslim figures. As a reminder, each *hadith* is made up of two parts. The first is the text or passage that was narrated and the second is the chain of narrators that goes all the way back to the original incident or utterance.

Bukhari relied on verifying that the original narrators of these sayings lived at the same time as the person/prophet/authority that was being cited and that there was verifiable proof that the original narrator had actually met that person or even the prophet Muhammad himself. Then he made a similar verification for the chain of narrators. This is crucial because other *hadith* collections do not always have such strong corroborative documentation or evidence. This is the reason why his collection is deemed the most genuine and accurate and why his *hadith* texts are called *Sahih al-Bukhari* – *sahih* meaning "authentic" or "genuine" in Arabic. Al-Bukhari's compilation is therefore a book of "authentic" narratives or *hadiths*.

Jihad as a holy war also appears in *Sahih Muslim*, another compilation of *hadith* passages put together by Muslim Ibn-al-Hajjaj. Like Al-Bukhari, Muslim Ibn-al-Hajjaj used a similar, tedious process to evaluate and verify the passages in his collection. And also like Al-Bukhari, he devoted an entire book of his collection to *jihad*: Book 19: "The Book of *Jihad* and Expedition."

Sahih Al-Bukhari and *Sahih Muslim* are both highly regarded canonical texts and *hadith* collections but other compilations view *jihad* in much the same light and they may devote an entire section to *jihad*.

Given the early history of Islam, this isn't all that surprising. Muhammad left his home city of Mecca (referred to as the "Hijra" or emigration) in the year 622 after being warned of a plot to assassinate him. He relocated to the city of Medina, where a small group of Muslims had earlier offered him their support. For the rest of his life – until 632 – Muhammad either participated in, or ordered scores of raids and expeditions against various tribes and peoples on the Arabian Peninsula that culminated in his conquest of Mecca in 630 and the defeat of his archenemy and nemesis there – the Quraysh tribe. The strategic purpose of these raids and expeditions was to spread Islam throughout the Arabian Peninsula, although some individual raids were aimed at acquiring financial resources or eliminating and punishing enemies. The Public Broadcasting System has produced an excellent chronological timeline of Muhammad's life[134] and there are numerous references listing his military accomplishments. There are numerous text and online references to Muhammad's military battles and expeditions.

It is no wonder that in the *hadiths*, *jihad* is portrayed less as the inward, spiritual struggle between right and wrong in the Koran and more as a physical fight or battle against those Muhammad perceived as the enemies of God. Hence the conflation between "*jihad* in the cause of God" and "fighting (*qital*) in the cause of God."

OFFENSIVE AND DEFENSIVE FORMS OF *JIHAD* IN WARFARE

In its militaristic sense of Muslims fighting unbelievers or infidels, *jihad* has both offensive and defensive forms. I think it is once again very

---

134. "Muhammad: Legacy of A Prophet," Public Broadcasting System website. Accessed July 15, 2017. http://www.pbs.org/muhammad/timeline_html.shtml.

important to reiterate that the word *jihad* is not conflated with warfare at all in the Koran – either offensively or defensively. The terms that are used for the two forms of *jihad* are terms that have been contrived by men – Islamic scholars who have rendered their opinions on Islamic rulings and jurisprudence over time.

The offensive form of *jihad* is called *jihad at-talab* and some Islamic scholars have cited verses from the Koran and various *hadiths* as evidence of the lawfulness of offensive war against the unbelievers even though those scriptures do not mention it specifically by name. Literally, *jihad at-talab* means "the *jihad* of the request" and the concept comes from one of the *hadiths* in the *Sahih Muslim* compilation in the book that specifically deals with military *jihad* where the prophet was heard to say:

> *Fight in the name of Allah and in the way of Allah, fight against those who disbelieve in Allah. Make a holy war; do not embezzle the spoils; do not break your pledge; and do not mutilate (the dead) bodies; do not kill the children. When you meet your enemies who are polytheists, invite them to three courses of action. If they respond to any of these, you also accept it and withhold yourself from doing any harm. Invite them to (accept) Islam; if they respond to you, accept it and desist from fighting against them. Then invite them to migrate from their lands to the land of the Muhajirs [i.e., Dar al-Islam] and inform them that, if they do so, they shall have all the privileges and obligations of the Muhajirs [i.e., those who have accepted Islam, become Muslims, and migrated to the Dar al-Islam]. If they refuse to migrate, tell them that they will have the status of Bedouin Muslims and will be subjected to the Commands of Allah like other Muslims, but they will not get any share from the spoils of war or Fai' except when they actually fight with the Muslims (against the disbelievers). If they refuse to accept Islam, demand from them the Jizya [i.e., a tax imposed on non-Muslims by Muslims]. If they agree to pay, accept it from them and hold off your hands. If they refuse to pay the tax, seek Allah's help and fight them.*[135]

---

135. *Sahih Muslim*, Book 19, Hadith 4294.

In the above *hadith*, it was clear that the Muslims in the Prophet Muhammad's time were allowed to confront the non-Muslims in their own lands and first ask, or request them to accept Islam. If they accepted Islam, then they would be asked to emigrate to the Realm of Islam and become Muslims therein with all the ensuing rights, privileges, and obligations.

If they did not accept Islam, then they would be asked to pay the *jizya* tax and if they refused, then the Muslims were allowed to "seek Allah's help and fight them."

Once again it is important here to stress the historical context of the *hadith*. It was during a time in Muhammad's life in which he was endeavoring to spread his faith throughout the Arabian Peninsula. Islam had not yet become a commonplace, worldwide religion. There was no Islamic Empire yet. The faith was still limited to a relatively small portion of the Arabian Desert. And as we know, the prophet spent the last ten years of his life fighting to spread Islam throughout the Arabian Peninsula and the instructions in the above *hadith* were said to be given to those commanders he sent out on military expeditions. And by "inviting (or requesting) them to three courses of action," those commanders were engaging in what Islamic scholars would eventually call the *jihad at-talab*.

Like specific issues in any religion, not every scholar has agreed with the concept of an offensive *jihad* against unbelievers or infidels. There are some who have pointed to the preceding historical context of Muhammad's time and have expressed an opinion that such verses relating to *jihad at-talab* have been abrogated. Others refer to the Islamic rules of warfare (which we'll discuss shortly) that indicate any permissible warfare can only be defensive in nature.

The scholars who favor the idea of an offensive *jihad* also point to several verses in the Koran for religious evidence. Foremost among these is the infamous Sword Verse that we discussed in chapter three:

And when the sacred months have passed, then kill the polytheists wherever you find them and capture them and besiege them and sit in wait for them at every place of ambush. But if they should repent, establish prayer, and give zakah, let them [go] on their way. Indeed, Allah is Forgiving and Merciful.[136]

From our previous examination of this scripture we know that several contemporary scholars hold that this verse (and similar verses in the same chapter) refers to a specific context involving polytheism and those who were denying the Oneness of God/Allah *in Muhammad's lifetime*. Nevertheless, it certainly is not uncommon for clerics in any religion to seize upon a single verse, pull it from its context, and render their own interpretation for their own purpose. Everybody has their own opinions and interpretations of the divine messages in virtually all religions and the situation with Islam isn't any different.

In any case, the majority opinion of the *ulema* over time seems to be that *jihad at-talab* is considered to be a "collective obligation" on Muslims rather than an "individual obligation." And the purpose of this offensive *jihad* is clearly to use military means, in conjunction with the *Da'wah* [i.e., "the call" or the non-violent Islamic missionary duty), to spread the religion around the world and impose God's law – the *Sharia* – throughout the earth.

There may also be some disagreement over the permissibility of offensive *jihad* among the four main *Sunni* schools of Islamic thought but the one which most Islamists claim to follow – the Hanbali school – largely equates *hadiths* with the Koran as primary source and evidentiary material in its religious rulings and *fatwas*. This gives them the religious cover and legitimacy to justify their violent and intolerant interpretation of *jihad* and *takfir*. The other schools rely on the Koran as the primary referential source for their religious rulings. (Note that there are several method-ologies used for rendering Islamic rulings. These are collectively called the "Fundaments of Islamic Jurisprudence" but a detailed discussion or examination of them is beyond the scope of this book.)

The defensive counterpart to *jihad at-talab* is called *jihad ad-dafa'* or the "*jihad* of defense." Unlike the concept of offensive *jihad*, there is universal consensus among the *ulema* that fighting to defend the Realm of Islam

---

136. Koran 9:5.

and the Muslims from any foreign aggression is an "individual obligation" upon all Muslims. Each individual is obligated to do whatever he or she can to avoid the suffering of other Muslims and the shedding of their blood.

This is merely self-defense, pure and simple, and any people, group, or community has the right of self-defense even under modern international law. In principle, nobody can argue the fact that anyone and everyone should have the right of self-defense.

The devil is always in the details, however, and much of the fighting and violence we are seeing in the Middle East today can be blamed on *jihad ad-dafa'*. In fact, the defensive *jihad* is really the key component at the heart of the rise of *Salafist* extremism, violence, and *takfirism* in that part of the world.

For example Osama bin Laden believed that expelling the Soviet invaders from Afghanistan during the eighties was a defensive *jihad*. He unquestionably saw it as an individual duty upon every able-bodied Muslim male to go to Afghanistan during the Soviet occupation and take up arms to free the Realm of Islam from an infidel invader. This defensive *jihad* was the seed from which today's aberrant, intolerant Islamism ultimately sprang.

In Syria and Iraq we see conflict and open warfare that is rooted in the *Sunni-Shia* rift where each side sees the other as an apostate and an infidel within the Realm of Islam who must be destroyed. In Yemen this same struggle is playing out between the *Shiite* Houthis, the majority-*Sunni* government, and the Al-Qaeda Islamists. It's the same story in Somalia, the home territory of Al-Shabaab, and in places like Mali, where the Islamist Al-Qaeda in the Islamic Maghreb sees non-Muslims occupying a Muslim heartland.

Sadly, given the scale of the hatred and bloodshed in the region – particularly in Iraq, Syria, and Yemen – the inter-Muslim and inter-Arab *jihad* shows no signs of abating anytime soon. Even though the Islamists hate us in the West for our democratic values and our freedoms, they hate apostates even more because they were once considered Muslims but they turned their backs on the One True Faith. The *Sunni* extremists refer to the *Shia* as the "Rejectionists" or the "Safavids" (their pejorative term for the Persians) and such Islamists absolutely despise them above everyone else. I suppose we can take some small comfort in that.

THE ISLAMIC RULES OF WARFARE

When we see the widespread killing and senseless violence in countries like Iraq or Syria, it would seem as if the phrase "Islamic rules of war" must be some kind of oxymoron. What kind of warfare allows the mass executions of military-age *Shiite* men or the genocide of some non-Muslim religious minority? Are we to believe that the mass beheading of Coptic Christians in Libya or the immolation of a caged Jordanian pilot at the hands of the Islamic State are being conducted according to some kind of Islamic law book? Are we to believe that when IS decapitates its prisoners by exploding detcord wrapped around their necks, drowns them in a cage, or crucifies them in a square that these punishments are somehow spelled out in the Islamic rules of warfare? Really?

I've often wondered if we could bring Ibn Taymiyyah back from the dead to see how the Islamic State is behaving today, would he be pleased? Would the Sheikh of Islam be happy that so much bloodshed is being carried out – even against innocent Muslims – by a group that justifies much of its atrocities under his own *Salafist* ideology and rulings? Is this the sort of barbarity that was practiced under the "pure" Islam during Muhammad's time? Did Ibn Taymiyyah believe that "pure" Islam was meant to be a religion of retribution, punishment, and fear? I'm no religious scholar so I guess that is a question for Muslims themselves to ponder and answer.

Yes, facing the steady parade of macabre videos, images, and stories emanating out of the "caliphate" – each more shocking than the last – it would seem absolutely ludicrous to us to discover that Islam does indeed have rules of warfare. Since the thugs in the Islamic State have pretty much violated all of them, it is yet another indication of the difference between Islam and Islamism and the need for us to constantly remind ourselves of this distinction.

Islamic rules of warfare are found in the verses of the Koran and in the *hadiths*. For example in the Koran we find:

Fight in the way of Allah those who fight you but do not transgress. Indeed, Allah does not like transgressors.

And kill them wherever you overtake them and expel them from wherever they have expelled you, and (strife) is worse than killing. And do not fight them at Al-Masjid al-Haram [i.e., the Sacred Mosque] *until they fight you there. But if they fight you, then kill them. Such is the recompense of the disbelievers.*

And if they cease, then indeed, Allah is Forgiving and Merciful.

Fight them until there is no more (strife) and (until) worship is (acknowledged to be) for Allah. But if they cease, then there is to be no aggression except against the oppressors.

(Fighting in) the sacred month is for (aggression committed in) the sacred month, and for (all) violations is legal retribution. So whoever has assaulted you, then assault him in the same way that he has assaulted you. And fear Allah and know that Allah is with those who fear Him.

And spend in the way of Allah and do not throw (yourselves) with your (own) hands into destruction (by refraining). And do good; indeed, Allah loves the doers of good.[137]

---

137. Koran 2:190-195.

The preceding verses are often cited as evidence that Muslims are only allowed to fight defensive wars. They are allowed to fight anyone who is fighting against them but if their enemies stop fighting, these verses enjoin the Muslims to stop doing so, as well. Muslims may fight as retribution against aggression but they must not be the aggressors.

There are several other verses in the Koran that admonish Muslims to stop fighting if their enemies stop fighting and that implication is further evidence that Muslims should only be fighting in self-defense. As noted, there is no universal consensus among all the scholars of the various main schools of Islamic thought on this subject.

The *hadiths* also provide guidance on how Muslims should conduct war and treat enemy combatants and prisoners. In the following *hadith*, Abu-Bakr al-Siddiq, a companion of Muhammad and his successor as the first of the "Rightly-Guided Caliphs," issued this instruction to one of his commanders during a military expedition:

> *I advise you ten things (relating to the rules of war). Do not kill women or an aged, infirm person. Do not cut down fruit-bearing trees. Do not destroy an inhabited place. Do not slaughter (animals) except for food. Do not burn bees and do not scatter them. Do not steal from the materials captured in combat, and do not be cowardly.*[138]

There is disagreement among the four main Islamic schools of thought on the authenticity of the above *hadith* so not everyone sees it as genuine.

There are other Islamic references to how Muslims should treat combatants and non-combatants during wartime. In a *hadith* within the Abu Dawud collection, Muhammad is quoted as saying: "Do not kill a decrepit old man, or a young infant, or a child, or a woman; do not be dishonest about booty, but collect your spoils, do right and act well, for Allah loves those who do well."[139]

---

138. *Al-Muwatta*, Volume 21, *Hadith* 10.
139. *Sunan Abu Dawud*, Book 14, Number 2608.

There are also ten rules for the treatment of enemy combatants and prisoners of war, according to the *Islam 101* website. The website is a project of The Sabr Foundation, which bills itself as a non-profit organization that promotes education about Islam. The website recaps these rules as follows:[140]

1. *Torture or punishment by fire is forbidden: The basis for this come from a hadith compiled by Abu Dawud that states, "Punishment by fire does not (behoove) anyone except the Master of Fire (i.e., God)."*

2. *Safety of the wounded: According to the Prophet Muhammad, "wounded soldiers who are not fit to fight, nor actually fighting, should not be attacked."*

3. *Prisoners of war should not be killed: The Prophet Muhammad said, "no prisoner should be put to the sword."*

4. *No one should be bound to be killed: Muhammad "prohibited the killing of anyone who is tied or in captivity."*

5. *Prohibition of looting or destruction in enemy territory: While the Muslims may plunder the battlefield of the enemy's wealth, goods, and equipment, they are specifically and expressly prohibited from destroying or taking any property from any person who is not engaged in fighting them.*

6. *Property rights: Muslims are forbidden from taking any property from the "general public of a conquered country" unless they pay for it. They may not take or use things that belong to the local population – even during a time of war – without that population's consent and permission.*

7. *Inviolability of corpses: Islam forbids the mutilation or disfigurement of enemy corpses.*

---

140. "Chapter Four: Rights of Enemies at War," *Islam 101* website. Accessed July 15, 2017. http://islam101.com/rights/hrM4.htm.

8. *Return of enemy dead: Here Muhammad's treatment of an enemy warrior's body after the Battle of Ahzab is cited as evidence that the corpses of enemy dead are to be returned.*

9. *Prohibition against breaching treaties: The website says that treachery in Islam is forbidden and uses Muhammad's adherence to the Treaty of Hudaybiyyah under a difficult circumstance as the proper example to be followed.*

10. *Declaration of war: Muslims may not commence hostilities against an enemy without first declaring war, unless the enemy has already begun hostilities against them. Koran verse 8:56 is cited as the authority: "If you apprehend breach of treaty from a people, then openly throw the treaty at their faces."*

The website does not always provide specific scriptural authority or evidence for each of the above but the preceding rules (or at least most of them) do seem to be commonly accepted in orthodox *Sunni* Islam. The website does offer an Islamic scholar's journal article as a reference for the rules.[141] They roughly equate to a Muslim version of the Code of Conduct that our own servicemen and servicewomen are expected to uphold in times of war. Groups like Islamic State, Boko Haram, Al-Shabaab, and Al-Qaeda have violated most – if not all – of these tenets and have proudly made videos of themselves doing it.

JIHAD OR TERRORISM?

But is the violence we are seeing in places like Iraq, Syria, and Nigeria today really a continuation of Muhammad's quest to spread the faith? Do the majority of Muslims in the world see the Islamic State's mass beheadings, crucifixions, and executions as some form of religious duty? Do they really think that Boko Haram's suicide bombings and mass killings and kidnappings of innocent Nigerians are part of a righteous and noble cause? Are Muslims around the world proud of Al-Shabaab's 2013

---

141. Sheikh Abu al-'A'la Mawdudi, "Human Rights in Islam," *Al-Tawhid Journal*, Vol. IV, No. 3, Rajab-Ramadan 1407 (H), (March-May 1987).

terrorist assault on innocent Kenyans at Nairobi's Westgate Shopping Mall? Are they exultant over the car bombs and suicide bombs that take innocent lives every day? Are the pictures of decapitated heads on poles and the mutilated and disfigured victims of bombings the image of Islam they want to present to the rest of the world?

I'm not a Muslim, but I don't think so. Neither does *Sunni* Islam's top cleric, Sheikh Ahmed al-Tayeb, the Grand Sheikh of Al-Azhar. According to an article published in the UK's *Daily Mail* newspaper on December 3, 2014, he characterized the Islamic State's actions as "barbaric crimes" at an international conference in Cairo to fight terrorism. He went on to say:

> *Militants are acting 'under the guise of this holy religion and have given themselves the name "Islamic State" in an attempt to export their false Islam.'*

> *'I wonder and ask why this blind division exists that has tainted Arab blood,' Sheikh Tayeb said, adding that religious, political and economic factors were behind the emergence of groups such as IS.*

While acknowledging that some Muslims may see Israel as "the root of their suffering" and, thus, the cleric claimed he could not rule out Israeli involvement in the region's extremist violence, nevertheless he was also quite clear on the need for the Muslim and Arab world to accept their share of responsibility for this extremism:

> *But we should not ignore our own responsibility for the emergence of extremism that has led to the formation of organizations such as Al-Qaeda and other armed groups.*

That is actually quite a stunning admission from such a powerful and influential Islamic figure. All too often we have heard from Arabs and Muslims about how they have been victimized by Israel, America, and the West. It's usually somebody else's fault. Finally we are seeing someone of the stature of Sheikh Ahmed al-Tayeb stepping up to accept Arab and Muslim responsibility for the Islamist phenomenon and that is a very healthy thing. You gotta own it if you're gonna fix it.

The Grand Sheikh isn't alone in his criticism of the bloodlust and savage brutality of groups like IS. An article from Qatar's government-funded *Al-Jazeera* in July 2014 cited the opposition of numerous *Sunni* clerics to Abu-Bakr al-Baghdadi's proclamation of a caliphate in Iraq and Syria. The article cited such *Sunni* notables as the influential Sheikh Yusuf al-Qaradawi, the leader of the International Union of Muslim Scholars, Abu Mohamed al-Maqdesi, a *Nusra* Front supporter, and Rachid Ghannouchi, the founder of Tunisia's Islamist *Ennahda* Party and all expressed opposition to, and "scathing criticism" of the IS caliphate. Some referred to Al-Baghdadi's followers as "deviant."[142]

And as we've noted before, a solid majority of Muslims are concerned about the growth of Islamist extremism. A median majority of 67% was either "concerned" or "somewhat concerned" about extremism in the results of a survey published by the Pew Research Global Attitudes Project on September 13, 2013. This poll was conducted across the Muslim populations of 11 states: Senegal, Lebanon, Tunisia, Malaysia, Nigeria, Pakistan, Egypt, Palestine, Jordan, Indonesia, and Turkey. Majorities registered concern over extremism in all but Turkey and Indonesia (which was split 48% concerned to 48% not concerned). The survey found that the overall support for suicide bombing from respondents (outside the Palestinian territories) had also dropped considerably.[143]

This kind of data and the level of criticism and opposition to IS expressed by such authoritative *Sunni* scholars make it pretty clear that most Muslims do not believe that what IS, Boko Haram, Al-Shabaab, or any other similar group is doing falls under the rubric of *jihad* in any way whatsoever. You can call it a pogrom, you can call it crimes against humanity, you can call it terrorism, but you cannot call it *jihad*. Period.

---

142. Shafik Mandhal, "Muslim Leaders Reject Baghdadi's Caliphate," *Al-Jazeera*, July 7, 2014. Accessed July 15, 2017. http://www.aljazeera.com/news/middleeast/2014/07/muslim-leaders-reject-baghdadi-caliphate-201.477.44058773906.html.
143. "Muslim Publics Share Concerns about Extremist Groups," Pew Research Center, September 10, 2013. Accessed July 15, 2017. http://www.pewglobal.org/2013/09/10/muslim-publics-share-concerns-about-extremist-groups/.

WORDS ARE IMPORTANT

As a linguist I know how very important words can be. A well-meaning (but inexperienced) translator might take the idiomatic English phrase "out of sight, out of mind" and translate it into "invisible and crazy" in the target language. Certainly "out of sight" could mean "invisible" and "out of mind" could mean "crazy," but that is obviously not the meaning of this expression. Words convey messages, emotions, and concepts and they must be carefully selected in order to render the correct meaning with all these other components that are also being communicated.

Since we have already shown that most Muslims don't believe that what Al-Qaeda, IS, or Boko Haram is doing can be called *jihad*, we should be calling it something else – anything else but *jihad*. Neither should we refer to the followers of those and other extremist groups as *jihadis* or *jihadists* or *mujahideen*. They are absolutely nothing of the sort.

I have heard American commentators and pundits say, "They refer to themselves as *jihadists* so that is fine with me," but that is an uninformed and even dangerous statement to make. Calling yourself a *jihadist* doesn't make you one any more than calling yourself an astronaut puts you into space. Our war with the extremists has a huge propaganda component and it's time that we became more mindful of how words can either hurt us or help us in that conflict. Semantics can have an extremely powerful impact inasmuch as we're saying what we mean and meaning what we say. It's also a lot cheaper than resorting to a military action or invasion.

As the aforementioned 2002 Gallup poll showed, Muslims may have differing ideas of what *jihad* actually means to them, but they universally see it as a positive and righteous struggle for a noble cause. Regardless of their religious and denominational backgrounds and differences, *jihad* is a good thing.

In the propaganda battle, our primary objective is to prevent the radicalization of vulnerable young people. As I've already noted, the fight against cancer is always more effective by preventing its occurrence altogether than through treatment once the disease has manifested itself. Terrorism must be handled the same way – through prevention rather than countering the threat once it appears.

I'm no psychologist but let's make a quick comparison between Nazi propaganda during World War II and the IS videos we are seeing now. The Nazis showed mass rallies and torchlight marches that conveyed a sense of unity and power – woe unto those who stood in the way of the Third Reich. These undoubtedly stirred patriotic feelings in the hearts of young German men and women on the eve of the Second World War and prompted many to enlist in the German military or serve in some other useful capacity. Only after Nazi Germany's defeat was the actual horror of the death camps revealed to the rest of the world when films were discovered of SS executions throughout Eastern Europe. Here it's worth pausing just a moment to note that Nazi experience is also a potent reminder that the dark side of humanity isn't limited to just one religion or ethnicity. The Nazis perfected death on an industrial scale that makes IS look like a bunch of rank amateurs.

The SS films and the IS videos are both about showing their respective group's power against a weak and defenseless foe, but I think that is where the similarity ends. The Nazis filmed executions almost like they were filming clinical documentaries as reports for their superiors. Soldiers doing their jobs and meeting their "quota" of dead Jews or Slavs. And to be objective, the Germans didn't have access to the social media venues that are so extensive and prevalent today.

The grisly videos by IS are different. The display of the Islamic State's omnipotence and power is obvious because they claim they are meting out Allah's judgment against unbelievers. But there is more here. These are recruiting videos, not documentaries. They are designed to appeal to a person who feels alienated and alone, someone who may feel as if his or her community has been slighted or insulted and is inclined to become part of something righteous – something larger than oneself. Somebody who wants to impose retribution on the iniquitous evildoers of the world with the same zeal as a young German man who resented the humiliations imposed on his homeland by the Great Powers after World War I. Both examples portray their fighters as being heroic in the face of sub-human enemies. And when you dehumanize your enemy, it makes him easier to kill. Think of how we portrayed the Japanese during World War II.

So, by using the terms *jihad, jihadist,* or *mujahideen* we are inadvertently lending legitimacy to these extremists and their grisly deeds in the same way that the German phrases for "storm trooper" or "master race" might have put deluded visions of mythical, Wagnerian ideals in a young German's head.

I'm sure that there are many ways to become radicalized, but let's take a hypothetical example where a young, Muslim man or woman in the West feels alienated and disenfranchised. They may not fit in with their peers at school. They may get teased by classmates for their religious beliefs or even their clothing, in the case of a young woman dressed in a *hijab* or other distinctive and conservative attire. Kids can be pretty cruel to each other, after all.

As the youth's resentment continues to build, he or she comes upon some online videos showing the exploits of Al-Qaeda or IS fighters who are heroically portrayed as battling against the evil unbelievers of the West. They may claim to be fighting to free Iraq or Afghanistan or some other land from US or Western aggression or occupation. The videos themselves may be of near-professional quality and have a stirring song with a militant, religious theme in Arabic (called a *nasheed*) as a soundtrack. Such videos may have scenes of suicide bombs or improvised explosive devices being triggered from a distance but they don't necessarily contain any gruesome images of beheadings, mutilated bodies, or the like. The fighters and martyrs featured in these videos are depicted as brave *mujahideen,* not cold-blooded killers. Thousands of these videos are available or disseminated on *YouTube, Facebook, Twitter,* and other social media outlets and dozens more are uploaded every day.

As he or she watches more and more of these productions, the youth begins to feel a sense of identification with the fighters on the computer screen. A sense of finally belonging to something larger than oneself begins to develop. The youth is too young and naïve to understand whether or not the cause – the *jihad* – on the videos is one that really is just and noble. The youth has very little grounding in the actual orthodoxy of his or her faith. He or she just wants to find somewhere they can belong – where they, as a proud Muslim, finally do fit in. It's a sentiment common to almost all adolescents at some time or other.

The youth's interest in what is called *jihad* may finally develop to the point of visiting some of the Islamist online forums and chat rooms and reading some of the discussion threads. That may progress to tentative online postings or discussions with other forum members – some of whom may be recruiters for extremist groups. The youth may start following the *Twitter* account of an IS sympathizer or even a recruiter. Now the recruiter has a direct contact with the recruit.

A recruiter might begin gradually introducing the youth to more violent and horrific material, explaining that the noble *mujahideen* have the moral courage to kill their enemies – and the enemies of Allah – with their bare hands unlike their Western adversaries – the pilots and soldiers who simply fire missiles or drop bombs dispassionately on some distant target while they remain safe and disassociated from the actual bloodshed. It's having the guts to carry out the intimate kill compared to the cowardice of death by Nintendo. The recruiter may ask, "Do you have the same courage as those *mujahideen*? Do you want to become one of them?" What do you think the youth's answer will be? It will be the Islamist version of Nazism's *Sieg! Heil!*

When we refer to these killers as *jihadists* or *mujahideen* we are sending the wrong message to vulnerable youths like the one in our example. They see that even the American government – the Great Satan – and its corrupt media are calling these groups *jihadist* and depicting their ghastly crimes as part of a *jihad*. They will think that if even their greatest enemy is calling it *jihad*, then it must really be true; it must be a real *jihad*. And since they don't have a deep knowledge of their faith to begin with, they don't understand the real concept of *jihad*, anyway.

We certainly do not need to give the bloodthirsty *takfirists* and extremists any more credit or legitimacy than they deserve – which is absolutely zero. The first step in this is to stop calling their terrorism *jihad*. Let's take the glamour out of wanton bloodlust and encourage all our allies to do the same. This is the first step in pulling the plug on their propaganda machine.

These people must rely exclusively on that one word – *jihad* or *jihadist* – in order to brainwash their hapless, uninformed, and unsophisticated recruits into believing that what they are doing is just and in the cause of Allah. We can take that away. We have the luxury of using many other words that are much more accurate descriptors of their actions and ideology.

For example, remember that the Arabic word *takfir* means to brand someone as an unbeliever, an infidel, someone who has turned his or her back on Islam. We know that such apostasy is viewed as a capital offense in Islam. The followers of nearly all of these Islamist extremist groups use *takfir* as their justification for massacring anyone who does not believe the same way they do. Since this violence, terror, and bloodshed is such an integral and intrinsic part of their philosophy and methodology, I suggest we start referring to these groups and their fighters as *takfirist*. After all, their objective seems principally to excommunicate and kill anybody that does not embrace their harsh, unforgiving, and austere brand of religion and render the adherents of any other faiths extinct.

In conjunction with their *takfirist* practices and philosophy, many of these Islamist extremists are in a fight to the death with modernity. They sternly believe that man's sole purpose on this earth is to worship God – Allah – and they have no time or use for modern conveniences whatsoever and are absolutely opposed to any innovation in, or evolution of Islam. They hearken back to the words of Muhammad when he said:

> *The people of my own generation are the best, then those who come after them, and then those of the next generation.*[144]

Therefore, they believe that emulating the life of Muhammad and his companions in the seventh century is the purest way of practicing Islam. As I mentioned in chapter four, this puritanical emulation of Muhammad and his contemporaries is called *Salafism*. It is a very conservative movement that has enjoyed some popularity in Arabian Gulf countries like

---

144. *Sahih al-Bukhari* 8:76:436-437.

Qatar, Saudi Arabia, and the United Arab Emirates and most observers believe it to be at the root of the violent, global *jihad* movement that began to gather steam with Osama bin Laden in the 1990s.

And while we're on the subject of *Salafism*, I think it's important to point out that I don't think very many of the Muslims Gallup surveyed in its 2002 poll would have wanted to give up all their modern conveniences and medical and technical advances to turn the clock back 1400 years. My experience from living in the Middle East is that the people there like driving their air-conditioned cars to the air-conditioned mall or supermarket and taking their frozen ice cream back to their air-conditioned homes to enjoy while watching their favorite programs on television. They're a lot like us in that respect and not very many are keen to give all that up to live in sackcloth and ashes in a tent in the desert. They want to go to the soccer stadium to watch soccer, not executions.

So, *takfirist* and *Salafist* are both much more accurate adjectives for the Islamist extremists and their groups that convey none of the potential legitimacy of *jihad*. Terrorist fits pretty well, too. The migration away from *jihad* and the transition to *takfirist* and *Salafist* by our allies and us may seem insignificant to the *incogniti* but it is a vital and simple first step in our comprehensive strategy and campaign to defeat the Islamist ideology. It doesn't cost us anything but it can be very rewarding in our heretofore-neglected propaganda campaign.

CHAPTER SEVEN

STEP TWO: LET'S SHUT THEM UP

"Unlimited tolerance must lead to the disappearance of tolerance. If we extend unlimited tolerance even to those who are intolerant, if we are not prepared to defend a tolerant society against the onslaught of the intolerant, then the tolerant will be destroyed, and tolerance with them."

– Plato

I find it disconcerting that the "Cyber Caliphate" of the Islamic State was able to hack into the *Twitter* and *YouTube* accounts of the US Central Command – the tip of the very spear that is tasked with "degrading" the capabilities of IS in Iraq and Syria.[145] While Washington simply downplayed this incident as just a form of cyber vandalism,[146] that misses the whole point of the attack.

In my mind it's yet another indicator that we aren't taking the information and media war against IS and extremist ideology very seriously. A rag-tag band of terrorists in the middle of nowhere have been able to tweak the nose of the most powerful military force in the world – much to the delight of their followers. It's a huge propaganda win for them and a humiliating embarrassment for us. We can read license plates from space,

---

145. Dan Lamothe, "U.S. Military Social Media Accounts Apparently Hacked by Islamic State Sympathizers," *Washington Post*, January 12, 2015. Accessed July 16, 2017. https://www.washingtonpost.com/news/checkpoint/wp/2015/01/12/centcom-twitter-account-apparently-hacked-by-islamic-state-sympathizers/.
146. Peter Singer, "It Doesn't Really if ISIS Sympathizers Hacked Central Command's *Twitter*," *Wired*, January 13, 2015. Accessed July 16, 2017. http://www.wired.com/2015/01/doesnt-really-matter-isis-sympathizers-hacked-central-commands-Twitter/.

drive rovers on Mars, and buy cars that will parallel-park themselves but our much-vaunted military – with all its various cyber commands and units – is apparently no more adept at protecting its own social media accounts than Hollywood celebrities. I believe we should expect better from our military and our counterterrorism enterprise.

Of course the Washington spin machine spooled up immediately to reassure us that this wasn't actually a hack into any Central Command or Pentagon computer systems. Whatever information the hackers could get from those *YouTube* and *Twitter* accounts was old and outdated and already available through open sources. Just about any teenager could have done it.

But, the point of the attack was for IS to show that it could pull it off and embarrass the US and its powerful military at the same time. There was never any serious intent to break into secure computer systems but even small victories like this are just going to encourage the "Cyber Caliphate" to try something similar again. This same sort of activity was seen a couple of years ago when the Syrian Electronic Army (a band of hackers supporting Syria's President Bashar al-Assad) gained brief notoriety when it disrupted the websites and social media accounts of such notable entities as the White House, Harvard University, and numerous Western media companies.

A key obstacle blocking better government performance is that our government doesn't really recognize that we actually still are at war against *takfirist* and *Salafist* ideologues who oppose everything that we represent. The "War on Terror" phrase so ubiquitous during the George W. Bush administration has fallen out of favor in Washington. It's just not politically correct anymore. Washington has forgotten that regardless of what it wants, the enemy always gets a vote. Many of our myopic politicians and policymakers erroneously believed that the terrorist boogeyman under America's bed died when Osama bin Laden met his just fate. But as we have seen, this war is far from over. Islamist extremism has grown exponentially since 1992 and we need a comprehensive strategy now more than ever.

As our enemies continue to evolve, we seem destined to make the same mistakes over and over while satisfying ourselves that a campaign of airstrikes and the retraining of a country's failed army is somehow going to succeed a second time when an intrinsic part of the problem in both Iraq and Syria is the lack of inclusiveness for the *Sunnis* in a *Shia*-dominated government and state. We are targeting and killing the commanders of a group who have already embraced martyrdom without doing enough to defeat the ideology they embrace. We are still treating the symptoms instead of the disease itself.

It's time for us to take our game to the next level and go on the offensive where our enemies have been effective: on the media, information, and propaganda front. In the previous chapter I made the case for not calling terrorism *jihad*. This next step involves depriving them of access to the media to spout their bile.

Terrorism needs a forum and a medium in order to have the desired effect. Creating videos of suicide bombings or a mass beheading or execution is pointless if you have no way of showing them to your desired audience. Pull a lion's teeth and the beast will starve. Let's shut down their access and starve the *takfirists* of the media attention they need to survive.

The nearly omnipresent availability of the world wide web and the proliferation of social media have made it possible for anybody with a smartphone to post and upload their opinions, images, and videos on virtually any subject. In the hands of a disgruntled US teenager, it is a tool for venting complaints against other kids, schoolteachers, or parents. But in the hands of a savvy terrorist group, the combination of a smartphone and social media becomes an extremely useful tool of asymmetric warfare against a superpower like the United States. The Internet is transformed into a force multiplier where a slickly produced and edited video can make a group appear much stronger and more influential than they actually are. If a picture is worth a thousand words, a well-made video is worth a million and there is no medium with more across-the-board impact than the visual medium. Television did supersede radio, after all.

Choking off the terrorists' media and Internet access is absolutely critical to our victory and it deserves much more attention and effort than it has been getting. Let's face it; the country that invented Madison Avenue, public relations, the Internet, and even social media is getting outplayed by a bunch of tech-savvy Islamist malcontents in a mud hut (alright, I do concede that these sympathizers can really be anywhere as long as they have reliable access to the web). We should be doing more about it.

THE CYBER CAMPAIGN

Let's acknowledge right from the get-go that any attempt at muzzling our adversaries and denying them access to any forum through which to spread their message falls right smack under the category of censorship. By its very definition, the objective of censorship is to block material from being seen, read, or heard and that is precisely what we would aspire to do.

In basic terms, what I am advocating here is an offensive in information warfare. It goes way beyond the World War II propaganda radiobroadcasts by Tokyo Rose, Axis Sally, and Lord Haw-Haw. While ultimately seeking to reset the clock back to the seventh century, these radical Islamists have become very adept at using our own modern information and communications technology against us. They are already engaged in their own information war on the Internet and they threaten to radicalize our most vulnerable youth in the process. We shouldn't even be giving them a chance. Depriving terrorists of media attention is the most effective means of shutting them up and moving them toward extinction. To accomplish this, we have considerably more assets and resources than do our Islamist foes.

There will undoubtedly be free speech advocates that would complain over any attempts to suppress freedom of expression – particularly if that effort comes from the government. But, we're not protecting somebody's artsy movie here, or debating whether somebody's magazine is publishing pornographic images. We're protecting kids – in many cases minors – from being exposed to graphic images for the purposes of their radicalization. We're endeavoring to prevent terrorism and the loss of innocent life. We are acting in the interests of protecting the United States of America and its citizens. According to the Constitution, that is what the government is *supposed* to do.

It's illegal to produce, distribute, and exhibit so-called "snuff" films in America that feature some unfortunate victim being purposely murdered or killed for the sake of the movie. How are the videos by the Islamist radicals we've seen over the years featuring the brutal and gruesome beheadings of Daniel Pearl, Nick Berg, James Foley, or Steven Sotloff any different? If we're not willing to allow a filmmaker to murder an actor or actress for the sake of "art" or box office sales, why should we allow the Islamic State to show thousands of videos of mass executions of innocent victims for the sake of their "religion" or, more accurately, their propaganda?

Murder is murder and the criminals that are committing this savagery are essentially doing so for their own bloodlust and twisted entertainment. Besides, they are not US persons and do not enjoy any privileges under US law or the Constitution. They deserve only what they are meting out. Let's remember that this is war, not some academic or hypothetical discussion over tea and crumpets.

Neither do we allow child pornographers the luxury of openly showing or marketing their disgusting videos and movies online. We've driven much of this perverted trade to the Dark Web and we should be doing the same to Islamist deviants.

As for the lectures and sermons by aberrant clerics like Anwar al-Awlaki or Sheikh Abu Hamza, these radicals have openly called for the killing of Americans or the destruction of our country. These acts constitute sedition since they call on US Muslims to rise up against their own government, so I don't believe they should be classified as "protected speech." Extremists like this condone the killing of innocent Americans in the furtherance of their intolerant beliefs and their desire to replace democracy and freedom with oppression, slavery, and death. If Supreme Court Justice Oliver Wendell Holmes ruled that free speech does not allow someone to falsely yell "Fire!" in a crowded theater in order to create mayhem and violence, it's hard to see how promoting sedition and open rebellion should be handled any differently.

I strongly disagree with any free speech activist who might be concerned over the potential muzzling of Islamist radicals and terrorists online (and elsewhere). This isn't about censorship, free speech, or the freedom of expression it's about prosecuting and winning the information war against those who are doing the same against us. I certainly don't see the IS supporting democracy or free speech. There's no reason whatsoever (legally or morally) to protect their rights to promote violent subjugation, sedition, treason, and institutionalized murder, or any combination thereof.

And there is an important aspect of this campaign we should remember. These horrible atrocities aren't necessarily going to go away just because we are denying IS a forum to show off their terrorist handiwork. These massacres and killings also serve the purpose of intimidating the populations IS already has under its control and forcing them to do its bidding. The objective of our campaign is to prevent them from radicalizing and recruiting others.

Now that we've answered the legal question over muting and censoring Islamists online, it's time to address some of the technical aspects of cyber – and information warfare.

Cyber operations can (sort of) be divided into passive and active categories.

On the passive side we find what I call cyber reconnaissance. This is the act of discovering what is really out there on the Internet and then cataloging and indexing it so it can be accessed later, if desired. This is a task that is constantly performed by large search engines (and intelligence agencies) often through the use of "bots" (short for robots) such as web crawlers and web scrapers. These tools are programmed to visit various websites and do things like take snapshots of their pages for the purposes of determining whether those websites still exist and are still active. Web crawlers and scrapers can also be programmed to search for specific topics and subjects. They are limited in their tasks by how they have been programmed (they can't think for themselves) but they are far more efficient and faster for the tedious task of web indexing than humans.

The major search engines use these bots to constantly roam cyberspace and index as much online content as possible into massive databases that are used to provide results to search queries. Search engines like Google and Yahoo must endeavor to categorize as much web content as possible so that when someone types in a specific request for "information about some celebrity," "how to install a gas water heater," "the demographic makeup of the population of Peru," or some medical question, it can find and rank the search results quickly and easily. In short, these search engines are constantly and continuously utilizing these bots and other, similar tools to ultimately find and catalog everything that is on the Internet.

That's a Herculean task and often someone putting up a new website will actually want to provide the new site's URL to Google or Yahoo to make sure it gets indexed right away. The mega-search entity that is Google will eventually find it with or without such assistance, but submitting the URL will likely get them noticed faster on any Google searches. The use of these web and search crawlers has become indispensable to indexing and categorizing all web content.

In fact, with its gargantuan effort to find and catalog virtually everything on the Internet, Google's web collection efforts scoop up the sensitive and private data of many millions of people every day. It would make a heck of an intelligence agency. Through its various applications, email service, instant messengers, cloud storage, and other features Google can quite easily build a complete profile of its users that would be far more accurate than those from any security service – foreign or domestic. Don't believe me?

When you're logged into your Google account, the search company tracks your every online move while using their servers. It was reputed to have 425 million Gmail users in 2012 and one *billion* users of its Android phone and tablet operating system worldwide in 2014. While NSA's systems intercepted around 200 million SMS text messages per day in 2014, Google's Android users send 20 *billion* text messages per day[147] Google can monitor your calls and messages, track your phone usage and online browsing habits, and read whatever unencrypted email attachments are stored in your Gmail account. And there's absolutely no judicial oversight or restriction on any of this activity. There are no limits on what Google can store or how long it can store it. Google's file on you is likely much larger than that of any intelligence or law enforcement agency and while *Facebook* and Yahoo may do the same, to a certain extent, their efforts pale in comparison to Google's conscious collection

---

147. James Ball, "NSA Collects Millions of Text Messages Daily in 'Untargeted' Global Sweep," *The Guardian*, January 16, 2014. Accessed July 18, 2017. https://www. theguardian.com/world/2014/jan/16/nsa-collects-millions-text-messages-daily-untargeted-global-sweep.

and utilization of personal information. The proof of the pudding is that NSA was actually intercepting Google's own unencrypted data as it was sending it to its various foreign data centers. Google was hoist with its own petard!

Intelligence agencies also have web search tools but their mission differs from that of the search engines in that they are not simply blindly collecting and cataloging data; they are ultimately attempting to sort through massive amounts of data in order to find specific messages, videos, images, or other files that have intelligence value.

To assist in that endeavor, the NSA developed an extremely utilitarian analysis tool called XKEYSCORE that is able to analyze large amounts of collected raw data in numerous ways with the ultimate goal of identifying and monitoring intelligence targets. The tool has been so effective that the agency has shared it with several of our allies.[148]

These passive measures are all well and good for identifying hostile targets on the web, but for the purposes of a cyber campaign to drive the Islamists off the Internet, we will have to engage in more active operations. This is the domain of NSA's Tailored Access Operations (TAO) units. These are rumored to be the ninjas of offensive cyber-warfare. They can conduct computer network exploitation (CNE) aimed at the surreptitious access of data stored on a network, monitoring the computers using the network, or planting targeted malware – you name it, and they can do it. Quite simply the hackers at TAO can identify, infiltrate, and monitor the computer networks of our foreign adversaries, usually without them even knowing it. How good are they?

We've heard about how the Chinese have a specialized military hacking organization called PLA Unit 61398 that has allegedly been responsible for the Chinese cyber espionage and cyber theft of sensitive US defense and industrial intellectual property. They have stoked our own righteous indignation over Chinese hackers apparently running amok in sensitive US computer networks and systems with nobody holding China to account over this debacle. Pundits cry foul as they point fingers of

---

148. Glenn Greenwald, "XKeyscore: NSA Tool Collects 'Nearly Everything a User Does on the internet,'" *The Guardian*, July 31, 2013. Accessed July 16, 2017. https://www. theguardian.com/world/2013/jul/31/nsa-top-secret-program-online-data.

accusation at China for the disastrous OPM hack. While these Chinese breaches have been serious and damaging, our media often portrays this shadow war as if the Chinese are the only ones doing the hacking. The reality of the situation is really quite different.

In June 2013, Matthew Aid ripped the cloak of secrecy from TAO in a profile he penned for *Foreign Policy* entitled, "Inside the NSA's Ultra-Secret China Hacking Group." That article reported that TAO had been roaming at will inside China's computer systems for "almost 15 years" without so much as a peep from the Chinese or even our own media. Aid quoted China's "top Internet official, Huang Chengqing," as claiming that Beijing had "mountains of data" proving the widespread US hacking of Chinese computer systems.[149] The Chinese hackers may be good, but apparently they're not in the same league as TAO's operators.

But that's not all:

> *Since its creation in 1997, TAO has garnered a reputation for producing some of the best intelligence available to the U.S. intelligence community not only about China, but also on foreign terrorist groups, espionage activities being conducted against the United States by foreign governments, ballistic missile and weapons of mass destruction developments around the globe, and the latest political, military, and economic developments around the globe.*[150]

During the 2007 surge in Iraq, the unit was credited with "single-handedly identifying and locating over 100 Iraqi and al-Qaeda insurgent cells in and around Baghdad."[151]

The TAO is the absolute best cyber-warfare unit in the world for several reasons. First, the National Security Agency has six-plus decades of experience using advanced, high-tech signals intelligence collection platforms. It has an established industrial base of experienced contractors with whom

---

149. Matthew Aid, "Inside the NSA's Ultra-Secret China Hacking Group," *Foreign Policy Magazine*, June 10, 2013. Accessed July 16, 2017. http://foreignpolicy.com/2013/06/10/inside-the-nsas-ultra-secret-china-hacking-group/.
150. *Ibid.*
151. *Ibid.*

it can collaborate to design, build, and operate similar systems for cyber collection and warfare.

The agency has a long history of hiring extremely intelligent and innovative people. It has employed some of the country's top mathematicians as cryptanalysts. It is constantly recruiting those who have a high degree of proficiency in a foreign language to work as linguists. It has scores of engineers and technologists who are evaluating collection missions of the future for targets that may not even exist yet. So, if NSA is attracting the best and brightest computer scientists, linguists, geeks, and hackers into TAO it should not come as a surprise. The agency will always be a leader in the technology on which the highest value targets are located.

And finally, the NSA and TAO have unrivalled worldwide access to international communications and computer networks. The agency operates from outposts all over the world – and even in outer space – at an incomparably high technical level that neither the Chinese nor even the Russians can match.

Russian cybercriminals may be able to pull off the theft of credit card data by installing malware on point-of-sale machines and the Anonymous group might tout its ability to launch distributed denial of service attacks against a targeted website. These incidents always get plenty of news coverage. But I do not believe that anybody has the talent, access, and infrastructure to match TAO. They're working 24/7/365 and rarely ever in the news, and that's the way the intelligence community likes it.

In short, TAO is the premier cyber-warfare player in the world today – bar none. And they would undoubtedly be the ones tapped to carry out any official, offensive, cyber operations – a computer network attack (CNA) in NSA-speak – against any websites of our radical Islamist entities. An attack that doesn't just disrupt IS and its ilk, but permanently destroys their data and equipment. A systematic and persistent attack that permanently drives them off the mainstream Internet and deprives them of the ability to disseminate their barbaric message. An attack that forces them to the Dark Web with the drug dealers and pornographers, a place where their influence is rendered ineffective and their voice is attenuated to the point of near silence.

Let's shut them down on social media. There's no place for these bastards on *Facebook, Twitter,* or *YouTube.* Take out their email accounts, too. If the "Cyber Caliphate" wants to play games with Central Command's social media outlets, let's show them what the *real* cyber warriors can do and put *them* out of business – permanently. Let's make it so difficult for them to maintain a web presence that eventually they become disconnected from their followers – immediately attack any new websites or social media accounts as soon as they appear. That forces them to allocate exponentially more resources just to maintain a presence while completely disrupting their propaganda capability.

Track down any online sympathizers who may be providing active support and turn them in to their respective government authorities. Make *them* look over their shoulder. "Hey, *takfiri,* watch your back – we're coming for you!" Two can play at their feeble attempt at a mind game.

Make no mistake; the Internet is a fundamental battle space that they have used to great advantage while we have held back. It's time to implement the modern military strategy of Anti-Access/Area Denial (A2/AD) and prevent these extremists from having any online opportunity or advantage. Let's put them back into the seventh century where they belong. What are we waiting for?

Any military commander knows that when you control the tempo of the battle, you will keep your enemy off balance and you will prevail. Until now we have been reacting and not taking the offensive. Just like our defensive counterterrorism posture, we have not been taking the initiative in the cyber battle space. Here again, we have not been fighting to win. That's no longer good enough if we are to prevent the kind of radicalization that can lead to the dreaded lone wolf attacks. It's time to take control over the operational tempo of the information war.

Now, I know what the response to this will be from some in the Intelligence Community. They may say, "But these websites are really a good source of information on what these terrorists are doing. If we take all of them down, we won't have any intelligence sources."

That excuse has some merit to it, but let's take a closer look at the issue. To begin with, if we were to attack the main *takfirist* chat rooms on the Internet and force them to shut down for an extensive period, this would play havoc with their communications. This would deprive them of a common place to post messages, ask questions, upload videos, etc. These chat rooms and forums offer an online place for these extremists and their sympathizers to meet that provides a perceived modicum of anonymity, safety, and security since the members and participants can conceal their true identities. Even though they know that NSA and other Western intelligence agencies are monitoring what goes on in these chat rooms, they still feel as if they are just out of the West's actual reach.

And I agree that these chat rooms can have some intelligence value. I've translated manuals on how to make explosives out of everything from fertilizer to goat poop, how to wire up a bomb, and documents on military and guerilla strategy that were all downloaded from terrorist chat rooms. I've translated extensive chat room discussion threads on how to surgically implant a functional bomb inside the body of a willing "martyr." Members and participants may discuss or recommend various computer security programs or lecture each other on operational tradecraft.

There might be a noticeable increase in the amount of discussion on a chat room about a particular subject, or just a higher level of activity. We've discussed that this is often what officials refer to as an increase in terrorist "chatter" or "buzz." Here the activity level itself becomes an indicator without any specificity about the target or timing of any potential attack. So while these chat room websites do have some intelligence value, it is extremely unlikely they will ever tip us off to any specific attack – especially now that homegrown terrorist attacks are becoming the norm.

But now imagine the effect on these *takfirists* if their chat rooms were taken down. Suddenly they are completely disconnected – unable to communicate with like-minded sympathizers. Their sense of unity is taken away. They are unable to use the chat room as a central resource for downloading manuals, reading various discussion threads, or answering Islamic legal questions. It would become much more difficult to pass instructions or operational planning. Their ability to promote their ideology and attract new adherents would now be severely constrained.

If they do wish to communicate with each other, they then have to do so without the perceived safety and anonymity of the chat room. What if all their *Twitter* and other social media accounts were closed almost as soon as they opened them? It would make it much harder for them to get their messages across and it would make it difficult for their online sympathizers to help them.

Flushing the extremists off the chat room into the open may actually give XKEYSCORE and TAO (along with all their other tools that we don't yet know about) a much better chance to identify and track individual extremists (maybe even groups). We would be hindering their communications, alienating them, and crushing their propaganda machine. Where's the downside in that?

This is how to fight and win the information war. We're not attacking state actors like Russia, China, or even North Korea. This isn't about cybercrime or cyber vandalism. We're taking down a deviant bunch of non-state-actor extremists and their sympathizers who must not be given any opportunity on the Internet to peddle their snuff films and cancerous philosophy. Take TAO off its leash and let's go after them! It's all about fighting to win in every single battle space, wherever our enemies our confronting us.

Of course, this cyber offensive against Islamist radicalism also must include cleansing all the existing *YouTube*, *Facebook*, and other social media accounts that contain pro-radical, anti-US, and graphic content. This is naturally going to be a controversial step and I can already hear the building crescendo of lawyers and free speech proponents beginning to squawk again, but I believe that there is a firm legal basis for this.

Let's take the case of the now-deceased Sheikh Anwar al-Awlaki as a case in point. The US Department of Justice prepared a lengthy memorandum in July 2010 concerning a legal analysis and opinion on the "Applicability of Federal Criminal Laws and the Constitution to Contemplated Lethal Operations Against Shaykh Anwar al-Aulaqi [sic]." The *New York Times* and American Civil Liberties Union successfully sued to have the details of the memo released, which was published in June 2014.

The United States Department of Justice deemed the US-born Al-Awlaki to be such a threat that it concluded the use of lethal violence against him did not constitute a violation of his Fourth Amendment rights, as they were "outweighed by 'the importance of the governmental interests [that] justify the intrusion.'" The rationale used by the Justice Department was summarized on the memo's last page as follows, "…the US citizen in question has gone overseas and become part of the forces of an enemy with which the United States is engaged in an armed conflict; that person is engaged in continual planning and direction of attacks upon U.S. persons from one of the enemy's overseas bases of operations" that would make his capture infeasible. He was engaged in activities that posed "a continued and imminent threat to U.S. persons or interests…"[152] Consequently, Anwar al-Awlaki was successfully targeted and killed in a US drone strike in Yemen in September 2011.

Some of the activities in which Awlaki was engaged included many video lectures in which he openly called for bringing down the United States and the implementation of Islamic law (as he interpreted it) all over the world. Because he was born in the United States, he was a fluent English speaker who had a charismatic appeal to Muslim converts that were not native Arabic speakers. He was especially popular among Muslim youth in the West who were susceptible to his propaganda and entranced by his charm, eloquence, and speaking ability.

But, if you go to *YouTube* and type in "Anwar al-Awlaki lectures" as the search term, you will get 61,400 search results (as of July 16, 2017). The service claimed to have removed links to his incendiary lectures and sermons back in 2012, but many of those videos apparently still remain. My question is, why? He shouldn't be there at all – period.

If this guy was a big and important enough terrorist for the US Department of Justice to sanction his assassination in Yemen – even though he was a US citizen – then why are we allowing his poison to survive on the Internet? If the whole point of killing him was to remove

---

152. Memorandum for the Attorney General dated July 16, 2010, "Re: Applicability of Federal Criminal Laws and the Constitution to Contemplated Lethal Operations Against Shaykh Anwar al-Aulaqi," American Civil Liberties Union website, June 23, 2014. Accessed July 16, 2017. https://www.aclu.org/sites/default/files/assets/2014-06-23_barron-memorandum.pdf.

him from being a clear and present danger to the United States, why are we patently ignoring the man's propaganda value, whose stock has risen immensely since he attained his status as a "martyr?" Why aren't we actively purging every trace of this terrorist's online presence and relegating him to anonymity and obscurity? Why are we still subjecting disenfranchised young Muslims to the threat of his radicalization? Since the whole objective of defeating the Islamist ideology is to prevent the creation of a future generation of terrorists, the eradication of Awlaki, IS, Boko Haram, Al-Qaeda, bin Laden, Ayman al-Zawahiri, Al-Shabaab, and any others of their ilk from any online or web presence whatsoever would seem to me to be a no-brainer.

With such a surfeit of lawyers inside the Beltway, do we still need to be reminded of what constitutes treason, sedition, or other great crimes against our country? Chapter 115 of Title 18 of the United States Code is entitled "Treason, Sedition, and Subversive Activities" and it seems pretty clear. Here are a few examples:

Title 18 Part I Chapter 115 § 2381 – Treason:

Whoever, owing allegiance to the United States, levies war against them or adheres to their enemies, giving them aid and comfort within the United States or elsewhere, is guilty of treason and shall suffer death, or shall be imprisoned not less than five years and fined under this title but not less than $10,000; and shall be incapable of holding any office under the United States.

Title 18 Part I Chapter 115 § 2382 – Misprision of Treason:

Whoever, owing allegiance to the United States and having knowledge of the commission of any treason against them, conceals and does not, as soon as may be, disclose and make known the same to the President or to some judge of the United States, or to the governor or to some judge or justice of a particular State, is guilty of misprision of treason and shall be fined under this title or imprisoned not more than seven years, or both.

Title 18 Part I Chapter 115 § 2383 – Rebellion or insurrection:

Whoever incites, sets on foot, assists, or engages in any rebellion or insurrection against the authority of the United States or the laws thereof, or gives aid or comfort thereto, shall be fined under this title or imprisoned not more than ten years, or both; and shall be incapable of holding any office under the United States.

Title 18 Part I Chapter 115 § 2384 – Seditious conspiracy:

If two or more persons in any State or Territory, or in any place subject to the jurisdiction of the United States, conspire to overthrow, put down, or to destroy by force the Government of the United States, or to levy war against them, or to oppose by force the authority thereof, or by force to prevent, hinder, or delay the execution of any law of the United States, or by force to seize, take, or possess any property of the United States contrary to the authority thereof, they shall each be fined under this title or imprisoned not more than twenty years, or both.

Title 18 Part I Chapter 115 § 2385 – Advocating overthrow of government:

Whoever knowingly or willfully advocates, abets, advises, or teaches the duty, necessity, desirability, or propriety of overthrowing or destroying the government of the United States or the government *of any State, Territory, District or Possession thereof, or the government of any political subdivision therein, by force or violence, or by the assassination of any officer of any such government; or*

Whoever, with intent to cause the overthrow or destruction of any such government, prints, publishes, edits, issues, circulates, sells, distributes, or publicly displays any written or printed matter advocating, advising, or teaching the duty, necessity, desirability, or propriety of overthrowing or destroying any government in the United States by force or violence, or attempts to do so; or

Whoever organizes or helps or attempts to organize any society, group, or assembly of persons who teach, advocate, or encourage the overthrow or destruction of any such government by force or violence; or becomes or is a member of, or affiliates with, any such society, group, or assembly of persons, knowing the purposes thereof—

Shall be fined under this title or imprisoned not more than twenty years, or both, and shall be ineligible for employment by the United States or any department or agency thereof, for the five years next following his conviction.

If two or more persons conspire to commit any offense named in this section, each shall be fined under this title or imprisoned not more than twenty years, or both, and shall be ineligible for employment by the United States or any department or agency thereof, for the five years next following his conviction.

As used in this section, the terms "organizes" and "organize", with respect to any society, group, or assembly of persons, include the recruiting of new members, the forming of new units, and the regrouping or expansion of existing clubs, classes, and other units of such society, group, or assembly of persons.

Title 18 Part I Chapter 115 § 2389 – Recruiting for service against the United States:

Whoever recruits soldiers or sailors within the United States, or in any place subject to the jurisdiction thereof, to engage in armed hostility against the same; or

Whoever opens within the United States, or in any place subject to the jurisdiction thereof, a recruiting station for the enlistment of such soldiers or sailors to serve in any manner in armed hostility against the United States—

Shall be fined under this title or imprisoned not more than five years, or both.

This is pretty serious stuff and what guys like Awlaki and all the others are doing is inciting others to rebel against the US Government, wage their deviant form of *jihad* in their nefarious cause, and actively conspire against the United States and its interests whenever they can. How can that not be the case when they are advocating killing Americans? How can it not be the case when they are calling for the downfall of the US Government and its replacement with their extremist version of Islamic law? How can calling for the rescission of all our democratic freedoms and values be considered anything but sedition and treason?

Now, some may reply that many of those posting these offensive and violent videos are not US persons so the above provisions of Title 18 US Code do not apply. Again, I disagree.

YouTube forces anyone opening an account with its website to agree to its terms of service. Paragraph 14 of that agreement (accessed July 16, 2017) clearly defines the *YouTube* service as being based "solely" in the US state of California. It goes on to state:[153]

---

153. "Terms of Service," *YouTube* website, June 9, 2014. Accessed July 16, 2017. https://www.youtube.com/static?template=terms.

These Terms of Service shall be governed by the internal substantive laws of the State of California, without respect to its conflict of laws principle. Any claim or dispute between you [i.e., the user] and YouTube that arises in whole or in part from the Service shall be decided exclusively by a court of competent jurisdiction located in Santa Clara County, California.

Even though the user may be located anywhere in the world, it is quite clear from the above that *YouTube* acknowledges being a US entity that is subject to California laws and, by default, all US laws and it therefore must compel its users to abide by those laws. This, in turn, infers that *YouTube* must consequently accept the responsibility that its service must be used in accordance with those US laws and prevent those using its service from violating those same laws.

In light of this, if there are any videos on *YouTube* that preach violence against the United States or Americans, call for a rebellion or insurrection, recruit persons for terrorist activities against America or Americans, or display any other such seditious content (and we already know these videos exist), does that constitute conspiracy? Is *YouTube* aiding and abetting our enemies or facilitating their conspiracy for sedition against the United States by allowing its users to upload and display such videos? Does *YouTube* have a responsibility to "censor" its users?

In fact, *YouTube* has already set such a precedent. If you remember, a video that was reputed to be anti-Islamic called "Innocence of Muslims" was voluntarily blocked by the video sharing service itself to several Arab and Muslim countries in 2012 after allegations that the video had sparked violence in the Muslim world and was responsible for anti-American demonstrations and protests, in particular demonstrations against the US embassy in Cairo and the notorious Benghazi attack in which US Ambassador Christopher Stevens and three other Americans were killed.[154] So, if *YouTube* can selectively and voluntarily shut down one video on allegations that it is anti-Islamic, what is stopping it from shutting down thousands of *anti-American* videos uploaded by deviant (and violent) Islamists – videos that at the very least violate the sections of Title

---

154. "Google Blocks Video Clips in Egypt, Libya Amid Concerns Over Anti-Islam Film," *Al-Arabiya News*, September 13, 2012. Accessed July 16, 2017. https://english.alarabiya.net/articles/2012/09/13/237659.html.

18 US Code listed above? The logic and content in these videos is every bit as offensive to innocent Americans as "Innocence of the Muslims" was to Islam and Muslims. This isn't freedom of speech or expression; it's anti-American and anti-democracy hate speech. Shouldn't we get the same rights as the countries and Muslims who opposed the 2012 film?

And if we're talking about videos that show gruesome, grisly, or extremely violent content, *YouTube* has a policy against those, too. As of July 16, 2017 paragraph 6.E. of the same Terms of Service states:

> *You further agree that you will not submit to the Service any Content or other material that is contrary to the YouTube Community Guidelines, currently found at https://www.youtube.com/yt/policyandsafety/communityguidelines.html, which may be updated from time to time, or contrary to applicable local, national, and international laws and regulations.*

Those guidelines prohibit the posting of "violent or gory content" that is intended to be "shocking." Permissible content does not include that which "promotes or condones violence against individuals or groups based on race or ethnic origin, religion…" That pretty much defines the sort of Islamist "snuff films" that many of these extremists like to post.

While I've focused on *YouTube* as an example, this problem exists throughout social media. *Facebook*, a for-profit US corporation listed on the NASDAQ exchange, has similar injunctions against posting hate speech or gratuitous or graphic violence in its Community Standards, too (as of July 16, 2017). Shouldn't we be expecting them to uphold their own policies and force users to remove offensive content? If you can't show hate speech or snuff movies on television or in a theater, why is it okay to do so on *YouTube*, *Facebook*, or *Twitter*? Why are we giving social media sites a pass on abiding by some of the most serious laws of the land?

With that said, there are some positive signs that the major social media networks have begun policing the content of their users. A January 2015 news story reported that *Twitter* had suspended the accounts of 18,000 IS supporters out of a total of approximately 45,000. The article stated that *Twitter*, *YouTube*, and *Facebook* began to take harsher action against objectionable content after IS uploaded the horrific video of its beheading of US journalist James Foley. *Twitter's* actions were taken against the most active IS accounts, while leaving others to be monitored and exploited by US intelligence. These moves were said to have a "devastating" effect on the terrorist group.[155] *Twitter* continued its fight against IS into 2016. It had reportedly deleted 125,000 accounts deemed related to terrorism from mid-2015 through February 2016.[156]

Letting TAO take care of foreign websites that are used by the terrorists to spread their propaganda and holding the social media giants in the US to the enforcement of their existing policies while obeying US laws will go a long way toward muzzling our enemies and denying them any advantage in our cyber information war. It is crucial if we are to prevent vulnerable young minds from being radicalized and recruited.

Depriving terrorists of attention is the equivalent of starving a malignant tumor of its lifeblood. If we don't do something to silence our enemies on the Internet, our personal liberties and freedoms will slowly be eroded further and further in response to security and counterterrorism concerns as radicalized, homegrown, lone wolves carry out (or attempt to carry out) attacks that could have been prevented if we would have done something to stifle the Islamist ideology in the first place. The First Amendment won't have any relevance in an America where our rights and liberties are always trumped by the state's safety and security policies, which will ultimately neither make us any safer nor more secure.

We, and indeed the whole world, are facing the same challenge from the malicious evil of Islamism. We must all band together to do whatever is necessary to mute these violent *takfirists* once and for all and deny them any forum to peddle their hate.

NEWS VS. SENSATIONALISM

The media business is (and always has been) intensely competitive but the twenty-first century has taken that competition to a whole new level. We

155. "War Against IS Group spreads to *Twitter*: Expert," *AFP*, January 28, 2015. Accessed July 16, 2017. http://www.spacedaily.com/reports/War_against_IS_group_spreads_to_Twitter_expert_999.html

156. Danny Yadron, "Twitter Deletes 125,000 ISIS Accounts and Expands Anti-terror Teams," *The Guardian*, February 5, 2016. Accessed July 16, 2017. https://www.theguardian.com/technology/2016/feb/05/twitter-deletes-isis-accounts-terrorism-online.

have an ever-increasing number of choices from which to get our news and information and all seem to have an insatiable appetite for something – anything – to report during the non-stop, 24-hour news cycle. It's almost impossible to find a dedicated television news channel that doesn't have one or more crawlers on the screen reporting stories in addition to the one that is being broadcasted. If you're not being oversaturated and stimulated with minutia, then you're not apparently getting good TV news.

To make matters worse, much of what we see on so-called news channels these days really isn't news. There is a plethora of commentary designed to pander to the channel's target demographic. Most of this seems aimed at either bashing one political camp, regardless of whatever it does, or defending another political camp, regardless of whatever it does. This "white noise" tends to reduce everything to a political dimension that often ignores the strategic interests of the United States and the American people and it likely contributes to the Washington gridlock. Spin constantly seems to exceed fact and the existence of any real strategy and that, in turn, has a negative effect on making policy. Unfortunately, we can't just make facts go away or ignore them just because they may be inconvenient to our political cause.

But when there is a really big news story, it often gets played and replayed (naturally there are a lot of gaps in that 24-hour cycle) even when there may be nothing new to report. We, as the viewing audience, have come to expect splashy graphics and videos whenever there is a significant story and the news channels, blogs, and networks know that such glitzy visual stimuli will attract even more viewers so they want to maximize that aspect of their reporting. News is now inextricably intertwined with entertainment so getting that viewer share is all-important to these providers. I don't think anyone would disagree that news channels sometimes push the envelope and resort to gimmicks to increase their viewer share.

Unfortunately groups like the IS do their best to provide the maximum visual impact and therein lies the rub. How many times have we seen doomed Western hostages in orange jumpsuits kneeling, with their hands bound behind their backs, posed next to some knife-brandishing coward in a balaclava looming over them? Guys like the so-called "Jihadi John" of the IS couldn't make it in the real world and the only way for them to act like a man is to tie somebody up and force them into a position of submission and subjugation. If he isn't even brave enough to show his own face, then apparently he does not have the actual faith in his supposed convictions. Bank robbers wear masks; those allegedly embarked on a supposed "*jihad* for the cause of Allah" shouldn't need to.

We see clips of IS "fighters" running a column of prisoners into a ditch, forcing them to lie on their bellies, and then shooting them in the back. We've seen them go down a line of captured Syrian soldiers in Raqqa, forced to kneel in the street, and shoot them in the back of the head.

Those actions are crimes against humanity and a slur against Islam, in whose name they are being committed. They are not the heroic battlefield exploits of righteous, noble, and honorable soldiers and warriors. These extremists are terrorists and criminals.

As long as our television and print media continue to make them look invincible, we are simply encouraging the religiously ignorant, alienated, and susceptible youth in the West to emulate their barbarity. *Charlie Hebdo*? Ottawa? The murder of British soldier Lee Rigby in Woolwich? Is this the kind of criminality that we want to encourage? Expect more of it as long as we – and our media – stand by and do nothing to stop the propagation of their contamination.

The January 2015 Paris attack on the *Charlie Hebdo* satirical magazine is a great example. Almost all the news broadcasts intentionally distorted the video image of the Muslim Paris policeman's assassination at the hands of the shooters, but what they did show of the video made these guys look fearsome and indomitable. We were complicit in the propaganda even as we refrained from showing an actual crime. Are we more interested in selling advertising than we are in protecting our own way of life?

I've got a better idea. Let's not show such videos at all. Let's not encourage anybody else who may be tempted to be a misguided copycat to attempt to do the same thing. The Paris attackers were criminals and we need not depict them as if they were insuperable marauders. We certainly don't need to give anybody the false impression that what they did was in any way heroic. It's pretty easy to be invincible when you're shooting unarmed and unsuspecting victims with an automatic rifle but that doesn't mean it's right. What it does mean is that the Kouachi brothers who carried out the *Charlie Hebdo* attack were every bit as deranged as Adam Lanza, the perpetrator of the horrific Sandy Hook Elementary School Shooting in Newtown, Connecticut. They were criminals, no better and no worse, and do not deserve to be called "*jihadists*" or given any other religious appellation. It's a crime. It's terrorism. Leave religion out of it.

Yes, the killing of Western hostages and the other brutal massacres and pogroms that are happening in the Middle East are important news and they deserve proper coverage. Show a hostage's picture but crop out the masked goon standing over him. Be careful that whatever video or images we do show will not put these murderers in a favorable light. They are not omnipotent and our media should be ethical enough not to succumb to sensationalism. Let me reiterate that depriving them of media attention will make it much harder to recruit others to their cause. That's the way to prevent future terrorism. Responsible journalism – accurate reporting without sensationalism – will contribute greatly to the achievement of that goal.

There may already be something of a precedent for this. If you remember, there was an incident in Moore, Oklahoma – an Oklahoma City suburb – on September 25, 2014 in which a worker who had been fired from his job at a food processing plant that day returned to the plant and beheaded one coworker and stabbed another. The assailant was a man who had allegedly converted to Islam in prison and made posts sympathetic to the Islamic State on social media. Other workers at the plant claimed that he had tried to convert them to Islam and the man's grisly beheading of an office worker shortly followed the similar killings of Americans James Foley and Steven Sotloff at the hands of IS.[157]

Officials quickly classified the crime as workplace violence, national coverage of the story faded almost immediately, and we have heard very little about it since. Even though this may have met the definition of lone wolf domestic terrorism, its classification as workplace violence served the purpose of quickly reducing and diverting the media's attention and, hopefully, prevented some other copycat to attempt the same

---

157. Mark Berman, "After a Beheading in Oklahoma, Debate Over What to Call
It," *Washington Post*, September 29, 2014. Accessed July 16, 2017. http://www.
washingtonpost.com/news/post-nation/wp/2014/09/29/after-a-beheading-in-
oklahoma-debate-over-what-to-call-it/.

thing. That same strategy didn't work with the Nidal Hassan shooting at Fort Hood, however.

ESTABLISHING A COUNTER-NARRATIVE

Where is our counter to the terrorists' narrative against us in the Arab world? An effective, credible counter-narrative is an essential part of our playbook that has been missing from day one. We didn't start on one after Palestinians hijacked their first US airliner in 1969, we didn't have one in 1979 when Iranian *Shiite* radicals poured over the walls of the US embassy in Tehran, and we didn't have one when *Sunni* extremists and Al-Qaeda started the war against us in 1992. A counter-narrative is extremely important; you can't win a battle of hearts and minds without one – and we haven't had one.

In its simplest terms, a counter-narrative is a counterargument. While Al-Qaeda, IS, and other groups all use essentially the same narrative to justify their actions and garner popular support, we have not effectively responded in kind. We've not successfully and convincingly answered the allegations against us by the Islamists. My educated guess for this is that our Washington leadership does not understand Muslim and Arab culture well enough to establish an effective counter-narrative of our own. It has failed to crack the region's cultural code. We're trapped like a deer in the headlights behind seeing everything through the lens of terrorism so we've become obsessed with how much mouthwash and shampoo people take on airplanes instead of effectively taking on, and countering the *takfirists'* ideology.

Naturally, since Al-Qaeda has emerged as an indigenous part of that Arab and Muslim culture, they have been very successful in developing a narrative that resonates with many in the Middle East. The group blames the West for all the indignities and humiliations that Muslims around the world are suffering. The West has installed or supported corrupt, secular, puppet leaders to protect Western interests at the expense of the Arabs and Muslims and the only way this oppression can be cast off is through violence and armed struggle. This will require self-sacrifice and a sense of "*jihad*" aimed at cleansing the *Dar al-Islam* from the occupation and influence of the despicable Christian Crusaders, who have brought nothing but pain and suffering on the *ummah*. Only after the Westerners are expelled and defeated and the *Sharia* becomes the law of the land will Muslims enjoy true peace, security, and prosperity for all.

This narrative promotes the concept of *Al-Wala wal-Bara'* [i.e., "Friendship and Disavowal"] that encourages Muslims to support each other while avoiding and mistrusting all non-Muslims – especially those who are Westerners. We've already seen how the Koran supports this view more than once and admonishes Muslims about getting too cozy with non-Muslims:

> *O you who believe! Do not take for guardians those who take your religion for a mockery and a joke, from among those who where given the Book before you and the unbelievers; and be careful of (you duty to) Allah if you are believers.*[158]

The above reference to "those who were given the Book" clearly warns Muslims to be wary and mistrustful of Christians and Jews. Another verse cautions:

> *O you who believe! Do not take the unbelievers for friends rather than the believers; do you desire that you should give to Allah a manifest proof against yourselves?*[159]

This Al-Qaeda message certainly at least strikes several chords with many Muslims. A large majority has believed for years that US support for Israel has kept their Palestinian brethren oppressed under the Zionist occupier since 1948. Many Egyptians harbor rancor against the United States, believing it kept the hated dictator Mubarak in power for over three decades. Iraqi *Sunnis* hate America for toppling Saddam Hussein and handing the country over to the *Shiite* apostates. Iranians hate us for engineering the coup that toppled Prime Minister Mossadeq six decades ago. Strict Saudi *Wahhabis* see us as corrupt and licentious unbelievers who are not welcome in their desert kingdom.

---

158. Koran 5:57.
159. Koran 4:144.

There's no shortage of antipathy in the Muslim world toward the West, in general, and the United States, in particular, so Al-Qaeda has been pretty successful in riding the coattails of that. Al-Qaeda's Islamist successors have clearly seen this and have kept up their anti-Western diatribe.

Now, while it is true that we have not successfully established our own counter-narrative to that of Al-Qaeda, it isn't completely fair to say we've never started one. We've discussed how the administration of President George W. Bush believed that promoting democracy in the Middle East would allow the common people to finally have a voice in their own governance. The Bush White House believed that its policy of hegemonic democratization would short circuit the so-called *jihadist* trend and create the atmosphere for peace, stability, and enlightenment.

Unfortunately, this policy was both ill-conceived and poorly executed. It's pretty hard to sell democracy when some of your best friends in the region are such democratic stalwarts as the Saudi royal family, Hosni Mubarak, Yemen's Ali Abdullah Saleh, and Tunisia's Zine El Abidine Ben Ali. No support for democracy there.

To our embarrassment, we found that democracy didn't always serve our interests or achieve the desired results. When the Hamas movement won the Palestinians elections by a landslide in 2006, we weren't too happy about it even though international observers certified the balloting process as being free and fair. Without a doubt the *Shiite*-dominated government in Iraq that was "democratically elected" has allowed Iran unparalleled influence in the country that once blocked its expansion into the Middle East, proper. So, are we only supportive of democracy when things go our way?

In the end, even moderates in the Arab and Muslim worlds have been reluctant to speak out in support of US policies and values because they cannot dispute much of Al-Qaeda's narrative. They cannot defend American policies that have supported autocrats and dictators while keeping the Palestinian people under Israel's thumb. We simply have a credibility problem that, at present, seems largely insurmountable without a significant effort and major policy changes.

And as we've already seen, our biggest miscalculation was trying to convince the Arabs to implement our style of democracy into societies that lacked the basic building blocks and institutions for that type of government. That effort was doomed to fail. The Arab societies do not have a free press, women are largely second-class citizens, and there is no formal separation of religion and state. Most often, Islam is recognized as the state religion. We were endeavoring to spin straw into gold while ignoring the crucial fact that our democratic evolution has taken nearly two-and-a-half centuries. Any attempt to impose our external form of democracy on the Arab world would meet with the same level of success as if our extremist enemies foisted the *Sharia* on us.

Since we have already pointed out that a majority of Muslims believe that Islam and democracy can coexist, we are going to have to let them design and build the form of democratic government that works for them. That's the way we did it and that is the best way for them to do it, too.

Given the fact that we have shot ourselves in both feet several times with our Arab and Muslim policies over the past half-century, building an effective and (most importantly) credible counter-narrative among Muslims must be viewed as a gradual and incremental process. We cannot afford any more grandiose missteps like hegemonic democratization and military invasions and occupations. We're going to have to crawl before we can walk, and walk before we can run. But, we absolutely have to do it and we have to get started right away.

As a suggested first step, we should make sure we amplify the voices of the victims of Islamist extremism all over the world. Our media (and the media of our allies) should be casting the spotlight on the terror these radicals are inflicting on indigenous populations. Let those enduring the persecution and violence speak and tell the world of their suffering and their horror without any additional commentary or editorializing from us. These victims have credibility in their own societies and cultures because they have been peaceful, ethnic and religious minorities in them for centuries. Make sure these stories flood the airwaves and newspapers throughout the Arab and Muslim worlds.

Next let's have these victims ask the Muslims in their societies whether the violence and carnage that IS, Al-Shabaab, or Boko Haram has inflicted upon them is really their idea of a religion of peace. Is mass butchery really *jihad*? This question must be asked of Muslims repeatedly – every single time an atrocity or massacre against innocent victims takes place. It is time for Muslims themselves to take some responsibility in what is happening and maybe they need to be shamed into it.

The goal here is to steadily begin chipping away at elements of the Al-Qaeda/Islamist narrative. Yes, the West does bear some responsibility for the Middle East's problems but the extremists' methodology isn't right, either. What purpose does Boko Haram's kidnapping of 200 Nigerian schoolgirls serve? Are those under the control of the Islamic State somehow better off than the population of Abu Dhabi? The people in Yemen and Somalia already have a difficult enough life, why repress them even more? Is that really the will of Allah? Should Arabs and Muslims be proud that this is how their "religion of peace" appears to the rest of the world?

We begin by planting seeds of doubt and misgivings about the way these radical groups are behaving and conducting themselves, drawing special attention to their harsh punishments and absolute intolerance of minorities who have enjoyed a shared, peaceful history in the region. Most importantly, the less obvious our involvement appears in this effort, the more successful it will be. Our reputation and standing in the region are already damaged goods. Let the victims speak for themselves directly to the Muslims of the region and the world and ask *them* these difficult questions. Muslims should be encouraged to ask themselves these questions, too.

When opportunities present themselves to enhance our counter-narrative, we shouldn't be reluctant or shy about seizing them. For example, after *Charlie Hebdo* there was a lot of negative reporting about the alleged alienation of the Muslim community in France and how that supposedly contributes to the radicalization of disaffected, isolated, Muslim youth not just in France, but also throughout Europe. That is undoubtedly true but it is not the entire story.

To illustrate, there is a positive and inspiring story that has gone under-reported. This story is about the heroism of Muslim police officer Ahmed Merabet, who was killed by the gunmen in the *Charlie Hebdo* attack. Here was a patriotic French officer, who just also happened to be a Muslim, who was killed in the line of duty against terrorists who struck civilians inside the French capital supposedly in the name of Islam.

Press coverage of officer Merabet and his dedication to duty should overshadow and eclipse that of the misguided Kouachi brothers who carried out the massacre. Don't focus on them, focus on the brave Muslim police officer who gave his life defending fellow Parisians. Terrorism thrives on the spread of irrational fear. Concentrate on the positive aspect while giving short shrift to the sensationalist portion that feeds that fear. We don't need to feel any sympathy whatsoever for the poor, little Kouachi brothers and their screwed-up cause. History needn't remember them.

The same is true for the Muslim deli worker at the Hyper Cacher kosher supermarket in Paris that was attacked on the same day as the *Charlie Hebdo* atrocity. Here 24-year-old Lassana Bathily, a Muslim originally from Mali, hid persons trapped in the supermarket inside the store's cold storage unit. This is an opportunity to contrast the brave, loyal, and humanitarian actions of one Muslim – hiding customers in a Jewish grocery store – with the nihilistic philosophy of the assailant, Amedy Coulibaly. Again, put the focus on Bathily's great courage and honorable conduct while relegating Coulibaly to oblivion.

And there are more opportunities for us. What about the several millions of Muslims in France (and elsewhere in Europe) who have *not* been radicalized? Wouldn't it be great to repeatedly and constantly publish their success stories and showcase them as productive citizens, something often neglected in mainstream media coverage of Muslim communities in the West? Who gives a damn about the killers? Let's focus on the positive while consigning the negative to a brief news item that will quickly fade away.

There are really two major benefits to this approach. First, it directly refutes the Al-Qaeda/Islamist narrative that the West is engaged in a war with Islam. By showing how Muslims are an integral part of Western society, we are confronting and disproving that portion of their argument.

Secondly this should help to attenuate some of the Muslim bashing that has become so popular – particularly in the United States. Those who practice it usually don't offer solutions; they just stereotype and criticize

Muslims. It wouldn't hurt us to change a few hearts and minds right here at home by publishing the success stories of American Muslims.

As I've noted before, many critics like to trot out the tired, old phrase, "Most Muslims may not be terrorists but most terrorists are Muslims," as if this – by itself – is some profound universal truth. They conveniently ignore the corollary to this statement: Most victims of terrorism are Muslims, too. Of course, real objectivity doesn't serve the Muslim bashers' agenda. Hate does.

The terrorists are even happier to attack the "near enemy" (those in the Arab and Muslim worlds they have branded as apostates) than they are to attack the "far enemy" (i.e., the United States). These "near enemy" targets are local, far easier to reach, and there are more of them. We just tire of news about car bombs blowing up scores of Iraqis in Baghdad every day.

For example, *Der Spiegel Online* reported in December 2009 that the Combating Terrorism Center at the US Military Academy at West Point looked at specifically acknowledged Al-Qaeda attacks and arrived at some interesting facts. Since the group has had difficulty in attacking the West, the report concluded that Al-Qaeda "maintains its relevancy by attacking countries with Muslim majorities." The researchers concluded that "non-Westerners were 38 times more likely to be killed" in an Al-Qaeda attack than Westerners. In fact, in 2007 some 99 percent of Al-Qaeda's victims were non-Westerners while this percentage was 96 percent in 2008.[160]

This report alluded to the problematic issue of identifying the religion of the victims since countries like Iraq have Christian, Kurdish, and Yazidi minorities that have been targeted by Al-Qaeda, but a significant number of terrorist victims in Iraq and elsewhere were also known to be *Shiite* Muslims – reviled by the extremists.

---

160. Yassin Musharbash, "Surprising Study on Terrorism: Al-Qaida [sic] Kills Eight Times More Muslims Than Non-Muslims," *Der Spiegel Online*, December 3, 2009. Accessed July 16, 2017. http://www.spiegel.de/international/world/surprising-study-on-terrorism-al-qaida-kills-eight-times-more-muslims-than-non-muslims-a-660619.html.

Just looking at the death toll from terrorist attacks in November 2014, the figures are quite striking. In December 2014 the UK daily *The Guardian* cited a report from the International Centre for the Study of Radicalisation:

More than 5,000 people, mostly civilians and overwhelmingly Muslims, were killed in jihadi attacks in November, according to a study documenting the toll of Islamist violence worldwide.

About 60% of these deaths were caused by the militant groups Islamic State and Boko Haram, suggesting a transformation in the nature of jihadi groups from terrorists to "more conventional forces that are fighting to gain or hold territory against state armies," the report by the International Centre for the Study of Radicalisation and the BBC, said.[161]

On July 31, 2012 the US National Counterterrorism Center published a statistical report entitled "Country Reports on Terrorism 2011" that also concluded that Muslims were disproportionally represented as victims of terrorist attacks. The NCTC published the following findings regarding victims of terrorist attacks just in 2011 (emphasis added):

Over 12,000 people were killed by terrorist attacks in 2011. The overall number of victims killed, however, decreased 5 percent from 2010. More than half of the people killed in 2011 were civilians and 755 were children. Although terrorism deaths decreased, the number of government representative and security force fatalities increased significantly. Muslims continued to bear the brunt of terrorism, *while attacks targeting Christians dropped nearly 45 percent from a five-year high in 2010.*

---

161. Michael Safi, "Jihadi Attacks – November's 5,000 Deaths Broken Down by Country, Victim, and Terror Group," *The Guardian*, December 11, 2014. Accessed July 16, 2017. http://www.theguardian.com/world/2014/dec/11/jihadi-attacks-killed-more-than-5000-people-in-november-the-vast-majority-of-them-muslims.

- *Although civilians were the largest single group of victims killed in terrorist attacks, their numbers over the past five years in proportion to the total number of deaths have gone down by 13 percent, decreasing from a 2007 high of 64 percent.*

- *The number of government employees and contractors killed in 2011 increased by over 60 percent from 2010, while the number of government officials killed in 2011 increased by over 13 percent. The number of police killed in 2011 also increased by over 15 percent.*

- In cases where the religious affiliation of terrorism casualties could be determined, Muslims suffered between 82 and 97 percent of terrorism-related fatalities over the past five years.

- Muslim-majority countries bore the greatest number of attacks involving 10 or more deaths, with Afghanistan sustaining the highest number (47), followed by Iraq (44), Pakistan (37), Somalia (28), and Nigeria (12).

- *Afghans also suffered the largest number of fatalities overall with 3,245 deaths, followed by Iraqis (2,958), Pakistanis (2,038), Somalis (1,013), and Nigerians (590).*[162]

This fact that Muslims represent the majority of the victims of terrorism provides yet another arrow to add to our counter-narrative quiver. It allows us to express empathy to the Muslim world for its victims, which *often number more every month* than the number of victims we lost on 9/11. Just stop and think about that for a minute. And with IS and Boko Haram on the warpath, that monthly toll in the Muslim world is more likely than not to continue rising.

Reaching out to those Muslim victims while emphasizing the fact that despite its alleged embracement of *Al-Wala wa al-Bara'* (i.e., "Friendship and Disavowal") and supposed support of the Muslims in *Dar al-Islam,*

---

162. "Country Reports on Terrorism 2011," National Counterterrorism Center, July 31, 2012. Accessed July 16, 2017. http://www.state.gov/j/ct/rls/crt/2011/195555.htm.

Al-Qaeda and the other misguided faith-based butchers are doing far more harm to Muslims than anyone else. How can these groups claim to be carrying the banner of Islam when the majority of their victims are Muslims? Constantly hammering this home to the Muslim world should already be a part of our counter-narrative and it would be an excellent way to start rebuilding good will and credibility with the people most harmed and affected by Islamist terror.

We cannot restore that good will and credibility overnight; it will be an agonizingly slow and arduous process. But the sooner we get started, the sooner we will begin to see results and, hopefully, the sooner we will start eroding support for Al-Qaeda and its ilk by disrupting and disproving key elements of their narrative. The ultimate aim of our strategy is to deprive and deny this ideology of terrorism of any support and sympathy it may derive from the Arab and Muslim populations. What is the benefit of supporting Al-Qaeda when most of the people it kills are Muslims? That's a pretty powerful question we should be encouraging Muslims to ask themselves.

Then there are serendipitous little plums that fall into our hands from time to time. Take, for example, the story of the IS recruit who traveled to Iraq from India with dreams of *jihad* in his head. Twenty-three-year-old Areeb Majeed left for Iraq with three friends but instead of participating in the "deadly offensive," he was forced to fetch water for the other fighters and clean toilets. Disillusioned by these menial tasks, Majeed returned home to Mumbai where he was arrested by the Indian National Investigation Agency for "terror-related" offenses, according to the *Press Trust of India*.[163]

And, of course, nothing says "band of brothers" like the mass executions of your own fighters. A December 2014 report originally attributed to the *Financial Times* revealed that Islamic State had executed 100 of its own foreign fighters who had tried to escape from Raqqa. The article claimed that Islamic State had created a military police force to handle any foreign fighters that were shirking their duties. Around a dozen Europeans who

---

163. "Indian IS Recruit Goes Home After Having to Clean Toilets: Reports," *AFP*, December 1, 2014. Accessed July 16, 2017. http://www.spacewar.com/reports/Indian_IS_recruit_goes_home_after_having_to_clean_toilets_reports_999.html.

had gone to fight for Islamic State were said to be disillusioned after they wound up fighting against other Syrian rebel organizations instead of the Syrian regime. These men were reportedly being held prisoner by Islamic State and they now wanted to return home.[164]

Many Muslim youth susceptible to radicalization may envision what IS calls its *jihad* as some noble endeavor where Arabian Knights sweep across the desert on horseback slaying infidels. The fact that IS fighters have become disillusioned and seek to leave – at their own peril, on pain of execution – should be published in every news periodical and shown on every television channel. Repeatedly.

Feature articles and programs should be made of the families whose misguided sons and daughters went off to Iraq or Syria only to perish. These vulnerable youths must constantly see the pain and suffering of these grieving parents as a constant reminder of how their actions may potentially hurt those whom they love the most.

The stories of young men and women who have been able to escape the clutches of IS or other groups and make their way back home should also get prominent coverage. Their mistreatment, the lies told to them by their recruiters, and the omnipresent death and destruction – narrated by these youths themselves – can be powerful counters to the notion that this "*jihad*" is somehow a glamorous adventure.

All of these things must be carefully and gradually woven into the fabric of our counter-narrative. We have a Muslim and Arab audience out there that is at least as concerned about Islamist extremism as we are – I mean, the violence and bloodshed is happening in their streets and in their own backyard. They are the ones knee-deep in bodies. Deep down inside, many of them would like to cooperate with America and the West in solving this problem but a half-century of bungled US policies in the region has left them reluctant to trust us – they may be sympathetic to our values but lack confidence in our actions and our commitment. If we can begin to restore our good will and credibility, if we can acknowledge

---

164. "IS Has Executed 100 Foreign Fighters Trying to Quit: Reports," *AFP*, December 20, 2014. Accessed July 16, 2017. http://www.spacewar.com/reports/IS_has_executed_100_foreigners_trying_to_quit_report_999.html/.

the suffering that terrorism has wrought upon the Muslims themselves, and if we can plant doubt in their minds about the truth of Al-Qaeda's narrative, we might find we have a more receptive audience than we thought. What do we have to lose?

The new Global Engagement Center (GEC) in the US State Department is responsible for the development and dissemination of this counter-narrative. According to its web page:

> *The Global Engagement Center is an interagency entity, housed at the State Department, which is charged with coordinating U.S. counterterrorism messaging to foreign audiences.*

> *It was established pursuant to Executive Order 13721, signed by President Obama on March 14, 2016. As stated in the Executive Order, the Center "shall lead the coordination, integration, and synchronization of Government-wide communications activities directed at foreign audiences abroad in order to counter the messaging and diminish the influence of international terrorist organizations," such as ISIL.*

> *The Center plays a key role in countering ISIL's messaging. Designed to be an agile, innovative organization, the Center uses modern, cutting-edge technology and takes advantage of the best talent and tools throughout the private sector and government.*

> *The Global Engagement Center replaced the Center for Strategic Counterterrorism Communications. The new strategy seeks to be more effective in the information space and is focused on partner-driven messaging and data analytics.*[165]

---

165. Global Engagement Center, Department of State website. Accessed July 16, 2017. http://www.state.gov/r/gec/.

The GEC's predecessor, the Center for Strategic Counterterrorism Communications, failed to counter the terrorists' narrative in the Middle East and Muslim world. For now the GEC seems focused on a more comprehensive strategy for accomplishing that mission and using "a global network of credible voices" to do so. I hope, with time, that the center expands from social media efforts to propagate our counter-Islamist and counter-*takfirist* narrative in the mainstream Arab media, as well.

Our message must penetrate and permeate throughout the Arab and Muslim worlds *every single day*. It must be a cooperative effort that is coordinated internationally among our allies and friends. Our mission and our goal is to debunk the main tenets of our enemies' narrative and plant doubt in the minds of the population about whether those terrorists are really acting in their best interests and the best interests of Islam. This is fundamental to our victory and we don't seem to be getting it done.

Information warfare has to be a form of psychological warfare in order to work. That means it is absolutely essential that we tailor our message and our counter-narratives to each target population. When we are addressing the people of Yemen, our counter-narrative message must be customized to the specific issues plaguing Yemen, like Al-Qaeda in the Arabian Peninsula (AQAP). The social, cultural, tribal, economic, and even religious dynamics must all be taken into account. A proper counter-narrative is not a one-size-fits-all kind of proposition. It has to *resonate with that specific population*. Otherwise we are missing the mark and wasting our time and potentially doing more harm than good – and we cannot afford to do that.

Likewise, our message to Egypt must be focused tightly for Egyptians, a counter-narrative that is harmonized to their attitudes and concerns. The same must be true for targeting Syria, Iraq, Lebanon, Somalia, Tunisia, Libya, and everywhere in the world. We have embassies and CIA stations all over the world; let's put their knowledge of the local countries to good use in crafting a uniquely tailored message and counter-narrative for each state. While our basic counter-narrative may consist of broad outlines, adapting them to appeal to specific audiences will have much greater effect.

An effective, targeted counter-narrative is one of the most useful and valuable smart weapons in our arsenal to defeat the terrorists' ideology. It doesn't have to be expensive, it doesn't need to be delivered by a multimillion-dollar jet or ship. But it does need to be out there in the wild.

If we're focusing on yet another US Government bureaucracy like the *Voice of America* to deliver our message, that's just one more strategic mistake. It has such a minuscule audience in the Arab world as to be nearly insignificant. Our counter-narrative needs to be showcased in the mainstream Arab media like *Al-Jazeera*, *Al-Arabiya*, and each country's national networks. It needs to be there every day. Our message is one of hope, life, and a better future while the Islamists preach hate, death, and the past. Only bureaucracy can make this effort more difficult than it needs to be.

A strong, credible, and persistent narrative that counters the message of our extremist foes and resonates with the target audience is arguably the most powerful and important tool that we can exploit to defeat the Islamist ideology. We will not be able to win without it.

CHAPTER EIGHT

STEP THREE: LET'S ADDRESS
FAILED AND FAILING STATES

"The events of September 11, 2001, taught us that weak states, like Afghanistan, can pose as great a danger to our national interests as strong states. Poverty does not make poor people into terrorists and murderers. Yet poverty, weak institutions, and corruption can make weak states vulnerable to terrorist networks and drug cartels within their borders."

– National Security Strategy of the Bush Administration

Remember the old 1960s television comedy "Get Smart?" In the show, Maxwell Smart (Agent 86 played by Don Adams) was a bumbling secret agent for CONTROL, a secret US intelligence agency, in the struggle with its archrival KAOS and the forces of international evil. Smart would hilariously screw up nearly every assignment and mission, yet somehow manage to save the day at the end of each episode ("Sorry, Chief, missed it by THAT much!"). Smart's deadpan demeanor and by-the-book attitude made his missteps all the funnier.

That show parodied the Soviet and US competition for geopolitical and geostrategic position and influence at the height of the Cold War in the 1960s. But the forces of chaos today are very real and very dangerous – especially the events taking place in the Middle East and Africa. As Islamism spills over into the West, our enemies seek to use our natural social tolerance and diversity as a tool against us – threatening one of the hallmarks of Western society. In confronting and eliminating this danger, we can't afford to simply keep on doing what we have been doing – that obviously has not been working. We cannot afford to make the kind of mistakes that Smart did as Agent 86 in the show.

The Black Plague of religious and sectarian violence is sweeping through the Middle East and Africa in cruel, unprecedented paroxysms that can leave thousands dead (or worse) in a single month. The staggering death toll from this constant brutality makes Ebola look like just a bad case of the flu and, unfortunately, no successful vaccine is yet in sight. The patient is in extremely critical condition.

The good news is that while the situation is desperate, it isn't necessarily hopeless. The bad news is that we will primarily have to rely on the patient to heal himself – external (i.e., non-Muslim) cures are simply not going to work. And it's probably going to take some time. This means that the potential is extremely high for the situation in that part of the world to get worse before it gets better.

Since the only places where Islamist terrorists and extremists can really set up shop is in failed or failing states, the success of our long-term strategy to eradicate Islamist ideology depends on stopping the slide of troubled states toward anarchy and chaos and turning them around and eventually reviving failed states and restoring proper governance in them. There's a term for this that absolutely nobody likes: nation building. Nevertheless, without restoring a system of law and order, without eradicating widespread corruption, without proper educational curricula that avoid prejudice and discrimination, without some kind of sustainable economy, without an Islam that stands up to Islamism, and without inclusive governance that promotes tolerance and a sense of worth and belonging, there will be no peace. Things have just grown too far out of hand. Unless the world finds some way to push the reset button, the region is simply going to sink deeper and deeper into a bottomless pit of hardening animosities and ceaseless violence.

This escalating violence will exert more and more destabilizing forces on countries that are already vulnerable, accelerating their collapse, and, more troublingly, potentially threaten or erode the stability of other countries presently deemed secure. This is the scenario we have seen being played out in the Middle East ever since the Arab Spring of 2011. Arab strongmen and dictators who had been in power for decades in countries like Tunisia,

Egypt, Syria, Libya, and Yemen suddenly found themselves an endangered species or out of power altogether. These seismic events took everyone by surprise – including the Arabs themselves – and the resulting power vacuums opened the door to power struggles to fill these voids. Often Islamist groups, parties, and forces that have seen themselves as oppressed for many years have become major players in these struggles. They don't represent a majority anywhere but they are the ones that have the guns and are the most organized and they are extremely adept at quickly moving to fill these power vacuums in the region whenever they occur.

This isn't just a Middle East problem. The effects of this violence and unrest have repercussions both inside and outside of the region. People seeking to escape the constant chaos, warfare, and death in their home-lands such as Iraq and Syria have fled in droves to neighboring states such as Lebanon, Turkey, and Jordan, and are continuing to do so. These huge numbers of refugees have placed a heavy burden on those countries' limited economic and humanitarian resources that adds to the possibility of further regional instability.

It's a human tragedy on a scale not seen since the end of World War II. Many of these refugees are so desperate to leave the Middle East and find new lives in some Western European country that they are willing to pay human smugglers to gain passage on rickety ships bound for Spain, Greece, or Italy. This trade is flourishing in places like Istanbul where many Iraqi expatriates with experience in smuggling refugees from Iraq's civil war are now cashing in on a constant stream of Syrian refugees. Many of these victims perish when overcrowding, poor weather, and abandonment by the smugglers cause their boats to founder and sink.

A similar fate claims many African refugees who are fleeing violence and poor economic opportunities in their homelands. Many of these follow a difficult overland journey into a lawless Libya where, if they survive, they are forced onto unsafe, inadequate, and unseaworthy vessels for an extremely hazardous voyage north. It is a trade that is extremely lucrative for the smugglers and often fatal for the refugees.

A news article issued by the United Nations High Commissioner for Refugees on September 16, 2014 estimated that 2,500 victims had either died or gone missing at sea so far that year.[166] A news article citing the International Organization of Migration two weeks later put the death toll even higher at 3,072 for that point in the year.[167] In August 2015 the agency revised the number of fatalities for the previous year upward to "3,500" and estimated that "2,500" refugees had either died or gone mission crossing to Europe in 2015.[168]

How many actually make it to Europe? The UN High Commissioner for Refugees estimated that 75,000 refugees arrived in Italy, Spain, Greece, and Malta during the first half of 2014 compared with 60,000 for the same period in 2013.[169] That pales in comparison to 2015, however, where the agency estimated *half a million* refugees had crossed the Mediterranean into Europe in the first nine months of the year alone.[170] The trend has continued throughout the winter of 2015-2016 and on March 4, 2016 the BBC reported that over 135,000 refugees had arrived in Europe by sea since the beginning of the year.[171] That sort of humanitarian deluge is not sustainable.

And while the total number of refugees arriving in Europe during the first half of 2017 is only 35% of the number who entered Europe during the same period in 2016, the number of those crossing the Mediterranean from Africa to Europe (primarily Libya to Italy) are up 40%.[172] With 2,000 deaths among the refugees seeking to cross the Mediterranean from Africa

---

166. "UNHCR Alarmed at Death Toll from Boat Sinkings in the Mediterranean," United Nations High Commissioner for Refugees website, September 16, 2014. Accessed July 17, 2017. http://www.unhcr.org/54184ae76.html.

167. "Record 3,072 Migrants Killed Crossing Mediterranean in 2014, Report Says," *France 24* website, September 29, 2014. Accessed July 17, 2017. http://www.france24.com/en/20140929-record-migrants-killed-crossing-mediterranean-2014-report/.

168. "Mediterranean Sea Crossings Exceed 300,000, Including 200,000 to Greece," United Nations High Commissioner for Refugees website, August 28, 2015. Accessed July 17, 2017. http://www.unhcr.org/55e033816.html.

169. "UNHCR Calls for Urgent European Action to End Refugee and Migrant Deaths at Sea," United Nations High Commissioner for Refugees website, July 24, 2014. Accessed July 17, 2017. http://www.unhcr.org/53d0e2d26.html.

170. "Refugee Emergency in Europe: UNHCR Appeals for USD 128 Million," United Nations High Commissioner for Refugees website, October 1, 2015. Accessed July 17, 2017. http://www.unhcr.org/560d34c26.html.

171. "Migrant Crisis: Migration to Europe Explained in Seven Charts," *BBC* website, March 4, 2016. Accessed October 31, 2016. http://www.bbc.com/news/world-europe-34131911.

172. Jane Onyanga-Omara, "United Nations Figures Show Big Drop in Number of Migrants Arriving in Europe," *USA Today*, June 13, 2017. Accessed July 17, 2017. https://www.usatoday.com/story/news/world/2017/06/13/united-nations-figures-show-big-drop-number-migrants-arriving-europe/102806878/.

to Europe, Amnesty International predicts that the mortality rate for these migrants will be the deadliest on record, triple that of 2015.[173]

Moreover, these fortunate ones often soon discover that being a refugee in Western Europe isn't what they thought it would be. Homesickness, unemployment, cultural isolation and alienation, and economic hardship soon cause many of these victims to wonder if they really are any better off with an uncertain future in a refugee camp in a strange country than they would have been staying at home in the first place.

As short-term humanitarian refugees eventually turn into a long-term drain on the economy, tensions begin to mount between the migrants and segments of the indigenous European population who perceive those refugees as causes of increasing crime and economic woes. Now, these mounting cultural tensions will simply add fuel to the East-West cultural clash that is simmering in the background. The best way to prevent this kind of problem is to find ways to stop the failing state process in the first place. Do that and you stop the endless flow and migration of refugees and the ensuing human misery that it will invariably cause to both the refugees and their hosts.

LIKE IT OR NOT, IT'S GONNA TAKE NATION BUILDING

Why is this our problem? I mean the Muslims and the Arabs really don't have anyone to blame but themselves for the *Sunni-Shia* violence in Damascus and Baghdad, right? You have Al-Shabaab Somalis fighting pro-government Somalis and Boko Haram Nigerians fighting pro-government Nigerians. The causes of this fighting don't have anything to do with the United States, Israel, or the West, so why should we even care if they all kill each other?

It's certainly a valid question but it ignores the fact they're not just killing each other. America and Americans have been in the crosshairs of our current enemies – the *Sunni* Islamist extremists – since December 1992. Islamists in Algeria targeted Westerners of all stripes when that country's

---

173. Kate Samuelson, "Amnesty: 2017 on Course to Be Deadliest Year Yet for Refugees Crossing the Mediterranean," *Time*, July 6, 2017. Accessed July 17, 2017. http://time.com/4845054/amnesty-2017-refugees-crossing-mediterranean/.

bloody civil war broke out in 1991. If we want to prevent attacks on our nation and ourselves, we have to become part of the solution to eradicate their ideology. Do we really want to just sit on the sidelines as a region that is awash in weapons and potentially even WMD technologies threatens to fragment and spill its violence into adjoining areas and countries? The turmoil isn't going to just go away because we'd like it to. Terrorism isn't just a rhinovirus or some minor allergy that will clear itself up in a few days. Islamism isn't a fad that will simply fade away in a few months when pop culture needs a change.

Our motive for nation building in the Middle East and Africa is foremost one of self-defense. Furthermore, as I have stated earlier in this book, any real answer to the ideology of Islamist extremism is going to have to come from inside the Muslim world itself. Successful solutions cannot be imposed from the outside.

Now there is no argument from me that most of the failed and failing states in the Arab and Muslim worlds have fallen into their respective tailspins on their own through widespread corruption, authoritarianism, and mismanagement – you name it and they've been guilty of it. Most of these places have been ruled by gangster politics for decades. The Islamic State may put a religious spin on it but it's still authoritarianism. Nevertheless, it's also pretty obvious that these failed countries are not, and will not be able to extricate themselves or their populations from the infectious, destabilizing circumstances under which they now exist. And if the extremists who have found a home in one failed state can destabilize and conquer another, they're going to do just that. We've already started to see how IS now has affiliates in places like Libya, Afghanistan, and Yemen. Further regional economic and social collapse just allows the contagion to spread further. That certainly is not in our best interests.

Corruption and authoritarianism are huge problems in the Middle East. Corruption trickles from the top on down to the very bottom of these governments. Bribery is often the only way to get anything done from the local police office all the way to establishing a regional office for a multinational corporation or signing a contract on a major commercial project. Officials have their hands out at every level.

The people know it and it disgusts them. Even we recognize it. Graft and corruption breed the desire for reform – often through violent means after decades of pent-up resentment and exasperation if no other alternative exists. People will want retribution for long years of suffering and oppression. The fact that Islamists in failed and failing states promise to offer reform and retribution at the same time may find resonance with a public that has had enough. A victimized population will be quick to make an emotional short-term decision rather than a deliberative strategic one. And bad times often encourage people to turn to religion. All this favors the Islamists.

We have paid a heavy price for keeping autocrats like Egypt's Mubarak and Yemen's Saleh in power. We have been duped into thinking that just slamming Islamists in jail and throwing away the key is the best way to eliminate the extremist threat. It isn't. It just breeds more terrorism and our shortsighted view of the situation does little except aggravate the problem and make it worse. It merely highlights our complicity with the tyrants at the people's expense. Perhaps it is time that we stepped back a bit, quit attempting to control or support regimes in the Middle East based merely on our assessment of them as "pro" or "anti" Islamist, and gave the responsibility to the Arabs to clean up their own backyard.

There must be an important precondition to any nation-building enterprise. It has to be an international and regional effort. *This is not a task that is to be bankrolled, managed, or run by the United States.* The vulnerable and failed states in the Middle East are a regional problem that requires a regional solution. We didn't break them and we cannot fix it for them. We cannot pay for it for them. It will not be a job for the US taxpayer. They will need to sink or swim in this by themselves as part of the larger Arab and Muslim solution to eradicate Islamism from within their own midst. They must have skin in the game for this to work.

The principal role for America in this enterprise is to be its guide, cheerleader, ringmaster, and chief proponent. We may have plenty of experience in nation building from our post-World War II Marshall Plan that resurrected Europe and Japan to the modern Peace Corps and Agency for International Development but this task must be handled and funded by the Arabs and Muslims themselves. We can cooperate, advise, support, and encourage but our regional allies and partners must be the ones putting the rubber on the road. This is part of forcing the Arabs and Muslims to recognize the need for reforms throughout the Middle East, not necessarily just in its fragile and failed states.

This is their time to shine. It is their time to develop a sense of collective maturity and to take ownership for the miserable state of affairs in their own region. They may say that Islamic State is a deviation that has connection to Islam. Fine, then it is time for them to step up, defend their faith, and show us what true Islam is supposed to look like. Stop being a victim and start acting like a real Muslim.

Show us that you can roll up your sleeves, lend a hand to a neighbor in need, and fix up the "distressed properties" in your own neighborhood. Show the world that you can bring your religion into the modern realities of the twenty-first century. Stop blaming others for your problems. Show us that you can be responsible leaders in today's international community!

Here is my suggestion on how they can get it done.

WHAT ABOUT AN ARAB PEACE CORPS?

I don't think we need to look any further than our own Peace Corps as an effective mechanism of humanitarian assistance and development. What if the Arabs established their own version of this venerable organization?

Okay, okay so I can hear the snickers and the laughter already. Eyes are rolling throughout the State Department. I mean, with the daily scenes of violence and carnage we see in Syria, Iraq, Yemen, and elsewhere in the Middle East, how could the words "Arab" and "peace" in the same phrase be considered anything other than an oxymoron, right? Certainly the level of chaos, brutality, and bloodshed in the region warrants some healthy skepticism in the concept but we shouldn't completely disregard it out of hand. Let me explain why I think the idea has plenty of merit.

We can start by looking at what our own Peace Corps does. It sends American volunteers for a two-year term abroad to assist in the social, economic, and technical development of a needy nation. These volunteers might work as educators, business consultants, or environmental engineers. They may be assigned to serve with a foreign government, a non-profit organization, or a non-governmental organization. American volunteers have helped foreign farmers boost their agricultural production, drill water wells for rural villages, and build schools and houses in isolated areas.

Our volunteers don't go to a foreign country to outwardly promote American culture and values. They do go there to show in deed what our values and our culture embodies. Those who serve in the Peace Corps are America's humanitarian ambassadors to that country's people. They aren't there to argue or discuss politics; they are there to perform a humanitarian service and to fill a need, often an urgent one. And as they demonstrate our caring, compassionate, and humanitarian side they also learn about the culture and values of the country and people they are serving. They epitomize the good things about America, its people, and their values. It is a rewarding experience for the volunteers as well as the people they are helping.

Correct me if I'm wrong, but this kind of thing would seem to be exactly what the Middle East needs. Anything to get the Arabs working together instead of shooting each other and blowing each other up would be a positive thing and whatever we can do to encourage them to move toward that objective would be in everyone's best interests – ours and theirs.

However, it is also important to emphasize at this stage that our Arab Peace Corps – like its US counterpart – is not in any way involved in promoting major government or political reforms in any way, shape, or form. It is meant solely as a tool for effecting social, economic, and technical development at the popular and humanitarian levels inside a fragile, vulnerable, Arab country. And those countries targeted for assistance would not be the totally failed states that have already crashed and burned like Iraq, Syria, and Yemen. They would be countries where this kind of intervention can still stop the slide toward total failure and prevent it from occurring. This effort would be aimed at preventing fragile states from becoming failed ones – with all the negative consequences that would result for everybody if that were to happen. They will have to deal with the total failures later.

To put an even finer point on this, political unions in the Arab world have all been dismal failures. And political organizations like the League of Arab States or the Organization of Islamic Cooperation are impotent bodies that have no teeth to enforce any of their own resolutions. Their only role is to grandstand and propagandize while doing nothing to actually accomplish Arab or Muslim unity on any cause.

This Arab Peace Corps must exclusively be a humanitarian enterprise that would have absolutely no political dimension of any kind. Its methodology and objectives would be very similar to those of our own Peace Corps but adapted for regional cultural and religious considerations.

The next question is who will create and sponsor our Arab Peace Corps? Naturally, this mission will have to fall to a country wealthy and stable enough to carry it out. It would have to be a country that has excellent relations and enjoys a good reputation with the other states of the Arab (and Muslim) world. Unfortunately, this also begs the question of whether or not any one Arab country – regardless of its wealth and stability – is up to the task of operating our Arab Peace Corps on its own.

In my opinion, no single Arab country does have the stability and resources to sponsor, create, and operate this type of humanitarian service organization by itself. Therefore, I nominate the Gulf Cooperation Council (GCC) as the best candidate for this job. It would be hard to find a wealthier nucleus of countries for our Arab Peace Corps than the six member states of the GCC: Saudi Arabia, Kuwait, Qatar, United Arab Emirates, Bahrain, and Oman. And while several of them have their own political and domestic problems, they are at least as stable as any other Arab country and more so than most.

There are some significant advantages for placing this organization under the aegis of the Gulf Cooperation Council. First, the GCC is a long-standing regional body that already has its own political and military dimensions. If one examines the council's objectives and areas of cooperation on its website (http://www.gcc-sg.org) he or she will find that this body is supportive of inter-Arab cooperation at all levels. It could almost be a "plug-and-play" sponsor for our Arab Peace Corps to provide humanitarian assistance at the popular level in vulnerable Arab states in the region.

Obviously, the GCC members already share the same culture and religion as the states that would be targeted for assistance. Many of the societal and Islamic sensitivities that complicate our efforts to provide assistance as a non-Arab and non-Muslim country would not apply to them. And whatever problems might arise could be resolved between two fraternal, Arab states that aren't separated by a cultural, linguistic, or technological divide.

The GCC has experience with joint venture projects, infrastructure integration (railroads, power grids, and water systems), and technological development among its member states. These are all potential areas of social and economic development that would be extremely useful in humanitarian assistance, as well. The council's proven track record in such efforts is a major plus.

This enterprise would offer a series of considerable benefits to the GCC states, too. The first of these would be a major expansion of the group's regional influence and prestige. The fact that these wealthy Arab states would undertake humanitarian assistance to their Arab neighbors and brethren independent of any political concerns and considerations would demonstrate a heretofore unprecedented level of collective maturity and responsibility among the GCC members.

And there is evidence that the council has begun to shift its gaze from the Gulf outward to the rest of the Middle East. Iraq, Jordan, Yemen, and Morocco have all expressed their desires to join the organization, which has taken the matter under consideration. (Iraq was once shunned by the GCC after its 1990 invasion and occupation of Kuwait but all has since been forgiven.) Jordan, Yemen, and Morocco are all located outside the Gulf proper, although Yemen is situated on the Arabian Peninsula. An expansion of the GCC outside the Gulf would naturally lend itself to an expansion of its humanitarian mission, as well.

An Arab Peace Corps may offer an indirect and unintended benefit to a growing problem in the Arab world in general, and the countries of the Gulf in particular: youth unemployment. The economies in the Gulf states are over-reliant on petroleum and they suffer from rigid, centralized planning. As a result, the institutions of these economies are more focused on the status quo than innovation for a more diverse economic future.

Young Arabs in these countries often have access to great educational facilities (either at home or abroad) but their prospects of finding a job that is worthy of their investment in higher education are not good – particularly outside of the petroleum and petrochemical industries. Service in an Arab Peace Corps (with a moderate stipend from the GCC sponsors) would give these youth an opportunity to gain valuable practical experience that they might not be able to obtain at home and save some money toward future goals like getting married, all while helping a fraternal Arab people. The GCC countries could benefit from an Arab Peace Corps that attenuates some of the pressures from the unemployed youth demographic.

This enterprise offers a golden opportunity to mold and shape young Arab hearts and minds and steer them away from Islamism. It's one that could represent a quantum leap forward in our fight against our common *takfirist* foes and their nightmarish and nihilistic view of the *Sharia* and Islamist society. It's also chance for our allies to beat the IS propaganda machine at its own game.

There has not been a single, orthodox, mainstream, Islamic authority or cleric who has recognized the Islamic State's declaration of its "caliphate" in June 2014. From the Grand Sheikh of Al-Azhar on down to the popular *Al-Jazeera* cleric Yusuf al-Qaradawi, the recognized *Sunni ulema* have universally condemned the Islamic State and its barbaric practices as being a deviant entity that has nothing to do with the religion of Islam. They have denounced IS mass beheadings and crucifixions, cautioned Muslim youth against joining the group, and expressed concern over the group's spread outside of Iraq and Syria into places like Yemen, Libya, Tunisia, and Egypt.

We know from the polling of Arab and Muslim populations by respected institutions like Gallup and the Pew Research Center that these societies are also worried about the spread of Islamist radicalism. They are, after all, the primary victims of Islamist terrorism in the Middle East.

An Arab Peace Corps – one that is wholeheartedly endorsed by the *ulema* – provides an effective mechanism to combat "deviant" Islamism and demonstrate to other Arabs and the world what true Islam really looks like. Here is a way to showcase Muslims helping other Muslims instead of brutally murdering those who don't agree with your ideology. Here is a rare opportunity to portray Islam in a positive light in the West. It is a chance to contrast the intolerant and unforgiving face of *Salafism* with the benevolent and compassionate face of modern Islam, where Muslims are quick to lend each other a hand and show respect for Christians and Jews – the Koran's "People of the Book." This is an opening to start scoring major points in the propaganda and information war that has been monopolized thus far by Islamic State and Al-Qaeda. It would affirm that Islam looks forward to a better future for all Muslims as opposed to the *takfirists* and *Salafists*, who only look backward to a harsh, cruel, and austere past.

What has made Islamic State so popular – especially among young people? It has skillfully and masterfully employed its narrative that the suffering of Muslims is the fault of the West and its lackey regimes in the region. It alone is standing up to the suffering and oppression against those Muslims and it has become so strong as to be invincible. America hasn't been able to defeat it; Russia hasn't been able to defeat it; and neither the Iraqi nor the Syrian regimes have been able to defeat it. This is the best evidence that Islamic State enjoys Allah's divine protection. That's their message in a nutshell.

The group resonates with disaffected Muslim youth because it has become bin Laden's "strong horse." Its messages and its videos are professionally crafted and quite effectively sell the message that Islamic State is stronger than its enemies and it will prevail, no matter what. It offers the alternative of a "strong" Islam to the view of some Muslim youth that Islam has become weak and subservient to the West and America. Certainly some of these young people are attracted to IS out of misguided good intentions, but they still voluntarily buy into, and embrace its ideology, nonetheless.

Now, imagine if we were able to actively choke off Islamic State's access to the Internet and social media while boosting the presence of an Arab Peace Corps on that social media at the same time. Let's take a page from the IS recruiting playbook and post professionally produced videos of Arab Peace Corps volunteers assisting others to counter the terrorists' narrative. Let's show young Arabs who don't have to run away from home to serve their religion; young Muslims who have a more hopeful and valuable future than a senseless "martyrdom" on a faraway battlefield somewhere in a false cause. How about recruiting messages for the organization from the Grand Sheikh of Al-Azhar and other notable *ulema*? What if these top clergy praised these young peace corps volunteers as true *mujahideen* and called their service to other Muslims the real *jihad* of the twenty-first century? Let's delegitimize the Islamists' monopolization of such terms. Where's the downside in that?

Let's remember that what's at stake here is the hearts and minds of Muslim youth. Those hearts and minds represent the future of Islam, the *ummah*, and the Arab world. Do we want them to be influenced and won over by the terrorists' propaganda and the Islamists' narrative or would we prefer that they stand up for their faith and embrace a better future for themselves and their countrymen? Those hearts and minds represent the strategic targets in this war and we have not done enough to attract them to our cause. An Arab Peace Corps gives them a real mechanism through which they can put their faith into action. Each of tomorrow's Peace Corps volunteers is one less terrorist and each volunteer's positive message about his or her volunteer experience to friends, siblings, and family potentially wins over that many more hearts and minds to our cause. It works to prevent future terrorists and terrorism. Such volunteer service provides an attractive alternative to those youth that are seeking to put the values of their religion into humanitarian practice. It discredits the terrorists' message that the existing Arab regimes are Islamic in name only and that they are doing nothing to actually support the religion.

There is an extremely important transformation that is going on in the Middle East, one that does not get much attention here in America. It's one that is largely driven by demographics – especially the growing percentage of younger people in the Arab world. They are not satisfied with the status quo of the post-war Middle East and they want their lives and their societies to change. They have embraced technology and are social media and Internet savvy and they want to have their say in government, society, and culture.

The best evidence that such a shift is underway is the 2011 Arab Spring. Young people represented a significant portion of the opposition in places like Egypt, Syria, Tunisia, and Libya. They used social media and the Internet to organize demonstrations, communicate with one another, and publicize abuses by the regimes. Their online presence at multiple levels became a useful weapon of asymmetric warfare against authoritarian regimes that were caught flatfooted and resorted to the predictable tactic of shutting the Internet down. That just further fanned the flames of the opposition and heaped international scorn and condemnation on those governments.

What Washington must now grudgingly accept is that the structure and shape of the old Middle East – the one before 2011 – is no longer sustainable. The demographics – the youth – will continue to force change whether we like it or not, and whether we are ready for it or not. The pace of change may not be as rapid right now as we saw in 2011, but the Arab Spring showed us that popular dissatisfaction could erupt overnight and cause conditions on the ground to change almost immediately. And it is the youth that will be the driving force that will be clamoring for change.

The proposed Arab Peace Corps would provide a constructive outlet for some of that desire for change. There are undoubtedly many youth who have flocked to IS out of a sense of frustration with the current state of affairs in the Middle East, which they view as un-Islamic. Until now Islamic State has been the only option for many of those disillusioned young people who want to support their religion in some active, physical way. The Peace Corps concept would offer these youth a positive alternative for doing just that, one that would steer them away from violence and *takfirism* and toward real humanitarian values.

In short, an Arab Peace Corps could be a modality for promoting positive change in the region. We should stop looking backward at trying to maintain the Middle East of yesterday and focus instead on encouraging helpful influences to shape the region's future. We cannot stop change from happening so we will need to accept it and work to make the best of it.

Creating a GCC-sponsored Arab Peace Corps would offer some significant benefits to the council's member states. First, it would be an enormous boost to the council's international political reputation. Even though this Peace Corps would have absolutely no political role whatsoever, the mere fact that the council had established such an organization would demonstrate a new and unparalleled degree of collective responsibility and maturity by the Gulf states. It's a move that would complement the council's political and military dimensions and offer a new and innovative approach to addressing the needs of some of the fragile states in the Middle East *before* they actually fail completely. It could be the start of a "neighborhood watch" system where the Arabs would begin policing their own backyard. That would be good for everyone.

The GCC has long ignored the usefulness of economic and humanitarian assistance as a means of soft power projection. The very fact that such assistance would be provided without any political (or religious) preconditions would be an extremely powerful tool for expanding GCC influence, particularly into Africa. For example Iran exploited soft power to establish a strong presence in Ghana, where it built a hospital and established an Islamic university as well as other institutions. Iran's success in that West African country – even while it was targeted by harsh economic sanctions – should be a lesson to the GCC on the strong impact soft power can have for a relatively low cost (even during an oil glut with depressed petroleum prices).

Likewise China has benefitted from its use of soft power on the African continent. Chinese construction companies are involved in projects of all sizes. They are welcomed because they are there to meet social and economic development needs. They are not there to preach politics.

GCC economic and humanitarian assistance through an Arab Peace Corps would have the potential to counter Iranian soft power influence (especially in Africa) while boosting the council's regional influence and prestige. Moreover, the GCC would likely get a greater payback at less cost than it does by spending billions on the latest and greatest Western weapons and military equipment every year.

In fact, it's hard to see where this Peace Corps concept would be a bad idea. It would allow the Arabs to demonstrate "true" Islam to the rest of the world, provide a golden opportunity to offer an effective counter to Islamist propaganda, alleviate potential unemployment among GCC youth, present a catalyst for an Arab "neighborhood watch" system, and create a tool for GCC soft power projection. And finally, by giving such assistance to fragile, needy, Arab states the GCC would be actively preventing the kind of humanitarian tragedy we see playing out every day from Syria.

The GCC and the Arabs aren't the only ones who stand to gain from creating their own Peace Corps; there is upside for America in this approach, too. For one thing, our own Peace Corps operations have been suspended in much of the Middle East due to the unstable security situation in the region. Given the level of volatility and violence there, our Peace Corps efforts will probably have to remain shelved for some time to come. An Arab Peace Corps opens the door to a continuation of organized humanitarian and social development assistance that might serve to ease some tensions in vulnerable Arab states. It could fill a need that our Peace Corps presently cannot.

In addition, this Arab Peace Corps could team up with other indigenous and external non-governmental organizations and relief agencies operating in the region for the sake of social and economic development or humanitarian relief. This would be a way for the Arab Peace Corps to gain from the operational experience of other agencies and improve the overall coordination of relief and development efforts in the Middle East (and East Africa). Such coordination and cooperation could represent a force multiplier that generates a synergistic outcome for the total effort.

Here, let me stress that I do not see this Peace Corps concept as a panacea for all the strife in the Middle East in and of itself. But as an inter-Arab and inter-Muslim enterprise that can address some of the humanitarian issues of the failed state process and one that is integrated with the other steps of the strategy in this book, it can play a significant role in our struggle. Since the ultimate solution for the ideology of Islamism must come from within the Muslim and Arab worlds, an Arab Peace Corps can actually be an essential part of that solution as it encourages them to stand up to the Islamist deviants and demonstrate the true nature and values of Islam.

If we were to assist and advise the GCC with the creation and establishment of this Arab Peace Corps while leaving the operation and management to the council members, we would start changing our image in the region from that of an invader and occupier to one of a facilitator. And since we would stay out of the nuts and bolts of the day-to-day operations, the organization would be free to succeed or fail on its own. We would have no fingerprints on its actions and decisions. This, again, would help to counter the terrorists' narrative that we are imposing ourselves on the Arab and Muslim worlds.

There would be a much-needed boost to our international political and diplomatic credibility, too. Does Russia or China have a Peace Corps? Could either one of those countries help to pull off such an ambitious effort? Are the Russian forces in Latakia showing Syrian farmers how to boost agricultural production or drilling water wells for isolated villagers? I don't think so.

Assisting our GCC allies to set up their own Peace Corps to assist their own neighbors would demonstrate real leadership by a global superpower that can project its power and influence without the need for drone or airstrikes. We would be helping our regional partners and friends to emulate an organization that has embodied the best of our own American and democratic values since 1961. For us to make a policy move of that magnitude, one that requires neither the Sixth Fleet nor a squadron of stealth bombers, would be a real breath of fresh air to everyone. Who knows? We might discover that we can actually accomplish more on the ground if we leave the hammer in the toolbox.

But before we get too used to the view through these rose-colored glasses, it is important to recognize a serious, potential threat to the success of this effort. We (and the GCC members) must acknowledge that the growing popularity of the *Wahhabist* and *Salafist* ideologies is largely due to the support that they have received from conservative Muslims in Saudi Arabia and the rest of the Gulf Arab countries. The Saudis and others may now have spoken out against the *takfirist* ideology of Islamic State and its predecessor, Al-Qaeda, but there are still plenty of traditional conservatives in the GCC countries that remain sympathetic to those *Salafist* values and philosophies. Qatar has been a known supporter of the Muslim Brotherhood. It has faced a diplomatic crisis with neighboring countries in 2017 including Saudi Arabia, Bahrain, United Arab Emirates, and Egypt because of Qatar's perceived support for terrorism.

Therefore, these GCC countries must implement a mechanism to vet any volunteers and prevent this Peace Corps from becoming a conduit for spreading even more hate and intolerance. This organization must not be usurped to become a tool for preaching *Wahhabism* and proselytizing other Muslims to that doctrine. That would irreparably distort the effort and make it part of the problem instead of part of the solution. The GCC Arabs must fully understand and comprehend this Peace Corps is not part of the *Da'wah* – the Islamic missionary endeavor. It is about people helping people.

So, where might this Arab Peace Corps be of use? One prime candidate would be Jordan, which is hosting around a million refugees from Iraq and Syria. Aid in the form of economic assistance to help Jordan manage its largest refugee camps at Al-Zaatari and Azraq would be welcome and take some of this burden off the Jordanian government. These camps have now become established little cities so Arab Peace Corps volunteers might be put to work performing health care duties, assisting refugees to establish small businesses in these camps, job training, and any other tasks that might make the refugees' lives more productive and useful inside those camps.

Jordan also has an agriculture sector that has been in decline for decades. It is in dire need of a top-down reassessment from the nature of agricultural land ownership to irrigation methods to crop selection and yields, to marketing. Jordan could use some outside expertise to resurrect this sector and put it on the path to greater productivity.

In conjunction with agricultural development, Jordan would benefit from the development of its rural areas. This may include anything from reliable electrical power to communications and Internet services to potable water supplies.

These are all functions similar to those that have been undertaken by our own Peace Corps; there is no reason that they could not be performed by an Arab version.

Similarly, Egypt is a country that is long on problems and short on answers. The Egyptians could use economic assistance and outside help to address a host of issues like a stagnant economy, high unemployment, agricultural and rural development, education, well... pretty much everything. Egypt could use whatever help an Arab Peace Corps could provide – and then some!

Once the Islamic State is defeated and the fighting stops in Iraq's Anbar Province, it will need outside assistance to rebuild the infrastructure that has been shattered there by decades of fighting and civil war. There could eventually be a major role for an Arab Peace Corps to play here since the *Sunnis* would distrust the motives of any Iraqi *Shia*.

The situation is the same in Syria, which has been even more devastated by its ongoing civil war.

Libya isn't exactly ready for anybody's peace corps just yet, either, but the GCC itself might play a positive role by agreeing to mediate among the various domestic powers and reach some sort of political compromise on governance that would be the first step toward internal security.

Yemen will need extensive Arab and outside help once the fighting stops there.

As I mentioned, an Arab Peace Corps could expand GCC soft power into East Africa. It would be suitable for development projects in Somalia, Sudan, and throughout the Horn of Africa.

It seems pretty clear there are present and future roles that an Arab Peace Corps could undertake and make a positive contribution to the region while countering the terrorists' propaganda machine. It all boils down to being a good neighbor and a good Muslim. Let's encourage our GCC allies to show the world what true and proper Islam is all about by setting up and operating its own Peace Corps.

Now, is there any guarantee that the GCC will embrace this concept? Will there be sufficient unity among its members to create, manage, and operate an Arab Peace Corps under the council's umbrella? The fact is, we won't know the answers to those questions unless we encourage them to give it a try.

We occasionally hear from politicians about the idea of an Arab regional land army and the need for such a force, along with US military cooperation, to stop the spread of radical Islamism in the Middle East. This concept presupposes that the only solution to Islamism is a military one and I think we've put that notion to bed. An Arab regional land army just perpetuates conflict without doing anything to kill the ideology. It just generates more martyrs for the bad guys and that is not the answer.

An Arab Peace Corps is aimed at winning those all-important young hearts and minds through humanitarian assistance while debunking the terrorists' narrative. It is aimed at convincing the GCC Arabs to demonstrate to the world what Islam truly stands for. It is about taking an entirely new, innovative approach that is based on building bridges instead of blowing up villages. History has proven to us that what we have been doing isn't working. Let's wise up and try something different for a change.

There will be more about new ideas and fresh approaches to our Mideast policy in chapter ten.

FRAGILE STATES AND BASKET CASES

So, who decides what states are fragile or failing and which ones have failed? Is there some kind of political definition of failed and failing states that depends on whether one is located in the Northern or Southern Hemisphere? Is it like the futile attempt to reach an internationally acceptable definition of what constitutes terrorism?

Nope. The process of identifying states vulnerable to failure is actually undertaken on an annual basis by a globally respected think tank called the Fund for Peace (FFP). This organization conducts research with the objective of preventing conflict and promoting sustainable development and security. To that end, FFP compiles its "Fragile States Index" every year that evaluates all member states of the United Nations.

The index evaluates each country based on 12 different social, economic, and political indicators. It assigns a score of one to ten for each indicator (high scores indicate less stability) and then totals these individual indicator scores to reach a comprehensive rating for each country. These ratings are classified as "Alert" (a comprehensive score of 90 or more), "Warning" (a score of 50 or more), "Moderate" (a score of 30 or more), or "Sustainable" (a comprehensive score of less than 30). "Alert" states are shaded red on the index map and "Warning" states are shaded orange. The index doesn't offer any timeline for when any particular state might fail but its annual scores can be plotted to evaluate whether the general trend in that country is improving or getting worse.

It's worth noting the scale of the failed and failing state problem in the Middle East. Every Arab country on the Fragile States Index is rated either under "Alert" or "Warning." Even the United States only earns a "Moderate" rating. (To be fair, only Canada, Australia, and the Nordic countries received a "Sustainable" score.)

The FFP has been in existence since 1957 and it has performed research for many governments around the world (like for our own State Department) and it has a deep library of publications. More about the FFP, its work, and its Fragile States Index can be found on its website at http://www.fundforpeace.org.

One common warning flag for failed and failing states seems to be human rights abuses. So if the objective, multi-level assessments of the Fragile States Index aren't good enough for you, there are annual reports on human rights abuses from our State Department and many other human rights watchdogs around the world.

Acts of terrorism in any state ring warning bells about its stability and security and any erosion in those areas might very well lead to a state graduating to a "failed" or "failing" status. Once again, our State Department publishes an annual report on terrorism around the world.

And of course, there is always the Mark I Eyeball. It shouldn't take more than a single look at places like Iraq, Syria, Yemen, and Libya to determine that they have already graduated to failed state status. These are countries where the authority of any central government is either nonexistent altogether or severely weakened. The resulting power vacuum has left the people living in large swaths of these countries utterly defenseless against the terrorists and extremists who may move in to fill that void. They are quite literally experiencing hell on earth.

Fixing each and every one of these would require a massive effort that would have to span decades and the economic cost would be enormous. The situation in each country is different. It has its own cultural dynamics, resources, tribal structures, and geography. Iraq's situation is quite different from Somalia's. What may work in one place may not work somewhere else.

We can't really do anything about them right now. They're just too far-gone and would require too many resources. Nevertheless, the human suffering and tragic situations in these countries must serve as our best motivation to try and save those states that are still salvageable.

***

Iraq once had a strong central government under Saddam Hussein with firm state institutions and a strong rule of law, albeit one that was oppressive and discriminatory. Iraq has always been a melting pot of *Sunni* and *Shia* but Saddam was the glue that held everything together – for better or for worse. The tribes in the *Sunni* heartland of northern and western Iraq enjoyed great favoritism and patronage under the Iraqi president, who was skilled at making alliances and agreements among these tribes to solidify his support.

When we routed Saddam's regime in 2003, we overturned a centuries-old balance of *Sunni* rule in the country that we replaced with a *Shiite*-dominated government that was more intent on retribution than democracy and proper governance. The country collapsed along *Sunni-Shiite*-Kurdish axes and our lengthy occupation, along with a sense of *Sunni* resentment and rancor at being alienated by the *Shia*, gave rise to a *Sunni* insurgency that eventually morphed into the anarchy and chaos we're seeing in the *Sunni* regions of Iraq today. The *Sunni* rebellion against the *Shiite* regime in neighboring Syria has just added to the dilemma. This messy situation is forcing refugees and violence to spill over into Jordan and Lebanon, ultimately threatening their stability.

The potential for the pre-2003 Iraq to rise phoenix-like from the ashes of today's crisis is slim to none. By removing Saddam and Iraq's *Sunni* ruling class we opened the door to making Iraq a proxy of the Islamic Republic of Iran, much to the chagrin of the Gulf Arabs, who fear an Iran that has become emboldened by its advances in Iraq and the successful defense (so far) of the Syrian regime will become more aggressive in meddling among the *Shia* in Bahrain and Saudi Arabia's Eastern Province.

Meanwhile, the open *Sunni-Shia* conflagration that has erupted shows no signs of abating. The *Sunnis* justifiably distrust the *Shiite* central government and see little to gain from any rapprochement with Baghdad. Thus, the Awakening Council strategy that was used so successfully against Al-Qaeda during the US occupation of Iraq is no longer viable since the *Sunnis* do not see a trustworthy, reliable, inclusive government partner in this fight. They are likely to seek greater autonomy for themselves instead.

Despite probes and forays by the Islamic State along the fringes of Iraqi Kurdistan, the Kurds have generally been able to maintain the integrity of their territories and generate a good income from the oil wealth of the region. This ethnic group was oppressed in Saddam's time and Kurds were often displaced and resettled so that *Sunnis* loyal to Saddam could take over their lands and properties. They have never had any great love for Baghdad or the Arabs and are quite content with the status quo. They are more than happy to keep their distance from the warring Arabs and they have already enjoyed a high degree of autonomy from the central government in Baghdad. They have neither a reason nor any desire to change that.

The large swath of land from Baghdad southeast to Basra is *Shiite* territory. The *Shia* have historically been repressed in Iraq and they endured mass executions and persecutions under Saddam's regime. They hate the *Sunnis*, view the fighters of IS as *takfirists*, and undoubtedly have greater allegiance to the *Shia* homeland of Iran than they ever did to Iraq. Religion nearly always trumps nationalism and patriotism in the Middle East. The increasingly passionate and vengeful tenor of the hate speech on both sides of the white-hot *Sunni-Shia* divide means that those passions will not subside any time soon and there isn't very much we can do about it.

I believe that history has also shown us that placing too much faith in the Iraqi Army in our quest to defeat Islamic State in Iraq has its drawbacks. The *Sunnis'* reversal of fortunes after the 2003 US invasion and occupation of Iraq from the country's ruling class to near refugee status in a now *Shia*-dominated government means that the *Sunnis* don't really have much faith in either America or Baghdad right now. They may not be happy living under IS persecution and oppression in Mosul, but they don't want to live under *Shiite* persecution and oppression, either. The toppling of Saddam's regime and its replacement with the hated "Rejectionist" government in the Iraqi capital has almost made them feel as if they are stateless citizens in their own homeland.

The Iraqi Army, with US and coalition support, will certainly be able to liberate Mosul, but then what? The tribes in the Sunni heartland will not accept an occupation by *Shiites* from Baghdad (and the *Shiites* probably won't want to stay there, anyway). Without some planning for inclusive governance that gives the *Sunnis* a real seat at the government's table, Anbar Province will very probably slide back into the same political vacuum that Islamic State was able to exploit in the first place. It would be a real tragedy if we allowed that to happen.

There has to be a viable plan to prevent that from happening *before* Mosul and the rest of Anbar Province and northwest Iraq is purged of Islamic State. Local governance of these areas is not a military issue and the long-term occupation of Anbar by a *Shiite*-majority force will likely cause more harm than good. It is worth remembering, too, that the Iraqi Army retreated *en masse* from the Islamic State fighters when they first swept into the province, leaving many of their vehicles and weapons behind.

We have a golden opportunity here to learn from the mistakes of the past and to plan for a future that goes beyond just the short-term objectives of liberating Mosul and Anbar Province.

As for fighters on the ground, the Kurdish Peshmerga are a much more effective fighting force than the Iraqi Army. They have already defeated Islamic State in pitched battles such as at Kobani, where they held IS fighters off for weeks and eventually turned the tide of the battle in their own favor. The Peshmerga know what it takes to win and they don't run away from a fight. But Turkey has been fighting a decades-long insurgency against the Kurds who want independence for their portion of Turkish Kurdistan and Iraq doesn't want to see the Kurds become any more powerful, either. The end result of the situation is that we cannot arm the best indigenous fighting force inside northern Iraq with better and heavier weapons because of the concerns of the Iraqis and Turks.

Now that the anti-IS coalition has freed Mosul and begun to move on the IS capital of Raqqa, let's hope that all of our partners in this campaign understand the importance of planning for how to maintain the post-liberation peace and prevent a recurrence of the past.

***

Iraq's neighbor to the west, Syria, is in its sixth year of open civil war. This civil war began at the zenith of the Arab Spring in 2011 as an uprising against a secular dictator. In the beginning, the opposition to Syrian President Bashar al-Assad wasn't limited strictly to Islamists. There were

Sunni dissidents who objected to the *Shiite/Alawite* Assad regime but there were also healthy numbers of secular liberalists in the mix who opposed the Assad dynasty because of its oppression of civil and political liberties. They had no plans to replace Assad with an Islamist state of any kind.

The Tunisian revolution saw President Ben Ali fall in just a few days. Egypt's Mubarak fell in a couple of weeks and Libya's revolution took approximately eight months to topple and kill Muammar Gaddafi. Syrian dissidents were initially optimistic that Assad would be driven from power within a reasonably short period of time.

But now in its sixth year, with hundreds of thousands of Syrians dead and millions of others displaced internally and externally, the optimism has gone. Assad has proven far more resilient in his ability to survive than anyone had ever dreamed possible thanks primarily to outside help from Russia, Iran, and Lebanon's *Hezbollah*. Nevertheless, despite raining Scud missiles, chemical weapons, and barrel bombs on Syrian civilians, Assad has not been able to gain the upper hand. And even though the opposition forces have "liberated" vast swaths of northern, eastern, and southern Syria and even carried out large-scale attacks in and around the capital of Damascus, they have not been able to deal a deathblow to the Assad regime. Neither side is winning and neither side is losing so the bloody stalemate continues and the human tragedy in the country plays on.

The conflict has now morphed principally into another *Sunni-Shia* war; the secular character of the opposition – what started out as the Free Syrian Army (FSA) composed of more secular moderates – has almost entirely been eclipsed by the rabidly anti-Assad and anti-*Shiite takfirist* groups. Unfortunately, we really don't hear much about the FSA anymore (there is a whole alphabet soup of opposition groups now) but we do constantly hear about the Al-Qaeda affiliated *Nusra* Front (now the *Fatah al-Sham* Front) and its allies in the *Jaysh al-Fatah* ("Army of Conquest"), the Islamic State, and a smattering of smaller *Sunni* extremist groups. They are all better armed and supplied than the US-supported "moderate" rebels and this has rendered those forces largely irrelevant in the current fighting. And no matter how many weapons we give them, their moment in the war as a potent and credible fighting force has passed.

Iran's entry into the war on the side of the Assad regime – its long-term mainstay ally in the Arab world – with troops and fresh arms changed the equation from a simple civil war into a religious battle along sectarian lines. *Sunni* passions were inflamed even more when Iran's Lebanese proxy, *Hezbollah*, entered the fray.

Sadly, the bloodshed and violence has not been limited to the *Sunnis* and *Shia* in Syria. The Christian Arameans of Ma'loula, for instance, suffered violence at the hands of the Islamists when they occupied the village. Similar atrocities have been inflicted on other ethnic and religious minorities in the country like the Kurds and Druze.

Nobody in Syria has escaped the ferocity and brutality of the war. Children in places like Aleppo and Homs have witnessed friends and schoolmates blown apart before their very eyes. Scud missile attacks have wiped out whole neighborhoods in the middle of the night. These Syrians live in constant fear of helicopters flying overhead, snipers, and random artillery fire. It's difficult to pick sides when you're caught in the crossfire. An entire generation of Syrian children will be psychologically scarred and traumatized even if the war ends tomorrow.

Social media and *YouTube* have brought scenes of all manner of atrocities, massacres, and inhumanity to the eyes of anybody in the world with a computer. Neither side is innocent. I've seen a video of a rebel fighter cutting the heart out of a dead Syrian soldier's chest and biting into it. I've also seen regime soldiers taunting and torturing opposition prisoners mercilessly and then summarily executing them, laughing the whole time. In fact, there is no shortage of execution videos carried out by both sides.

You can watch a horror movie with the best special effects, but you always know in the back of your mind that it's a movie. The ghastliness of these videos lies in the fact that you know it's real. It's not a movie. Beheading and crucifixion are not the ways that you want to meet your demise.

Can there ever be a happy ending to such a bitter, vehement, vicious, and primal struggle? I don't think so; this is a war where nobody wins and everybody loses. In the first place, just look at the level of destruction the entire country has suffered. Complete cities, towns, and villages have been virtually wiped off the map. Large numbers of persons who have been displaced by the war will not have any home to go back to.

Next consider the demographics of the country. Syria's population is about three-quarters *Sunni* Muslim. When this bloody war does eventually end, do you think they will tolerate another *Shiite/Alawite* replacement for the Assad regime? Not after all that they will have sacrificed in blood and property.

And if Bashar is replaced by a *Sunni* regime, what do you think will happen to the roughly ten percent of Syrians who are *Alawites*? Is everybody just going to shake hands as if nothing ever happened? I don't think so.

Don't forget that Iran and *Hezbollah* have a lot invested in Syria, too. They're not going to just give up on Assad and the *Alawites* after shedding this much blood. More probably, they will do whatever they can to maintain the status quo and keep Assad and his sect in power. In other words, Assad, Iran, and *Hezbollah* win by not losing.

If that's not complex enough, then the *Sunni-Shia* violence in Syria has now become inextricably linked to the sectarian strife that has spread into Iraq. It will be almost impossible to reach any kind of peace in one country without finding a way to do the same in the other.

And just when we thought things couldn't get any worse in Syria, Russia interjected itself into the already-crowded scrum of US and coalition forces battling the Islamic State, the various opposition and dissident fighting groups battling the regime, Iran, Hezbollah, and Syrian government forces.

Russia is carrying out airstrikes from an airbase in Latakia to prop up Assad and provide air cover for his army to retake territory lost to Syrian rebels in the north and northwest of the country. On the surface, Putin's gambit in Syria seems to be saving Bashar and keeping him in power. Certainly there are tangible benefits to Russia for doing so.

But perhaps there are other, more strategic objectives behind Russia's military moves in Syria. One of the most significant of those would be to curry favor with Iran and lay the framework for a strategic partnership. There are a multitude of reasons for this that would benefit both Iran and

Russia and we'll look at this in greater detail in the next chapter. Sadly for Syria, however, it means that in addition to the *Sunni-Shia* conflict, being a battleground against Islamic State, and the human tragedy played out daily in the civilian population – from Scud missiles and chemical attacks to barrel bombs, it has now become the scene of a proxy war between Russia/Iran and the West.

***

Yemen is another failed state where there are more questions than answers, more problems than fixes. It is a country with an identity crisis with a modicum of petroleum wealth that barely dents the population's crushing poverty. Yemen's modern history has been characterized by sectarian and civil warfare and, following the reunification of North and South Yemen in 1990, a largely corrupt and ineffective central government.

Frankly, if Yemen didn't have bad luck, it wouldn't have any luck at all. Much like some medieval prisoner being drawn and quartered, Yemen is being pulled in several directions at once. The tragedy is that because the country is so poor and the people are so isolated, no matter who wins, everybody still pretty much loses. It's an unfortunate but common theme throughout all the region's failed and failing states.

We don't have to go back much further than about 50 years to get a gist of the country's miseries. North Yemen fought a civil war throughout much of the 1960s that pitted royalists, aided by Saudi Arabia, Jordan, and Great Britain, against republicans, who were actively supported and assisted by Egypt. Although the republicans eventually won the day, Egypt's disastrous involvement in Yemen, which included its use of chemical weapons, would eventually become known as "Egypt's Vietnam." Although there are no accurate figures, estimates of civilian casualties from the war range from 100,000 to 200,000.

While this civil war was going on the British were in the process of decolonizing from the southern Yemeni city of Aden. This eventually led to the establishment of an independent communist state known as the People's Republic of Yemen, which was changed a few years later to the People's Democratic Republic of Yemen when a more Marxist element took power. The northern and southern parts of Yemen coexisted peacefully for a short time but the honeymoon didn't last forever. Another civil war broke out that eventually saw the forcible removal of the Marxists and an uneasy reunification of the north and south portions into a single Yemen in 1990.

In 1994, civil war erupted yet again when the south attempted to secede from the north. That ended badly for the south and, after a few months, Ali Abdullah Saleh became the leader of a Yemen that was once again united. Nevertheless, there is still a very strong and popular movement in southern Yemen that favors secession from the north. The movement's demonstrators intermittently engage in violent clashes with Yemen's security forces but this unrest has largely been off the US and Western radar screens.

Additionally, the Houthis are a community in northwestern Yemen that is an offshoot of *Shia* Islam that has engaged in an on-again, off-again insurgency with the Sanaa government since 2004 in a bid for greater autonomy. The insurgency is now definitely on again since the Houthis have taken control of the government in Sanaa and toppled the country's president. Their reach eventually extended all the way south to Aden as the government officials and ministers scrambled to neighboring *Sunni* countries for their own safety. The anti-Houthi coalition was eventually able to claw its way back to the outskirts of Ta'iz, but the war has largely been a stalemate ever since.

This is extremely worrisome to the Saudis, who are concerned about an Iranian proxy on their southwest border. This concern escalated to direct military action in 2009 when Saudi ground forces and warplanes attacked the Houthis during a particularly active period of their rebellion. In any case, no one is quite sure yet what to make of the Houthis' capture of the country's capital and how it will affect the nation and the region. The current round of Saudi airstrikes seems to be killing as many innocent Yemenis as Houthis.

And while all this is going on, we cannot forget the presence of Al-Qaeda in the Arabian Peninsula. Al-Qaeda has fought its own insurgencies with the central government, attempting to form its own emirate in the southeast of the country. Its activities have made Yemen a stage for international intervention since the United States has been involved in training Yemeni armed forces while also conducting drone strikes against leaders of the terrorist group.

Given all the war and fighting the Yemenis have had to endure, it should come as no surprise that the country is also absolutely awash in weapons. It's not unusual to see child soldiers in the country carrying Kalashnikovs almost as big as they are.

According to the World Bank, Yemen's per capita income was $1,040 per year for 2016.[174] Much of what doesn't get spent on weapons does get spent on qat, leaves from a specific plant that are chewed to induce a stimulant effect. Use of qat inside Yemen borders on endemic but it's easy to see how living in a harsh, desert country that has been constantly beset by wars might encourage a daily escape from reality.

And if human beings didn't make life hard enough in Yemen, Mother Nature occasionally throws some additional suffering into the mix. The country lies on the juncture of the Arabian, Somali, and African tectonic plates and it has experienced devastating earthquakes. A 1982 temblor caused nearly 3,000 casualties and resulted in widespread damage to buildings that were primarily constructed of mud brick and adobe.

Yemen's disintegration along internal fault lines also allows it to become a proxy battleground for external forces. The rise of the *Shiite* Houthis and their takeover of the central government by force raises fears about Yemen falling into the sphere of Iranian influence, certainly a nightmare scenario for the Saudis and other conservative states of the Arabian Gulf. They aren't going to let that happen and they don't care how many innocent Yemeni civilians must be sacrificed to prevent it.

The United States has also been heavily engaged in fighting Al-Qaeda in the Arabian Peninsula in parts of southern and southeastern Yemen. The weapon of choice in this effort has been drone strikes and airstrikes, although Yemen's army has also been involved. Regardless of whether US drone strikes create more terrorists than they eliminate, the strikes haven't made us very popular with isolated, rural Yemenis and the ongoing violence has done little to stabilize an extremely volatile (and poor) part of the country where loyalties are based on tribal alliances. Decades of neglect by Sanaa have fostered deep antipathy and distrust of the central government.

---

174. "Yemen, Rep.," Data from the World Bank website. Accessed July 17, 2017. http://data. worldbank.org/country/yemen-rep?view=chart.

Yemen is the very essence of a nation-building project and such a project must eventually be the primary responsibility of the wealthy Gulf countries. As I noted earlier, they have the necessary cultural ties (and money) and stand to lose the most if the country becomes a haven for terrorism or Iranian influence. Nevertheless, like Iraq/Syria, the situation will likely get worse before it gets better.

***

Libya is another Arab country that quickly collapsed into anarchy after its strongman dictator, Muammar Gaddafi, was toppled and killed in the fall of 2011. Much like Iraq, Libya is a nation with a strong tribal and desert character that overshadows any sense of Libyan nationality or national identity. During Gaddafi's four-decade grip on power, he was very adroit in using those tribal alliances and relationships to his advantages – sometimes playing one tribe or clan against another. He was careful to restrict his real power to a small circle of close associates whom he could trust to carry out his orders without question or remorse.

The Libyan dictator was enamored with the idea of being a revolutionary and fancied himself an Arab nationalist leader in the mold of Egypt's iconic Gamal Abdel-Nasser. Other Arab leaders viewed the mercurial Libyan with amusement, disgust, or a combination of both. In any case, he never gained any wide acceptance or respect as an Arab statesman so he turned his attentions to making himself a figurehead of pan-Africanism. Gaddafi involved himself in African politics where he unsuccessfully tried to gain control over the uranium-rich Aouzou Strip in neighboring Chad. His brinksmanship with the United States and involvement in terrorism made him a regional pariah and many Arab, European, and African leaders were happy to keep him at arm's length or just ignore him altogether.

But, he was the glue that held all the disparate tribes and communities together inside Libya. Gaddafi's record on human rights and democracy was about as dismal as they come and the Islamists of Cyrenaica were frequent targets of Gaddafi's suspicion and his security services.

The eastern Libyan cities of Derna and Benghazi had long been strongholds of extremely conservative Islamists and since Islamists had been the first real, organized opposition to Gaddafi's regime, they made up a significant percentage of the country's political prisoners.

He attempted to craft his own philosophy (his "Green Book") by blending his personal view of Islam, revolution, and politics and it just made the Islamists hate him even more as an apostate. He and his sons doled out support and favors to those they liked and heaped oppression, scorn, and deprivation on those they distrusted – which turned out to be most of the country.

Ever the survivor, Gaddafi managed after decades of conflict with the United States to restore diplomatic ties with his former adversary and cooperate in the hunt for Islamist terrorists and extremists. His renouncing of WMD and the destruction of his cache of chemical weapons bolstered his newfound status as a US ally in the war on terror. For its part, Europe saw Libya as a nearby source of cheap oil and a market for its military industries. All was quickly forgiven and Gaddafi was welcomed back into the international community.

Unfortunately for him, the little dictator's world began to unravel in February 2011 when the people of Benghazi erupted in open revolt against his regime at the height of the Arab Spring. Eight months later he was dragged from a culvert in his hometown of Sirte and killed. His sons and family were either killed or captured, with the exception of a fortunate few who made it safely into exile.

As it turned out, Gaddafi and his regime were the only institution of state in the country. With his death, the country fell into complete anarchy and chaos as various groups and militias jockeyed for position and competed for power.

Like the toppling of Saddam in Iraq, the death of Gaddafi left a huge power vacuum. In Iraq, that vacuum was initially filled by the US occupation that promised to rebuild the country and help usher in democracy. At first, the *Shiite* majority there was so ecstatic about the end of Saddam's rule that they welcomed us with open arms. After something between six months and a year, that honeymoon ended as Iraqis just wanted us to leave so they could go about getting started with their own civil war.

In Libya there was no occupation after Gaddafi's fall. It twisted aimlessly in the wind for a while as abortive attempts were made to form one government after another. Various political factions couldn't agree on anything. Militias steadfastly refused to disband and turn their weapons over to a largely impotent central authority; they weren't about to concede their influence. The country has not been able to save itself nor has Gaddafi's exit eased the suffering of the Libyan people. If anything, it's become worse.

The Islamists didn't necessarily represent the majority of those who had risen up and fought Gaddafi, but at the end of the conflict their militias were the ones most organized and holding the most weapons. Governance in the country is now largely nonexistent as two rival governments – a secular one in Tobruk and an Islamist one in Tripoli – wrestle each other for dominance. Now we see yet another failed Arab state being transformed into a breeding ground for ruthless extremism as the opportunity for a better future is exchanged for revenge and the horrors of the medieval past.

Mali and Somalia are two non-Arab countries that do have a strong Islamic history and lie on the periphery of the Arab world. Ethnic tensions, vast underdeveloped areas, and weak central governments in both countries have given Islamist extremists the opportunity to fill the existing void and exploit those tensions for their own benefit.

Somalia's descent into chaos began with the collapse of the corrupt central government of Siad Barre in 1991 and the subsequent eruption of its civil war. The country went through a series of warlords and autonomous regional governments and finally began struggling to establish a central, federal system of government in the early 2000s. The fact that this struggle is still continuing despite the shadow of terrorism cast by Al-Shabaab is no small feat and great credit must be given to the Somali people for their perseverance under the most difficult of circumstances.

The Al-Shabaab movement, which has declared its affiliation to Al-Qaeda, evolved from what was originally called the Islamic Courts Union in the south of the country and proclaimed its intent to govern Somalia in accordance with the *Sharia*. It was one of the first Islamist groups to successfully attract recruits from the United States. Unhappy and disillusioned Somali refugees – many in the American Midwest – were persuaded to return to their homeland and join the terrorist movement.

Although the federal government is still weak, African Union (AU) peacekeepers have been mostly able to protect Mogadishu from Al-Shabaab, which has been critical to the government's development. The AU forces have also successfully engaged the movement elsewhere in the country and driven them from various areas, although the group is far from defeated.

These are positive signs – signs that failed states can be revived. They don't have to become permanent havens for barbarism and brutality that are carried out under some religious banner. We may be able to take advantage of some of the things that have worked in Somalia in other trouble spots.

The Republic of Mali lies in northwest Africa as something of a bridge between West and North Africa. It has a history of being a conduit for trans-Saharan trade. Tuareg nomads populate the arid, northern half of the country while southern Mali's population is concentrated in lush lands along the Senegal and Niger rivers. The Tuaregs have felt little affiliation to Mali's central government in Bamako and have aspired to greater autonomy and even independence, having little in common ethnically and culturally with those in the south, whom they see as countrymen in name only.

In 2012, Tuareg attempts to declare independence from Mali and create their own state of Azawad were hijacked by Islamist militants affiliated with Al-Qaeda in the Islamic Maghreb, who exploited the political and security vacuum in northern Mali with the intent to set up their own Islamic emirate. Naturally, these militants were neither Mali nor Tuareg but a collection of Arab, Pakistani, and other insurgents that had been displaced from other countries and battlefields. They quickly set about implementing their version of *Sharia*, publicly flogging members of the population for such things as buying or smoking cigarettes, and tearing down and destroying ancient archaeological treasures in World Heritage sites like Timbuktu that they believed were un-Islamic and idolatrous.

In January 2013, French troops moved in to combat the Islamist forces, keep them from moving southward, and drive them out of the Tuareg north. *Operation Serval*, the French military campaign in Mali, succeeded in these objectives and Bamako did its part by holding fresh presidential and legislative elections. While *Operation Serval* was terminated, the French have continued to maintain a presence in Mali and prevent the Islamists from returning.

The situation in Mali has stabilized for now, even though tensions and mistrust still remain between the Tuareg north and African south of the country. The present security situation is entirely dependent on French forces remaining in Mali; their withdrawal would simply open the door for the Islamists to come back – something the Tuaregs themselves do not want.

The Tuareg people have fought since early in the twentieth century to establish their own independent homeland. The latest attempt in Mali in 2012 was carried out by the National Movement for the Liberation of Azawad (French acronym MNLA) and its objective was to create an independent, secular Tuareg state. The movement briefly allied with Islamist forces in their common fight against the forces of Mali's central government, but the MNLA quickly saw that they were simply trading subjugation to Bamako for subjugation to the Islamists' view of *Sharia*. The majority of Tuaregs may be Muslims, but they do not share the harsh, medieval ideology of the *takfirists* and they have no desire to share their homeland with them.

EVERYBODY ELSE HAS A CASE OF THE SNIFFLES

In addition to the preceding basket cases, the Arab world has plenty of other countries that are facing pressures and threats. In fact, one could say that just about all of the Arab states face one or more serious challenges. They might not fall under the category of failed or failing states yet, but they could eventually find themselves in that situation in a few years if things don't change.

Algeria: Algeria has faded from many observers' memories now, but Algeria fought a very bloody civil war from 1991-2002 after the country's ruling National Liberation Front (FLN) canceled elections, fearing that the Islamic Salvation Front (FIS) had become sufficiently popular to threaten its dominance. The military took to the streets, the Islamists took up arms, and the bloodshed was on for the next decade.

The conflict is notable because it was an early example of "radical Islam" seeking to overthrow the government of an Arab state and replace it with an Islamist regime. Bear in mind that this conflict broke out a full year before Al-Qaeda's first attack against the US in December 1992. Although exact figures are likely unknown, one research paper put the number of casualties in the civil war at 150,000.[175] The Islamists did carry out attacks in Algiers but they roamed quite freely in the countryside and brutally killed many innocent Algerian civilians. The violence was considered quite savage in its day.

These massacres at the hands of the Islamists didn't win many hearts and minds among the Algerian population. Although we don't hear too much about Islamist violence in Algeria today, clashes between Algerian military and police and Islamists continued for another ten years or so after the end of the civil war. In addition, it's worthwhile to remember that the January 2013 attack on Algeria's natural gas facility at In Amenas was carried out by Islamist terrorists and over three dozen foreign workers were killed in the incident. It took everybody by surprise (Algeria included) and it reminds us that bad things can still happen without warning in the country.

The country's president, Abdelaziz Bouteflika, has been in power since 1999 and even though there were calls for regime change inside the country a few years ago, the guy was elected to a fourth term of office in April 2014. He had spent much of the previous year in France recovering from a stroke, had not campaigned for reelection, and was shown casting his vote from a wheelchair.

Given the president's obvious health issues, one wonders who is really pulling the strings in Algeria and whether the population's desires for change will ever find receptive ears. And what will happen in the country when Bouteflika eventually passes on?

Bahrain: The Kingdom of Bahrain is an island nation located near the western shores of the Arabian (Persian) Gulf. According to the 2015 "CIA World Factbook," approximately 55% of the country's population of around 1.3 million is made up of migrants. About three-quarters of the nation's export revenues come from petroleum production and

---

175. Jonah Schulhofer-Wohl, "Civil War in Algeria 1992-Present," University of Virginia website, 2007. Accessed July 17, 2017. http://faculty.virginia.edu/j.sw/uploads/research/Schulhofer-Wohl%202007%20Algeria.pdf.

processing but it continues to be a worldwide center of Islamic finance and its strategic location makes it valuable to international companies as a regional headquarters.

The major problem facing this country is that it is a *Sunni* kingdom with a majority *Shia* population. The 2011 Arab Spring sparked violent demonstrations and public unrest in the country as the *Shia* demanded greater representation in government and expanded religious freedoms. The country's government promptly responded by calling for assistance in quelling the protests from its Gulf Cooperation Council allies.

Bahrain's heavy-handed reaction to the popular demonstrations in 2011 led to numerous deaths and injuries among the demonstrators and the imprisonment of those deemed to be opposition ringleaders. The lack of any real subsequent reform and a high unemployment rate among the country's youth means that tensions still continue to boil over in acts of violence and protest.

Egypt: Once one of America's most reliable allies in the Arab world, since the 2011 Arab Spring Egypt has faced one upheaval after another. When Hosni Mubarak was toppled that year many observers in the West likened the situation to the fall of the shah of Iran in 1979 and feared the potential for Egypt – the Arab world's most populous country – to fall into an Islamist orbit.

However, the Egyptians surprised everybody when they opted to hold the first real democratic presidential elections in the country's history. Television talk shows in Cairo buzzed excitedly almost every day about the country's transition to real democracy. When Mohamed Morsi, an affiliate of the long-banned Muslim Brotherhood, won the presidential election it seemed to be a sign that the political scene in Egypt had finally changed.

The honeymoon didn't last long. Morsi began giving himself more and more powers and authorities while stacking the constituent assembly responsible for drafting a new constitution with conservative Islamists. In 2013, almost exactly one year from his election, General Abdul Fattah El-Sisi and the Egyptian military had had enough. Morsi was arrested and jailed along with other Muslim Brotherhood leaders and figures. The group was soon banned once again and two large encampments of Morsi supporters were ruthlessly broken up by the military and security forces.

Meanwhile, Muslim Brotherhood supporters who had voted for Morsi began taking their frustrations out violently on Egypt's community of Coptic Christians, whom they viewed as complicit in the military's coup. They targeted Egyptian soldiers and police and organized protest marches demanding that Egypt's first democratically elected president be restored to power. Sisi completely ignored those demands even as he traded in his military uniform for the civilian mantle of President of the Republic after engineering a victory in the 2014 presidential elections. He has quickly become a strongman leader in Mubarak's image.

Egypt has witnessed periods of extended protests and violence off and on ever since the 2011 Arab Spring. Tensions have remained high and the brutal 2013 crackdown against pro-Morsi demonstrators has caused deep resentment among the Muslim Brotherhood's supporters against Sisi, the military, and the police. This anger has subsided to some degree, but it still boils under the surface.

These periods of violence have not done Egypt's tourism industry any good. A stagnant economy with a high unemployment rate (a record 12.6% during the second quarter of 2012[176]) has created economic pressures that add to the political and social turmoil.

And if that wasn't bad enough, Egypt is facing the threat of Islamist extremism in some areas of the Nile Delta and the Sinai Peninsula. The *Ansar Bayt al-Maqdis* ("Partisans of Jerusalem") group has carried out a series of deadly attacks that have killed dozens of Egyptian soldiers and civilians. The group began ramping up its attacks after Morsi was overthrown and remains a thorn in the government's side despite extensive campaigns by the Egyptian army to defeat it. The group has pledged allegiance to the Islamic State and now calls itself simply the Sinai Province. Neither the Islamists nor the army is anywhere close to declaring victory in this simmering conflict.

---

176. Hend El-Behary, "Egypt's Unemployment Rate Hits Record High in Second Quarter," AhramOnline website, August 14, 2012. Accessed July 17, 2017. http://english.ahram. org.eg/NewsContent/3/0/50405/Business/0/Egypts-unemployment-rate-hits-record-high-in-secon.aspx.

While Sisi has kept the lid pretty tight on the domestic security situation for now, none of the root causes of Egypt's problems has been resolved. One major terrorist attack by the Islamists, a popular demonstration that gets out of control, or more economic bad news could easily cause the violence to return to a full boil.

Jordan: Although it never captured the same level of media attention as the seismic revolutions in Egypt, Tunisia, Syria, and Libya, Jordan went through its own period of unrest during the 2011 Arab Spring. Like their brethren in the neighboring countries, Jordanians took to the streets to demonstrate for political and economic reforms and Islamists and *Salafists* were well represented in these protests.

Islamists have a relatively long history in Jordan. The country's branch of the Muslim Brotherhood was formed in the 1940s and, despite an early attempt at political participation, it evolved to become more involved in social and charitable programs. It does have a political arm that is called the Islamic Action Front. The Brotherhood has taken a novel position that while it supports the establishment of an Islamic state that is based on the *Sharia*, it does not oppose the monarchy. King Hussein generally enjoyed relatively cordial relationships with Brotherhood leaders and figures but his son and successor, King Abdullah II, seems lukewarm even to so-called "moderate" Islamists.

The country does have *Salafist* groups and leaders, most notably in the cities of Zarqa and Irbid. These groups began to gain in number and influence within the country when Jordanian fighters began returning home from the war in Afghanistan in the late 1980s. Note that the late commander of Al-Qaeda in Iraq – Abu Mus'ab al-Zarqawi – was a Jordanian from Zarqa. Many of these *Salafists* have adopted a much harsher line against the monarchy in Jordan than the Muslim Brotherhood. In 2012 Jordanian authorities thwarted a major Al-Qaeda attack against multiple targets including the US embassy in Amman, proving the existence of supporters for the terrorist group inside the country.

The Jordanian society is beset by an assortment of stressors where each contributes its own fair share of pressure on the country. Without a doubt, the Palestinian-Israeli struggle has historically been a major stressor on the country. Due to Jordan's administration of the West Bank Palestinian territory, the 1967 Six Day War and Israel's occupation of the West Bank forced Palestinian Jordanians out of the West Bank and into Jordan, proper.

Tensions began to mount as these displaced Palestinians called for Jordan to be governed by the PLO. Palestinian terrorists hijacked several Western aircraft and parked them in a disused British desert airfield in the country. By September 1970, King Hussein took action and eventually drove the PLO out of the country altogether in a military campaign dubbed "Black September" by the Palestinians. Nevertheless, sympathy to the Palestinian cause and opposition to Jordan's peace treaty with Israel remain strong among Jordanians.

The country was caught in the middle in the 1990-91 Iraqi invasion and subsequent occupation of Kuwait that prompted the *Desert Shield/Desert Storm* response to evict Saddam's army from that Gulf country. Saddam Hussein was a popular figure in Jordan due to his prominent support for the Palestinian cause and for providing Jordan with petroleum at heavily subsidized prices or even for free. When Saddam invaded Kuwait, Jordan's monarch was hesitant to denounce the Iraqi leader's move since Iraq's cheap oil was vital to Jordan's economy and budget, which suffered chronic deficits. Many Iraqi families, wanting to get out of Iraq before the shooting started, moved to Amman and rented apartments. In some neighborhoods of the Jordanian capital, Iraqis nearly outnumbered Jordanians. But since Jordan abstained from a clear denunciation of Saddam's Kuwaiti misadventure, good relations continued between the two countries and – most importantly – Jordan continued to benefit from cheap Iraqi oil.

When the United States invaded Iraq in 2003, Jordan found itself in a unique position at the end of the war. It was able to capitalize on its location as a gateway into Iraq for Western governments, businesses, and contractors as billions were poured into rebuilding Saddam's devastated country.

Today many Jordanians still admire Saddam Hussein. His toppling and eventual execution has not replaced his friendly *Sunni* government with an equally amicable *Shiite* one, evoking concerns of Iranian meddling in Jordanian affairs. This has been aggravated by Iran's overt support and assistance to Bashar al-Assad in Syria and has encouraged a surge in Jordanian *Salafist* fighters crossing the border to fight Assad's armed forces in the Syrian civil war.

The flood of Syrians fleeing the fighting in their homeland has been devastating to Jordan's economy. As of December 2016, Amnesty International put the number of Syrian refugees in Jordan at 655,675.[177] For its part, the "2015 CIA World Factbook" quantifies Jordan's refugee population as follows: 55,509 Iraqis (2013), 2.070,973 Palestinians, and 597,328 Syrians (2014 figures). Regardless of the figures, the added strain on the already-limited national and economic resources doesn't do the internal situation in the country any good.

Jordan is a country lacking in oil, water, and just about every other natural resource. This has made the country heavily reliant on foreign assistance. The "2015 CIA World Factbook" reports that Jordan suffers high unemployment and poverty rates (both at around 14%). The per capita GDP for its population of just under eight million is only $6,100, giving the country a world ranking of 151.

The country occupies a geographic location that makes it prone to be a refuge for displaced Palestinians, Syrians, and Iraqis. Much of the country is arid desert with limited agriculture, water, and natural resources. The economy is perennially weak and unemployment and poverty add to an already meager existence for much of the population. There is ample cause for unrest in the country if the cost of fuel or bread rises by even a tiny amount.

The 2011 protests demanded greater political freedoms such as a parliament that wasn't just a rubber stamp for the king and a popularly elected prime minister instead of one appointed by the royal palace. In a worrying turn, the *Salafists* were also publicly critical of King Abdullah himself and this criticism offers a revealing glimpse of what could happen in Jordan if they were able to take the reins of power.

The barbaric execution of Jordan's captured pilot by the Islamic State has galvanized popular opinion against the extremists in Syria for now, but Jordan's economic woes are not going away anytime soon. Bad times are always good recruiting opportunities for religious parties and some Muslim Brotherhood members have defected over to the more

---

177. "Syria's Refugee Crisis in Numbers," Amnesty International, December 20, 2016. Accessed July 17, 2017. https://www.amnesty.org/en/latest/news/2016/02/syrias-refugee-crisis-in-numbers/.

conservative Islamist parties. Unfortunately, this signals that we should expect the king to face a continuing threat from the Islamist and *Salafists* for the foreseeable future.

Lebanon: The tiny and beautiful country of Lebanon has had to endure more than its share of suffering over the past 60 or so years and most of it has not even been of its own making. The country has been subjected to Israeli invasions from the south and Syrian invasions from the east. It still plays host to nearly half a million Palestinian refugees who fled their homes during the 1948 creation of the State of Israel.

Syria engineered the assassination of Bachir Gemayel, Lebanon's president elect, in 1982 and the country's prime minister, Rafik Hariri, in 2005. Lebanon was historically once a part of Greater Syria and Syria has remained a major player in Lebanon's domestic politics under the dynasty of the Assad family. The Syrian military actually invaded Lebanon in the mid-seventies and remained a dominant presence there for decades.

Violence from the ongoing civil war in Syria has spilled over into Lebanon on numerous occasions with pro-Assad and anti-Assad factions battling it out in cities like Tripoli. Insurgents fighting the Assad regime have infiltrated into Syria from Lebanese border villages like Arsal, which has suffered Syrian airstrikes in return. Adding insult to injury, tens of thousands of Syrians fleeing the violence in their own country have streamed into Lebanon seeking refuge. Like Jordan, Lebanon already has a sizeable Palestinian refugee population and cannot easily accommodate even more from Syria.

Hezbollah carries out Iran's bidding in Lebanon and in Syria, rushing to the defense of Bashar al-Assad. The party has become an extremely potent force in Lebanese politics. That, in turn, opens it up for reprisals by *Sunnis* opposed to the Assad regime in Syria.

But despite all these tribulations, Lebanon and its people have remained extremely resilient. The Lebanese have learned to carry on and go with the flow as they are buffeted by dynamics and forces that are outside of their control. One wonders what this tiny gem of a country could really achieve if the lion and the lamb were to lay down together and peace were to descend on the region. Of course this is the Middle East and that is unlikely to happen anytime soon.

Mauritania: Like Mali, this North African country is not exactly on the radar of most media and news organizations. The country gained independence from France in 1960 and attempted to annex a portion of the Spanish Sahara but abandoned the effort after three years of raids by the Polisario Front that is seeking its own independence for the same territory. President Taya seized power in a military coup in 1984 and controlled the country for the next 20 years. Mauritania has attempted to transition to democratic rule but this has proved difficult. Ethnic tensions between the Arab-Berbers and the African Mauritanians remain strong.

The 2015 "CIA World Factbook" ranked the country 190th in the world in per capita GDP at $2,200. With 40% of its population of 3.5 million living below the poverty level and 30% unemployment, Mauritanians face harsh economic circumstances in addition to their ethnic problems. The country is viewed as being threatened by terrorism from Al-Qaeda of the Islamic Maghreb.

Saudi Arabia: The House of Saud may not be in imminent danger of collapsing but that doesn't mean that the edifice isn't showing a few cracks and signs of wear. Saudi Arabia is the birthplace of Islam and home to the religion's top two shrines: the Great Mosque of Mecca and the Prophet's Mosque in Medina. In recognition of that, the Saudi king is also called the Custodian of the Two Holy Mosques.

Widely seen by Westerners as a bastion of religious conservatism, Saudi Arabia prohibits any form of gambling or alcohol consumption, bans women from driving motor vehicles, does not permit the sale or consumption of pork, and actively censors images and articles in magazines that are deemed too licentious or critical of the royal family. It isn't uncommon to pick up a magazine from a Saudi newsstand in which the images of various advertisements and articles have been blacked out by hand with a permanent marker. Similarly programs and movies that are shown on television have romantic scenes and kisses edited out of the broadcast, along with any other behavior deemed too racy by the censors (such as holding hands), and the random excision of blocks of film often makes the plot line difficult to follow. Television broadcasting and stores mandatorily shut down during each day's five prayer times and women and children are segregated from the men even in fast food restaurants.

Nevertheless, there are some Muslims who think the royal family and the constitutional monarchy system of government needs to go for not being strict enough, while critics in the West encourage greater personal liberties in the desert nation such as allowing women to drive. Oddly enough, this (sort of) puts the royal family in the position of being moderates in a very strict and religiously conservative nation. The judicial code is based on the *Sharia* and beheadings and floggings are still common punishments for serious violations of Islamic law.

However, the very existence of a royal family and a manmade government in any form is absolute anathema to many strict conservatives in the country who see the *Sharia* as the only form of government that is needed. After all, Allah Himself handed the *Sharia* down to mankind and revealed it through the Prophet Muhammad in the very land of Saudi Arabia. As the Koran has instructed, He has no associate or partner so there is no need whatsoever for man to meddle in what Allah has already provided.

This strict version of Islam originated with an eighteenth Saudi cleric and preacher named Muhammad Ibn Abdul-Wahhab who believed that various acts popular with Muslims at the time like visiting tombs and shrines had become a form of idolatry and should be purged from the faith. He advocated a return to an austere and puritanical form of Islam that emulated the practice of the religion in the prophet's time; hence *Wahhabism* – the dominant Islamic sect in Saudi Arabia – became aligned with today's *Salafism*. Abdul-Wahhab formed an alliance and pledged the loyalty of his faction to a young local chieftain named Muhammad Bin Saud and that alliance between *Wahhabism* and the House of Saud has endured into the 21st century.

Not all *Wahhabis* and *Salafists* have been happy with the royal family, however. Osama bin Laden was absolutely mortified and enraged that the Saudi king had allowed US and Western "infidel" armies to "occupy" the Muslim holy lands in the Arabian Peninsula during the 1990-91 *Desert Shield/Desert Storm* campaign to expel Iraq from Kuwait. The founder of Al-Qaeda saw the Iraq-Kuwait crisis as purely an Arab and Muslim matter and the presence of Western soldiers and forces was a "defilement" of sacred land. This set the stage for sporadic terrorist attacks against Saudi military forces, officials, and Western expatriates in the kingdom.

Al-Qaeda sympathizers in Saudi Arabia eventually joined forces with their compatriots in Yemen to form Al-Qaeda in the Arabian Peninsula. They see the Saudi government and royal family as apostates and "near enemies" deserving only of *takfir* and punishment (i.e., death).

Dissident political movements have been established such as the UK-based Movement for Islamic Reform in Arabia (MIRA) and the Committee for the Defense of Legitimate Rights (CDLR). Both the United States and the United Kingdom have attempted to tie these movements to Al-Qaeda (with some success) and the movements themselves have attempted to justify their opposition to the Saudi royal family on human rights grounds to the Western media while blasting the family's legitimacy to rule under the *Sharia* in Arabic.

Moreover, the fact that *Wahhabism* is now synonymous with *Salafism* – the radical form of Islam behind much of today's terrorism – and it is the state-sponsored form of the religion in Saudi Arabia prompts many Americans to wonder what side the Saudis are really on in the Global War on Islamism. There has been no shortage of wealthy Saudis who have generously contributed funds and support to Al-Qaeda and other *Salafist* groups – including even the Islamic State. Add this *Wahhabist/Salafist* connection to a history of rabidly anti-Jewish public school curricula in the country and, "Houston, we have a problem."

Obviously *Wahhabism* cannot be classified as moderate so how can we classify the Saudis as "moderates" when their state is actually promoting and teaching *Wahhabism* as the proper form of Islam? There is an obvious inconsistency here that absolutely begs to be answered and it's going to take more than a couple of token airstrikes by Saudi warplanes on IS targets in Iraq or Syria to convince me that the Saudis are really on our side. I'll discuss ideas for dealing with the Saudis a little later in the book.

But even as the Saudis face their own challenge from the conservative *Wahhabist* corner, there is also a restive minority of *Shiites* concentrated in the kingdom's Eastern Province who have been consistently clamoring for greater religious and personal freedoms. Since *Wahhabism* is vehemently and virulently anti-*Shiite*, the *Shia* in the country have often faced persecution and arbitrary arrest and imprisonment. Naturally, the plight of the *Shia* also creates frictions with Saudi Arabia's neighbor across the Gulf – Iran.

There have been national *Sunni-Shiite* dialogues in Saudi Arabia to discuss the situation, but as long as the *Wahhabists* remain firmly entrenched and in control of the Saudi state religious establishment, any reform will be very slow going – if it occurs at all. Of course, that doesn't exactly bode well for the wider *Sunni-Shia* open warfare that is going on in neighboring Iraq and Syria.

Yet, it is on human rights matters where the Saudis face the greatest criticisms from the United States and the West. There are matters related to religion such as the rights of religious minorities (like Christians) to openly practice their faiths in the kingdom. Personal maids and servants brought in from Asia and elsewhere are often treated little better than slaves, enduring beatings and constant verbal abuse. Women certainly find themselves at a much different level in Saudi society than men, unable to go shopping or even travel out of the country without the permission or accompaniment of a male relative. Gaining the ability to drive might be a symbolic victory for women in the kingdom but I think they have bigger and more important rights issues that should be tackled first.

Since there is no freedom of expression in the kingdom, the quickest way to find yourself locked up in a Saudi jail is to express opposition to the government, criticize the royal family, or insult Islam. And they're not kidding. Canada's *Toronto Star* was one of a number of newspapers that reported the case of a Saudi blogger named Raif Badawi, who was sentenced to ten years in prison and 1,000 lashes – 50 lashes at a time per week – for "insulting Islam." Fortunately for Badawi, after his initial public flogging on January 9, 2015, his corporal punishment has been suspended and delayed "for medical reasons." Sharp international criticism of the Saudi's imprisonment and punishment has also likely encouraged the Saudis to put the whips away for a while.[178]

And Badawi doesn't seem to be alone in his dissent against the Saudi system of government. The "Country Reports on Human Rights Practices for 2014" published by our own Department of State reported plenty of anecdotal evidence that the Saudi Ministry of Interior tortures prisoners

---

178. Jillian Kestler-D'Amours, "Saudi Arabia Postpones Flogging of Blogger Raif Badawi," *Toronto Star*, February 20, 2015. Accessed July 17, 2017. http://www.thestar.com/news/world/2015/02/20/saudi-arabia-postpones-flogging-of-blogger-raif-badawi.html.

and coerces confessions from them, despite official denials.[179] Such confessions may lead to anything from imprisonment under substandard conditions all the way up to execution.

This is exactly the type of autocracy that has gotten America in trouble elsewhere in the region and around the world. If we are truly to be the Beacon of Democracy and Reagan's "Shining City on the Hill," should we be hanging out with dictators who jail and torture their opponents and stifle any form of dissent? Haven't we learned our lesson from our close, continuing, and enduring friendships with such popularly reviled dictators as Ferdinand Marcos, Anastasio Somoza, Hosni Mubarak, and Shah Reza Pahlavi?

Some may say that this is the price we have to pay to gain the upper hand against the terrorists but if we aren't going to allow torture ourselves (or even "enhanced interrogation techniques"), should we be getting friendly with those who do? If we were justified in our criticism of the North Vietnamese torture of our pilots and airmen during the Vietnam War, what makes it right for us to look the other way now when our "friends" start hooking up battery cables to suspects? I have no sympathies for the terrorists but we should be absolutely cognizant that we are playing right into Al-Qaeda's narrative about us when we condone such abuse.

Let's face it. There isn't much daylight between the Islamic State and Saudi Arabia when it comes to crime and punishment (the quantity of their victims, notwithstanding) and the level of tolerance toward any internal dissent seems to be about the same, too. It's a problem we seem reluctant to address.

Saudi Arabia is not immune from domestic opposition. It is not a champion of human rights and we should keep that in mind in our dealings with them. I've repeated this time and again throughout this book – while the state is firmly in control today it's worth remembering that nobody foresaw the consequences of the 2011 Arab Spring to the entrenched leaders of Tunisia, Egypt, Syria, or Libya, either.

---

179. "2014 Human Rights Reports: Saudi Arabia," 2014 Country Reports on Human Rights Practices, Department of State website, June 25, 2015. Accessed July 17, 2017. http://www.state.gov/j/drl/rls/hrrpt/2014/nea/236620.htm.

Sudan: In contrast to Saudi Arabia, Sudan is an extremely poor country that has seen nearly continuous ethnic, tribal, and religious struggles. The independence of South Sudan in 2011 hasn't led to the complete cessation of hostilities between the Arab Muslim north and the largely animist and Christian African south since both sides have their eyes on the oil wealth in the southern part of Sudan and how those revenues are to be split remains a subject of contention between the two sides. Territorial disputes also remain unresolved. South Sudan has been in its own civil war since 2013 so there is plenty of unrest to go around.

Sudan has been run primarily by Islamic-oriented military governments since its independence in 1956. Since the 2011 independence of South Sudan, fighting has broken out between the Sudan People's Liberation Movement-North in South Kordofan and Blue Nile states and the central government in Khartoum, which has resulted in 1.2 million internally displaced persons.

Violence in the western state of Darfur has been ongoing since 2003, displacing nearly two million people with an estimated 200,000 – 400,000 deaths. Much of this violence has been perpetrated by Muslims against non-Muslims.

The 2015 edition of the "CIA World Factbook" put the unemployment rate in the country at 20% and the percentage of the country's population living below the poverty level is 46.5%. GDP per capita is a meager $2,600, ranking the country as 182nd in the world.

It's worth remembering that Osama bin Laden took up residence in Sudan for about five years from 1991 to 1996 after falling out of favor with the Saudi government. Sudan welcomed him with open arms at the time, on the condition that he would make considerable investments inside the country. Bin Laden did invest significantly in various infrastructure and agricultural projects through a bank and construction company that he established.

But, with bin Laden in the country, Sudan made its way onto the US State Department's list of state sponsors of terrorism. By 1996, America was pressuring Sudan to expel the Al-Qaeda founder and he moved on to Afghanistan that year.

Sudan paid an expensive price for hosting the Saudi extremist. In 1998 the United States destroyed the Al-Shifa Pharmaceutical Plant in a cruise missile strike in retaliation for the Al-Qaeda twin bombings against US embassies in Tanzania and Kenya. Soil samples collected at the site made them suspect that Al-Qaeda was using the facility to manufacture chemical weapons but there was never any solid evidence to prove this.[180] It is quite possible that the factory only produced normal pharmaceutical drugs and medicines and the plant's loss just made the lives of the Sudanese who needed those drugs that much more difficult.

The country's backing of Saddam Hussein in his 1990 invasion of Kuwait certainly strained relations with the United States even further. The fact that such other noted terrorists such as Carlos the Jackal and Abu Nidal lived in Khartoum during the early nineties put Sudan on a collision course with US foreign policy in the region.

The Embassy of the United States in Khartoum has provided a recap of the frosty relations between Sudan and America on its website. It notes that there has been no US ambassador in the country since 1998 and the embassy has undergone periodic closures and reopenings. While publicly supporting US counterterrorism efforts, Khartoum opposed US strikes in Afghanistan and a widening of this effort to other countries. Government-sanctioned violence in Darfur led the Bush administration to impose new economic sanctions in 2006.[181]

The government in Khartoum remains in control of the country but often faces demonstrations from university students who are protesting the poor economic conditions and lack of jobs in the country. Many also seek greater political freedoms and reforms. The lack of jobs in the country has forced many to risk their lives to migrate in hopes of finding better lives in Egypt, Libya, Israel, and Western Europe. It also has sparked a lucrative trade in human trafficking. The

---

180. Vernon Loeb, "U.S. Wasn't Sure Plant Had Nerve Gas Role," *The Washington Post*, August 21, 1999. Accessed July 18, 2017. https://www.washingtonpost.com/archive/politics/1999/08/21/us-wasnt-sure-plant-had-nerve-gas-role/3ed5ab71-f050-44e6-817c-eefa717e84bf/.

181. "What You Need To Know About U.S. Sanctions," U.S. Department of the Treasury, Office of Foreign Assets Control, July 25, 2008. Accessed July 17, 2017. https://www.treasury.gov/resource-center/sanctions/Documents/sudan.pdf.

one bright spot in its economy is oil, but that is in limbo as long as problems with South Sudan remain unresolved. China – which has played a main role in developing Sudan's petroleum industry – might be a candidate for mediating this dispute although we would certainly not be happy to see a boost in China's image at either the African or international level.

Sudan may not be classified as a failed state just yet but it isn't exactly on the international community's dean's list, either. With a history of ethnic violence that has no end in sight, an autocratic leader, and a stagnant economy, the country's future looks as bleak as ever.

IS TUNISIA AN ARAB SPRING SUCCESS STORY?

Given the path that Tunisia has followed since the Arab Spring of 2011, the country has had its ups and downs but it has largely overcome some daunting challenges in its transition to democracy and may provide a good example of what an Islamic democracy in the Middle East can look like. It's also interesting to compare the much different results of the first two revolutions in the Arab Spring: Egypt's and Tunisia's. The former has returned to authoritarianism while the latter seems firmly on a path to democratization even though it is facing some very serious security challenges from Islamists. In fact, the success of Tunisia's democratic experiment is the prime motivator behind the Islamists' terrorist attacks as they seek to cripple Tunisia's tourism-dependent economy. At the same time they do not wish to see any Arab or Muslim state in the Middle East become a haven of democracy – especially the country where the Arab Spring revolution against autocrats and tyrants began.

Eva Bellin, the Myra and Robert Kraft Professor of Arab Politics at Brandeis University's Crown Center for Middle East Studies, wrote a compelling comparison of the two cases that was published in December 2014 on the website of the Project on Middle East Political Science (POMEPS) at the Elliott School of International Affairs.[182]

---

182. Eva Bellin, "Explaining Democratic Divergence: Why Tunisia Has Succeeded and Egypt Has Failed," Project on Middle East Political Science website, December 10, 2014. Accessed July 17, 2017. See http://pomeps.org/2014/12/10/explaining-democratic-divergence/.

Bellin pointed out the very different roles of each country's military institution, civil society, leadership attitudes, luck, and several other influential factors in shaping the trajectories of Tunisia and Egypt after their respective revolutions. For example, the military in Tunisia is a relatively small institution that has not played a leading role in the country – especially in politics. It has no great military history. It has developed an attitude of acceptance to civilian supremacy and leadership.

In Egypt, the military is a much larger and more prominent state institution. It has supplied presidents to the country ever since the Free Officers Revolution and Gamal Abdel-Nasser. It has fought numerous conflicts with Israel and it is portrayed domestically as the victor of the 1973 October War. As such, the Egyptian military has enjoyed a status of respect and influence among the Egyptian people that is far different from the standing of the Tunisian armed forces among that country's population.

The civil society in Tunisia was already more politically diverse at the time of the Arab Spring than Egypt's was. Bellin observed that this civil society did a better job of playing "the watchdog" on Tunisian leaders and politicians to make sure they did not stray from democratic ideals.

In contrast, Egypt's society was more polarized with the country's first presidential election boiling down to a holdover from the old regime or a candidate from the previously banned Muslim Brotherhood. Both sides were evenly split and both were adamantly opposed to the other side's victory.

The democratic election of the Muslim Brotherhood candidate, President Morsi, was initially hailed as the success of the democratic experiment in the country. But the optimism faded as Morsi began making himself an Islamist president with nearly absolute powers who was beyond judicial and even legislative oversight. He worked to isolate and marginalize the opposition, just making the domestic scene that much more divided. Egypt had merely traded a secular dictator for an Islamist one. After a year, the military stepped in and Morsi was done. The country has been in varying states of turmoil ever since.

In Tunisia, the victory by the Islamist *Ennahda* Party initially rang alarm bells in the West but the situation was quite different from what happened in Egypt. Bellin commented:

> *Rachid Ghannochi* [i.e., the founder and leader of *Ennahda*] *distinguished himself by reaching out to the non-Islamist camp and by pressing his base to compromise on key issues such as the role of sharia in the constitution, the ban on blasphemy, and the issue of gender equality. He argued quite eloquently that even if Ennahda had had the power to push through its views unilaterally, it should not, that in building the country's foundational political institutions the country ought to come together and strive to build consensus. He counseled his base to take the long view, not to win in the short term only to lose in the long.*[183]

Other factors may include Tunisia's remoteness from the Arab-Israeli conflict, the absence of any leading role in Arab and international politics, and the existence of a much healthier economy. The country, much smaller in population and geography, does not have the same societal pressures as Egypt does.

Although Tunisia is still fighting Islamist terrorist insurgents in the country and it did go through periods of post-revolution political assassination and unrest, it does seem now to be establishing the principles of political tolerance and power sharing. These components, so critical for laying the foundations of a successful democracy, bode well for the country's transition to a diverse, multiparty political system. As I referenced earlier, this is why the Islamists are so intent on doing whatever they can to thwart this process.

The Egyptians, in contrast, attempted to carry out a democratic presidential election without first laying a foundation composed of the necessary democratic components. The experiment failed and the country boomeranged back to autocratic rule – first by an Islamist, then the military. This is an important reminder that democracy, regardless of whether it is a Western or Islamic one, can only flourish

---

183. *Ibid.*

after a certain amount intellectual and political enlightenment has established the proper underpinnings and framework. We can't expect Cairo to become Cleveland overnight.

The previous information is critical for understanding the gravity of the present situation in much of the Middle East and North Africa. I trust that you can now see why preventing fragile states is such a high priority. We cannot allow them to fail completely. We cannot allow the formation of any more sanctuaries like Iraq, Syria, Yemen, Libya, and Somalia for groups like Islamic State, Al-Qaeda, or Al-Shabaab.

But, this is a job for Arabs and Muslims, not us. We can help and provide advice and support, but we will always be outsiders in the region. An Arab Peace Corps under the auspices of the Gulf Cooperation Council – the wealthiest and most politically stable Arab countries – provides an indigenous mechanism for assisting fragile states and countering the Islamists' narrative in the heart of the Arab world.

The demographics in the Middle East are going to force changes whether we like it or not. Let's encourage our Arab allies to do whatever they can to steer those changes in a positive direction in the part of the world that needs them the most.

CHAPTER NINE

STEP FOUR: LET'S BE SMARTER
WITH MILITARY FORCE

"The supreme art of war is to subdue the enemy without fighting."

– *Sun Tzu*

The best thing about hitting ourselves in the head with a hammer is that it feels so good when we stop. This statement seems eminently applicable to our constant use of the military in what was formerly called the Global War on Terror. Did we win the war in Iraq? Are we winning the war in Afghanistan? Yes, I know that we toppled Saddam Hussein and the Taliban, but did we win in Iraq and are we winning in Afghanistan?

In a word – no. I don't know what your definition of winning a war is, but the current state of affairs in either country – particularly Iraq – isn't what I think "winning" looks like. The reason for this is that we've over-relied on the military to solve a problem that is not inherently a military problem. Somebody once said that if the only tool in your toolbox is a hammer, every problem starts to look like a nail. We obviously need a better assortment of tools and that is the whole purpose for this book – adding more effective tools to our toolbox.

Don't get me wrong here. The military has performed its job magnificently. It is the politicians and the policymakers that have let us down – specifically our servicemen and servicewomen (and their families). They have endured numerous deployments, often at the expense of their personal lives and health, and yet we are no closer to strategic victory. I don't think our leaders have done right by them.

From the mid-nineties to the early 2000s, the neoconservatives chirped noisily like a nest full of hungry baby birds for "regime change" in Iraq. Saddam just had to go. The 21st century was going to be the American Century, according to their calculus, and the Iraqi dictator had thumbed his nose at the United States and the international community for far too long. He was unfinished business.

The Bush administration assembled dubious evidence about secret Iraqi WMD programs, garnered UN Security Council cover for military action, and invaded Iraq in March 2003. In just a matter of weeks, on April 9th of that year, Saddam's statue in Baghdad's Firdus Square came down and the remnants of his regime collapsed along with it. Unfortunately, that was also the end of the US strategy in the country. Once the Iraqi dictator was thrown out, we had no game plan for what was to come next. If a lawyer should never ask a witness a question for which he does not already know the answer, then a superpower shouldn't go around invading and occupying countries and changing regimes without knowing what the strategic consequences of those actions might be.

This neoconservative obsession with toppling Saddam was a strategic blunder of Biblical proportions. They had no idea of the cultural and religious history or dynamics inside the country – and you don't just change a country's regime in a political or cultural vacuum. Their myopic mistake was the geostrategic equivalent of the introduction of rabbits to Australia. Only in this case, proliferating Islamists replaced the proliferating rabbits down under. Years of economic sanctions under Saddam had already made Iraq an extremely difficult place in which to live and we made it even worse with our invasion, regime change, and subsequent occupation. Many Arabs justifiably hold us responsible and accountable for that.

Yet, now we hear many of the same figures that called for the 2003 invasion of Iraq clamoring for more and more military deployments in the Middle East. But, aside from *Desert Storm* in 1991, when was the last time we had a successful US military campaign in the Middle East that ended with a lasting peace and a stable US ally?

And every time the balloon goes up somewhere in the Middle East or Southwest Asia, we hear the same, old, tired, voices making the same, old, tired suggestion: "Send in the drones." But we've been using drones for over a decade in Afghanistan and Pakistan and yet the terror threat there hasn't subsided one iota. If anything, it's worse. The same is true for Yemen. Drones kill people, but people can always be replaced. Drones do nothing to kill the Islamist ideology. On the contrary they just create martyrs and that only plays into the Islamists' ideology.

I'm sure we've got lots of high-tech, skilled workers putting drones and Hellfire missiles together so you can make a case that they are important for jobs. They make for "must see TV" in the Combined Air Operations Center (CAOC) in Qatar so you can certainly make a case for giving real-time intelligence to military officers and civilian policymakers. But, you can't make a case that they are winning the war on terrorism. More specifically, they are not winning the war on Islamism. They are simply a tactical weapon with tactical benefits, nothing less and nothing more.

Unfortunately, calling this conflict against extremist ideology a war implies that the military *should* be the fundamental component for our victory. You do use soldiers, sailors, airmen, and Marines to fight a war, don't you? But, ours is not a war against Nazi Germany or Imperial Japan. It is not a war against another state or belligerent nation. It is a war against an ideology. It is a war of hearts and minds. Let's remember that we didn't win the Cold War by bombing Moscow and the Soviet Union into oblivion. We won it by defeating the communist ideology. It was the ballot box, the free economy, the stores stocked with food and merchandise of all kinds, and the American Dream that won that war. We may not be perfect, but we still have all that to offer. What, besides martyrdom and oppression, do the Islamists have to offer?

We have invested heavily in weapons and weapon systems that have become smarter and smarter and ever more lethal (and expensive) but such investments are only at the tactical level. What are we investing at the strategic level of this fight? What are we investing to actually *prevent* the next generation of terrorists? What are we investing to delegitimize and eradicate the causes of Islamist extremism in the Muslim world? What are we investing in strategic victory? Not very much, I'm afraid.

Military action and the use of deadly force absolutely does have to be part of our strategy against radical Islamist ideology if for no other reason than to protect the populations that are threatened with genocide at the extremists' hands. That's obvious. I am completely supportive of the *smart use* of US military force *within the confines of an overall strategy aimed at completely and strategically defeating our enemies and their ideology once and for all,* not just "degrading" them.

This may mean that sometimes we have to react to small-scale military targeting opportunities that present themselves such as our operations to eliminate Osama bin Laden, Anwar al-Awlaki, and "Jihadi John," to name a few. These achievements boost our morale and bring justice to the evildoers but the targeted killings of these and other terrorists will not end the war any more than our killing of Admiral Yamamoto ended World War II.

Such reactions must still fall within the outlines of our comprehensive strategy. We must not base our actions on reaction alone. Without a doubt we must have a strategy and a policy that allows us to drive the tempo of the battle and keep our enemies off balance and on the defensive, not just on the physical battlefield, but in the information war, the political and diplomatic arena, and in cyberspace, too. That's Battle Management 101. That's how we can win.

Conversely, the long-term, grand and expansive campaigns like Iraq and Afghanistan force us into the hated role of occupier, which is not a winning move when the goal is to win those hearts and minds. Moreover, the only strategy we had for getting into those operations was regime change. We accomplished that pretty quickly, so it became clear that we didn't really have a strategy for getting out of either country. The plan and the strategy ended with the fall of the regime. Then mission creep started us down the nation-building road for which we were unprepared financially, culturally, and administratively. We wasted precious lives and riches getting bogged down and trying to figure out what the end game was and, ultimately, while we won every battle, we still lost the war. We just can't afford to keep making such strategic mistakes of this magnitude. Short, sharp, violent operations that bestow a healthy dose of "what the hell just happened?" on any surviving enemies without getting into a protracted occupation or long-term misadventure are the key to success in the smart use of our military power. General H. Norman Schwarzkopf once said: "We need to destroy not attack, not damage, not surround. I want to destroy the Republican Guard." Pretty solid advice from a military strategist and commander who knew a thing or two about fighting and winning.

It's the kind of bold, successful leadership our Pentagon sorely needs today. "Degrading" is an ambiguous term in a war that desperately needs some clarity. How do we define it in military terms? What metrics are used to measure it? When has an enemy been suitably "degraded?" On the other hand, words like "victory" and "defeat" need no explanation or clarification.

Use military power sparingly – only when it is absolutely needed – but when it must be used, employ it with overwhelming force and violence. Killing the enemy violently, quickly, and in large numbers will have more of a deterrent effect on Islamist recruiting than any gradual approach to "degrade" our *takfirist* adversaries. A gradual campaign may actually improve Islamist recruiting because our enemies believe they win by simply not losing to the world's only remaining superpower.

There are many in our society who believe that the Islamist terrorism or extremism problem can only be solved militarily. Such people downplay and belittle diplomatic and political efforts to engage with Muslims in any attempt at reaching a mutual solution to the problem of radicalism. They postulate that we are indeed at war with all of Islam and all Muslims. According to them, Islam is a religion born out of violence, hatred, and intolerance and a faith that is completely incompatible with the Western values of freedom and democracy. The terrorists and *Salafists* in IS committing atrocities and crimes against humanity are somehow representative of all Muslims – even the ones that the IS terrorists have often videoed themselves beheading or killing.

The implication seems to be that we will have to militarily fight, defeat, or kill all the world's Muslims to survive. That's somewhere between one and two billion people worldwide, give or take. Although estimates vary widely, even World War II only managed to kill around 85 million victims.[184] Does anybody really think that killing 20 times the number of all the people who died in World War II is a serious policy option – one that can be justified as "self-defense" where the rest of the world will just look the other way?

---

184. "By the Numbers: World-Wide Deaths," website of the National WWII Museum. Accessed July 17, 2017. http://www.nationalww2museum.org/learn/education/for-students/ww2-history/ww2-by-the-numbers/world-wide-deaths.html.

Causing death on that scale would be virtually impossible with conventional weapons and I don't think the Russians and Chinese would be happy to just look the other way as we unleash our nuclear arsenal upon the Muslim nations throughout the Middle East and the rest of the world along their borders.

Let's take a moment to step back and reflect on the historical effectiveness of the military solution. As we have noted in chapter two, in 1258 the Mongol warlord Hulagu invaded and sacked Baghdad – the seat of the Abbasid Caliphate, the capital city of Islam itself at the time. The Mongols were the premier fighting force of their day. When they took the city they killed the caliph and they destroyed Baghdad's Islamic libraries. They made pyramids of skulls in the streets, killing thousands of the city's Muslim population.

Nevertheless, Islam went on to survive for the next 760 years – right up to the present day. The world's best military force of the times – like the US military is today – was unable to completely eradicate Islam even though it destroyed the capital city and killed the caliph himself. Islam survived because it had become a religion, an ideology, and a culture whose importance throughout the depth and breadth of the Muslim population of that time transcended that of the caliph and even the city of Baghdad. It is a lesson that is still very relevant for us today.

Using a more recent example, the Syrian regime has pounded the Islamic State and its ilk in six years of civil war. The Syrian military has become a battle-experienced force (albeit one that is also battle-weary and nowhere equal to either the Mongols or the US armed forces) that despite indiscriminate mass bombing, shelling, and Scud campaigns, has been unable to defeat and exterminate these groups. On the contrary, IS has even spread into neighboring Iraq to carry out its atrocities and terrorism there.

Now, to be fair, the Syrian military has tactically abandoned some areas that it could not hold due to the manpower limitations of its army. Nevertheless, there are situations where the Syrians have fought very effectively – especially when bolstered by Iranian or *Hezbollah* (and now Russian) allies. But they're still nowhere close to actually defeating and declaring victory over their foes.

Moreover, IS now has franchises in dozens of countries around the region and the world like Libya, Yemen, Egypt, and Tunisia. Even when we are able to deal a deathblow to the group in Mosul and Raqqa, we'll still have to deal with these other offshoots, according to the calculus of the military solution. Attempting to impose a military solution for Islamic State will simply lead to the group's subdivision and perpetuation. It will always live on somewhere else.

Still not convinced? Okay, I've mentioned that we killed Osama bin Laden, Anwar al-Awlaki, and many other terrorist leaders. Yet much like the results of the Mongols' sacking of Baghdad in 1258, Islamist extremism is still there and flourishing. We've killed and captured all sorts of terrorist figures and icons, but in the end we only killed men. We did not kill the ideology that stood behind them. Worse yet, we made them martyrs. That's the fallacy of banking on the military solution as the exclusive option to win a global war on Islamist terror. And that's the problem. We're focused on fighting the wrong war with the wrong tool. We should be fighting the ideology that breeds the terrorism and that takes a completely different strategy with different tools.

The obvious proof of this is that groups like the Islamic State and Al-Shabaab continue to pop up 16 years after 9/11. It is the best evidence that Washington has not, and does not have a strategic grasp of the problem. As long as we are not defeating the ideology, we will have to continue sending US warriors to deal with problems like IS and AQAP. The very existence of such groups proves the failure of our leaders – elected and otherwise. Unfortunately, the military gets stuck with cleaning up a mess that didn't have to happen if our government was doing its job properly in the first place. A regional Arab/US land army isn't the answer. Troop "surges" are short-term tactical solutions that do nothing to attack the strategic target of Islamism. Some politicians like to hold up the surge in Iraq as an example of great success, but let me ask you once again, did we actually win that war? Was that surge a part of a larger, successful strategy? Did it lead to an actual strategic victory in which Iraq became a stable democracy that is friendly to the United States? We all know the answers to those questions.

Turning to the fight against the Islamic State in Iraq and Syria, it is important to understand the difference between propaganda and reality.

The Islamic State propaganda peddled by our alarmist media tells us that IS fighters are ten feet tall and invincible. The reality is that IS can only survive by intimidating and repressing the populations it controls inside an area comprised of territory seized and occupied from two failed states. It needs a constant supply of clueless foot soldiers to replace desertions, combat losses, and even executions of its own men. Many people under its thumb are eager to throw off its oppression. While the organization's propaganda arm paints a picture of the inevitable triumph of the Islamic State over the infidels, in truth the self-proclaimed "caliphate" is becoming more brittle and more vulnerable every day. It is more corrupt and oppressive than the secular regime it has replaced.

Nevertheless, once such a terrorist organization has grown big enough to hold vast amounts of territory, once they engage in wanton genocide, we have no choice but to engage and destroy it militarily. It's the end product of the failed and failing state dilemma discussed in the preceding chapter.

Unfortunately, for much of the campaign against Islamic State, we've not had a sophisticated plan from Washington. Airstrikes. Drone strikes. Do more of the same tomorrow.

We waited too long before taking effective action. Our leaders spent more time putting constraints on how our military could fight instead of giving our warfighters the resources to win. Washington's hesitancy and deliberation only served to prolong the conflict and paint us as weak in the eyes of the Islamists and their vulnerable sympathizers.

Waiting to act has caused the suffering of millions of innocent victims. It allowed Islamic State to utilize its propaganda machine to radicalize and recruit tens of thousands more young people whose lives are now either ruined or over. Our delay gave IS an opportunity to metastasize to other countries and regions and encouraged its supporters to commit acts of terrorism. Getting rid of IS now is going to be a lot messier and will take a lot longer than if we had pounced on the group early on, well before it had even declared its caliphate.

It's the cancer analogy again. Removing an abnormal mole early is far more effective than attempting to successfully treat melanoma that has spread throughout the patient. That should be what swift, sharp, and violent military action is all about – more results with less footprint.

Now that the military campaign against IS is actually underway, the Pentagon, State Department, and White House have hopefully first established what the endgame will be in Iraq and Syria before we get too carried away with any use of military force whose only objective is to defeat Islamic State. Unless we know what will *follow* IS after they have been defeated and eradicated, simply engaging in yet another regime change will be pointless and possibly counterproductive; it won't get us out of the quagmire we are seeing in the *Sunni* portion of Iraq. We should actually define our strategic objective *before* we start ramping up military force.

That objective should be the effective, inclusive governance of the *Sunni* heartland in Anbar Province. One cautionary note in relying on the Iraqi Army to liberate places like Mosul and Ramadi is that the *Sunnis* already believe that it and Iraq's *Shia* central government are nothing but an instrument of oppression against them. The problems in Anbar Province are directly the result of Baghdad's persecution of the *Sunnis* and they will want nothing to do with that government; it is nothing but a proxy for the hated Iranian "Safavid rejectionists."

To make any form of governance work inside Anbar, the *Sunnis* will need the same degree of autonomy that the Iraqi Kurds enjoy inside Iraqi Kurdistan. If we were to remove the *Shia* government oppression and interference from the equation in the province, the *Sunnis* would be much more willing to throw off the yoke of Islamic State tyranny. If we were to communicate that the endgame objective is for the *Sunnis* to simply govern themselves – just like the Kurds – and leave the Baghdad *Shia* out of the province's affairs, they would have a reason to turn against Islamic State and take back their own cities, towns, and villages. They would have a reason to cooperate with us just like the Awakening Councils did during the occupation. Baghdad is Tehran's lackey and we are just potentially making things worse in Iraq by counting on them to help reclaim Anbar Province. Baghdad is seen there as the problem, not the solution and we must be attentive to *Sunni* concerns in this regard.

Hopefully, we have clandestinely established contact with some *Sunni* leaders already. If we were able make contact with partisans in Yugoslavia and islanders in New Guinea during World War II and the Northern Alliance in Afghanistan in 2001, then we can figure out how to establish contact with a nucleus of *Sunni* chieftains in today's Iraq. But, before we create another political and power vacuum by getting rid of Islamic State, let's have something that can immediately move in to fill that void waiting on the sidelines. Our efforts at the political, military, and diplomatic levels must be synchronized and coordinated.

We should always thoroughly consider the regional and cultural consequences of our military actions. We shouldn't stay too long or be seen as an occupying force and we always must be aware that all the various players in the region have their own interests foremost in their minds. That means that sometimes, not even the victims we are trying to save will be our friends for very long. The Middle East has always be a region of shifting alliances. We should keep the old Arab adage in mind: "The enemy of my enemy is my friend."

As for the fate of Islamic State in the wake of any military campaign, as long as the organization's ideology survives and as long as it can maintain a virtual presence in cyberspace to promote that ideology, it will continue to be a threat and problem. It may shift its focus to one of its affiliates in another country or it may be satisfied with being a "virtual caliphate" for a time, but it has far too many sympathizers around the world for it to simply vanish because of its loss of Iraqi and Syrian territory. It has become the standard bearer for Islamism. If anything, its reversal of fortunes may even encourage many of those sympathizers to carry out individual acts of terrorism. The group itself may ramp up terrorist operations – particularly in the West – just to demonstrate it has survived and is still a force with which to be reckoned. Many of their foreign fighters will undoubtedly try to escape to their homelands once they see that the Islamic State in Iraq and/or Syria is inevitably doomed. We should actually expect all this to happen as they lose territory on the ground.

Military action is not the strategic solution to our war. Even in the case of Islamic State, the now-required use of military force will simply push the conflict into another phase with its own, unique problems and difficulties.

RUSSIA'S SYRIAN GAMBIT

As if the situation inside Syria couldn't get any more complicated, Russia decided to interject itself into the mix inside the country by sending several dozen of its fixed – and rotary-winged combat aircraft to Latakia, in the northwest of the country. These Russian planes began an ambitious program of airstrikes in September 2015 that seemed aimed more at "moderate" Syrian dissident fighters than at Islamic State targets. Russian President Vladimir Putin justified the intervention as supporting Syria's legitimate, elected authority (i.e., President Bashar al-Assad).

Russian observers in the West, who had largely been out of a job since the collapse of the Soviet Union, suddenly warned of a resurgent Russian bear that had emerged from hibernation and was hungry from two-and-a-half decades of slumber. They pointed to Russian support for the rebels in eastern Ukraine, Russia's annexation of the Crimean Peninsula, increased long-range patrolling by Russian bombers, Russian aircraft buzzing US warships, and all sorts of worrying signs that Putin was positioning his country for another Cold War against America and NATO.

There's another aspect to this, too, though. This kind of posturing plays well for Putin's domestic audience because it temporarily takes Russians' minds off the desperate economic situation at home. Punitive Western sanctions on Russia because of the Ukraine and the low price and over-supply of oil have undoubtedly painted Putin (and the Russian economy) into a financial corner. Ukraine does actually border on Russia and it has a significant percentage of ethnic Russians so it was unlikely to stand idly by as Ukraine's pro-Russian president was chased out of office in 2014 (we weren't very passive during the Cuban Missile Crisis or the invasion of Grenada, either). Putin is an old Soviet KGB officer and I'm sure that he does finally enjoy some opportunities to tweak the West's nose here and there. But Russia's military is a mere shadow of what it once was during the Soviet era and nobody wants to escalate minor provocations into a shooting war – Putin included. Nevertheless, NATO's expansion in Eastern Europe all the way to the Baltic states on Russia's western border, the perceived threat to ethnic Russians in Ukraine, and the threat to Russian interests in Ukraine and Syria have undoubtedly sparked some "aggressive" pushback from the Russians.

Aside from reminding the West that it is still a Great Power, Russia's intervention in Syria seems to have two main, strategic objectives. First it is in Russia's interest to maintain the status quo in the country and that means protecting the Assad regime. At the very least it means that if Assad is eventually replaced, his replacement will be friendly to Russia. During the heyday of the Soviet Union, the Russian navy had friendly anchorages in Syria, Egypt, Libya, and Yemen. Its facility at Tartous, Syria is the only one left and its only remaining toehold in the Mediterranean.

If Putin does have ambitions of restoring Russia to the status of a global superpower, it would certainly be in his interests to hold onto that facility.

There is another aspect to this that doesn't get too much discussion in the West but the Assad dynasty has been a good and loyal client first of the Soviets, and now of the Russians. The Syrian regime has been a frequent military customer of Russian arms and technology. The Russian embassy in Damascus has historically had a very large contingent and it has served as the primary nexus of Russian diplomatic, military, and intelligence activity in the region. With Assad gone and replaced by a regime hostile to Russia, all that would go away.

In addition, by standing with Assad during his hour of need, Putin is sending a message to other despots out there – Russia won't abandon you the way America and the West abandoned their allies like Mubarak and Saleh. If you ask us for help, we'll be there with military force to back you up, if necessary. Russia and Putin are reliable partners, not like the untrustworthy politicians of the West. The Russian president cultivates a tough-guy image; he rides horses bare-chested, chops wood, flies bombers, and drives tanks. It is a strong message that resonates with dictators in tough neighborhoods all over the world.

And one thing is for sure – Assad urgently needs Putin's help. The fact of the matter is that even with Russian air support, Assad's army has had difficulty claiming territory it had lost in the northwest of the country. What Assad really needs is the one thing that Putin cannot provide him: manpower (although there are rumors of Russian mercenaries active in the country). Without Iranian and *Hezbollah* forces on the ground in Syria, Assad would really be in trouble.

I think an accurate reading of Russia's involvement in the Syrian civil war distills down to a wobbly-legged, desperate Assad who is on the ropes and unable to save himself. Ever the survivor, he cannot go on without Iranian, *Hezbollah*, and now Russian support and assistance. He has used all sorts of conventional and chemical weapons along with ballistic missiles against his own people. His country is in shambles, millions of his countrymen are dead or displaced, internally or externally, and aside from these few "friends" he has no one to whom he can turn. By accepting Iranian, Russian, and *Hezbollah* help he has made his deal with the Devil. When they decide his time is up, they – not the Syrian people – will replace him.

However, the second strategic objective of Putin's Syrian gambit is much more intriguing. Obviously, by allying himself with the hated, *Alawite, Shiite,* Assad regime in Damascus, the Russian leader has alienated himself from pretty much every other Arab country in the region. He has drawn the ire of every *takfirist* and *Salafist* anywhere in the Arab world and they're probably all lining up to martyr themselves in Moscow's Red Square.

At first blush that would seem to be a real dumb move until you realized that the real prize in this conflict isn't Assad or Syria. The real prize would be Putin's establishment of cooperative and friendly relations with Iran. Here is a country with vast natural, petroleum, and human resources. It is a close neighbor to Russia's southwest along the Caspian Sea and a staunch and permanent thorn in the side of America and the West. With his newfound friendship with Tehran, Putin moves from being Khomeini's "Lesser Satan" to Iran's anti-American neighbor and potential ally to the north. He becomes the ayatollahs' pal and savior.

Because of its warming ties with Iran, Russia enjoys far more influence and cooperation inside Iran's proxy and vassal of Iraq than we would like – even after our eight-and-a-half year occupation, two trillion dollars of national treasure, and nearly 5,000 American lives.

There is no better evidence of this than the recent tripartite military cooperation arrangement between Iran, Iraq, and Russia. The Russians certainly obtained tacit Iranian and Iraqi concurrence before firing their salvo of Kalibr cruise missiles from the Caspian Sea since those missiles had to overfly those two countries enroute to their targets in Syria. Even more significantly, Russia staged bombers used to attack "terrorist" targets in Syria at an airbase in Iran. These countries all share a common threat from the *Sunni takfirist* menace in the region so you can bet this little partnership includes some serious intelligence and security information sharing.

It takes two to tango so this warming in Russian-Iranian relations equally serves Tehran's interests. Iran just went through a prolonged, hostile, and unsatisfying period of negotiations with the United States and the West over its nuclear program and the resulting agreement was one with which nobody was happy.

Russia, on the other hand, lent a mediating hand when needed and offered potential solutions that were agreeable to Iran. Moreover, the two countries already have a precedent for nuclear cooperation since Russia completed Iran's power reactor at Bushehr. As a permanent member of the United Nations Security Council a friendly Russia offers Iran the chance for some political and diplomatic cover. And of course Russia's anti-Western and anti-American credentials are unassailable. A Russian-Iranian marriage would be a match made in heaven for the two of them and an absolute nightmare for us.

Thus, Putin and Russia have very little to lose from the Russian military presence in Syria and an awful lot to gain. Regardless of whether or not Assad survives or falls, Putin has cast his and Russia's lot along with Iran's and in doing so, has earned a significant measure of Iran's trust.

There's undoubtedly some business acumen at work here, too. Putin knows that once Iran's economic sanctions are lifted, it will be in sore need of updating and upgrading its military and civilian aircraft fleets and even the infrastructure for its petroleum industry. Russia likely hopes that Tehran will show its gratitude for Russia's support for Assad by placing orders for some big-ticket items with Russia. Moreover, the two countries would have a mutual interest in joining forces to influence matters involving the international petroleum market.

RUSSIA'S EXPEDITIONARY FORCE IN SYRIA IS AN INTELLIGENCE GOLDMINE

Russia's deployment of an expeditionary force to Latakia is often portrayed as an entirely negative development. To some, it all harkens back to the days of the Soviet Union where Russia's military was nearly always portrayed in the West as being up to some kind of nefarious and diabolical mischief. For others, it's hard to see how this deployment has a positive side to it, but that would ignore the trove of data, information, and intelligence we can collect about current Russian military capabilities because of this move.

Russia hasn't projected such a military force outside its borders since the 1979 Soviet invasion of Afghanistan. Its airbase inside Syria certainly isn't on a scale with the invasion and occupation of Afghanistan but it provides a wealth of clues about Russian logistics and supply capabilities. How long did it take the Russians to prepare their airfield? How well can they feed and support their soldiers and airmen at Latakia? What about medical care? Can Russian air force maintainers keep their aircraft combat ready? (There is already some anecdotal news reporting that Russia is struggling to keep its aircraft in the air due to maintenance issues.)

The Russian force in Syria offers some unique SIGINT exploitation opportunities. Even if much of their communications are encrypted, you can tell a lot about their communications by looking at their technical parameters. What kind of satellite and other communications are they using? How much bandwidth? With what other support or intelligence facilities are they in contact internally and externally? Little analytical tidbits like these can offer clues about everything from how much data they can push to potentially even the quality and timeliness of their intelligence. Since we have a lot of practice in expeditionary operations, we know what it takes to support a force of a certain size. How does the Russian deployment compare with our own experiences?

Now we have a golden opportunity to see what their modern S-300/S-400 air defense systems look like in a deployed mode. Collecting and analyzing those signals and their associated communications and telemetry offers us a great chance to find technical ways of exploiting and defeating those systems. What operational frequencies do the surveillance and tracking radars use? How well do these systems handle the desert environment? How long are the radars and other components down for maintenance? How effectively do the various launchers, radars, and other components communicate with each other? There is a wealth of technical data on these systems that will now be available to us from a real combat deployment.

How well can Russian airplanes actually prosecute their air war? How effective are their airstrikes? Are they using primarily unguided, dumb bombs or precision weapons? (Again, anecdotal news reports suggest Russia is dropping mostly dumb bombs on its targets.) What is the combat performance and effectiveness of today's Russian pilots and aircrew compared with their Soviet predecessors?

Russia sent its Blackjack, Bear, and Backfire strategic bombers from bases in Russia on actual long-range combat missions over Syria. What intelligence can be gleaned from these operations about their long-range, strategic aviation capabilities?

The Sukhoi SU-34 Fullback is Russia's new, premier, tactical attack bomber. How well did it stand up to expeditionary operations, especially in the desert? What sort of missions did the Russians use the Fullback for compared to its older stable mate, the Sukhoi SU-24 Fencer? How effectively did it employ its weapons? What can we tell about the aircraft's sensors, radars, and communications from all the various signals it emits? What can we tell from cockpit video imagery provided by Russia's Ministry of Defense? Amassing a technical library about the Fullback's different emitters gives us valuable information on how to defeat the aircraft if that is ever required.

It's too bad that we were not able to encourage a Fullback aircrew to defect with their plane to Turkey, Cyprus, or Greece? When Russian pilot Viktor Belenko flew his MiG-25 Foxbat to Japan in 1976 and defected to the United States it gave US and Western experts and engineers a close look at an aircraft that represented the cutting edge of Soviet technology at the time. Let's hope there will be an opportunity in the future of repeating the Belenko intelligence coups and getting our hands on a Fullback.

In October 2015, Russia demonstrated its technological prowess by firing 26 of its new Kalibr cruise missiles from the Caspian Sea that were intended for targets 900 miles away in Syria. Four of those missiles (about 15% of the total) crashed somewhere in Iran before reaching their objectives. Do we know why they crashed? What does that tell us about the quality and reliability of Russia's naval cruise missiles and how does that square with the performance of our own Tomahawk weapons?

In the summer of 2016, the Russian navy deployed a task force led by its sole aircraft carrier, the Admiral Kuznetsov, all the way from northern Russia to the Eastern Mediterranean. What does that deployment tell us about Russia's ability to project its naval power? What is the assessment of Russian carrier and air operations?

How well do Russian soldiers adapt to expeditionary deployment? Do morale problems negatively effect force deployment? Is a largely conscripted force able to accomplish the mission?

While it's a no-brainer to concede that adding a couple of dozen Russian combat aircraft on their own airstrikes into the crowded aerial furball over Syria adds an unwanted complication to our own operations, we do stand to gain a real goldmine of intelligence about a very broad range of Russian combat capabilities. There is a very real bright side to Russia's Syrian deployment.

Besides, like us, the Russians will likely find out soon enough that airstrikes alone won't really have much effect on the fighting on the ground or the strategic balance of forces. As noted previously, Assad's army is just too weak to regain or hold much ground and airstrikes can't hold territory.

US SPECIAL FORCES IN SYRIA

A *CBS News* report on October 30, 2015 broke the news that "the US is sending a small number of special forces into Syria." According to the story, "less than 50 special operators will be based in Northern Syria... to work with groups like Kurdish Peshmerga forces." The White House did not consider this either a combat deployment or a change in the administration's mission, it merely would "further intensify" the working elements of the US strategy.

The corollary to that must be that there were elements of the US strategy against Islamic State that were *not* working.

So, despite 13 months of White House proclamations of "no boots on the ground" in Iraq and Syria, the October 30, 2015 *CBS News* story heralded the first installment of a subsequent steady trickle of US special and support forces into Syria. While the White House and Pentagon have not given their official tally of US forces in Syria, the media has provided some educated guesses on those numbers.

A *Washington Post* story dated March 15, 2017 estimated that there were "about 500 U.S. Special Operations forces" already in Syria deployed with the Syrian Defense Forces (SDF). In addition, there were "about 250 Rangers and 200 Marines." The story also reported on plans to deploy "up to 1,000 more troops into northern Syria in the coming weeks" before the offensive on the IS capital of Raqqa. These new troops might possibly come from the 24th Marine Expeditionary Unit and elements of the 82nd Airborne Division, which was already sending 2,500 of its troops to Kuwait.[185]

The Special Operations forces are primarily in Syria to advise and train the SDF but the Marines are manning an artillery battery capable of shelling targets in and around Raqqa. As for the Rangers, they have been deployed near the Syrian city of Manbij as a "visible sign of deterrence" to prevent Turkish forces and Kurdish fighters from attacking each other. And in a bit of Pentagon gimmickry, any troops in Syria (including the Marine artillery detachment) that serve "less than 120 days" are "not counted as part of the force levels authorized by the White House" for that country.[186]

The obvious reason for the buildup of US forces in Syria is to advise and train the Kurdish and SDF forces in preparation for the assault on the IS

---

185. Thomas Gibbons-Neff, "U.S. Military Likely to Send as Many as 1,000 More Ground Troops into Syria Ahead of Raqqa Offensive, Officials Say," *Washington Post*, March 15, 2017. Accessed July 17, 2017. https://www.washingtonpost.com/news/checkpoint/wp/2017/03/15/u-s-military-probably-sending-as-many-as-1000-more-ground-troops-into-syria-ahead-of-raqqa-offensive-officials-say/.

186. Luis Martinez, "Marines Arrive in Syria to Provide Artillery Support in Fight Against ISIS," *ABC News*, March 8, 2017. Accessed July 17, 2017. http://abcnews.go.com/International/marines-arrive-syria-provide-artillery-support-fight-isis/story?id=46006062.

capital of Raqqa, now that the Iraqi city of Mosul has been liberated. In addition to the advisory role, the Special Operations forces may also be involved in the gathering of vital intelligence since a persistent presence on the ground with access and contact with the local population provides some valuable opportunities to study the enemy's strengths and weaknesses.

Moreover, it is a sign of the evolution and progression of the war against Islamic State. After the near-total reliance on airstrikes to fight IS in Iraq and Syria by the Obama administration, the fight has reached the point where cities must be liberated and territory must be captured and held. That cannot be accomplished by airstrikes alone; it requires sufficient ground forces.

Likewise, the US presence serves to protect our SDF and Kurdish allies. The Russians have been prone to targeting all Syrian rebels, including these SDF and Kurdish fighters, in their airstrikes. Embedding US forces with them makes it less likely that Russian aircraft will bomb them since I doubt that the Kremlin would intentionally strike a target where US personnel are located.

And those US forces in Syria have demonstrated that they will defend themselves and our allies not only from Islamic State, but from Syrian and Iranian forces that get too close or too aggressive. In late May and early June 2017 at its training garrison at Al-Tanf near the Syrian-Jordanian border, the US struck a pro-regime convoy that penetrated a 34-mile deconfliction zone and it downed an Iranian-made Shahed 129 drone that was probing that zone in the same area. According to a *CNN* report, America officials credited Russia with trying to calm the situation.[187]

Similarly, a US Navy F/A-18E shot down a Syrian Su-22 after the Syrian aircraft conducted an airstrike on an SDF position near Tabqah, Syria on June 18, 2017. The Syrian jet ignored US warnings and dropped its bombs near the SDF forces as regime soldiers "equipped with tanks, artillery and technical vehicles" were advancing on the SDF position. The coalition used the deconfliction hotline with the Russians in an

---

187. Barbara Starr and Ryan Browne, "US Officials Credit Russia for Calming Tense Situation in Southern Syria," *CNN*, June 9, 2017. Accessed July 18, 2017. http://www.cnn.com/2017/06/09/politics/us-russia-syria-al-tanf-isis/index.html.

attempt to defuse the situation and stop the regime attack but in this situation, that attempt failed.[188]

And thanks to those US forces, we now have an integrated, operational air-ground task force in Syria to prepare, train and support the SDF and Kurdish forces in their attack on Raqqa. And, just as importantly, we have demonstrated that the US will defend itself and its allies from the Islamic State and the Syrian regime without hesitation.

It's further proof that, when it comes to allocating military resources, battlefield conditions should always trump silly proclamations made solely for domestic political considerations.Our military is made up of many tools from riflemen to special forces to aircraft and submarines. If the use of military force is required, we should allow our commanders to select the tool that is appropriate to accomplish the given mission and achieve the desired objective within our comprehensive strategy. Limiting our military's resources to accomplish their mission because of domestic political concerns makes that mission more difficult.

***

Military force should never be used in the absence of complementary political and diplomatic efforts in the region. We must understand the consequences of that action and be prepared in advance to deal with them. And, as in our delay to strike IS when it was still in its nascent stages, we should also remember that not taking military action at the right time with the right resources has a cost, too.

Sun Tzu had it right all along: "The supreme art of war is to subdue the enemy without fighting." That's what the majority of this book is about: finding ways of defeating our Islamist enemies without the need for military action.

But sometimes the use of military force is required. When that happens, we must hit so hard and fast that there is no doubt to either our enemies or our allies of the outcome.

---

188. Ryan Browne, "New Details of US Shoot Down of Syrian Jet," *CNN*, June 21, 2017. Accessed July 18, 2017. http://www.cnn.com/2017/06/21/politics/us-syria-russia-dogfight/index.html.

CHAPTER TEN

STEP FIVE: LET'S ABANDON CONVENTIONALISM AND START THINKING BOLDLY AND CREATIVELY

"There is only one duty, only one safe course, and that is to try to be right and not to fear to do or say what you believe to be right. That is the only way to deserve and to win the confidence of our great people in these days of trouble."

— Winston Churchill

Isn't it amazing that we have such a multitude of political pundits and commentators who represent nearly every point on the political spectrum, yet 24 years after Al-Qaeda's first attack on US interests, they haven't figured out that our real war is against an ideology? They don't seem to look back strategically and realize that our game plan is not working. We collect mountains of intelligence data every day. We've got smarter bombs, smarter drones, unblinking satellites, and the best-trained and most-capable forces on the ground and in the air over the battlefield. Yet, despite our tactics on the front lines evolving over the years with the introduction of new weapons and technology, I don't think we have had a real *strategy* to defeat Islamism since the terrible attacks on 9/11. Unless we come to grips with the fact that our real enemy in this war is the Islamist ideology, an enemy that will require the use of other tools besides the hammer, then we are simply doomed to continue repeating our mistakes.

The members of both houses of Congress have a limited grasp of the real problem. There is often a tendency to frame everything within the confines of political gamesmanship that serves neither the interests of our great country and people nor those of the West, in general. Many members on both sides of the aisle are satisfied to break the Middle East down into the good guys (i.e., the Israelis) and the bad guys (i.e., anybody who isn't an Israeli). They don't really know the difference between Hamas and *Hezbollah* or a *Shiite* and a *Sunni*. For the most part, neither they nor their staffers are Middle East observers or experts and they don't really have a comprehensive understanding of the religious and cultural dynamics that are driving our *takfirist* foes. They are not up to speed on the demographic changes in that region that are having a significant impact on the worldview of the Arabs and Muslims. And since they are politicians, the opinions and views that our representatives and senators do have may be shaded and influenced by the sentiments of their constituents and their potential impact on any reelection chances.

Political gridlock in our nation's capital is a serious problem but the real obstacle to winning our war against Islamist ideology is intellectual gridlock. Trying to use a twentieth-century mindset to solve a twenty-first-century problem whose origins trace back to the seventh century is bound to fail. It's a fundamental reason why the Israelis and Palestinians can't agree on a peace settlement – both sides are mired behind twentieth-century "red lines," i.e., their respective negotiating points on which each side believes there can be no compromise. As the Palestinians point to UN resolutions of "international legitimacy" supporting their positions and calling for returns to 1948 or 1967 borders, the Israelis simply annex more land and build settlements. The Palestinians would do well to start looking ahead rather than looking behind; at some point there may not be very much left for them on which to negotiate.

The same is true about us. We are stuck in a post-9/11 time warp where the counterterrorism enterprise has continued to grow ever larger to counter every conceivable terrorist threat and we have grown accustomed to sending our military off to tackle whatever the next emerging terrorist group is in the region. When does this end? Notice how nobody ever talks about victory in this war anymore? More on that in chapter eleven.

One wonders whether anyone inside the Beltway really wants the status quo to change. Bureaucrats have the opportunity to grab larger and larger slices of the budget pie while contractors line up to sell their latest security, defense, and intelligence technology and services at premium prices. Everybody wins except the American taxpayer, yet we are no closer to delegitimizing and eliminating the ideology that actually breeds the terrorism.

In a time of threatened sequestration and tightening federal budgets, the federal government's counterterrorism enterprise has become a solid growth industry for bureaucrats and contractors, alike. Criticizing the counterterrorism establishment at any level and for any reason has become the McCarthyism of the twenty-first century. As more and more personal freedoms, liberties, and privacy are bulldozed for the sake of national security, anyone raising any objections or concerns is branded unpatriotic. It's our own form of *takfir*. After all, what do you have to fear if you're not doing anything wrong?

What we desperately need to do is recognize that our strategic fight is against the phenomenon of Islamist radicalism and not terrorism, which is only a symptom or manifestation of the radicalism issue. It's my same mantra. Eradicate the extremist ideology and you put the brakes on the radicalization of vulnerable youth. That, in turn, works to dry up the flow of recruits to terrorist organizations like IS and Al-Shabaab, shutting down the next generation of Islamist terrorists and withering support for their ideology. Moreover, as that radicalism begins to wilt, the growth and expansion of these *Salafist* groups is prevented. In practical terms, that means we can spend less federal dollars on military deployments and the replacement of military equipment that gets worn out in the process.

In fact, keeping the hammer in the toolbox and only using it when necessary has several benefits. Avoiding long-term invasions and occupations of Muslim countries not only saves us a lot of money, it removes one of the primary irritants that promote Islamist extremism and radicalism in the first place – the occupation of Muslim territories by non-Muslims. By redirecting a portion of those resources we don't have to spend on military operations and investing them in an Arab and Muslim partnership to discuss the seeds of Islamist extremism and the methods for its eradication, we can get a much higher return on our investment. Diplomacy will always be cheaper than the deployment of military forces and it has the added advantage of being less provocative. It's not a weaker option it's a smarter one.

STARTING OVER

From our reality check in chapter one, we can clearly see that what we have been doing has not been working. We've made a lot of mistakes and miscalculations in what we thought was a war on terrorism so our best approach now is really just to start over again from scratch with a clean sheet of paper. There really isn't much point in trying to salvage elements of a failed approach or policy that hasn't worked for nearly a quarter of a century. Let it go and figure out a new strategy that will focus on the proper threat, one that does have a chance to succeed. Obviously, that is what the steps outlined in this book are all about – improvise, adapt, and overcome.

Perhaps the first step in this process is for us to accept several fundamental truths. The first of these is what I have been harping about since the very beginning of this book. We are not in a war against global terrorism; we are in a war against global Islamism. And since Islamism is a deviant ideology, that means we must think of this fight as an ideological war, not a religious one. Did we cast the Cold War primarily as a religious war of Western Christianity against Soviet atheism? No, and we should not do it with our war against Islamism, either. Constantly framing this struggle in religious terms adds passion and emotion that makes the necessary objectivity of our strategy all but impossible and it plays right into our enemies' narrative.

The second fundamental truth is that we cannot win this war by ourselves and we cannot impose change on the Middle East from the outside. We cannot just wave a magic wand and turn the Arab and Muslim worlds into little democratic Americas. It is narcissistic folly for us to think so. Real change in the region will have to come from the inside. The best we can hope to do is encourage the Arabs to recognize the need to embark on a process of change and reform and then support them from the sidelines. They will need to devise and implement reforms that are consistent with their own values and their societies and do so at a pace that they can sustain.

And the final fundamental truth that I think we must accept unconditionally is that the Islamists simply cannot win in the end. There is no way that all the world's 7.5 billion souls are going to accept living in a *Salafist* world under the *takfirists'* interpretation of *Sharia*. It is ridiculous to think that 99.999% of the world's Arabs and Muslims want to live under a "caliphate" like Islamic State. It's just another form of autocratic, tyrannical oppression that is being carried out this time under the guise of religion.

Let's get real for a minute. Young, frustrated Arabs were the ones who drove the 2011 Arab Spring and they did not want to exchange a secular oppressor for a religious one. They wanted a better future for themselves and their families and children. Many of these youths are highly educated and enjoy being part of the modern connected world. They don't want to live in a mud hut or a cave.

We don't see 20 million young Egyptian men lining up to fight among the ranks of IS in Iraq and Syria. We don't see hordes of Arab and Muslim youth flocking to Al-Qaeda's little slice of Yemen. The Islamists offer only martyrdom and death and that does not resonate with young people and the populations of emerging states with their whole futures ahead of them. The extremists' message of violence, intolerance, and brutality only strikes a chord with a disenfranchised, unhappy, and maladjusted few.

Nevertheless, many Arabs and Muslims are inclined to approve of the fact that Islamism tweaks Uncle Sam's nose. They view US policies in the region and blind support for Israel as anti-Arab and there is no shortage of *Schadenfreude* among them when they see us getting what they think we deserve.

No, the Islamists do not enjoy mass appeal. But the ideology of Islamism has been shown to be resilient. Islamic State picked up the black flag after Al-Qaeda Central stumbled and fell. Islamic State will be ultimately and inevitably be defeated but some other group will eventually emerge to carry on unless we destroy that ideology once and for all.

Islamism is really just a hybridized gang/cult that is based on *some* tenets of Islam while it ignores most others. As a cult, it appeals to the same sort of misfits that joined David Koresh in Waco, Texas or Jim Jones in Guyana but it does not have mass appeal among broad and expansive components of the Arab and Muslim worlds. As a gang, it appeals to those with dark urges to commit violence and acts of inhumanity against others under the justification of religion. The vulnerable see it as a source of identity and structure in a world where they don't fit in. But, while Islamism can hold small populations hostage for a time and threaten the rest of the world with acts of terrorism, it can never take over and dominate the entire globe. International demographics and public opinion just won't allow that to happen. *Salafism, takfirism,* and Islamism will always just be fringe elements that do represent a serious terrorist threat to the world, but there is no question that we will inevitably prevail over them. The only real unknown variable in this equation is the human and material cost that we and the rest of the world will pay in the process.

When we look at the situation that way, our task becomes one of hastening the demise of Islamism and the suffering it is causing. Our role is to promote reform and positive change in the Arab world while encouraging Arabs and Muslims to stand up for their faith and uproot the cancer of Islamism from their own midst.

Let's stop portraying this struggle as a fight against *Islamic* extremism. That strategy and approach has not been successful. Continuing down this path will just waste more taxpayer dollars, prolong and perpetuate our fight, and lead to greater loss of life among all parties involved. It will just generate more violence, chaos, and death at home and abroad. It is *Islamism* that we should be putting in the crosshairs.

Starting over means that we must recognize that our strategic objective is Islamist ideology and that we must treat this as an ideological war, not a religious one. It means acknowledging our need to build trust and credibility with our Arab and Muslim allies and partners and work side-by-side with them to eradicate the Islamist philosophy from their society and culture. It means embracing strategic optimism in the sure knowledge of our ultimate triumph over this phenomenon. It means recalibrating our entire approach to the problem.

AN IDEOLOGICAL CONFLICT, NOT A RELIGIOUS ONE

As I mentioned, Islamism is a cult/gang hybrid that uses some elements of Islam and disregards all the rest. As a result, we may be better off using some of the tactics to fight gang and cult membership in the war against this radical ideology. But, one thing that will not work is to make this a religious war against Islam.

We can make this a war of hearts and minds. We can make it a war of basic human rights and crimes against humanity, but we cannot make it a religious war because we are not fighting a religion. We are fighting the ideology of a cult and a gang. Decoupling religion from the conflict would remove much of the passion, emotion, hoopla, and disinformation on all sides of this struggle that do nothing but obscure objectivity and truth. Let's give it a rest. We are fighting a cult, not the Crusades.

Fortunately we've had some experience with this kind of warfare. During the Cold War, the ideology of free markets, personal freedoms, and democracy trumped that of communism. It didn't take a genius to compare the standards of living in the United States and most Western European countries to their Warsaw Pact counterparts and realize that communism had very little to offer. Farmers in America were feeding the world; farmers in Russia couldn't even feed Russia. The Soviets' Eastern European allies erected fences and walls to prevent their own populations from escaping, not to stop Westerners from flocking into their so-called "workers' paradise."

By the 1980s, West Germany's post-war *Wirtschaftswunder* was putting its drivers in luxury BMWs and Mercedes while their brethren in East Germany were relegated to Trabants and Wartburgs that were powered by little more than a two-stroke lawn mower engine. And they had to wait lengthy periods even to buy them. Supermarkets and department stores in the West were always fully stocked with exotic foods, produce, stylish clothing, and luxury goods while stores behind the Iron Curtain were often nearly empty. Want an avocado or a banana? Good luck! The Soviet system eventually just imploded economically.

The lesson from our Cold War victory is that we have already won a war of hearts and minds; we can do it again.

Our conflict is also one about basic human rights. The crux of the problem with Islamism in the contemporary world is not one that is really predicated on religion at all. The fundamental problem with this ideology lies in its outright disregard for basic human rights. The ideology's rigid and prescribed intolerance of anyone who does not believe in, and follow its harsh *Salafism* violates these basic human rights at every level. Killing or enslaving those perceived to be "infidels" and confiscating their homes, lands, and other property should be discussed and treated as human rights issues, not religious ones. They are crimes against humanity that are being committed by a criminal cult, not an organized religion.

These extremists could be secularists from the Great Purple Poodle Party who subject anyone who does not follow their political beliefs to torture, persecution, and death. It isn't about Islam or Great Purple Poodles. It is about basic human rights, and the right to stay alive and live free of persecution is about as basic as it gets. It is about criminal cult behavior and human rights abuses. This is the sort of approach we take with rogue states like North Korea, for example. We don't see that conflict as Christianity versus communist atheism. It is democracy and freedom against a cult of personality and tyranny. How are the abuses in Iraq and Syria any different than those in North Korea?

We cannot allow those with prejudices and biases to portray our fight as one against Islam because they are misrepresenting the true enemy and complicating our fight at the international and domestic levels. We absolutely have to restore the Arabs' and Muslims' trust and confidence in us if we are to encourage them to join us in this ideological war against the cult of Islamism. We have already seen how the overwhelming majority of Muslims have turned their backs on Islamism and view it as a threat and a danger to them. They share our concern. We must rely on Arabs and Muslims to effect changes from within their societies and communities if we are to eradicate Islamism and we cannot do that by wrongly stereotyping them all as our enemies. This sort of inflammatory hyperbole is completely and totally untrue and it is harmful and counterproductive to our mutual cause. We won't convince them to be our partners if we're alienating and attacking all Muslims.

On the domestic front, we must find ways to engage American Muslims in our fight against this corrupt and intolerant ideology. Muslims in this country must be encouraged to stand up and defend their faith against this cult of hatred and violence. Muslim families must be the ones to steer their vulnerable youth away from radicalism. They must be our partners in this war and that will be difficult to accomplish as long as there is a steady stream of anti-Muslim rhetoric in our media.

In any ideological war between the modern world and the cult of Islamism, we should win that struggle hands down. Our orientation is toward a bright and prosperous future for everybody. We espouse democratic values and personal freedoms and liberties. Citizens of the modern world are free to practice whatever religion they desire and pursue the occupational path of their choice.

At best, the cult of Islamism can only offer its followers martyrdom. It is a stark acknowledgement that the cult cannot help you to live a better future in this life; your best bet is to die and hope you're dealt a better hand in paradise. The cult offers no democratic values or personal freedoms – just oppression, persecution, and misery. And if they catch anyone practicing any other form of religion, they will suffer a cruel and barbaric death.

Our philosophy believes in the value and worth of the individual. We allow people to grow and flourish and achieve their potential. You can be whatever you want to be.

Under the cult, people have only one purpose: to worship Allah. There is no need for anyone to enjoy life or fulfill personal goals and ambitions. You have no say in government and you don't get a vote for the next caliph. One's marriage is arranged with all the romance of selling a camel. It's no wonder that this grim ideology only appeals to ignorant and gullible misfits.

It doesn't matter if it is Aum Shinrikyo, the Branch Davidians, Heaven's Gate, Peoples Temple, or Islamic State. None of these cults – including Islamism – was ever about religion; they were only about control and nothing else. None of them – including Islamism – ever allowed its followers any free thought. The followers were brainwashed into thinking that they had no individuality. Their sole purpose was to carry out the wishes of the cult and its leaders. They had no personal life or worth beyond their value to the cult. I'm sure many of those who joined up with these groups realized the error of their ways pretty quickly but they were not allowed to leave. The door to most cults and gangs only swings one way and Islamic State is no different from the others.

Winning this war on an ideological and human rights basis should be like shooting fish in a barrel. The Islamists have even less to offer humanity than the Soviets did. There is absolutely no way they can win this war. Fight Islamism like the cult and gang that it really is and leave religion out of it. We'll gain the Arab and Muslim friends and allies we need and reach the finish line a lot faster.

If we start thinking outside the box it will force everybody else to do the same. It recalibrates the paradigm – and that is a good thing. We have all been stuck in the same old ruts for too long.

A TIME TO BE BOLD

America wasn't settled and tamed by a bunch of shrinking violets and wallflowers. During the nineteenth century – the truly formative period of our nation – settlers were willing to risk everything just to find a new life over the western horizon. The westward expansion of the United States brought great risk but also promised great reward to those with a spirit of adventure and a willingness for hard work.

The neoconservatives foresaw the twenty-first century as the so-called American Century. It can still happen if we quit thinking that we have to fight the entire world. Let's put the hammer down and extend our hand to our friends. Working to turn the rest of the world against the extremists and their ideology will be more effective than all the drone strikes in the world.

Allying ourselves with Arabs and Muslims to stamp out Islamist radicalism holds the promise of great reward if we are willing to put in the hard work. This effort will require patience, diplomacy, and dialogue. It will mean that our partners and us will have to agree to disagree on some issues while still persevering toward a common goal of eliminating an ideology that threatens us all. Typically, we like to do all the talking and dictating but in this enterprise, it will be incumbent upon us to shut up and listen. A successful partnership depends on mutual trust and nobody likes a mouthy, arrogant, egotistical, know-it-all for a partner.

We must first learn to talk and engage with our partners on this issue and stop using the hammer so often. Killing people creates martyrs and martyrs simply perpetuate the ideology of the cult of Islamism. As noted, there is a time for selective military force but it must only be used when necessary. Besides, engagement, diplomacy, and dialogue is cheaper than using a $30 million aircraft to drop a $200,000 missile on a $50 IED. If nothing else, we should at least be doing the math to see if we're getting our money's worth out of our military operations.

Let's initiate a dialogue with Muslims at all levels – official, popular, and even clergy – to discuss the root causes of this extremist ideology in the first place. This phenomenon has emerged from their own backyard so let's let Muslims discuss why this deviant philosophy exists and how they can go about countering it. We are not a Muslim country so let's keep our government out of any religious debate and leave that to the Muslims and Arabs (including those in the United States) to discuss among themselves. Remember, it's an ideological and human rights issue, not a religious one. We want to recruit Muslims and Arabs as allies; we do not want to alienate them.

We must stop stereotyping Arabs and Muslims and thinking that they are all the same. They may not have the same level of cultural and religious diversity that we enjoy, but they're certainly not so one-dimensional as to be all the same. Each country has its own social and cultural dynamics that we should respect and understand. As was noted in chapter two, environment is everything.

AT THE POPULAR LEVEL

One of the more effective tools we utilized against communism during the Cold War was to invite people to come and visit the United States to see our culture and our values first hand. We encouraged young foreign students to come to America to study in our colleges and universities. We sponsored thousands of foreign military officers and personnel to come for training in the United States. We wanted to highlight the openness of our society and representative government while showcasing the cultural benefits of our way of life. Our objective was to instill a positive view of our American way of life that they would take back and share with their own people. We hoped some of our values would rub off on them if they ever rose to leadership positions in their own countries.

Granted, the carefree days of peace and prosperity as portrayed on *Leave it to Beaver* have long since been superseded by one daunting societal question after another about such gritty topics as LGBT rights, drug use, online violence, and race relations. But, just the mere fact that we are willing to raise and discuss such questions openly (at least most of the time) still says something important about us as a people and about America as a nation. We may have extremely spirited exchanges that are filled with rhetoric and hyperbole in a highly charged and emotional atmosphere between two diametrically opposed candidates, yet our candidates and our people respect the power of the ballot box and the sacred principle of the peaceful exchange of power. Wouldn't it be great if we could encourage others to do the same?

Maybe the real benefit lies in showing our society – warts and all – to our visitors and letting them understand that the need for tolerance and patience in a hyperactive twenty-first century is more important now than ever before. Look at how the world has become a much more chaotic place since the breakup of the Soviet Union. The bipolar glue that once kept many regional and popular disputes from flaring up has broken down and left many countries and regions with restive segments of their populations that are determined to finally achieve their own autonomy and settle age-old scores with their perceived oppressors. Obviously, the Middle East is no stranger to this unrest.

What do we have to lose by bringing people over to the United States and elsewhere in the West to initiate a discussion and a dialogue about the causes of Islamist radicalism? And for starters, let's let them do most of the talking. We have spent way too much time treating this problem the wrong way and we haven't really listened to the views of the Arabs and Muslims on why this ideology has evolved. Why don't we be quiet and listen to them for a change?

While we're listening, let's make sure we listen to everyone. Muslims, Christians and other religious minorities, secularists, businessmen, teachers, doctors, lawyers, *Sunnis*, and *Shiites*. Let's invite people from Egypt, Pakistan, Iraq, Yemen, Malaysia, Indonesia, Turkey – every country in the Muslim world. It may take awhile, but at some point we're going to get a pretty accurate assessment at the popular level of the root cause or causes of Islamist radicalism in their societies. These popular assessments are likely to be our best tool at getting to the core of the problem because they won't be going through any government distillation process or filters that might distort the results for political reasons.

As we're inviting Arabs and Muslims to come here to discuss the causes of Islamism and its appeal in their homelands, we should be doing our best to send Americans to visit Arab and Muslims countries. Perhaps groups visiting America from somewhere in the Islamic world would be willing to host a similar exchange from the United States to visit them and see their country firsthand while continuing the dialogue.

The cultural gap between the Muslims and us continues to widen and we need to find a way to bridge that gap and gain a better understanding of each other. In my view, the best way to do that is through conversation and dialogue. Our respective societies and communities face the same threat from the cult of Islamist terror so we both stand to benefit from its eradication. We're better off working together than working against each other.

This effort will take time to bear fruit. The results of each exchange should be carefully recorded since these dialogues are intended to get the popular opinions on why extremism exists in the Muslim and Arab worlds and what causes people to be attracted to it. Our strategic imperative is to keep the enterprise going, maintain the discussion, and build trust with our partners.

Once again I can see the naysayers clucking their tongues and shaking their heads at the prospect of establishing and maintaining such a dialogue with so many Arab and Muslim countries, but we haven't been doing so well by relying on military force to contain or degrade this or that group. Talk is cheap, but can be effective. The more people we can get to talk to us, the less they are lining up to shoot or bomb us. Once again, what do we have to lose?

An added benefit of establishing a continuous dialogue at the popular level is that, hopefully as trust builds between our people and the Arabs and Muslims, they will begin to open up about some of their societal, cultural, and governance concerns above and beyond Islamism. We can use this dialogue as an opportunity for Arabs to begin discussing the reshaping of their culture and society themselves. Let's encourage discussion about groups that aren't well represented in the traditional, male-dominated societies of the Arab world. What can be done to enhance the roles of women and young people in the Middle East? Is there a way to turn their frustration, unemployment, and alienation around so that these groups provide positive energy (such as suggested in chapter eight)? How can education and health care be improved? Perhaps a discussion of some of the benefits of globalization might help assuage some of the Arabs' fears that globalization will mean the loss of their cultural identity. Perhaps they need some reassurance that the times are unavoidably changing for everyone, not just them. After all, the nihilism of *Salafist* Islamism is symptomatic of the abandonment of any hopeful or optimistic future in exchange for an escape to the past.

When we reach the point where we are constantly taking the actual pulse of an Arab or Muslim society it will be worth far more than any intelligence estimate that is based on the assessment of a handful of intelligence community analysts who may have never even visited the target country. This is real, open source intelligence that would reflect actual popular sentiment about the state of the people's hopes, dreams, and fears in a specific country or potential regional trouble spot. It would come straight from the horse's mouth, as the saying goes, without the need for a lot of sophisticated espionage and technical gadgetry. Knowing the environment is key to evaluating the threat and determining how to neutralize it – in this case defeating the Islamist ideology and helping and encouraging disadvantaged and even oppressed peoples to devise their own forms of democracy that are consistent with their cultural and religious values. Some aspects and ideals of our unique American democracy will undoubtedly be worthy of emulation but the actual nuts and bolts of how to do it in other countries should be left for the people in those countries to figure out. It's not our place to dictate or impose.

This dialogue doesn't necessarily have to always happen in the United States. Our embassies in Mediterranean or Asian countries can host sessions on various topics and social media can be employed as yet another tool for gleaning information and data. We can encourage other Western, Asian, and African allies to take part, too. The important thing is for we Americans to keep the effort going and to listen more than we talk. In doing so, this continuing dialogue and listening endeavor will rise to become an integral cog in our own counter-narrative. Had such an effort been in place prior to the Arab Spring, we (and a lot of Arab dictators) may not have been caught so off guard.

This is how we rebuild *real* credibility in the region without resorting to cruise missile strikes over out-dated and ill-conceived "red lines." The people who seem to have no other plan but military action show a decidedly twentieth-century mindset that completely ignores the realities of today. Nobody in the world wants us to be the global sheriff and a pretty large segment of our own population doesn't think we should be playing that role anymore, either. That gig has cost us dearly in lives and treasure since 9/11 without achieving the desired result – like I've said, we've got more Islamist terrorists now than we've ever had. It will take more courage for us to admit we've been wrong, change our attitude, and turn in our sheriff's badge, but I think doing so will put us on a much wiser path toward our ultimate victory.

AT THE OFFICIAL LEVEL

I know that getting Arab governments to talk to us honestly about the roots and causes of Islamist extremism in their respective countries will be difficult. Most of the time these governments have plenty to hide. By their very nature, these administrations are designed to deflect any opposition or criticism and most often their primary concern is the survival of the ruler and his immediate family. Prime ministers and cabinets will come and go but dictators are eternal (unless the Grim Reaper comes a-calling).

Nevertheless, we have to make the effort. We cannot expect that these governments will ignore our effort to cultivate a dialogue at the popular level about the reasons for the existence of the Islamist phenomenon in Arab and Muslim societies without some form of parallel effort at the official level. We're likely to hear some standard party line responses about how this ideology originated from somewhere else and that it isn't indigenous to this or that culture or society. We already know that the first rule of thumb in the dealings with any Middle Eastern government is that it usually loves to blame somebody else for its problems – nothing is ever its fault.

Because of that, the first order of the day is not to point the finger of blame at anyone in the government or even in that society. We must come from the angle that this problem of extremist ideology is one that exists throughout the Middle East and Arab world. We are endeavoring to confront and eradicate this ideology, which is going to be the common goal of virtually all of the Arab governments in the region. Once again, it is not a religious problem but a cult/gang/human rights issue that is plaguing that particular country and society along with many others. It may have originated externally but now it must be dealt with internally if we are all to exterminate it.

In the past we've simply overlooked the ideology and relied on unscrupulous rulers to imprison Islamist dissidents and torture them to find out about their plans and accomplices. Our policy of rendition allowed us to fly prisoners around to various locations and outsource their interrogations to regimes that were not averse to using pain as a form of persuasion.

This is yet another damning piece of the terrorists' narrative against us that has not helped our credibility with the Arab man on the street. It's difficult to convince people of our commitment to democratic values such as the right to *habeas corpus* when it's common knowledge on that street that the CIA has been flying detainees to this or that country so that the regime there can interrogate and torture them.

If we or some corrupt Middle Eastern regime imprisons, tortures, or even kills detainees in either our or its custody, all we've really done is create yet another martyr. Creating martyrs just creates more recruits and foot soldiers. We've simply added yet another root to the Islamist ideology and worked against our own interests to eradicate and eliminate it. This is one cycle we have to break.

Senator John McCain has called our own enhanced interrogation techniques, such as the use of waterboarding or stress positions, torture. I would submit that since the senator experienced torture himself while detained as a prisoner of war in North Vietnam, he personally knows what torture is and if he says that waterboarding is torture, then I'm prepared to agree with him.

And the jury is still out on whether torture really does any good. CIA Director Brennan acknowledged that subjects who had undergone enhanced interrogation techniques did provide valuable intelligence, however there was no clarification on whether they did so while enduring these interrogation procedures or at some other point during their

318

detention. Such behavior may yield an occasional tactical benefit but it is an obvious strategic mistake and we should not have done it.

We need to immediately and permanently distance ourselves from "friendly" autocratic dictatorships that have eagerly done our dirty work for us. It will not make us any safer, it will not make them any safer, and it will ultimately work against our effort to defeat the extremist ideology. The politicians and bureaucrats who claim otherwise often use counterterrorism and homeland defense as a justification for such action yet there is no definitive evidence, as of yet, that enhanced interrogation ever stopped any terrorist plot. Does the international community ever admire anyone who stoops to commit torture? Think for a minute, are we going to attract support for our cause by copying the way Nazi Germany, North Vietnam, Argentina, Chile, and North Korea treated their detainees?

Egypt is a problematic case in point. The imprisonment and torture of dissidents in any form has become so institutionalized that it's more than likely going to happen regardless of who is in charge of the country. And it's precisely this perception of oppression by the Islamists in the Sinai, Upper Egypt, and elsewhere in the country that actively fertilizes the ideology of radicalism. General Sisi's continuation of these policies and actions is nothing but active recruitment for the Islamist gang and cult. How did that strategy work for his predecessors Sadat and Mubarak?

Libya's Gaddafi was determined to lock up and eliminate Islamists in his country during his four decades of tyranny. He ordered the massacre of over a thousand prisoners his regime had jailed at the infamous Abu-Salim Prison. That is because the Islamists wound up being a thorn in his side almost from the very beginning. They were the most organized as well as being the best funded and best armed of any group of dissidents that the Libyan dictator ever faced. Nevertheless, in the end, Gaddafi's corpse was the one on display in a macabre, carnival atmosphere where Libyans posed to have their pictures taken with his lifeless body. The various Islamist gangs are the ones now fighting over what's left of the country.

This dialogue won't be necessary everywhere. In Iraq we already know that the wider problem is *Sunni-Shia* violence and civil war. There won't be very much to discuss unless and until that conflict burns itself out. In other places such a dialogue won't be welcomed.

In countries like Yemen, there isn't anybody or any government left with which to even have any kind of conversation, let alone one on the origins of Islamist radicalism. It's finally graduated from a failing state to one that has failed.

However, this downward spiral in the region as a whole is the very reason why we have to start convincing governments there to start looking honestly at the reasons why Islamist radicalism exists in their respective countries and what they can do to not just confront it, but also to eradicate it. We, along with the Arab and Muslim people, recognize the danger of further chaos and if we do nothing it will only make the problem that much worse. We must find ways for recalcitrant governments to acknowledge the threat and pull their heads out of the sand even if it means appealing to their sense of survival. It goes back to preventing the fragile states (and we saw in chapter eight that all the Arab states are fragile) from actually failing.

To be honest, the governments with which we most need to have this conversation are the very ones that are the least likely to open a dialogue with us. Here, I am specifically referring to the conservative Gulf nations like Saudi Arabia, Kuwait, Qatar, and even the United Arab Emirates. These countries are the very breeding grounds of the *Salafist* and *Wahhabist* ideologies that are behind Islamist radicalism and its unyielding intolerance. They may very well tell us what they think we want to hear while saying the exact opposite to their own people. Deep down inside they may even support this ideology. This kind of duplicity is an everyday occurrence in the Middle East in general, and the Arab world, in particular.

If we cannot initiate an honest discussion with these countries about the causes and effects of this Islamist radicalism, are we simply dead in the water? Is there a way forward in the face of such obfuscation? I think there is.

The answer in such a situation is to find a proxy. It must be someone who enjoys our credibility, trust, and respect who also enjoys that of the various Gulf (and other) rulers. It must be someone with strong cultural and religious ties as well as someone whom these other rulers can see as a peer. And, naturally, it must be someone who has a deep, first-hand understanding of the problem of Islamism.

I think an excellent candidate for such a proxy and ally is King Abdullah II of Jordan.

The Jordanian monarch is the ideal person to discuss radical Islamism in our stead with virtually any other Arab leader in the region. In the first place, his country is shouldering the brunt of the burden when it comes to housing refugees who are escaping the violence from extremism in Syria and Iraq. Jordan has been an active participant in the anti-Islamic State coalition and when its pilot, First Lieutenant Kasasbeh, was captured and then burned alive inside a cage by the IS it galvanized public opinion in the country against extremism. King Abdullah is intimately familiar with both the radical ideology of Islamism and the Israeli-Palestinian conflict and his nation has a vested interest in finding solutions to both. He is widely respected in the United States and the West, as well as throughout the entire Arab world. He will surely know when his counterparts are being honest with him and he will surely know when they aren't.

Asking King Abdullah to take on the hard cases of the Gulf is asking a pretty big favor but I believe he would be the right man for the job. The Saudis, Kuwaitis, and the others would never talk to us as equals. The cultural, political, and religious gaps are just too great. But Abdullah is a Muslim, an Arab, and a king. He doesn't have to bridge those gaps.

Moreover, by virtue of his Western education and native fluency in English, King Abdullah understands us perhaps better than any other Arab or Muslim leader. We can communicate directly with him without having to go through some kind of filter. He is not put off by either our culture or our politics. As a result, he can be an extremely valuable resource in our effort to first identify the origins of Islamist ideology in the Middle East (and especially the Gulf) and ultimately exterminate it. I think we would find in the king a willing and knowledgeable partner whose country faces the same extremist threat as we do.

Going one step further, I firmly believe that not only would King Abdullah be onboard with such an idea, he represents probably the best hope for engaging the entire region before it goes down in flames. He already has the respect and credibility that we lack and he can hit the ground running. Any efforts we make at the official level will likely take time to spool up that we really cannot afford.

Finally, let's try to do this quietly. We do not need our close association and collaboration in this enterprise to either thwart the king's efforts or tarnish his reputation and standing in the region. Let the king take the lead in who he wants to talk with and when and we can communicate through back channels. The less US hands are seen in this activity the better. We can't change a light bulb in the State Department without ten ambassadors and two hundred staffers. Let's let the king go about his task quietly and if he has any other suggestions in our quest, it would be in our best interests to listen to them. He could be an invaluable source of guidance on how to proceed with encouraging social, educational, religious, and governmental reforms. He would be an ideal sounding board for our ideas and policies for the region.

King Abdullah's activities might even evolve into a regional inter-Arab partnership of governments whose objective is to confront and eliminate the Islamist ideology. This effort would go well beyond another regional counterterrorism organization. Such a coalition could take on the tasks of tracing the funding of Islamist extremism, encouraging Islamic religious authorities to bring the faith into the twenty-first century, and promoting educational, governmental, and societal reforms. Again, having a well-respected Arab ruler guide this process would be far more successful than anything we could ever do from the outside.

Let me emphasize that shifting our approach (and that of our allies) to Islamic State and Islamism and treating it as a criminal cult and gang that has no religious standing whatsoever will remove the religious passion and hyperbole from the equation. These Islamists are no different than child pornographers, human traffickers, and drug dealers and they are preying on young, vulnerable minds to spread their propaganda and filth. They and the ideology that stands behind them have no place in any society in today's world.

Since nothing happens in the Middle East for free, the price we would likely have to pay for the king's cooperation would be to push Israel back to the negotiating table with the Palestinians. The chances for success would improve greatly if we could gently press the Israelis to give up some of their historical "red lines" while Jordan did the same with the

Palestinians. Maybe if we could start these negotiations from scratch the two sides would have a better chance of reaching an acceptable, permanent settlement to their conflict. Such optimism may not be realistic at this stage but obviously the existing, historical positions of both sides haven't gotten them anywhere. Both the Israelis and the Palestinians could use some creative thinking of their own and they could start by looking toward the future instead of fixating on the past. We are all going to get run over by change in the Middle East if we do not adapt to accommodate it.

And restarting the peace process is really a small price to pay compared to the benefits we may reap by fighting the cult of Islamist ideology at its very source.

AT THE RELIGIOUS LEVEL

America has tended to tiptoe along the political correctness line whenever it has addressed the issue of the religious nature of Islamism. Washington and all manner of federal, state, and local officials typically reiterate that Islam is a religion of peace, that most Muslims are peace-loving and law-abiding people, and that the extremists are practicing a deviant form of Islam that has nothing to do with the true religion. While those platitudes may be largely true, by continuing to hold ourselves hostage to the concept of Islamism as a deviant form of religion rather than a cult or gang, we are continuously on the defensive about our own policies and our treatment and characterization of Muslims inside our country and around the world. We are perennially painting ourselves into a corner where we will always anger someone no matter what we say.

That's not right. Since this ideology has originated from within the very Muslim world that now seeks to disavow it, it's time now for honesty, not more political correctness. If what Muslims claim is true – that Islamism is a deviation and distortion of their faith – then they need to do more to stand up to it and send that ideology to the rubbish heap where it belongs. There can be no argument that we and the Arabs and Muslims have the same fight. We should all be dropping any religious cover whatsoever for Islamism and call the groups that follow that ideology what they really are: gangs and cults. This isn't about religion, it's about brainwashing and criminal and terrorist activity. We must all agree on this.

As I mentioned before, Arab governments and Muslims in the region often like to blame someone else for their problems. The United States and Israel are almost always their guilty culprits and scapegoats. However the current violence we are seeing in the Middle East is most often pitting Muslims against other Muslims or other indigenous minorities in the region. As we encourage the Muslims and Arabs in the Middle East to start taking responsibility for their own neighborhood, they will have to acknowledge that many of their current problems really have nothing to do with us.

The *Sunnis* and *Shia* in Iraq are fighting and killing each other in a grotesque and bloody civil war. We witness car bombings and atrocities that take place in Baghdad and elsewhere in the country every day. It is now so commonplace that the Arab media is about the only source for any reporting on it anymore. These are Muslims fighting Muslims in the name of Islam and *it has absolutely nothing to do with either the United States or Israel.*

In Yemen we see *Shiite* Houthis fighting remnants of the *Sunni* regime while Al-Qaeda in the Arabian Peninsula is taking advantage of the chaos to expand its own territory and influence inside the violence-wracked country. Yemeni Muslims are killing other Yemeni Muslims in the name of Islam and *it has absolutely nothing to do with either the United States or Israel.*

In northeastern Nigeria and its neighboring countries Boko Haram has kidnapped children, bombed and terrorized villages, and even set off bombs in the country's capital city. It has declared its loyalty to the Islamic State. These are Islamist Nigerians killing other Nigerians in wanton bloodlust in the name of Islam and *it has absolutely nothing to do with either the United States or Israel.*

In Somalia Al-Shabaab – an Al-Qaeda franchise – murders and bombs its way through the country and mounts terrorist attacks in Kenya to punish that country for trying to keep the peace in Somalia. These are Somali Africans killing Somali and Kenyan Africans in the name of Islam and *it has absolutely nothing to do with either the United States or Israel.*

In post-Gaddafi Libya we see Islamist Libyans fighting other Libyans for control over the country. Recent videos have apparently shown an Islamic

State franchise in the North African country beheading 21 Egyptian Coptic Christians. Other Christians have been kidnapped and killed. These are Libyans who call themselves Muslims kidnapping and killing other Muslims and non-Muslims under the banner of Islam and *it has absolutely nothing to do with either the United States or Israel.*

Not to mention we have Egyptian-on-Egyptian violence, Syrian-on-Syrian violence, Lebanese-on-Lebanese violence, and Tunisian-on-Tunisian violence. *None of these conflicts has anything to do with either the United States or Israel.* This is violence that is almost exclusively being perpetrated by one Muslim community against another and it *has absolutely nothing to do with either the United States or Israel.*

In fact Muslim-on-Muslim violence is consuming a large portion of the Middle East and Arab world. If you claim Islam to be a religion of peace, then why are you killing each other? I would encourage the Muslim community worldwide to stop blaming the West, the United States, and Israel for all their problems. Let's go back and review chapter eight. If you have a rusting junkyard crawling with all manner of vermin in your own backyard it's kind of hypocritical to complain about a neighbor who hasn't mown his lawn for two weeks. As Matthew 7:3 in the Bible points out: "And why beholdest thou the mote that is in thy brother's eye, but considerest not the beam that is in thine own eye?"

Anyone who has ever spent time in the Muslim or Arab world would recognize the Arabic phrase *Insha' Allah.* The phrase means "God willing" and it is used virtually every time something about the future is being discussed. "Let's go to dinner tomorrow evening, God willing" or "Your order will arrive next week, God willing." The inference is that God (Allah) has already willed and ordained the outcome of whatever event is supposed to happen. If it is God's will, we will go to dinner tomorrow evening or your order will come in next week. It's kind of an easy way to dodge some level of responsibility – the order didn't arrive but it wasn't my fault, it was God's will!

Now if Muslim parents are blessed with a baby, that infant will on a daily basis soil his or her diaper numerous times. It may be God's will, but the parents are still going to have to change that diaper. In fact, caring for that baby through childhood and adolescence is going to allow them to learn many of God's lessons about life, love, and faith. God may ordain for there to be numerous tests and tribulations along the way, but the parents are obliged to deal with those crises and to protect and nurture their child because God gave them a sacred responsibility that accompanies the creation of a human life. With the blessing and gift of a child's birth comes a heavy responsibility and obligation on the parents.

If Islam is a divine blessing and gift to mankind from God (Allah), then don't Muslims have the same individual and collective responsibility to nurture and protect their faith from harm the same way parents have an individual and collective responsibility to protect their children? Don't they have the same obligation to God (Allah) to protect His gift and blessing to all of mankind?

Well, they're not doing a very good job. Cults and gangs like Islamic State, Boko Haram, Al-Qaeda, and Al-Shabaab are soiling Islam's image every day. They have hijacked the religion and are thumbing their noses at the rest of the world – and especially at the Muslims. Isn't it time that the Muslims themselves did something about it? This is a perverse and evil ideology that has come from within the Muslims' own community so how can they blame the West and Israel for many of their problems, on the one hand, while relying on the West to clean up their mess, on the other?

It is time for the Arabs and Muslims in the Middle East to be honest with themselves. What's happening in their neighborhood is not only a public relations nightmare for their religion, it is an obscene affront to the humanitarian values and principles of every other religious community in the world. No other major world religion permits its followers to put decapitated heads on sticks and then upload the image to the rest of the planet as if it is some perverted act of piety. I cannot imagine that this is the image of Islam they want the world to see.

The Muslim clergy in the Middle East have to go farther than just refer-ring to the Islamists as "deviant." The *ulema* – at every level – must com-pletely strip any religious connection and legitimacy from the carnage the Islamists are committing in Islam's name. From the Grand Sheikh of Al-Azhar on down, they must use the *takfir* weapon against the *takfirists* themselves and brand the Islamists as apostates and infidels, not Muslims. Islamism must be acknowledged as just a nihilistic death cult whose followers face eternal damnation. They are not just misguided, they are "enemies of Allah" in every sense of the word.

This is a critical step if future generations of vulnerable youth are to be steered away from radicalization. Having the clerical community brand the Islamists as unbelievers and apostates will also go a long way toward drying up any financial support they may be receiving from "conservative" Muslims. This is a time for every Muslim clergyman around the world to stand up and take the most important and significant action possible to defend the real faith from the Islamist imposters.

Unfortunately, the Grand Sheikh of Al-Azhar University, the pinnacle of Sunni Islamic knowledge and jurisprudence, has refused to do so. On April 14, 2017, the English-language sister publication of *Al-Masry Al-Youm, Egypt Independent*, reported criticism of Al-Azhar and its Grand Sheikh Ahmed al-Tayeb for not utilizing *takfir* to brand Islamic State and its followers as apostates and unbelievers. This came in the wake of IS attacks on Coptic Christian churches in Egypt on Palm Sunday that killed scores of victims.

Egyptian media outlets had criticized Al-Azhar for maintaining extremist teachings in its curriculum that some may perceive as legitimizing "the killing and slaughtering" being practiced by the group. Some in the Egyptian media see Al-Azhar's refusal to use *takfir* against Islamic State and its followers as "contributing to generate [sic] numerous members affiliated to IS."

According to the report, Grand Sheikh Ahmed al-Tayeb provoked further controversy with his statements in December 2015 when he publicly declared that "he does not have the right to declare IS an 'apostate' group since IS members believe in God and doomsday." Instead, Tayeb considers Islamic State and its followers to be "Khawarij," i.e., sects that rebelled against Islam's leaders after Muhammad's death and committed sins. However, the sheikh stated that Islamic law ordered that the "Khawarij" be killed and slaughtered for "practicing corruption in Earth." He added that IS members deserved "similar punishment."

The article added that Islamic affairs researcher Ahmed Maher believed the sheikh's reasoning for not branding IS followers as apostates was "not persuasive" since Al-Azhar "has previously considered many public figures who have different views as 'apostates.'"[189]

Since Tayeb has told the West that IS is not an Islamic caliphate and its actions are deviant and Islamic, is this an example of *taqiyya*? Is he telling the West one thing and telling the Arabs and Muslims something else? Is Al-Azhar secretly harboring and supporting extremist ideology and teachings? There certainly seems to be some controversy (and hypocrisy) in Tayeb's statements. There is no better way to delegitimize Islamic State than to brand the group and its followers as 'apostates' and 'infidels.' Anything less – including the "Khawarij" classification – just does not go far enough. Besides, there are nine or ten rules involved in invoking *takfir* and I'm sure that Tayeb and Al-Azhar could find the necessary legal grounds if they tried hard enough.

Defeating the Islamist cult ideology must be seen and portrayed as both a *fard ayn* (a personal religious obligation) and a *fard kifaya* (a collective religious obligation on all Muslims) on every member of the *ummah*. Allah is testing Muslims to rise up and protect their true faith.

Finally, it seems to me that there is a pretty logical religious argument for proving the fallacy of the whole *Salafist* philosophy. Allah has created time to move forward, not backward and He has not given us the power to travel to a time of our own choosing. If He has foreordained a Muslim to be born and to live at the contemporary time, then He has already willed for that Muslim to face the challenges and tests of the twenty-first century. Thus, it is not the will of Allah for that Muslim to decide for him – or herself to live in the past because He has already made that decision for that Muslim and He needs no associate.

Moving forward, a good start would be for American Muslim clergy to establish its own dialogue with senior clergy in the Muslim world such as the popular *Al-Jazeera* cleric Yusuf al-Qaradawi, the Grand Sheikh of Al-Azhar, and others. All these respected religious leaders must reach a

---

189. Taha Saker, "Why does Egypt's largest Muslim beacon, Al-Azhar, refuse to declare IS 'apostate'?," *Egypt Independent*, April 14, 2017. Accessed July 18, 2017. http://www.egyptindependent.com/why-does-egypt-s-largest-muslim-beacon-al-azhar-refuse-declare-apostate/.

consensus on officially and religiously calling groups like Islamic State and Al-Shabaab what they really are: non-Islamic, criminal cults and gangs. Islam is going through a negative and retrogressive transformation right now that is not beneficial to either the religion or the *ummah*. In contrast, the faith needs to be updated and reinterpreted for modern times. If Islam's scholars do not do this, then there will be nothing but death and violence on the horizon forevermore. The blowback from that will continue to be detrimental to the West, in general, and the United States, in particular and judging by the amount of anarchy in the Middle East, it won't do the Arabs and Muslims there any good, either.

Sheikh Yusuf al-Qaradawi is a very controversial cleric among US pundits and policymakers because he allegedly issued a *fatwa* during the US occupation of Iraq that sanctioned attacks against Americans in that country during the occupation. Accordingly, Qaradawi allegedly reasoned that the Americans were a foreign force that was occupying Iraq and the Iraqis had the right of self-defense against this foreign occupation, which included attacking and even killing these occupiers. Thus, Qaradawi supposedly was not calling for Americans to be killed simply because they were Americans or even infidels, he was justifying attacks against them because they were foreign forces that were occupying Iraq.

For his part, the cleric denied making any such *fatwa*. Nevertheless, some of his contentious rulings on other subjects such as female genital mutilation, homosexuality, and wife beating have prompted many observers and bureaucrats alike to brand him an extremist even though he has moderated his views on some of these subjects in recent years. These views and controversial opinions, as well as his long-time relationship with the Muslim Brotherhood, have earned him a ban on entering the United States and the United Kingdom. He has also publicly backed away and changed his mind on some matters.

Qaradawi is also a controversial and polarizing figure in contemporary Islam. Many Muslims and Arabs have accused him of being a supporter of the Muslim Brotherhood and Islamist extremism but he has also made some remarkably moderate statements – positions that we should be able to work with. The fact that his weekly religious television program on *Al-Jazeera* reaches tens of millions of Muslims worldwide speaks to his religious influence.

We can agree to disagree on some (and maybe even many) issues, but Qaradawi has spoken out and condemned the violence of extremism and condemned the Islamic State. He sees a role for women in Islam and believes the faith needs to be updated and reinterpreted in the light of modern technical innovations and advancements. Engaging with such an influential cleric who has taken a public position on many religious issues that is consistent with our own should not be something that we simply overlook. Some Islamist hardliners have even publicly condemned him. While that may not be a ringing endorsement of him, neither is it an indictment against him. Convincing someone like Qaradawi to label Islamist groups as actual criminal cults and gangs would certainly discredit them among many vulnerable youth and even their potential financial supporters.

In our history we've had diplomatic relations with such scoundrels as Muammar al-Gaddafi, Adolf Hitler, and Saddam Hussein. We've found ways to negotiate with the Taliban and even the brutal Hermit Kingdom of North Korea. We even sponsored negotiations with Yasser Arafat, who many Americans saw as the icon of terrorism. It shouldn't be impossible for us to find some acceptable way to use Qaradawi to promote areas of common ground. Let's be honest and accentuate areas where we agree and draw clear lines where we don't.

Remember, if we start thinking boldly and creatively it forces everybody else to do the same. There's the potential for a synergistic effect to result from that. As I've emphasized throughout this book, maintaining the status quo and refusing to cross "red lines" will simply perpetuate the conflict, make the extremists stronger, and ultimately cost us more in lives and treasure (see chapter one). Continuing to do what we have been doing just does not work.

Having a rational dialogue with respected, orthodox Muslim clerics will be an important part of that. Just like the establishment of a continuing dialogue at the popular level, having a constant discussion about Islamist ideology at the clerical level (senior and otherwise) is a good thing. How can Islam uproot radicalism while bringing itself to accommodate the modern age? These are questions that only the Muslims themselves can answer. American Muslim clerics can, and should encourage the *ulema* and the *ummah* to begin asking themselves these questions. They should encourage them to openly and constantly refer to the leaders and followers of these Islamist cults as apostates. They should encourage them to turn the weapon of *takfir* on the Islamists themselves as often as possible as a means of defending their faith and its image around the world. They should demand of every single mufti and senior Islamic cleric in every Muslim and Arab state to simultaneously, publicly, and unanimously declare those who follow the Islamist ideology to be apostates. At the same time they must declare all those who sympathize with them or support them financially to be apostates and traitors to the true faith.

This single step would deprive Islamists like Islamic State and Al-Qaeda of any religious legitimacy. It would send a clear signal that the *ummah* will no longer tolerate its ideology, intolerance, and violence and any Muslim who continues to follow, support, or sympathize with such cults faces *takfir* and whatever consequences may result from that. It would put the Islamists on notice that the *ummah* considers them to be criminals and terrorists and nothing more. And, not insignificantly, it would boost the worldwide image of Islam, its clerics, and its followers considerably – especially in the West where that image has taken a constant beating.

And since Qaradawi, the Grand Sheikh of Al-Azhar, and other prominent clergy have publicly denounced and condemned the terrorism and extremism that is being committed by terrorists in Islam's name, we do have the right to hold their feet to the fire until they actually take such a stand and until that ideology is completely eradicated. That must be the Muslim scholars' promise to us and we must hold them to it.

This is the Muslims' fight and they must step up if they are to prevent the Islamists and *Salafists* from hijacking their religion. We can assist them but the problem came from within their world and the answer is going to have to come from within their world, too. They are perhaps even more threatened by this terrorism than we are.

AT THE INTERNATIONAL LEVEL

Naturally, since pretty much the whole world (Muslim and non-Muslim) is threatened by this cult of Islamist extremist ideology, this full court press has to extend to the international level and include international associations and organizations and non-governmental organizations (NGOs). As we move forward in combating radicalism as a violation of basic human rights, the international arena will provide us with advantages and disadvantages – like any other forum – but it is one we should not neglect and it may prove more effective with Muslim populations than Muslim governments if we play our cards right. That's okay because this is a war for "hearts and minds."

For instance if we take a look at many of the governments in the Middle East, we find that they have an abysmal record when it comes to human rights. The governments of Egypt, Iraq, Iran, Yemen, Somalia, Libya, Syria, Saudi Arabia, and the Gulf states (to name just a few) have historically ranked at the bottom of the human rights scale. The laws and militaries in most – if not all – of these states have been designed to protect the government and the rulers from the very people they govern. They have met the enemy and it is them!

The freedom of speech and expression – a basic human right – is virtually nonexistent in these countries. They have ministries of information to tell the press what it can, and cannot print or broadcast. Opinions on anything that would clash with the official government line are simply not allowed. Journalists and bloggers who violate these press laws often go to jail.

Women in many Muslim countries are second-class citizens who do not have the same rights as men. They may not be able to own property or even attend school, in extreme cases. In some countries they are not allowed to drive or even go out to shop by themselves. They may not be allowed to leave the country without the permission of their husbands or a male relative. In places like Afghanistan and Pakistan, women are often the ones blamed when they are raped. They get to be the victim of both the crime and a perverse justice system.

Likewise rights of religious minorities in the Arab and Muslim worlds are often restricted or abridged. In many countries Christians, Jews, and members of other faiths are persecuted or prevented from openly practicing their religions. Such persecution may even extend to *Shia* and *Sunnis* when they are in the minority, such as *Sunnis* in Iraq and Iran and the *Shia* in Saudi Arabia.

In all cases religious persecution such as forced displacement, imprisonment, death, torture, rape, starvation – you name it – comes down to a violation of basic human rights. Nowhere is this any more obvious than in the harsh, intolerant, and unforgiving ideology of Islamist extremism.

Is there some sort of accepted international standard when it comes to basic human rights? You bet. It's the Universal Declaration of Human Rights (UDHR)[190] that was adopted by the United Nations General Assembly on December 10, 1948. The 30 articles of the UDHR, the International Covenant of Civil and Political Rights, and the International Covenant on Economic, Social, and Cultural Rights form much of the basis of international human rights law but there 18 different human rights instruments that have been enacted by the United Nations. Of those 18, the United States has ratified five while, surprisingly, Saudi Arabia has ratified eight of them. Egypt and Libya have ratified ten and eleven, respectively, while Yemen has ratified ten of those instruments and Syria, eleven.[191] Yet do any of these countries have a better human rights track record than the United States?

Nevertheless, the cornerstone of basic human rights at the international level is the UDHR and while most Muslim UN member states in 1948 voted in favor of the declaration, Saudi Arabia was a notable exception, claiming that the UDHR violated *Sharia* law. Some Muslims criticized the UDHR at the time as being too reflective of Western values, but all the other Arab Muslim member states in 1948 (except for Yemen, which neither voted nor abstained) cast their votes in favor of the document. So, at least in principle, we in the United States and much of the Arab and Muslim worlds agree on what constitutes basic human rights at the international level.

Moreover, even though the UDHR is not an international treaty on its own the fact that it was adopted to clarify terms such as "human rights" that are used in the United Nations Charter – a document that is binding on all member states – it is the opinion of many legal scholars that the declaration does have legal standing for member states of that body. Despite that opinion, Saudi Arabia and a few other Muslim states have

190. "The Universal Declaration of Human Rights," website of the United Nations. Accessed July 18, 2017. http://www.un.org/en/universal-declaration-human-rights/index.html.

191. "Status of Ratification Interactive Dashboard," website of the United Nations Office of the High Commissioner for Human Rights. Accessed July 18, 2017. http://indicators.ohchr.org.

remained opposed to the UDHR because they perceive the declaration to be inconsistent with Islamic law – the *Sharia*.

These Muslim countries sought to reach a compromise with the rest of the international community when the Cairo Declaration on Human Rights in Islam was adopted at the Organization of the Islamic Conference (now known as the Organization of Islamic Cooperation) in the Egyptian capital in 1990. This document fell far short of the United Nations' Universal Declaration of Human Rights since it retained restrictions on human rights allegedly allowed in the *Sharia* like those pertaining to women, corporal punishment, and the freedom to express one's opinion. Attempts by OIC members to legitimize the Cairo Declaration on Human Rights in Islam and classify it as complementary to the UDHR have completely failed.

The good news here is that despite staunch holdouts in the Organization of Islamic Cooperation (OIC) to the UDHR like Saudi Arabia, the general attitude within the OIC on basic human rights seems to be shifting. The organization created an advisory body on human rights in 2008, the Independent Permanent Commission on Human Rights (IPHRC), and it has sought to amend the Cairo declaration and bring it much closer to the UDHR.

The bad news is that the OIC has no enforcement authority over its members to implement any of its decisions, including those of the IPHRC. The governments of the OIC member states are free to either adopt the organization's resolutions or disregard them, as they deem appropriate. Thus, while the attitudes of some OIC members may be shifting to become more supportive of the principles expressed in the UDHR, others – like Saudi Arabia – remain steadfastly opposed to the UN document.

But, it's hard to believe that Riyadh's objections to the UDHR would stand in the way of their opposition to the brutal and genocidal atrocities being carried out at the hands of Islamic State and Boko Haram extremists. Regardless of how the Saudis might feel about what constitutes universal human rights, they would undoubtedly be on board with categorizing the crimes of such terrorist groups as violations of basic human rights. Anything else would simply put them in the untenable position of defending the actions of the Islamic State and others. In fact, aside from North Korea, I can't think of anybody who wouldn't be willing to classify the actions and atrocities of these terrorists as basic human rights violations and crimes against humanity.

Now, much of what we do through international organizations like the United Nations and others is going to be window dressing. It's not going to result in a lot of concrete actions against the Islamic State, Al-Shabaab, or Al-Qaeda in the Arabian Peninsula. Again, our war against Islamist ideology is one of hearts and minds and the more international forums in which we can make the case that this is a criminal cult/gang/human rights issue and not a religious one, the more chances we have to chip away at the terrorists' narrative that the United States is at war with Islam. As I've stated, we should be availing ourselves of any and every opportunity on the global stage to counter that narrative and to do so on a constant and continuous basis. Most significantly, branding the Islamists as a criminal cult at every level goes beyond just countering their narrative to actually stripping away any of their perceived legitimacy.

A second benefit to these actions at the international level is that it may open the door for us to finally get some results from some of our "allies" in this enterprise. For example, Saudi Arabia has been notoriously reluctant to provide banking information about potential Saudi sources of funding for Islamic State and Al-Qaeda. However, if they agree with us on the international diplomacy stage that these groups, acting as criminal gangs and cults, are violating basic human rights and committing crimes against humanity, then it gives us some added leverage to encourage them to step up and help with investigating those who may be funding these groups.

This is a war against extremist ideologues and their philosophy and we must be engaged in it at every level. In warfare you sometimes reap great dividends from seemingly inconsequential efforts. We must be more active in the public and international domain so as to state our case and regain the public relations initiative that we have all but ceded to our enemies. One way to achieve this is to make sure everybody – Muslims and non-Muslims – agree to consider Islamic State and its ilk as a form of criminal gang and cult.

This must be an all hands effort. We will require constant engagement at the popular, religious, official, and international levels. We must constantly hammer away at the fact that this issue is one of human rights and crimes against humanity by criminal cults and gangs. How can anybody possibly disagree with that?

Finding common ground and areas of agreement at all of these levels provides us with opportunities on which to further build and reinforce our relations with Arabs and Muslims who are facing the same threat from radicalism as we are. It unifies our mutual positions. It provides solid evidence that we are willing to work *with* them to solve this problem and that we have a comprehensive strategy for victory that goes beyond just airstrikes and drone strikes. And in the process of cultivating friends and allies in the Muslim world, we are also encouraging them to make reforms where they are needed.

Our war against Islamism and its ideology will be a marathon, not a sprint. Getting universal international agreement to brand Islamist groups as criminal gangs and cults would be a great start and I cannot imagine very much pushback from Muslim countries that have already labeled these groups as "deviant." It's a simple way to defuse the entire "religious war" issue that causes so much passion. This step eliminates any religious legitimacy for Islamist groups and their sympathizers, thereby blowing their entire narrative out of the water.

This international *takfir* of Islamism unifies everybody's position on the issue without the need to dance around religious sensitivities. It puts an arrow through the heart of Islamist ideology not just in the Middle East, but throughout the world. Let's be bold. Let's be creative. Let's get it done!

GETTING OUR DUCKS IN A ROW HERE AT HOME

What About Rehabilitation?

The steps in this guide are aimed at defeating Islamist ideology, thereby ultimately preventing the radicalization of future terrorists. But what about the tens of thousands of existing *Salafists* and *takfirists*? What should we do about them? Are they beyond redemption, fit only to be killed or locked up forever or is there any hope of reeducating and rehabilitating them? Can they be restored to some sort of productive role in their religious and social communities?

I have my doubts about the overwhelming majority of fighters who have gone so far as to join the Islamic State, Al-Shabaab, or some Al-Qaeda franchise. There may be a few of these who became disillusioned with the so-called *jihadist* life after being tasked with menial jobs or austere living conditions. Perhaps these individuals were more inspired by fantasies of adventure than desires to wage the Islamists' cruel form of *jihad* against other human beings. Watching atrocities on *YouTube* is much different than seeing people being beheaded or crucified in person. Not everybody will be cut out for that level of brutality and this small number of disillusioned defectors may be suitable for rehabilitation.

However, for the true *Salafist* believers, I don't think reeducation will do any good. Once a person has fought and killed in the name of his Islamist masters, it's too late. Shedding innocent blood in the cause of Al-Qaeda or the Islamic State means that the individual's soul has probably become as black as the iconic flags that symbolize those groups. They have crossed the point of redemption. Rehabilitation, then, becomes all but impossible, so our only option is to either destroy them or incarcerate them forever.

But, what about those vulnerable youth who have been radicalized but haven't yet taken the step of joining a terrorist group? What about those still here at home whose immature and susceptible minds are still in the process of being radicalized, the less-hardened recruits? Is there any hope of reeducating them?

Unfortunately, the results of Islamist terrorist rehabilitation are a little murky. There are rehabilitation programs in Muslim-majority states like Saudi Arabia, Yemen, and Egypt as well as non-Muslim countries such as Canada and the United Kingdom. While these programs have had some success, the rehabilitation of terrorists has also scored some notable failures so the jury is still out on whether rehabilitation works.

Not every program compiles recidivism statistics on attendees who return to the terrorist fold. Some programs provide a level of aftercare to attendees after their "graduation" while others simply release them back to society to fend for themselves after they finish the program, possibly falling victim to radicalization once again. One wonders how a fundamentalist, *Wahhabist* Saudi Arabia fares in reeducating extremists whose ideology does not differ greatly from the kingdom's own state brand of Islam.

Nevertheless, Saudi Arabia's rehabilitation program has been put forward as a model for much of the rest of the Middle East. According to an article by Jessica Stern in the January/February 2010 edition of *Foreign Affairs* magazine, Riyadh's Care Rehabilitation Center had a recidivism rate of 10-20%, a rate far lower than that seen for rehabilitation in the criminal system. Despite that, 11 of the program's graduates had still made the country's most wanted list.[192] Yet to be fair, it's unrealistic to think that every single person can successfully be reeducated and returned to society. After all, many of these individuals had become hardcore insurgents.

The Care Rehabilitation Center is housed in a luxury resort setting and the program's cost and level of detail may be difficult to emulate elsewhere.

For example, the staff and even the participants are constantly providing input on updating the program. "It includes psychological counseling, vocational training, art therapy, sports, and religious education." Former detainees at Guantanamo who complete their rehabilitation course "are given housing, a car, money for a wedding – even assistance in finding a wife, if necessary. They receive help with career placement for themselves and their families."

It doesn't all abruptly end when the participants are released, either. The program's graduates are carefully monitored. The philosophy behind the Saudi rehabilitation efforts is that the *jihadists* "are victims, not villains" who require remedial assistance that is customized and tailored to their individual circumstances rather than a one-size-fits-all approach.[193]

An effective and successful rehabilitation program relies on knowing and understanding the motives that lie behind a person's radicalization in the first place. What motivates a young Saudi or Egyptian to extremism may very well be quite different than what affects a young Muslim in Western Europe or the United States. Economic, psychological, cultural, and educational factors will have varying degrees of influence according to a person's geographic location and personal/family background.

---

192. Jessica Stern, "Mind over Martyr: How to Deradicalize Islamist Extremists," *Foreign Affairs Magazine*, January/February 2010. Accessed July 18, 2017. https://www.foreignaffairs.com/articles/saudi-arabia/2009-12-21/mind-over-martyr.
193. *Ibid.*

Exploring the extremist rehabilitation programs in the United Kingdom, the Netherlands, Belgium, and Canada to see what works in those and other Western countries would provide some guidance for the establishment of our own such program in America. The United States should have some sort of official rehabilitation program for radicalized youth who have not yet committed any crime. We don't throw kids away because of drug use or some other youthful mistake; we shouldn't throw them away for falling victim to Islamist radicalization. Let's find them and fix them *before* they go to Iraq or Syria or *before* they attempt some terrorist crime.

Since some of these vulnerable youth may feel disenfranchised and alienated in a Western country as part of a Muslim minority, they may be searching to belong to something larger than themselves, something that is strong and powerful. These are motivations similar to those that drive secular youth to gangs or cults, so some of the same strategies used to combat gangs and gang membership might be useful in a de-radicalization and rehabilitation program.

This kind of effort would also offer the chance for America's Muslim community to play a leading role in steering these errant youth back onto the right path. All too often, the Muslims in this country complain that they are treated as suspects instead of citizens. They feel that openly practicing their faith often subjects them to discrimination and religious and ethnic profiling and they have a valid point.

By taking responsibility for the proper religious reeducation of these radicalization victims, America's Muslims would be doing a favor to their own faith as well as our society. Muslims in this country suffer prejudice and discrimination because of the actions of groups like Islamic State and Al-Qaeda. Terrorism in Islam's name does not do them any good. Giving them such an open and positive role would certainly contribute toward improving the undeserved and negative perceptions that followed the tragic events of 9/11. Building inclusive bridges to the Muslim community in the United States and drawing it into our society rather than building walls around it would have a positive impact on everyone. The more we talk and interact with each other the less mutual suspicion we will have of each other. Suspicion breeds distrust and that works against our unity as Americans – *E Pluribus Unum.*

Even though the rehabilitation and de-radicalization field needs further study, it's pretty clear that the United States should have some kind of organized and official program. It isn't something informal that should be merely relegated to local Islamic centers; it needs a real curriculum that is based on science and fact. The approach may be tailored to each victim but it still has to be based on solid evidence. Understanding what has driven a person toward radicalization may provide the key to undoing that motivation, reeducating the individual, and preventing the creation of a new terrorist. That's a good thing.

In parallel, I think it would be a great idea for Muslim communities in this country to establish youth radicalization prevention programs with any rehabilitation effort. That would help to ensure that the young people in their Islamic centers receive proper instruction on the orthodoxy of Islam right from the start. Since it has been shown that many of the recruits to the Islamic State, for instance, have a weak knowledge of the actual fundaments of Islam, they would likely not have been so easily radicalized had they possessed a thorough education of their faith starting in childhood. Perhaps senior Muslim clergy at the national level in the US should discuss an appropriate religious education curriculum for its communities.

However, even as we work to reeducate and rehabilitate the misguided and radicalized youth in our communities, we have to be firm in our resolve to isolate any hardened terrorists who might return to our shores from the battlefields of the Middle East and Africa. Again, once a person has become a committed fighter for the Islamic State, Al-Qaeda, Al-Shabaab, or any other such group, they are too far-gone for rehabilitation and reeducation. Our only option with these Islamists is eternal isolation and incarceration. We cannot afford to have them metastasize and spread their malignant ideology to others in our society.

To me, this is an argument for maintaining the detention camp at Guantanamo Bay in Cuba and maybe even expanding it. Regardless of whether these terrorists were born in the United States or became US citizens at some point, in my view they have abrogated their rights as Americans by virtue of their treason against our country. If they swore allegiance to the Islamic State or some other group, then they are no longer Americans. The case against Anwar al-Awlaki has already set that legal precedent. By keeping them isolated in Cuba we are preventing them from having any contact whatsoever with members of our society except, perhaps, their lawyers. In fact, in countries like Yemen, where jailbreaks are very common, we should consider transferring their detainees to Guantanamo.

In conjunction with encouraging the muftis of every Arab state to denounce all Islamist cults and their followers and classify them as apostates who have no connection whatsoever to Islam, we should encourage every Islamic center in America along with every imam and Muslim cleric to do exactly the same thing. This would standardize everybody's position on Islamists and their atrocities. It would sever the link between Islam and Islamism once and for all so that the actions of these terrorists could no longer be attributed to Islam and Muslims, in general. A universal public statement by all US imams and Islamic centers and mosques that states unequivocally that Islamism is a criminal and apostate cult and its followers have turned their backs on true Islam would reassure all American non-Muslims and quiet all but the most biased and prejudiced antagonists.

By their public *takfir* of the cult and ideology of Islamism, American Muslims no longer would need to feel like they and their religion have been victimized. Their avowal that Islamism does not have any legitimacy under Islam and has no relationship to their religion whatsoever totally disconnects religion from the equation. This is another way American Muslims can be part of the solution.

Conversely, any reluctance to do so by any imam or mosque – especially after the denouncements by the Arab muftis and other US clergy – would justifiably raise questions about the loyalties and ideology of that imam and mosque. Let's not leave anyplace where this false ideology can hide.

What About Prison Radicalization?

As our media commentators and counterterrorism officials ring the alarm bell over the threat from a few hardened terrorists from the Islamic State with American or Western passports returning to wreak havoc in the United States, there is another matter that is not often discussed in the media and may not be well understood. Here, I refer to whether or not there is a terrorist threat resulting from the radicalization of prisoners incarcerated in our federal, state, and local prison systems who have converted to Islam.

Unfortunately, not a lot of scientific or statistical studies have addressed this issue so the degree of the threat from the terrorist radicalization of prisoners is often one of opinion. Some people exaggerate the threat while others downplay it.

The issue has been discussed several times by Congressional bodies such as the House Committee on Homeland Security, but the results do not seem to have been conclusive. The chairman of that committee, Rep. Peter King (R-NY), once cited an unsubstantiated and uncorroborated guess from the 1990s that up to 80% of mosques in the United States had been radicalized. He has since retracted that statement but it does show that officials in high places are not immune from potentially letting their own opinions, biases, and emotions get ahead of actual data.[194]

Luckily, the one person who has studied the subject is a criminology expert, Indiana State University criminology professor, Mark S. Hamm. Dr. Hamm submitted a federally-funded paper to the Department of Justice in December 2007 entitled: "Terrorist Recruitment in American Correctional Institutions: An Exploratory Study of Non-Traditional Faith Groups Final Report."[195]

In his 129-page report, Hamm cites estimates from other researchers that 30,000 – 40,000 prisoners in municipal, state, and federal correctional institutions convert to Islam every year. The reasons for their conversions vary. Some convert because they are seeking spirituality and they admire the self-discipline of other Muslims they see in prison. Others convert for protection because they see Muslims in prison as being the strongest group. Still others convert because of the charisma of the leader of some prison group. Many prisoners spend much of their incarceration bouncing from one religion to another so those who convert to Islam today may also convert to something else tomorrow.

194. Glenn Kessler, "Peter King's Claim About Radical Muslim Imams: Is It True?," website of the *Washington Post*, March 10, 2011. Accessed July 18, 2017. http://voices. washingtonpost.com/fact-checker/2011/03/peter_kings_claim_about_radica.html.

195. Mark S. Hamm, "Terrorist Recruitment in American Correctional Institutions: An Exploratory Study of Non-Traditional Faith Groups Final Report," December 2007, website of the National Criminal Justice Reference Service. Accessed July 18, 2017. www.nij.gov/journals/261/pages/prisoner-radicalization.aspx.

As well, Hamm found that there are many interpretations of Islam in America's prisons, not just the orthodox *Sunni* and *Shiite* versions. Moorish Science Temple and Nation of Islam are unique American forms of Islam that have been aimed at the Black prison population and these are universally disdained by the traditional *Sunni* and *Shia* branches of the faith – even in prison. In fact, a lack of qualified prison chaplains means that some prisoners make up their own versions of Islam that often import and combine aspects of other beliefs.

Hamm found the "potential for ideologically-inspired criminality" exists in maximum security prisons where "there are few rehabilitation programs; a shortage of chaplains to provide religious guidance to searchers; serious gang problems; and more politically charged living areas than in lesser-custody institutions."[196] While the prison environment can be conducive to radicalization, it is important to remember that the category of Islam in the prison system refers to a broad range of faiths and many of them have nothing to do with the extremist *Salafist* or *Wahhabist* forms of *Sunni* Islam.

The criminologist also assessed that while extremist groups may believe correctional facilities to be fertile grounds for recruitment, the known facts about radicalization in prison have shown that it does not yield a large number of recruits and seems to happen "only in the rarest of cases." He also found that radicalization is not limited to Islam.

However, when Islamist radicalization does occur, it has led to some very notable incidents. Hamm cited the case of Jose Padilla – "the dirty bomber" – who converted to Islam after serving time in South Florida's Broward County Jail in 1992. There is "shoe bomber" Richard Reid, who converted to Islam in the mid-1990s while in a British institution for young offenders for a string of muggings. Jamal "el Chino" Ahmidan was the mastermind of the 2004 Madrid train bombing who embraced radical Islam during his incarceration in a Spanish detention center in 2002. And Muktar Ibrahim, a British citizen, was part of a cell that attempted to carry out a follow-on attack to the London 7/7 bombings of 2005. Like Reid, he converted to Islam while serving time in a British youth offender institution.

---

196. *Ibid.*

One prison radicalization plot does stand out in Hamm's research: the case of the Jam'iyyat al-Islam al-Sahih or JIS ("The Assembly of True Islam"). Hamm laid out the story of the JIS and its leader, Kevin James, in the *National Institute of Justice Journal* No. 261[197] that was published in October 2008.

James began serving a ten-year sentence for robbery in 1997 at the California State Prison in Tehachapi. He had been a follower of the Nation of Islam but migrated toward a *Sunni* fringe group that was known as the JIS. He eventually took over JIS and began preaching the need for Muslims to attack their enemies with violence. He incorporated his own beliefs into a document called the JIS Protocol in which he justified the killing of infidels, the necessity of new members swearing allegiance to him personally, and the requirement to keep the existence of JIS a secret.

In 2005, James recruited two of his followers in prison to carry out an attack on a US Army recruiting station scheduled for September 11, 2005 – the fourth anniversary of 9/11. Once the two men were out of prison, they began raising money for the planned attack through a series of gas station robberies. Their sloppiness and incompetence as criminals led to their capture and the subsequent unraveling of the JIS terrorist attack but according to Hamm, at the time the FBI considered the JIS plot to be the most operationally advanced threat since the 9/11 attacks.

The perceived threat from prison radicalization is not limited to just the United States. Hamm's aforementioned examples of cases in the United Kingdom and Spain point to the issue being one of international proportions.

The January 2015 *Charlie Hebdo* attacks in Paris shed light on the problem in France. According to a BBC article dated February 5, 2015, there is evidence that two of the attackers, Amedy Coulibaly and Cherif Kouachi, were followers of Djamel Beghal in prison – a militant said to have links to Al-Qaeda. The article named several others who became radicalized in French prisons: Khaled Kelkal, a member of an Algerian group involved

---

197. Mark S. Hamm, "Prisoner Radicalization: Assessing the Threat in U.S. Correctional Institutions," *National Institute of Justice Journal No. 261*, October 2008. Accessed July 18, 2017. www.nij.gov/journals/261/pages/prisoner-radicalization.aspx.

in the deaths of eight persons in France in 1995; Mohamed Merah, who killed seven in a shooting spree in Toulouse in 2012; and Mehdi Nemmouche, who killed four in Brussels in 2014. The article claimed that 60% of France's 70,000 prison inmates have Muslim origins and criminal backgrounds that make them susceptible to radicalization.[198]

Here in the United States National Public Radio ran a similar story on the problems of French prison radicalization on January 22, 2015. Its story noted the similar cases of the high numbers of Muslims in French prisons and a US prison population dominated by American Blacks and Hispanics. Both prison systems are overcrowded, lack resources, and lend themselves to an environment where radicalization can occur.[199]

One of the takeaways from Hamm's research seems to be that prison radicalization to the point where someone becomes a follower committed enough to actually perpetrate violence for the sake of his cause is relatively rare. Neither does radicalization and recruitment occur in large numbers. But when that committed follower does follow through with some kind of attack, the results can be quite deadly. The trend appears to favor low-probability, high-consequence incidents. He points out:

> *The danger to U.S. security is not the number of adherents to Islam, or to white supremacy religions, but in the potential for small groups of true believers to instigate terrorist acts upon their release from prison. A miniscule percentage of radicalized inmates will join terrorist networks, and they are likely to be fresh converts—the newly pious, those with an abundance of emotion and feeling—who are highly secretive about their intentions.*[200]

---

198. Henri Astier, "Paris Attacks: Prisons Provide Fertile Ground for Islamists," website of *BBC News*, February 5, 2015. Accessed July 18, 2017. http://www.bbc.co.uk/news/world-europe-31129398.

199. Dina Templeton-Raston, "French Prisons Prove to be Effective Incubators for Islamic Extremism," website of *National Public Radio*, January 22, 2015. Accessed July 18, 2017. http://www.npr.org/sections/parallels/2015/01/22/379081047/french-prisons-prove-to-be-effective-incubators-for-islamic-extremism.

200. Mark S. Hamm, "Terrorist Recruitment in American Correctional Institutions: An Exploratory Study of Non-Traditional Faith Groups Final Report," December 2007, website of the National Criminal Justice Reference Service. Accessed July 18, 2017. https://www.ncjrs.gov/pdffiles1/nij/grants/220957.pdf.

In his October 2008 paper, Hamm made several recommendations to address the problem of terrorist radicalization and recruitment in US prisons.[201] These have been summarized and paraphrased below:

- Hire more chaplains: The American Correctional Chaplains Association recommends one chaplain per 500 inmates. The ratio is four and even five times that in some states like California and Texas. These chaplains represent a religious authority figure to the prisoners that discourages "prison Islam" offshoots of the faith that may often result from prisoners' lack of knowledge about the religion.

- Diversify corrections personnel: For example having more Muslim corrections staff reduces the alienation of the Muslim prisoner population.

- Staff training: Corrections personnel need further training on gang recruitment tactics inside the prison and they should be kept apprised of changes in the balances of power among prison gangs and inmates. (There's that radicalization/gang connection again.)

- Encourage further study and research on the aspects of prison life that encourage radicalization and terrorist recruitment.

One cautionary note that I would add to Hamm's first recommendation is to require some form of certification or accreditation from chaplain applicants or at least an approved path to gain that certification. The objective here is to verify that any prison chaplain applicant (Muslim or otherwise) does have the actual education, training, and experience to adequately perform the duties of that position. The applicant's background should be thoroughly vetted to ensure the individual has no radical ties or beliefs. States should not rush to fill chaplain vacancies by appointing just anybody to the job. Doing so might cause more harm than good.

---

201. Mark S. Hamm, "Prisoner Radicalization: Assessing the Threat in U.S. Correctional Institutions," *National Institute of Justice Journal No. 261*, October 2008. Accessed July 18, 2017. www.nij.gov/journals/261/pages/prisoner-radicalization.aspx.

This is a problem for which government has no current solution at either the federal or state levels. They don't even seem to have a strategy aimed at creating a solution. If we are allocating resources to prevent battle-hardened IS terrorists from returning to American soil, we should be doing the same when it comes to potentially radicalized, hardened criminals who are being released from our own prisons.

Something else we should bear in mind as that the longer we delay in dealing decisively with IS, the greater their recruitment appeal will be. That will translate into a greater threat for members of the vulnerable population (regardless of whether or not they are in prison) to become radicalized. Ex-convicts who may have converted to Islam in prison may be more susceptible to radicalization than their counterparts who are still incarcerated simply because they will have greater access to all forms of media once they are on the outside. Their newfound prison religion may spur them toward violence as a way of proving their commitment to their faith.

American Muslims as Active Partners Against Extremism

There is no doubt that the 9/11 attacks unjustifiably cast all American Muslims in an unflattering light. Suddenly they were collectively portrayed as a "fifth column," a community of anti-American terrorist sympathizers who preached hate and violence behind the closed doors of their mosques. It was an emotional time when people whispered about interning Muslims in camps just like Americans of Japanese heritage had been confined during World War II. Widespread American ignorance about Islam and passions ratcheted up to high gear made Muslim bashing a popular activity, equating every Muslim with being a potential terrorist. Then, as now, we have not been very successful in differentiating between Islamism and Islam.

The natural response to this behavior by American Muslims was to withdraw among themselves. It's a normal in-group response to an out-group threat. There were sporadic acts of violence against Muslims in the wake of 9/11 and some of the ensuing media coverage – such as that of Palestinians celebrating the attacks in the streets – did little to dampen emotions and assuage the white-hot American anger. American Muslims were victimized by the attacks themselves – as were all Americans – and many felt victimized a second time because they – and all Muslims – were being stereotyped as terrorists.

It's ironic that a country like the United States that has been built from such a diverse collection of nationalities and communities can have such a history of racial, ethnic, and religious bigotry. American Muslims are often still the unfair targets of prejudice and bias even 16 years after 9/11. I believe the best way for those Americans to fight and debunk that injustice once and for all is to stand up as a community, denounce Islamism, and be active partners in the fight against Islamist extremism. And while many American Muslims have already done this, their message is often disregarded or unheard. They must keep repeating that message with one voice until the whole nation finally does hear them.

Many American Muslims and Arabs may disagree with US policy in the Middle East and express dissatisfaction at the American bias toward Israel at the expense of the Palestinians and other Arabs. But such political disagreements are quite common in our society and they don't make someone a terrorist.

Plenty of American Irish Catholics were sympathetic to the Irish Republican Army during "the troubles" in Northern Ireland. Many of them might even have quietly provided financial support for the cause just as American Muslims might donate to charities active in Gaza and the West Bank. And Americans of German heritage supported Hitler in the thousands prior to the US entry into World War II. We didn't lock them up after the war broke out. Were they all terrorists? Isn't freedom of expression intrinsic to the American identity?

It is well past time for all Americans – Muslims and non-Muslims alike – to stop feeling like victims and start playing an active role in defeating the ideology of Islamist extremism and the terrorism that emanates from it. We all have to take off the blinders of ignorance, prejudice, and intolerance and work together as a nation to defeat our foes. Casting off our stereotypes and prejudices is one of the things that distinguishes us from our intolerant enemies.

Earlier I discussed the importance of engaging Arab and Muslim countries and populations at the popular, official, religious, and international levels. We can do many of the same things domestically.

For example, what if Muslim clergy all over the United States reached out to every Christian and Jewish congregation in their communities to explain the difference between Islam and Islamism and to denounce Islamism as the deviant, criminal cult that it is? Reaching out at the local and community level like this would go a long way toward clearing up the atmosphere of suspicion and mistrust that has fallen upon Muslims in America. Christian and Jewish clergy would then be given a similar opportunity to appear before Muslim congregations. And such exchanges should happen on a regular basis, not just once in a while. These mutual visits would allow us all to view each other in a non-threatening environment where we can all see each other as neighboring members of the same community.

The value of these religious exposures at the popular level should not be underestimated. This isn't about proselytizing it's about educating ourselves about our differences so that we can all dispel the clouds of mistrust and bigotry that may be obscuring our objectivity. The more we understand one another the less we have to fear from each other. It's about fear and suspicion giving way to understanding and compassion, or at least some level of reassurance. And the clergy who become experienced at such exchanges might then become great candidates to do the same thing at the international/popular/religious levels.

We want to embrace American Muslims in our war against extremism. They must start feeling like partners in this campaign instead of victims and this would be a great role for them to play. Showing non-Muslim Americans that Muslims have just as much to fear from Islamist extremism as everyone else would also serve to defuse the doubts about the loyalties of American Muslims. Encouraging them to constantly play highly visible roles to counter the many forms of Islamist radicalism would certainly contribute to boosting their image among the masses. Swift, public, and clear denunciations of any Islamist terror that occurs anywhere in the world would be far more productive for the American Muslim community than hunkering down and keeping a low profile. Many people will simply interpret the lack of any clear condemnation by this community as an indicator of its latent sympathy for the terrorists.

A natural progression of this would be encouraging American Muslims to join the discussion of the root causes of the Islamist ideology at the national and international levels. People who have come to America from a Muslim or Arab country will have a first-hand cultural perspective that will be impossible for any American diplomat or intelligence operative. The more minds we have working on identifying and countering these root causes, the better.

Bringing people together instead of driving them apart is supposed be what American democracy is all about – Inclusion versus exclusion. Let's encourage American Muslims to stand up against Islamism and defend their faith. Let's stop treating them with suspicion and distrust.

Recalibrating Our Notion of National Security

In the wake of the Cold War and the collapse of the Soviet Union, we have encountered a much more unstable and uncertain world than we ever expected. When the Berlin Wall came down politicians and pundits began talking about bringing Russia into the community of nations and "peace dividends" resulting from the slashing of unnecessary military spending. Everything seemed so rosy in the early nineties of the past century but reality didn't actually turn out quite that way.

The loss of a bipolar world created much more instability than we ever anticipated. Ethnic and religious tensions and rivalries that had simmered all over the world suddenly began to boil like superheated water in a runaway nuclear reactor. No place seemed to fragment so quickly and violently as the former Yugoslavia but similar events happened in many other places around the globe. The half-century stare-down between two superpowers with mind-numbing nuclear arsenals suddenly gave way to peoples settling many centuries worth of old scores with machetes and knives. Even now, Vladimir Putin is being increasingly portrayed as a stalwart Soviet as the Russian Bear begins to flex his muscles once again. So much for the peace dividend.

The world is obviously a much different place than it was in 1991 when the Soviet Union collapsed. If anything, we have many more commitments, crises, and threats now than we ever did during the Cold War. During the Cold War we were blissfully unaware of many of the simmering ethnic and religious tensions that we are now facing in the twenty-first century. In light of this, it behooves us to recalibrate our notion of "national security."

The term "national security" encompasses both offensive and defensive connotations that are based on a triad of sorts. The first leg of this triad is our armed forces. Our military is used to project force internationally when it is in our national interests to do so and, obviously, to defend our country in the event enemy forces attack us. This might take the form of anything from positioning an aircraft carrier task force off the coast of an unfriendly nation to "send a message" all the way up to all-out nuclear war.

The exercising of military force is a state's clear use of hard power to either destroy an enemy or force or compel him to do something. A good example of this is *Desert Storm* when an international military coalition forced Saddam Hussein out of Kuwait. It's usually thought of as a last resort when international diplomatic, political, or economic pressures (i.e., soft power) have not had the desired effect. Most countries usually don't go to war as the first step in a confrontation; they try to remedy the situation through soft power channels first.

The second leg of the triad is international diplomacy. This could be represented in anything from international trade agreements to attempting to pass a Security Council resolution against a perceived foe or offender of some kind. We sign international treaties and join international groups and alliances when we think those things are either in our national interests or will serve to defend them. These treaties and agreements may, in turn, call for exercising military force as a final option if diplomatic and economic leverage does not achieve the desired result.

International diplomacy usually has the advantage that you are trying to attract a nation or group of nations into cooperating with you on some matter. Sometimes, such as in the case of Iran and its nuclear program, it is about rallying support for economic and political sanctions. But, usually it is about playing nice with others within an international system of laws and customs. It can be utilized to promote our foreign policies, our economic interests, and our cultural values and, as such, it represents a far more utilitarian and non-aggressive tool than does military force on its own. Nobody likes a bully.

The last leg of the national security triad is represented by the law enforcement/counterterrorism/counterintelligence enterprise. It is responsible for keeping us safe and secure domestically. The counterterrorist component seeks to protect us against terrorists – both foreign and domestic – that would attempt to do America or Americans any harm in the further-ance of their anti-American cause. The counterintelligence component works to prevent the penetration of our government by foreign powers or the co-opting of Americans to work on behalf of any such entities. Both those components rely on law enforcement at the federal, state, or even local levels to execute their duties and carry out their missions. In addition, law enforcement protects our civil society against criminals and upholds the law and order that this society relies upon for everyday functioning. Without law enforcement our society would descend into chaos and anarchy – the very antithesis of national security.

These three legs of the national security triad don't go away when we talk about recalibrating our notion of national security, but it is time we assessed whether or not the legs and tools we are relying upon the most are getting us where we want to be. Are they moving us toward victory against our Islamist foes? The answer to that question is a clear, resounding, and unequivocal "no." As I've been addressing from the very beginning of this book, whatever we have been doing, particularly since the rise of Al-Qaeda in 1992, has not worked. We have tens of thousands more extremist fighters and probably hundreds of thousands more sym-pathizers (or even millions) than we ever had in 1992. We've resorted to the use of military force when it wasn't warranted (e.g., the 2003 invasion of Iraq) and then wrung our hands and waivered when we should have used it decisively (e.g., against IS). These strategic missteps have cost us dearly in blood and treasure and have actually worsened the problem of extremist ideology. They have worked against our national security and national interests, not in support of them.

We must have a strategic leadership in Washington that realizes that there is not going to be a military solution in our battle to eradicate the ideol-ogy of terror and violence. But that leadership must still be wise enough to understand that when military force must be used in our ideological struggle, it must be used forcefully and decisively.

As I have shown earlier in this chapter, the lead role will fall at the diplo-matic level. Our international popular and official efforts will be aimed at encouraging the Muslims themselves to find the causes of Islamism in their countries, clearly condemn and denounce it, and devise and implement solutions to eradicate it. We will need to develop mutual trust, credibility, and confidence in order to make this happen and that will require more carrot than stick.

As we have already discussed, one of the most important elements in this equation is our counter to the terrorists' narrative that we are at war with Islam and all Muslims. Developing and disseminating that counter-narrative must become a much higher priority if we are to change the Arabs' and Muslims' opinions of us on the information battlefield – arguably the most important field of battle in this war. Raising the visibility of the role of American Muslims in our efforts will also greatly help in challenging the terrorists' allegations against us and lend credibility to our campaign and our intentions.

Our investment in law enforcement and counterterrorism has been on steroids ever since 9/11. But as we have seen, numerous high-profile terrorist attacks and incidents still took place even when the government had foreknowledge of them. As I said before, the terrorists only have to be lucky once; we have to be lucky every time. No level of counterterrorism investment will yield protection all the time.

Big isn't necessarily better as growth often comes at the expense of agility. Government employees are skilled at creating wondrous bureaucracies with policies and procedures for nearly every insipid and inane activity. Knowledge and information in such an environment represent power and professional bureaucrats are inclined to share it carefully. After all, in the bureaucratic universe the prime directive is to survive and grow. The actual performance and fulfillment of an organization's mission isn't so much aimed at getting results as it is at fulfilling that prime directive. Hence, whenever a government institution is perceived to have failed at its job, the answer more often than not is to throw more people and money at the problem. To bureaucrats, size does matter.

The Department of Homeland Security has been embarrassed by very public lapses and failures at the Transportation Security Administration and even the Secret Service. It was an ordinary policeman who stopped two terrorists attempting to storm the Prophet Mohammed cartoon event in Garland, TX.[202] The G-Men had no idea about the plot. If the Department of Homeland Security were a commercial enterprise, would you hire it to protect your home or business?

Government employees must be evaluated every year so maybe it's time we did an open and objective evaluation of each government agency every year to see if they are actually meeting their responsibilities and to force them to do corrective actions if they're not.

Our national security triad today is out of balance. We are relying almost exclusively on the two legs of the triad that cannot achieve victory in our war while neglecting the most important leg and the only one that can – that of international outreach and diplomacy. Killing men won't defeat terrorism, eradicating the ideology that spawns it will. We don't have enough drones and missiles to kill everybody. We have to cooperate internationally with allies and partners if we are to triumph. Diplomacy is always cheaper than military action and with the innovative ideas in this plan it will be far more effective. Redirecting just a small fraction of the Pentagon's spending on its expensive weapons systems and gadgets that have no place in this war would be money better spent.

But, unfortunately the national security imbalance is a much more complicated problem than just rebalancing the legs of its triad.

One of the clear and present dangers to national security is our national deficit. The problem is further aggravated when we spend a limited number (albeit a large one) of tax dollars on items we don't need at the expense of other items that we do need urgently. Budget games, sequestration, and brinksmanship have all elevated party politics and one-upmanship ahead of the honest and responsible stewardship of the government's fiscal resources.

Simply put, the 535 members of the House and Senate must begin to put the needs and interests of the country and its people ahead of their political games. We must achieve a balanced budget. Either we find ways

---

202. Holly Yann, "ISIS Claims Responsibility for Texas Shooting But Offers No Proof," *CNN* website, May 5, 2015. Accessed July 18, 2017. http://www.cnn.com/2015/05/05/us/garland-texas-prophet-mohammed-contest-shooting/index.html.

to increase the revenues to pay for all the services we spend money on or we limit the number of services (and the resulting expenditures) the government provides. If members on one side of the aisle remain adamant about not passing any tax increases while members on the other side are just as adamant about not cutting current spending levels, the situation will continue to get worse. The House and the Senate must work seriously to find common ground on this issue. Their squabbling certainly does not benefit our national security posture and it does not befit the stature of either institution.

Like any other government organization, it's time for Congressional performance to be evaluated, too. Some might say that having elections every two years satisfies that function but I'm not so sure. We have many in both houses who have been fixtures in Congress for decades, even as the institution's favorability rating among the population has plunged and gridlock has increased.

I've often heard people assert that government should be run more like a business. This statement is usually made when we all hear about how much money the federal government spends (or wastes) on various programs that are deemed unnecessary or too extravagant. Maybe government and government officials should be evaluated like a corporation not just for the purposes of efficiency and productivity, but also for accountability.

Let's take the story of Enron and its executives as a somewhat recent example of what I mean by accountability. The Enron scandal came to light in October 2001 when it was revealed that the 60-billion-dollar energy trading company had been cooking the books for years and misleading shareholders and stock analysts alike about its financial performance. The company was forced into bankruptcy and several of its top executives were indicted, tried, and sent to jail for deliberately lying about the state of Enron's finances and business and bilking shareholders and investors out of tens of billions of dollars.

Just two-and-a-half years after the Enron scandal broke, we invaded Iraq under false pretenses that Saddam Hussein was concealing weapons of mass destruction programs that had been banned by the UN Security Council and the international community. The director of the CIA and our secretary of state presented inconclusive and dubious evidence of an Iraqi biological weapons program to the UN Security Council in early 2003. It was the absolute antithesis of Adlai Stevenson's eloquent and convincing presentation of photographs of Russian missiles in Cuba to the same body four decades earlier. Nevertheless, US forces were ordered to invade Iraq on March 19, 2003.

We all know the result. No WMD were found and we wound up occupying Iraq for the next eight-and-a-half years. The Iraqi misadventure cost us more than two trillion dollars and nearly five thousand American lives, not to mention hundreds of thousands of Iraqi ones. Yet, not a single politician or policymaker was held accountable for the exorbitant cost of this terrible error.

If we can hold Enron executives accountable for cheating shareholders out of billions of dollars, then why can't we hold politicians responsible for *thousands* of Iraqi and US dead and *trillions* wasted? Instead of holding our governmental officials accountable, we reelect them!

No board of directors in any legitimate US corporation would allow its officers to spend more money every year than the company made. Yet, our representatives and senators have not passed a balanced budget in decades. I'm sorry, but if we're going to operate government like a business then we must make any legislator in Congress ineligible for reelection if that body does not pass a balanced budget during his or her tenure. Allocating and spending government money is the sole purview of Congress and if it cannot do that fundamental job reliably then we need to turn out the entire membership until our Congress can accomplish its financial mission responsibly.

Unless we truly get serious about holding our representatives and senators accountable for their budget performance, the unacceptable situation we see in Congress today will never improve. Continued deficits and a spiraling national debt represent an obvious danger to our national security that Congress must not only address, but also rectify. Doing so will require a lot of fresh thinking, cooperation, and compromise.

Refreshing the American Brand

When you put all these new approaches and ideas together, it comes down to polishing and refreshing the American "brand." In the world of commerce, a customer only patronizes a business for one of two reasons: either he or she wants to or the customer has to. For example, Apple is seen as an innovative, cutting-edge company that has worked to craft its brand in such a way that its customers will line up to buy just about anything it produces. It has consistently exceeded its customers' expectations so that now virtually any product it introduces to the market will become an overnight success. People don't have to buy stuff from Apple; they buy stuff from Apple because they want to. They believe in the company and they believe in its products.

Once, during the fifties and sixties of the last century, the American brand was popular all over the world. It luxuriated in the post-war economic boom in the West that contrasted sharply with the gray, grim face of communism. We lent a hand to resurrect our erstwhile enemies in Germany and Japan. People all over the world believed in us and our values and they wanted to live the American Dream.

But the American brand has lost a lot of market share around the world in the past half-century. Our trademark has become shabby and threadbare. All too often we have been seen as the sheriff – and the bad cop, at that. We've used military force to impose our will and protect our interests without really considering the interests of others in the process. Many in the Third World accuse us of stealing their natural resources. Nearly everyone in the world can find some excuse to hate us if they want to. It is a strategic marketing mistake for the country that invented marketing in the first place.

Our brand needs a facelift. We need to find ways for the "customers" around the world to believe in our brand once again and to do "business" with us because they want to, not because they feel they have to. We must make ourselves credible and relevant again.

Apple constantly has its finger on the pulse of its customer base so when it comes out with a new product or technology, it already knows that the product will knock its customers' socks off. Can our leaders and diplomats take a lesson from Apple and craft US policy in a way that will "refresh the American brand" around the world? I hope so. We can still make this the American Century if we are willing to be bold.

Unfortunately Washington has historically been a toxic environment for new thinking and fresh ideas. You can look back at the four-decade parade of past presidents to see that regardless of whether or not one was a Washington insider or outsider, nothing much changed inside the nation's capital. Politicians come and go. They may debate policy but bureaucrats are the ones who run the government and the country on a daily basis. And bureaucratic and intellectual inertia combined with a blind and ignorant preference for the unsuccessful (but safe) conventionalism and fiscal irresponsibility we've followed for decades all pose huge obstacles to our ultimate victory.

A new and unconventional strategy that features fresh thinking and innovative ideas and approaches that emphasize diplomacy and communication over military force is the way to go. The old thinking hasn't gotten us anywhere so what do we have to lose by taking a new direction? The twenty-first century will be hard enough. It will be even more difficult if we're too stubborn to realize the need for boldness and creativity in our thinking.

CHAPTER ELEVEN

STEP SIX: LET'S START BELIEVING IN VICTORY AGAIN

"Remember that all through history, there have been tyrants and murderers, and for a time, they seem invincible. But in the end, they always fall. Always."

– Mahatma Gandhi

February 19, 2017 marked the 72nd anniversary of the Battle of Iwo Jima, an extremely brutal battle against 22,000 heavily fortified but abandoned Japanese who had been ordered to fight to the death; only about 200 were captured alive at the battle's end. Joe Rosenthal's iconic photograph of five Marines and a Navy Corpsman raising the American flag on Mount Suribachi on February 23, 1945 endures as an eternal tribute to the spirit of those fighting men who persevered for yet another full month before eventually winning the battle that cost the lives of 6,821 of their comrades.

As a proud veteran of the Marine Corps, I am humbled by the honor, courage, and commitment of those Marines and Sailors on Iwo Jima. Many knew they would not survive yet they continued to fight and die for their buddies on their left and right. They did whatever it took to achieve a final, unconditional victory over the Empire of Japan. Even when they were terrified, they stood fast and did their duty. And while they were doing the fighting, millions at home did whatever they could to support the war effort. Indeed, they were America's Greatest Generation and to them – service members and civilians alike – defeat was unthinkable. It was a dark time in our nation's history with no shortage of sacrifice but our ultimate, unconditional victory was the objective and no one hesitated to say it.

But something has happened between 1945 and today. Nobody ever talks about victory in our global war against Islamist radicalism. We never hear our president even mention the word. It's the same with our policymakers and government bureaucrats. Why? Is it because they don't really know what we're fighting against? Is it because they don't know what victory in this war will look like? Is it because they don't have a real strategy for victory? By now, I think we've seen that it's all of the above.

Our leaders stopped talking about victory against what they initially called terrorism pretty quickly. Granted, they have never grasped that the fight is against radical Islamist ideology but, nevertheless, they do seem to have given up on victory altogether shortly after 9/11. The very subject of victory in the global war on Islamist ideology is anathema to them. Today's generation of politicians – at every single level of government – prefer to sandbag. They would rather downplay future policy results and achievements so that there won't be any negative spin when their policies fail. And they will fail because our government has been – and still is – fighting the wrong war, with the wrong tools, against the wrong target.

In the absence of a clear strategy for victory from a courageous and visionary leader who sees the ideology of Islamism as our strategic target, we are left with a series of unsatisfying campaigns against one group after another. Al-Qaeda. Al-Shabaab. Islamic State. Indecisive campaigns that only guarantee that some other Islamist group will come along even though an administration's media handlers and press secretary will reassure us that our enemies have been degraded. Can we honestly look back at this fight since 9/11 and claim that we are winning? Must we accept conflict without end?

I believe that Washington has let us down. Fighting and beating an ideology is difficult but not impossible. We proved that it could be done with our victory over communism in the Cold War. However, our government's failure to recognize Islamism as our strategic objective means that it is destined to maintain the status quo of perpetual conflict. Our leaders do not seem to know what else to do.

The status quo is good for the military-industrial-security complex and it's good for the growth of government at all levels. The only ones for whom the status quo is bad are the American people, the taxpayers, and, of course, the poor victims in the Middle East who are being slaughtered. We deserve much better and we must start demanding it from our policymakers and our government.

First, I believe that Americans should hear from their chief executive that Washington's goal must be to prosecute the war against this extremist ideology all the way to victory. The president should hold all our policymakers to that pledge. We should all be united in our belief that we will triumph over our Islamist enemies and their nihilistic ideology and we should hear our leaders using the word "victory" often.

If they are afraid to articulate the word, then we don't need them. If they want to fret and worry in front of the TV camera about how hard the "terrorism" problem is, we don't need them. The American people want to know that their government is unanimous in its resolve for nothing less than absolute victory. Our government's lackluster performance at all levels since Al-Qaeda's opening volley against us in 1992 has not been its finest hour. We deserve results, not excuses.

This is a time for all of us Americans to dig down and find greatness inside ourselves once again. Let's take a strategic step back and think for a minute about who and what we are fighting. Our enemies are barbarous monsters that want to take us back to the seventh century. Once again, do any of us think that the majority of the world's seven plus billion people are going to buy into that vision? Of course not!

Let me also reiterate that the fighters in these Islamist groups are not invincible. They're just terrorists, not warriors who are skilled in the military arts. It doesn't take much courage or skill to kill someone whose hands are tied behind his back or to shoot unarmed people on the street with an automatic weapon. It is beyond belief that any authentic major world religion – including Islam – would claim to reward such criminal behavior in the afterlife with a harem of beautiful maidens in paradise.

While we wring our hands over legalistic balderdash like an Authorization for the Use of Military Force, the *takfirists* video themselves killing people in the most brutal manner and then they spread this obscene propaganda worldwide over social media. Our hesitancy has allowed them to engage in an organized pogrom to exterminate other religious minorities unopposed. Would the heroes of World War II and the Greatest Generation be proud of what we have become?

In this chapter's opening quotation, Gandhi nailed it. Germany's Hitler, Japan's Tojo, and Italy's Mussolini seemed invincible at the height of their power during World War II. But, they all fell and fell hard.

The Soviet Union collapsed and took its European Warsaw Pact satellites crashing to the ground with it. Countries like North Korea may survive for a time because of gulags and a tight control over the population but that control never lasts forever. The Hermit Kingdom's Kim dynasty will eventually wind up in the dustbin of history. It's inevitable.

Osama bin Laden is dead along with many of his Al-Qaeda cohorts. Gaddafi was toppled and killed by his own people. Mubarak languished for years in prison. Dictators and totalitarian regimes invariably must defend themselves against their own people and at some point they just can't keep all the plates spinning anymore.

And so it will be with Abu-Bakr al-Baghdadi of the Islamic State, Abubakr Shekau of Boko Haram, and all the others At some point their crimes will catch up to them. History has shown us that the downfall and demise of such tyrants and oppressors is inevitable.

While our victory may be certain, it would happen a lot sooner if our leaders were confident and headed in the right direction. As they wander in the wilderness following glimmering mirages of counterterrorism, regional armies, drone strikes, and "boots on the ground" they have stopped talking about victory because they've already settled for second place.

Our mistake is a strategic one. It lies in the erroneous belief that we are fighting only men in a war against terrorism. As I've noted, the problem with this approach is that the men may die but the ideology they follow continues on. That's why the old groups like Al-Qaeda morph into something else like Al-Qaeda in the Arabian Peninsula and new groups like Al-Shabaab and Islamic State pop up. We haven't grasped that the real enemy isn't terrorism or IS or even Al-Qaeda. The true enemy is their common ideology. Once we defeat that, we defeat the terrorism that springs forth from that ideology. Body counts don't matter strategically. Hearts and minds do.

At the beginning of this book I pointed out that what we have been doing since December 29, 1992 hasn't worked. We've been lulled into thinking that Islamist terrorism is largely a law enforcement problem. We've fooled ourselves into believing we can somehow "contain" terrorism much like we "contained" communism in Eastern Europe after the Iron Curtain fell over that continent. But containment is not the same thing as victory. Containment by its very definition does not eliminate the problem, it simply forces it to evolve and manifest itself somewhere else. Quarantining the patients of a disease doesn't cure the disease. The terrorist adherents who follow the radical Islamist ideology have found ways to evolve and break our quarantine. This should be pretty obvious to us by now. Most of the insurgents from IS came from somewhere else. The same is true of AQAP, Al-Shabaab, and Al-Qaeda in the Islamic Maghreb. Containment isn't victory and it just does not work.

We've spent hundreds of billions to gain fleeting, temporary benefits but this approach is ultimately doomed to fail. Repeating this misguided strategy over and over again is not going to yield a different result. Most significantly, it certainly is not going to lead us to victory and *if we are not fighting to win, what the hell are we fighting for?*

Let's take a moment to do something that the media and the Islamophobic fearmongers never do: take a deep breath and objectively examine the danger of the threat from Islamism from the strategic perspective. The world is not ever going to be conquered and dominated by either Islam or Islamism. The Islamists' ideology calls for every inch of the earth's surface to fall under the rule of their version of *Sharia*. Everyone should just get serious for a minute. Is Paris going to fall under Islamist dominion because of the horrific terrorist attacks that killed 129 innocent people? Are Americans going to suddenly wake up some day to find that the Stars and Stripes have been replaced by the black flag of Islamism? Will the Islamists take over Alaska, Siberia, the South Sandwich Islands, and Vanuatu? Of course not! We are more likely to be invaded and conquered by aliens from space than we are by the crop of maladjusted misfits parading as pious Islamists.

In the West and the majority of the world that is *not* failing, the best these cavemen can do is carry out terrorist attacks. Don't get me wrong – these potential acts of brutal and barbaric terrorism are a serious threat. The perceived threat from such attacks has already changed how we live our lives, how we travel, and how we view the rest of the world. We stay at high alert, especially around major holidays, and we seem to give little thought to giving up more and more freedoms and liberties under the guise of being safer.

But, will we actually be any safer? Every time we lose a freedom that is integral to being an American, we lose something unique and irreplaceable. Once Washington takes these liberties and freedoms away from us, we will never get them back. Think about that for a minute.

As Americans, we value individual life *because* of our freedoms and liberties. Once you start taking those things away, you start chipping away at the very essence of what it means to be an American. At some point, we start to lose our exceptional identity as Americans and trade away living in freedom for just existing in fear. Will we be relegated at some point in the future to cowering in the basement until Big Brother tells us it is safe to come out? If we are in an existential threat with anyone, it isn't the Islamists; it is with ourselves and the exaggerated terrorism fears of our own making.

Yes, in America, the West, and even most of the rest of the world, the Islamists can engage in crimes of violence and murder. They can disrupt civil societies, sow fear, and cause material and human losses, but they cannot take over our lands. They will not impose their *Sharia* over us They cannot win. This is a time for us to stop fearing their victory and to start believing in our own.

Yes, there are places in the world facing the danger of being overrun by Islamists and we've already talked about most of them in chapter eight. It is in the Middle East, Africa, and Southwest Asia where weak and fragile states are threatened with falling under the shadow of Islamist conquest. It is all the more imperative that we act fast to prevent any more of these countries from failing if we are to prevent Islamic State and the others from gaining a foothold there and causing greater human suffering. Eliminate Islamism there and you get rid of the ideology and the terrorism that goes with it.

Let's all start believing in victory again. This book offers a six-step approach in a real strategy for defeating – not just containing – the true enemy: Islamist ideology. It is a strategy that focuses on a better and more effective utilization of resources. It's a strategy that will result in draining the Islamist swamp once and for all instead of buying citronella candles and cans of bug spray, but it will require the implementation of all six steps, not just one or two. We, along with all of our allies and partners around the world, must apply the whole plan for it to be successful. It can be summarized as follows:

- **Ceasing calling terrorism *jihad*:** We shouldn't be taking any chances on giving the terrorists any legitimacy they don't deserve. *Jihad* has positive connotations in Islam; what these Islamist bastards are doing is neither positive nor *jihad*. It's simply terrorism. They can call themselves whatever they want; we should just use the truth.

- **Shutting the terrorists up:** Terrorism cannot survive without attention. Denying them a cyber presence and access to the media would go far in reducing the ability of groups like IS to recruit and spread their propaganda. At the same time, we must be much more engaged and much more effective at countering the Islamists' anti-US narrative. We really haven't been doing this very effectively.

- **Addressing failed and failing states:** The power vacuum in failed and failing states allows these terrorists a place in which to set up shop. We need an indigenous, Arab effort to stop the spiral of state failures in the Middle East and Africa. We must *guide and promote* this effort, not do it on our own. It's up to the Arabs and Muslims to bankroll and implement it.

- **Being smarter with military force:** Military force should not be the only tool in our toolbox. But when we do use force, it should be done with maximum violence of action for the shortest duration of time. Think *Desert Storm*. Let's start allocating the resources for achieving military victories in the shortest period of time instead of restricting the means available to our forces for domestic political reasons.

- **Thinking boldly and creatively:** What we are doing isn't working so it's time to do something radically different. Let's forget the "red lines" of old-fashioned conventionalism and start taking back the operational tempo of the conflict at the strategic level, where the bad guys can't really counter us. Engaging Arabs and Muslims at the popular, official, religious, and international levels would do wonders for disrupting the Islamists' narrative and rebuilding bridges of trust and credibility and this work has offered a number of new proposals for doing just that. Doing so puts us back in the position of being a responsible and respectful superpower and encourages the Muslim world to find and implement the solutions to eradicate extremist ideology from within. We cannot impose such solutions from the outside. We need them and they need us.

- **Believing in victory again:** Olympic champions (and US Marines) are winners because they believe in themselves. They visualize their triumphs before ever stepping into the arena. Our leaders in Washington must have that same unshakeable faith in our ultimate victory over the ideology of extremism and they must regularly communicate that faith to the American people. We must expect no less.

Let's abandon petty partisanship and return to the democratic values that have made America what it is today. Let's read more Abraham Lincoln, Thomas Jefferson, and Thomas Paine because their words can remind us that our great nation has encountered very real existential threats during its history that were far more dangerous to it than the present scourge of Islamist terrorism.

A new approach and a new strategy will restore our image to the rest of the world and encourage others to work with us as allies and partners. It will make us stronger, not weaker. It's the only real way to win this or any war. There is still time to make this the American Century. We can do it, we must do it, and we will do it. Let's start believing in victory again.

EPILOGUE

*"Numerical superiority is of no consequence. In
battle, victory will go to the best tactician."*

– George Armstrong Custer

Custer no doubt had some final misgivings about that statement at the
Little Big Horn. His quote emphasizes that while the shortcomings of a
bad strategy can be self-evident, it's also worth remembering that even
good strategies can fail if their execution is poor.

But you must have a strategy first. The White House has already acknowledged that its strategy to confront the Islamic State is incomplete while
the Pentagon has sometimes questioned Iraq's commitment and ability
to fight the terrorist group. Even our own commitment to eradicate and
eliminate these *takfirists* has been long in coming. The group's fortunes
will likely continue to ebb and flow but it is a long way from being
defeated and eliminated and that is largely our fault.

President Obama's National Strategy for Counterterrorism was dated
June 2011 and it nearly exclusively focused on countering Al-Qaeda and
its affiliates.[203] In its 26 pages, it didn't mention anything about defeating
the Islamist ideology behind the group. As a strategy, it was overtaken by
events and it was completely irrelevant to the fight against IS since that
organization didn't even exist then. The ideology did, though.

You'd think by now we would be able to see that Whack-a-Mole isn't
working. We can bomb a convoy of extremists into perdition but it won't
matter. We can kill or kidnap the occasional terrorist leader to temporarily

---

203. "National Strategy for Counterterrorism," website of the Obama White House Archives,
June 28, 2011. Accessed April 28, 2017. https://obamawhitehouse.archives.gov/sites/
default/files/counterterrorism_strategy.pdf.

disrupt one group or another but some other extremist is quickly promoted to fill the sudden vacancy and events just move on. We cannot win by continuing to fight this way. Without destroying Islamism's ideology we will never defeat the terrorism that it spawns.

The whole concept of martyrdom means that whenever we kill these fighters and commanders, it means nothing to their cause or their comrades. They want to die "in the cause of Allah," anyway. To them it is the act of martyrdom itself that matters, not its result. They are dead-enders to begin with and we are just playing their game, wasting our own blood and treasure in a futile endeavor that only perpetuates the struggle without ever winning it. It may make us feel good to kill "bad guys" but the body count metric in Vietnam didn't mean anything then and it doesn't mean anything in our fight against Islamist extremism now. The Mongols did not eliminate Islam when they sacked and destroyed Baghdad and we will not eliminate Islamism when Raqqa is liberated and Islamic State is driven out of Iraq and Syria.

It doesn't have to be this way. This book has offered some historical context about Islam and the Arabs and provided insight into the origins of Islamism and why our enemies hate us. It has reviewed the challenges we face in the Middle East along with pointing out some opportunities that we have not yet exploited.

Our strategic target for winning this war is not the individual groups or terrorists. It's the Islamist ideology, itself. The groups and individuals are merely manifestations of that ideology. Defeat the ideology and you stop the recruitment of fighters and terrorists into its pipeline. Defeat the ideology and you defeat the terrorism that emanates from it.

This work provides a six-step, comprehensive, and innovative plan for doing just that. We're fighting the wrong war and we're not fighting to win. This plan focuses on the real objective and shows us how to achieve real victory. Our ultimate triumph will not be quick, but it doesn't have to take generations, either. These six steps will allow us to regain our credibility in the Arab and Muslim worlds as we act in a responsible and collaborative manner that polishes our image as a superpower. We just need to start focusing on the right objective and fighting smarter – not just militarily, but diplomatically and politically, too.

I've made a point of hammering away repeatedly on numerous themes in this book. They are the foundations upon which the elements of my strategy are based:

- We are not fighting terrorism; we are fighting the ideology that generates that terrorism.

- America is not at war with Islam; it is at war with Islamism. We must do better at making that distinction and stop stereotyping Islam and all Muslims.

- What we have been doing hasn't worked. Why do you think we have so many more terrorists now than we did in 1992 or even after 9/11?

- Counterterrorism is a defensive posture and we haven't historically been very good at it. Defense does not win wars and the best defense is usually a good offense.

- We are in a war of hearts and minds and we have done little to counter the terrorists' narrative and their manipulation of the press and social media on the most important front: the information battlefield.

- We have over-relied on the use of force to solve a problem that is not intrinsically a military problem. And when the use of force really is required, we have been too slow and indecisive in its employment.

- Killing men only creates martyrs and this is actually counterproductive to killing the ideology that our enemies embrace.

- Our key to victory lies in engaging Arab and Muslim populations at multiple levels in peaceful, ongoing dialogue to reform their societies and governments and to find and eliminate the root causes of Islamism and extremism. These populations are every bit as concerned about the rise of Islamist extremism as we are and they are most often the victims of its terrorism. They don't want to return to the past, either. This phenomenon originated in their world and they must ultimately be the ones to find a solution for it. It cannot be imposed from the outside.

- It is necessary to strip away any religious legitimacy from Islamism and call it what it really is: a nihilistic death cult. Muslim orthodoxy must threaten the ideology's followers with *takfir* and the Muslim and Arab worlds must offer their youth a positive alternative in which to practice their Islamic values rather than Islamism's dead-end path of violence and martyrdom.

- There is no way the entire world of 7.5 billion people will buy into Islamism. Our victory in this war is assured; the only variable is the human and material cost because of our missteps and mistakes.

All too often we take too narrow a view and focus on what we are fighting *against* instead of what we are fighting *for*. We aren't just fighting *against* one specific Islamist group, we are fighting *for* a better future for all of mankind: one free of Islamist terrorism. This can still be the American Century if we are willing to put the hammer back in the toolbox and restore real superpower credibility and confidence in our political and diplomatic statesmanship and leadership. This book provides a roadmap for doing just that; it is nothing less than a roadmap for *victory*.

Honor, courage, and commitment. These are the core values that we discussed at the beginning of this work that have stood the United States Marines in good stead since 1775. As I said at the very beginning, they'll work for the rest of us, too.

Let's drain the damn swamp once and for all!

GLOSSARY

Alawite | A branch of Twelver *Shia* Islam that reveres Muhammad's cousin, son-in-law, and first male follower, Ali Ibn Abi Talib. Members of this religious sect are concentrated along the Syrian coast and are reviled by *Sunni* extremists as apostates and heretics.

Baath | Arabic word meaning "renaissance" in English. *Baathism* as a movement began in Syria as a blend of Arab nationalist, socialist, and anti-colonialist ideology following World War II. The movement was initially popular in many of the Arab countries but really only survived politically in Iraq and Syria.

Basiji | A member of Iran's paramilitary *Basij* resistance force. The force is a volunteer auxiliary organization that falls under the command of the Islamic Revolutionary Guards Corps (IRGC). During the Iran-Iraq war in the 1980s, these members were often marched across minefields to clear the way for the soldiers behind them to advance against the Iraqis.

Bedouin | A Semitic Arab nomad of the Arabian Desert, although Arab nomads outside the Arabian Peninsula are often colloquially known as Bedouins, as well. These Arabian tribesmen formed the basic military component that spread Islam first through the Arabian Peninsula, and from there all the way to the Atlantic Ocean in the West and the Indus River in the East within just a few decades.

Caliphate	An Islamic religious form of government whose ruler is a caliph. The word "caliph" comes from the Arabic word for "successor" (*khalifah*) since the caliph is considered the rightful successor to Muhammad as the leader of the Muslims.
Dar al-Harb	Arabic for the "realm of war." This refers to the lands and portions of the world that are not under Islamic rule or governed by the Sharia. This is a term that was contrived by scholars; it does not appear in the Koran.
Dar al-Islam	Arabic for the "realm of Islam." This refers to the lands and portions of the world that are under Islamic rule or governed by the Sharia. This is a term that was contrived by scholars; it does not appear in the Koran.
Da'wah	The "Islamic Call" to non-Muslims to convert to Islam. The Islamic missionary message.
Deen wa Dawla	Literally, Arabic for "a religion and a state" or "religion and state." Originally the phrase was used to illustrate that Islam was both a religion and a framework of state governance. Some devout Muslims have also used the phrase to show that their loyalty to their religion is above and beyond any loyalty to any state.
Fard Ayn	The term *fard ayn* refers to an obligation that is a religious duty incumbent upon each individual Muslim. An example of such an obligation would be the necessity of the Muslim to perform his daily prayers or to fast during the month of Ramadan.

Fard Kifaya	The term *fard kifaya* refers to an obligation that is a collective religious obligation on a group of Muslims. If one or more Muslims of that group fulfill the religious obligation, that is sufficient. It is sometimes also known as an "obligation of sufficiency." An example of this would be when a group of Muslims witness a car accident. One or more members of that group (but not necessarily the entire group) have a religious obligation to save or help any potential victims resulting from the accident.
Fatwa	A religious legal opinion rendered on a specific subject or matter by a *mufti* – a person who is qualified as a jurist to render such rulings. A Muslim may ask any *mufti* for a *fatwa* in order to clarify any aspects of his faith or problems of life that are not clear to him.
Feda'y	Singular form of *fedayeen*, a freedom fighter prepared to sacrifice himself in a greater cause. The term was widely used to refer to Palestinian guerillas during the 1960s, 1970s, and 1980s. With the exponential increase in suicide bombings and operations, the term has been supplanted nearly universally by *shahid* or "martyr."
Hadith	Arabic for "narrative" or "account," the term refers to the oral narratives and accounts of Muhammad's sayings, conduct, and behavior. The "authentic" oral narratives were ones that could be traced back to the prophet himself and were compiled in respected collections such as *Sahih Al-Bukhari* and *Sahih Muslim* a couple hundred years after Muhammad's death. These narratives are considered to be a major source of reference in Islamic law and jurisprudence in addition to the verses of the Koran.

Hezbollah	Arabic for "The Party of God." *Hezbollah* is Iran's religious proxy in Lebanon. It came into being in the early 1980s and made a name for itself kidnapping and killing Americans and Westerners in Lebanon during that decade. The group was also responsible for the 1983 bombings of the American Embassy in Beirut and the US Marine barracks. It has become a major player in Lebanese politics and is actively supporting the regime of Syrian President Bashar al-Assad.
Hijra	Arabic for "emigrate." The Prophet Muhammad was forced to emigrate from his home city of Mecca to Medina in the year 622 to escape a plot on his life. When he moved to Medina he began setting up history's first Islamic city-state there. Thus, the Muslim *Hijra* calendar begins with Muhammad's flight to Medina.
Islam	Arabic for "submission," Islam is the last of the three Abrahamic religions of Judaism, Christianity, and Islam. Adherents of the faith are known as Muslims. They believe that Islam is the perfect, final, and complete version of a divine message that was revealed earlier by various Jewish and Christian prophets. A major characteristic of Islam is that there is only one God (Allah) and man's sole purpose in life is to worship and serve Him.
Islamism	Sometimes known as "political Islam," Islamism is an ideology unique to *Sunni* Islam that is characterized by an extremely harsh interpretation of the *Sharia*. It is based on *Salafism* and seeks to emulate the practice of Islam during the time of the Prophet Muhammad. Islamism calls for the elimination of all non-Muslim influences (i.e., Western influences) on Muslims' daily life and the branding of anyone who does not follow the ideology as an "infidel," or unbeliever. This is considered a capital offense.

Isnad	The portion of a *hadith* that relates the uninterrupted chain of authorities upon which that *hadith* is based.
Istishhad	Arabic for "martyrdom." When Islamist terrorists or insurgents carry out suicide bombings or operations, they are referred to as "martyrdom" operations.
Jihad	It literally means "struggle" in Arabic. In the Koran it is used in the context of a struggle of good against evil, such as a Muslim struggling to resist temptation and sin. In the *hadith* collections, however, *jihad* takes on a more militaristic meaning where Muhammad was fighting against non-Muslims in his quest to spread Islam throughout the Arabian Peninsula. Islamists universally see *jihad* as a war against unbelievers that will only end when every inch of the earth is governed by the Sharia.
Jihad ad-dafa'	A manmade term not found in the Koran that means a *"jihad* of defense." An example of this would be when a portion of the "realm of Islam" is invaded or occupied by a foreign, non-Muslim power. It would be the individual religious obligation (*fard ayn*) of each able-bodied Muslim to go to that location and fight to repel the foreign invaders.
Jihad at-talab	A manmade term not found in the Koran that literally means a *"jihad* of the request." This is an offensive form of militaristic *jihad* (war) where a Muslim force enters the "realm of war" (i.e., non-Muslim territory) and asks the non-Muslims to embrace Islam, emigrate to the "realm of Islam," or pay the *jizya* tax that Muslims assess on non-Muslims. A positive response to any of those requests from the non-Muslims will avert war but if they refuse all these requests, it will lead to war between the Muslims and non-Muslims.

Koran	Arabic for "The Recitation." This is the Word of Allah that the angel Gabriel dictated to Muhammad over the course of over two decades that eventually were compiled into Islam's holy book. It consists of 114 *suras* (or books/chapters) that are arranged by length from longest to the shortest. Unlike the Jewish Torah or Christian Old Testament, the Koran does not follow a linear or chronological structure.
Madrassah	Arabic for "school." In an Islamic religious context, a *madrassah* is a school in which young boys learn to memorize and recite the Koran.
Majlis	Arabic for "council." The word sometimes refers to a national assembly (or parliament) or smaller meetings such as the weekly councils convened in Saudi Arabia by the country's king and royal family.
Matn	This is the main body or text portion of a *hadith* that is authenticated by the chain of authorities listed in the *isnad* for that oral narrative.
Muhammad	According to Islam, God's final prophet. Muhammad was the person to whom God/Allah revealed the Koran – His final and complete message. Muhammad was born in Mecca and lived from 570-632.
Mujahid	A *mujahid* is a "holy warrior" or a fighter fulfilling his religious obligation in a *jihad*. The plural form is *mujahideen*.

Salafism | An ultra-conservative, puritanical, and fundamentalist *Sunni* ideology that eschews any modern innovation in Islam and seeks to emulate the practice of the religion during the time of Muhammad. The term originates from the Arabic word *salaf*, which translates to "ancestors." Adherents are known as *Salafis* or *Salafists* and they view anyone who does not embrace their strict ideology as "infidels" and enemies of Islam.

Shahid | Arabic for "martyr," the term has become synonymous with those who carry out suicide operations for either *Sunni* or *Shiite* extremists. As suicide operations became the norm for Palestinian fighters, *shahid* has now largely replaced the previous Palestinian term for "freedom fighter:" *feda'y* (plural *fedayeen*).

Sharia | The precepts of divine Islamic law as contained and revealed in the Koran and the *Sunnah*. It is considered to be the final authority on virtually every aspect of a Muslim's life from hygiene and commerce to marriage, diet, crime, and clothing. Interpretations of *Sharia* law vary from one Muslim country to another.

Shiite | An adherent of *Shia* Islam, the second major denomination that represents about ten percent of all the world's Muslims. The followers of this denomination believe that Ali, Muhammad's cousin and son-in-law, was the rightful heir to succeed Muhammad after the prophet's death. The term *Shiite* originates from the Arabic referring to a "follower of Ali." *Shia* is the plural form in Arabic.

Sunnah	The collective words, actions, and teachings of Muhammad that provide proper examples for other Muslims to emulate and also represent elements of Islamic law.
Sunni	An adherent of *Sunni* Islam, the majority denomination of Islam. Since the *Sunnah* refers to the deeds and teachings of Muhammad, the "People of the Sunnah" became known as *Sunnis* as a means of differentiating them from the *Shia*.
Sura	A chapter or book of the Koran.
Takfir	The practice of one Muslim declaring another Muslim to be an apostate or infidel. Since Islamists see *takfir* as a capital offense, it is a common tactic that they use to eliminate other religious minorities and anyone else who does not agree with them. The *Shia* use *takfiri* or *takfirist* as a pejorative term for Sunni extremists.
Taqiyya	The lawful dissimulation or deception about one's Muslim faith that allows the Muslim to lie about, or even deny his faith and commit unlawful acts if he believes himself to be under threat of persecution. Semantically, *taqiyya* is seen as a *Shia* tactic but the *Sunnis* have a similar concept called *idtirar* that translates to "coercion." It allows religious deception by a *Sunni* Muslim.
Twelver	The Twelver sect is the dominant sect in *Shia* Islam. There are twelve imams (not caliphs) who are the rightful spiritual successors to Muhammad. These *Shiites* believe that the twelfth and final imam is Muhammad Ibn Hasan al-Mahdi, born in 869. They believe he is still alive and being held in "occultation" or "hidden" from humanity. He will eventually emerge together with Jesus to bring peace to the world.

Ulema | The term for a group of Islamic religious scholars who engage in Islamic jurisprudence and issue rulings on matters of the *Sharia* and Islamic law. Muslims may disagree on the standards and credentials that are required for inclusion in this elite body of scholars.

Ummah | The worldwide collective of all Muslims. The Muslim world.

Wahhabism | The Saudi brand of *Salafism* embraced by the eighteenth century cleric Muhammad Ibn Abdul-Wahhab. He formed a relationship with Muhammad Bin Saud, whose family would eventually rule Saudi Arabia. *Wahhabism* is the state-sponsored, conservative form of Islam that is taught and followed in that country today.

DAVID M. ENEBOE

ABOUT THE AUTHOR

David M. Eneboe graduated from the 47-week Arabic language course at the prestigious Defense Language Institute as a young Marine in December 1975. He graduated at the top of his class, with honors, and in the four decades since that achievement, he has had ample opportunities to apply his education.

Following language training, Mr. Eneboe received technical training in the signals intelligence (SIGINT) field as a Voice Intercept Operator (the Marine Corps now calls its language graduates Cryptologic Linguists). He was subsequently assigned to 2nd Marine Division, Force Troops, 2nd Radio Battalion at Camp Lejeune, NC. Consistent with the expeditionary nature of the Marines, Mr. Eneboe was continuously deployed domestically, abroad, and aboard ship for nearly the entire period of his assignment to the battalion.

After his honorable discharge from the Marines, Mr. Eneboe's position required him to routinely brief Senior US Officials, such as Ambassadors and cleared members of visiting Congressional Delegations.

Mr. Eneboe was certified in Arabic as a Language Analyst in 1990 and he was awarded numerous honors and citations, including an NSA Letter of Appreciation for his contributions during *Desert Shield/Desert Storm*, and a Most Valuable Player award from his component.

In the early nineties, the author returned to the United States after an unexpected tragedy made family considerations a higher priority. He founded Sahara Consulting Services and began working as a contract Arabic linguist for the intelligence community and that relationship grew to include various special projects and collection/reporting responsibilities focused on counterterrorism and counterproliferation. He was instrumental in pioneering early Internet research tradecraft and received a personal commendation from the Director of the Foreign Broadcast Information Service (now the Open Source Center) for his work on Mideast counterproliferation.

In addition to his work for the intelligence community, Mr. Eneboe also provides translation and other services to commercial clients.

In his leisure time, he is an active pilot and aircraft owner who enjoys flying for charitable and humanitarian causes. He and his wife live and work in Arizona.

Mr. Eneboe's biographical material has been reviewed for classification and compliance with legal obligations.

INDEX

Made in the USA
San Bernardino, CA
20 February 2018